M0007643

Figures

Tables

Summary

The Developing World has never been more important to the People's Republic of China (PRC) than it is today. China views its ties to developing countries as critical for securing natural resources, developing export markets, expanding its geostrategic influence, and gaining advantages in its global competition with the United States. During the Cold War, the Developing World was a symbolic cause that China used to differentiate itself from the two superpowers, the United States and the Soviet Union, and trumpet mainly rhetorical support for the poorer countries of the globe. In the post-Cold War era, since the 1990s, the Developing World has become a real arena for competition with the United States and the site of significant Chinese political, economic, and military interests. This report evaluates China's strategy toward and involvement in the Developing World and assesses its engagement on a regional basis: Southeast Asia, Oceania, Central Asia, South Asia, the Middle East, Africa, and Latin America and the Caribbean. This regional analysis is complemented by a focus on relations with five particular countries—Russia, Pakistan, Iran, South Africa, and Venezuela—with which China has developed deeper partnerships because of their significance to their particular neighborhoods and to China's interests.

China's Approach to the Developing World, 1949 to Present

The PRC has long seen itself as a leader of the Developing World. In the early years of the People's Republic, founder and first leader Mao

Zedong presented China as a champion for the Developing World and provided China's partners—particularly revolutionary governments and anti-colonial liberation movements—with both military and development assistance. The PRC identified itself as a developing country offering vocal and substantive support to the Developing World. In the late 1970s, following Mao's death, China focused its "reform and opening" policy on developed economies that could help the PRC advance economically and technologically; nevertheless, China simultaneously sought to gain access and influence in developing countries through military aid, arms sales, and rewards for switching diplomatic recognition from the Republic of China on Taiwan to the PRC. Then, in the early 1990s, China invigorated and broadened its outreach to the Developing World. China's fast-growing economy required new sources of raw materials for Chinese factories and new export markets for Chinese-made products.

Figure S.1
China's Four Rings of Insecurity

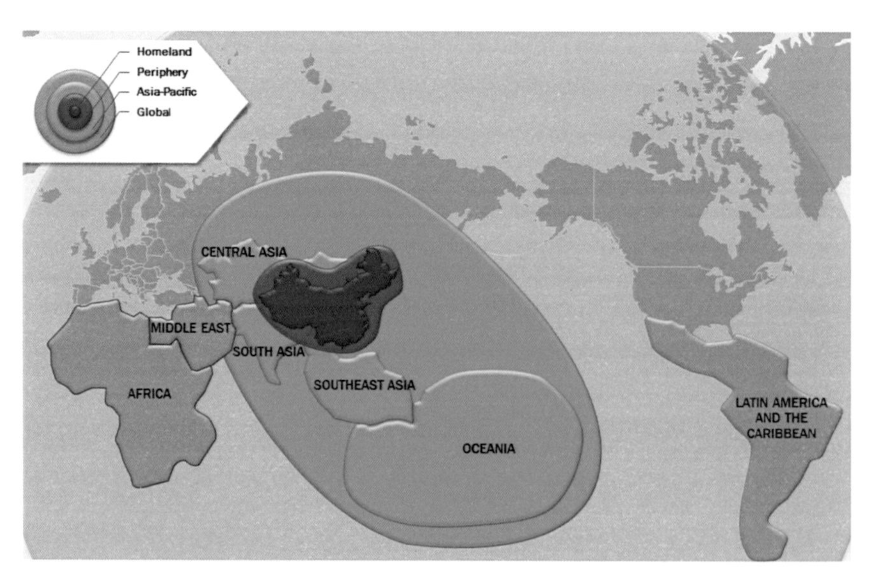

SOURCE: RAND, derived from Andrew J. Nathan and Andrew Scobell, *China's Search for Security*, New York: Columbia University Press, 2012, pp. 3–7.
RAND *RR2273A-S.1*

Since 2013, under President Xi Jinping, China has embarked upon an ambitious initiative to advance China's engagement with the Developing World. Xi has promoted an extremely ambitious effort to build a vast web of infrastructure—roads, railways, ports, canals, and pipelines—intended to link China to its neighborhood and the wider world. Originally labeled One Belt, One Road and as of 2017 known as the Belt and Road Initiative, it includes an overland "Silk Road Economic Belt" and an over-water "Maritime Silk Road." The former consists of a series of proposed networks linking Central Asia to South Asia, the Middle East, and onward to Africa and Europe; the latter envisions shipping routes through the South China Sea and the Indian Ocean toward South Asia, the Middle East, Africa, and Europe. With Belt and Road taking shape, we evaluate China's activities in the Developing World through the dawn of Belt and Road to note the trajectory of relations and where they are likely to head.

China's Rings of Insecurity and Drivers of Engagement

China's conceptualization of the Developing World is driven by Beijing's insecurity about stability at home and around China's periphery and results in special attention to its own neighborhood. Indeed, China sees its security environment in terms of four concentric circles (Figure S.1). The first and innermost ring encompasses China itself (including Taiwan, which it claims). China's second ring contains the territory and bodies of water directly adjacent to China's own land and maritime borders, including portions of Southeast Asia, Central Asia, and South Asia. Chinese leaders believe that peace on China's periphery is essential to domestic harmony, and this leads China to seek extensive influence in these regions and limit influence by outside powers. The third ring includes China's entire Asia-Pacific (including portions of Southeast Asia, Central Asia, South Asia, and all of Oceania), while the fourth ring includes everything beyond Asia—the rest of the globe: the Middle East, Africa, and Latin America and the Caribbean.

Four drivers propel China's desire and need for more engagement with the Developing World. First, China seeks to sustain its domestic economic growth and sees the Developing World as offering significant economic potential. Second, China wishes to work with developing countries to increase its global influence. Third, with expanding international investments and growing numbers of PRC citizens living, working, and traveling abroad overseas, Beijing has concluded it must work to ensure the safety of these overseas interests. Finally, China seeks to increase its engagement and activism in open, accessible, and underdeveloped regions around the world to compensate for the less welcoming, constricted, and more developed regions—Northeast Asia, North America, and Europe—which tend to be dominated by the United States and its allies.

China in Southeast Asia

For China, Southeast Asia is the most important of the world's developing regions. It contains some of China's most significant trading partners, is the conduit for much of Chinese global trade through the South China Sea and the Straits of Malacca, and is home to more overseas ethnic Chinese than any other region of the world. China has three overarching interests in Southeast Asia. First, Beijing aims to protect Chinese sovereignty and territorial integrity, including upholding Chinese claims to features in the South China Sea and increasing China's maritime presence and capabilities. Second, the PRC looks to promote and protect trade, investment, and other linkages to the region to support China's economic growth. Third, Beijing looks to promote and expand Southeast Asia cooperation with China as well as minimize the influence of other external actors.

Politically and economically, Beijing seeks to increase cooperation with its neighbors and regional influence through greater connectivity and trade. China's economic engagement with Southeast Asia in the past decade has been greater than with any other developing region. Unlike other developing regions, China's trade with the region is weighted much more heavily toward two-way trade in manufactured items rather than by China's purchase of raw materials. All ten members of the Association of Southeast Asian Nations (ASEAN) were among the 57 prospective founding members of the China-led Asian

Infrastructure Investment Bank (AIIB), widely seen as a vehicle for funding the Belt and Road Initiative.

China in Oceania

Oceania—a developing region that includes the developed countries of Australia and New Zealand as well as 14 developing states and a number of non-sovereign territories—is, on the one hand, China's least important region in the Asia-Pacific. On the other hand, its strategic importance to China is growing. Within the region, China prioritizes Australia and New Zealand, the largest geopolitical and economic actors in Oceania and the only two countries in the region with which China has signed "strategic partnerships." Although Australia is a close U.S. ally and New Zealand is a key U.S. partner, Beijing believes that political and economic exchanges could discourage both from supporting U.S. measures to contain China or counter China's maritime claims.

Economically, Beijing is principally interested in Oceania for its natural resources. In 2006, China established the China-Pacific Island Countries Economic Development and Cooperation Forum (CPIC) to provide a forum for high-level regional dialogue and cooperation, such as the delivery of concessional loans to finance infrastructure development. China's trade with Oceania is dominated by trade with Australia and New Zealand, from which China imports mostly crude minerals and mineral fuels and to which it exports manufactured goods and machinery. Beijing's rapidly growing stock of foreign direct investment (FDI) in the region is concentrated almost entirely in Australia.

China in Central Asia

Central Asia has been a high priority region for China since 1991 when Beijing first engaged with the newly independent post-Soviet republics. Beijing focused on developing a cooperative and constructive relationship with this bloc of neighboring states. In the 2010s, Beijing has four overriding interests in the region. China's first interest is to ensure its domestic stability and national unity, particularly by countering unrest among the minority Tibetan and Uighur populations in western China. The second interest is in maintaining peace, predictability, and secularism in Central Asia, principally by resolving border disputes and collaboratively managing cross-border minority populations. A third interest is increasing Chinese influence and limiting the influence of other outside powers, in large part through the multilateral Shanghai Cooperation Organization (SCO). A fourth interest is to promote and protect PRC economic interests in the region and beyond, in particular by constructing the infrastructure needed to access Central Asian oil and gas.

Although Russia views Central Asia as its sphere of influence, Beijing and Moscow have found opportunities to collaborate on regional initiatives through the SCO, and Beijing sees Russia—although geographically on the periphery of Central Asia—as its most critical partner in the region. Central Asia is also important as the first stage in President Xi's Silk Road Economic Belt, and China has funded a range of infrastructure projects in the region. Although China dominates the region's trade, Chinese investment—which is concentrated overwhelmingly in the Kazakhstan hydrocarbon sector—represents a small share of the overall stock of FDI in the region. China has pursued mining, oil, and gas deals in the region, especially in Kazakhstan and Turkmenistan. China has also engaged in a proactive program of high-level military visits, military-to-military exchanges, and combined exercises focused on anti-terrorism operations, suggesting that the region's security is a high priority for China. Through deft use of high-profile diplomacy, infrastructure investment, and military cooperation, Beijing has promoted the image of a powerful and benevolent China.

China in South Asia

South Asia has become a key region of expanding Chinese interests, influence, and involvement. China's primary goals in the region are to mitigate regional threats to its internal stability, principally Uighur nationalism stoked by Islamists from Pakistan and Afghanistan; to offset India's growing geopolitical and economic strength; and to safeguard Chinese investments and commerce in South Asia.

Unlike with most other developing regions (but like Southeast Asia), China's imports from South Asia include a high proportion of manufactured items, most of which originate in India. Nevertheless, China's closest partner in the region is Pakistan, which Beijing sees as the key to countering New Delhi—long China's principal regional rival—especially as India grows stronger economically and more powerful militarily. China has little cultural influence in South Asia; indeed, it seems more concerned about the flow of the region's cultures—particularly Islam and Tibetan Buddhism—into China. Whereas most of China's regional trade is with India, most of its investment has gone to Pakistan. In large part, this investment has focused on efforts to construct roads, railways, and an oil pipeline to connect China's Xinjiang province to the Pakistani port of Gwadar. This aspirational transportation infrastructure—critical components of the Belt and Road Initiative—would facilitate oil and gas imports from the gulf and, potentially, allow Chinese exports to be sent overland to a deepwater port on the Arabian side of South Asia. Since 2000, China has been a key supplier of major conventional weapons to South Asia; Pakistan and Bangladesh purchased more than half of China's total arms exports from 2000 to 2014.

China in the Middle East

The Middle East is of growing importance to China—and rivals Africa as the most important region to Beijing outside of the Asia-Pacific. Beijing has three overarching interests in the Middle East. First, China seeks to maintain its access to the region's energy resources (which comprise more than half of China's oil imports), continue trade flows, and protect Chinese investments and the approximately half a million PRC citizens in the region. Second, China works to enhance its stature and influence in a region of key geostrategic importance through involvement in high-profile issues, such as the Iran nuclear negotiations. Third, Beijing focuses on preserving internal and external stability and security around the periphery by preventing moral and material support for militant ethnic groups or heterodox religious sects. The Middle East is a central node of both the land and water parts of the Belt and Road Initiative. To date, China's imports from the Middle East are dominated by petroleum, and it has been involved in many infrastructure projects in the Gulf States and Iran.

China military involvement in the region has been extremely modest. Nevertheless, the People's Liberation Army (PLA) has been increasingly active, including participating in United Nations peacekeeping missions, conducting dozens of port visits, engaging in antipiracy patrols off the coast of Somalia, and operations to evacuate PRC civilians from regional trouble spots, notably in Libya (in 2011) and Yemen (in 2015).

China in Africa

Long a key area of the globe for Beijing, Africa's importance to China has grown, as have China's influence and involvement. China currently has four overarching interests in the continent. First, Beijing seeks access to natural resources, particularly oil and gas. Second, China looks to enhance international political legitimacy as a global power and leader of the Developing World, and support the principle of noninterference in sovereign countries' internal affairs. Third, Beijing is interested in export markets for Chinese manufactured items. Fourth, China desires sufficient political stability and security in Africa to assure the safety of its citizens and economic interests.

China ensures ongoing high-level engagement with African countries bilaterally and multilaterally, the latter through the Forum on China-Africa Cooperation (FOCAC), under the auspices of which China announces regional engagement strategies; launches educational and cultural initiatives; and unveils large bilateral trade, investment, and aid initiatives and aspirations. China has engaged in a vigorous public diplomacy campaign in Africa to counter negative public perceptions of China. This includes a massive outreach campaign by Chinese state media and the provision of thousands of scholarships, job training programs, and people-to-people exchanges under FOCAC auspices. China's foreign aid—roughly half of which goes to Africa—is by official pronouncement intended to produce mutual benefit rather than mitigate poverty. Much of China's aid to Africa is given in the form of concessional loans and, in some cases, grants intended for construction and infrastructure development, tied to the purchase of Chinese goods and services.

While China had long maintained a hands-off approach to security matters in Africa, terrorism, kidnappings, anti-Chinese protests, and civil unrest have affected Chinese citizens. Beijing decided to take a more proactive approach to security by building host nation capacity and making greater use of private Chinese security firms. China has expanded its participation in peacekeeping operations on the continent, including those in Mali, Liberia, Congo, Sudan, and South Sudan. This expansion culminated with the establishment of a base in Djibouti that China refers to as a facility to provide logistical support but that others have subsequently described as China's first overseas military installation.

China in Latin America and the Caribbean

Latin America and the Caribbean is the least important region of the Developing World for China. It is geographically distant and comprises a small share of total Chinese trade. China has three overarching interests in the region. First, Beijing pursues cooperation with Latin American countries to build regional support for PRC international initiatives. Second, Beijing seeks expanded trade and investment opportunities to support China's economic growth. Third, Beijing targets strengthened political legitimacy in the form of public acknowledgement in Latin America of the PRC being the sole political representative of China and the weakening of Taiwan's footholds in the region.

Although Chinese trade with and investment in the region has increased dramatically in the last decade, it is still low compared with Chinese economic engagement with other developing regions. Latin America has been a source of food for China and raw materials for Chinese manufacturing as well as an export market for Chinese manufactured goods and machinery. China seeks to strengthen trade with major regional economies and has been willing to provide significant financial support in exchange for resources. To reduce the share of raw materials in China's trade with the region, Beijing is increasingly focusing its investment on infrastructure, agriculture, and local production of value-added products. Countries that are in political turmoil or in financial crisis, such as Bolivia, Ecuador, and Venezuela, have particularly welcomed Chinese investment.

Pivotal Regional Partnerships

While China has formally established partner relations (*huoban guanxi*) with many countries around the globe, Beijing deems some capitals to be more important than others and tends to dub these "strategic partnerships" (*zhanlue huoban*). In fact, in almost every region examined in this study, China appears to have identified one particular state as being pivotal within the specific geographic region and sought to establish comprehensive, long-term strategic partnerships there. We label these states "pivotal regional partnerships" (PRPs). It is noteworthy that in only two regions—Southeast Asia and Oceania—can no single PRP be identified. The former is China's most important region in the Developing World, while the latter is one of its least important. In Southeast Asia, Beijing appears to perceive multiple PRP candidate states, depending on whether the primary criterion is economic (Malaysia), political (Indonesia), trustworthiness (Thailand), or geostrategic risk (Vietnam). In Oceania, the two largest states—Australia and New Zealand—are the clearest PRP candidates, but their close ties to and security alignments with the United States preclude either having a more robust relationship with China, at least for now.

PRPs Straddling the Second and Third Rings: Pakistan and Russia

The highest priority is afforded to those PRPs that straddle China's second and third rings of insecurity—countries that are on the PRC's immediate periphery. Two of China's five PRPs—Pakistan and Russia—sit in both the second and third rings.

Russia is China's PRP in Central Asia. Although Russia is not geographically located in the region, by dint of its size, proximity, history, and enduring influence in the six landlocked states that comprise the region—Kazakhstan, Kyrgyzstan, Tajikistan, Turkmenistan, Uzbekistan, and Mongolia—Moscow is, without a doubt, Beijing's most important partner in Central Asia. Russia's strategic value to China is underscored by the extended land border the two share. Although coordination between Moscow and Beijing has its limits, the two capitals have pursued significant cooperation in both military relations and energy affairs. Within Central Asia, Russia concentrates more on military activities while China is focused more on economic efforts, but they share significant interests in countering terrorism, extremism, separatism, and Western ideas of democracy and human rights.

Pakistan is China's PRP in South Asia. For decades Islamabad has been the linchpin of Beijing's South Asia policy precisely because it is a counterweight to New Delhi. But Pakistan appears to have become far more important for China than simply as a balance against India. Beijing's close, abiding partnership with Islamabad is linked to Pakistan's importance in managing the threat posed by Islamic extremists and ethnic groups who spill across international borders, including into China and Afghanistan. Thus China works with Pakistan to maintain internal security and quash unrest among ethnic minorities, notably the Uighurs in westernmost China. China is also keen to nurture stability and economic development in Pakistan and beyond, which has led Beijing to commit significant investments in Pakistan's transportation and energy infrastructure.

Fourth Ring PRPs: Iran, South Africa, Venezuela

China has three identifiable PRPs in the fourth ring—one in the Middle East, one in Africa, and one in Latin America. Certainly Beijing actively engages with multiple capitals in each region, and China has expansive relations with numerous states. Thus there are multiple viable candidates for Chinese PRPs. Nevertheless, China has deep, longstanding, and enduring ties with Iran, South Africa, and Venezuela, and each of these states seems to be viewed by Beijing as the centerpieces of its regional strategies.

China seeks friends in the oil-rich Middle East that are influential but neither beholden to nor engaged in direct hostilities with the United States; that is, the Islamic Republic of Iran. Both China and Iran tend to think of themselves as having been great powers for millennia and as heirs to splendid ancient civilizations. Ostracism by Western capitals drove the PRC and Iran to significant and broad collaboration in political, economic, and military spheres. Beijing provided Tehran with military materiel during the Iran-Iraq war, and China continued to trade with Iran (and provide military technologies) during years of Western sanctions, which strengthened their high-level political and economic ties. China was a key actor in the signing of the 2015 Iran nuclear deal and stands to benefit considerably from the lifting of international economic sanctions.

In Africa, China's strongest partner is the Republic of South Africa. South Africa has been a destination of choice for Chinese businesses because of its strong financial sector, rule of law, and infrastructure. While there are other significant partner states on the continent for China, including Angola, Nigeria, and Sudan, which are major oil exporters, and Ethiopia, where many Chinese companies have opened factories to take advantage of cheap labor, Beijing has singled out South Africa for a long-term relationship since at least the 1990s. As the most diversified economy on the continent, South Africa ranks as China's most significant trade partner and a leading destination for Chinese investment. Moreover, South Africa's reliable infrastructure and rule of law make it a convenient base from which Chinese businesses can access other African markets. In 2010, Beijing sponsored Pretoria's bid to become a member of the BRIC group (Brazil, Russia, India, and China), turning it into the BRICS group (Brazil, Russia, India, China, and South Africa), a sign of the value China assigns to South Africa.

In Latin America, although China has engaged with many regional states, Venezuela stands out based upon an array of economic and military indicators. Venezuela's large oil deposits made it an attractive partner for China, which rapidly offered Caracas significant levels of investment, military materiel, and loans, most of which Venezuela will pay for through future oil exports (if, given its economic collapse, it ever pays). Beijing continues to support Caracas despite its severe (and largely self-inflicted) economic crisis because there is money to be made and because Venezuela's ability to pay back many Chinese loans is dependent on continued commodity exports.

Ranking Regions by the Numbers

Our detailed examination of Chinese involvement in seven different regions using a common template permits us to compare them using the same criteria (Table S.1). An analysis of the movement and magnitude

Table S.1
Chinese Economic, Political, and Military Engagement by Region

	Southeast Asia	Central Asia	South Asia	Africa	Middle East	Latin America	Oceania
Economic							
Goods Trade $B (2000, 2014)	39.5 479.8	2.1 52.3	5.7 106.1	9.6 210.0	17.0 290.4	12.5 259.4	9.8 144.1
Investment $M (2003, 2012)	587 28,238	57 10,490	45 4,215	477 21,370	520 6,467	376 7,094	472 15,089
Political							
High-level visits (2003–2014)	94	55	40	91	40	45	18
Confucius Institutes (2014)	25	11	8	34	11	32	16
Military							
Arms sales $M (2000–2014)	1,635	0	7,204	2,246	1,495	550	0
Field exercises	26 (2005–14)	27 (2002–14)	24 (2002–14)	3 (2009–14)	1 (2014)	4 (2010–13)	6 (2004–14)

SOURCE: Data sources described in the text.

NOTE: The countries with the highest levels of each indicator are highlighted in a darker color for each category.

of China's economic, political, and military engagement can serve as indicators of Beijing's relative priorities of Developing World regions. Each dimension is represented by two data points. To assess economic engagement, we provide the total value of two-way goods trade in 2000 and 2014 and the total value of China's outward FDI in 2003 and 2012. To evaluate political engagement, we provide the number of senior leader visits (that is, PRC president, vice president, premier, minister of foreign affairs, and state councilor for foreign affairs) from 2003 to 2014 and the number of Confucius Institutes in 2014. To consider military engagement, we ranked the volume of arms sales from 2000 to 2014 and the number of military exercises the PLA conducted between 2000 and 2014, showing the dates of the first and last field exercise.

These data show that Southeast Asia is China's top priority region in the Developing World. Economically, Southeast Asia is far and away the most important of the seven regions with the largest trade volume—$479.8 billion or 31.1 percent of China's total trade—with the Developing World in 2014 and the recipient of the largest amount of China's outbound foreign direct investment in 2012: $28.2 billion or 30.4 percent of China's total stock of FDI in all seven regions. In terms of political attention, China sent more high-level leaders to Southeast Asia than to any other region of the Developing World. Between 2003 and 2014, top PRC leaders visited Southeast Asia countries 94 times; that is 24.5 percent of all high-level visits to the Developing World. On military measures, Southeast Asia ranks third in volume of arms sales between 2000 and 2014, with $1.635 billion (behind South Asia and Africa), and second in the number of field exercises conducted between the PLA and regional militaries, with 26, behind only Central Asia.

Beyond the Asia-Pacific, Africa is China's second most important region in the Developing World and Beijing's most important region outside of the Asia-Pacific, at least according to this analysis of Chinese resource allocations. Note, however, that Africa also has the most countries, which would inflate some of the numbers. Africa was the second largest recipient of the stock of Chinese FDI in 2012 with $21.4 billion—almost a quarter of the total (23.0 percent) Beijing sent to the entire Developing World. Africa ranks fourth in terms of the value of the two-way trade China conducted with all seven regions—$210 billion in 2014 (behind Southeast Asia, the Middle East, and Latin America). Africa is also home to the largest number of Confucius Institutes—34—of any single region, 24.8 percent of the total in the Developing World. Africa ranks second in terms of the most visited region by top-level PRC officials, well ahead of other regions, with 91 visits between 2003 and 2014, or 23.8 percent of the total. Africa ranks second only to South Asia in terms of the value of Chinese arms sales: $2.25 billion between 2000 and 2014. Although Africa ranks low in terms of the number of military exercises, if one includes other measures of military presence, such as the number of port visits (35) between 2000 and 2014, PLA operational deployments on United Nations peacekeeping missions in 2014 (seven), or establishing a naval facility in Djibouti in 2017, then this all only serves to underscore the level of importance Beijing attaches to Africa.

The Middle East ranks as China's third most important region in the Developing World and its second most important region outside of the Asia-Pacific. If one factors in the Middle East's role as a critical source of China's imports, its key linkages to China's internal security, and its geopolitical significance for China, then the Middle East at least rivals Africa's importance to Beijing. Nevertheless, the Middle East ranks ahead of Africa—and second only to Southeast Asia—in terms of the value of two-way trade China conducts with regions of the Developing World. However, the Middle East ranks sixth in terms of the level of stock of Chinese FDI, ahead of only South Asia. The political indicators, meanwhile, almost certainly do not do justice to the level of importance Beijing attaches to the region. The relatively low numbers of high-level political visits and Confucius Institutes in the region say more about Chinese political sensitivities and wariness where the Middle East is concerned. Chinese military attention to the region is limited but noteworthy; $1.5 billion in arms sales between 2000 and 2014, as well as anti-piracy task forces in the Gulf of Aden since 2008, 44 port visits between 2009 and 2014—more than any other region—and small PLA detachments on United Nations Peacekeeping Operations (UNPKOs) make the PRC a small-time military player in the region.

Central Asia is China's fourth most important region in the Developing World and second most important developing region in the Asia-Pacific by the numbers. Economically, this region may not be hugely important—it ranks last in terms of the value of China's two-way trade—but it ranks fourth in terms of the value of Chinese investments in the seven regions. Politically, Central Asia is an important focus of PRC high-level leadership visits, ranking third behind Southeast Asia and Africa. Militarily, Central Asia is considered particularly important at least in terms of the number of military exercises conducted in the region between 2002 and 2014: 27. This is the highest number the PLA conducted in any region of the world. This number becomes even more important given that the region has only seven countries, suggesting a high level of per-country activity.

South Asia is the fifth most important region in the Developing World and the third most important developing region in the Asia-Pacific. Economically, South Asia does not rate highly for China, with a low level of trade and ranking sixth, ahead of only Central Asia. Nevertheless, the region has a respectable volume of high-level leadership visits but ranks last in terms of the number of Confucius Institutes. It is in military metrics that South Asia truly stands out. It is first in terms of the value of Chinese armaments sold in the Developing World, and South Asia ranks third in terms of the number of military exercises China conducts. Indeed, more than half of China's total arms sales in the Developing World between 2000 and 2014 were to South Asian countries, and more than a quarter of China's military exercises between 2002 and 2014 were conducted with South Asia states—mostly with Pakistan.

One of China's least important regions, Latin America and the Caribbean, is of increasing significance to China. Economically, the region is of growing importance and ranks third in terms of two-way trade in 2014 and fifth in terms of a recipient of the stock of Chinese FDI in 2012. Politically, Latin America is a significant destination for high-level Chinese leaders—40—and ranks second only to Africa in terms of the number of Confucius Institutes. Moreover, the region takes on even greater political significance to China as home to a dozen states, as of 2014 (Panama broke ties with Taipei in 2017), that continue to maintain ambassador-level diplomatic ties with Taiwan. This represents the largest single bloc of holdouts to recognizing the

PRC and the government of China. Militarily, China's profile in the region is extremely small as measured by arms sales and field exercises.

While Oceania ranks last to China by the numbers as a region in the Asia-Pacific and low as a part of the Developing World, it is by no means unimportant to Beijing. Indeed, Oceania is of growing economic significance to China; it ranks third in terms of the stock of FDI—behind Southeast Asia and Africa—and fourth in the value of Beijing's two-way trade. Much of this economic activity is focused on one country—Australia—but China is also economically engaged across this sprawling maritime region. Oceania plays host to the fewest number of senior leader visits but is home to a respectable number of Confucius Institutes. China also directs few military resources at the region, conducting only a handful of exercises and a negligible volume of arms sales.

Conclusions

China has been more active economically, diplomatically, and militarily all across the Developing World, particularly since the 1990s. Beijing's activism has only increased in subsequent decades. China's growing presence in the various regions of the Developing World is likely to continue to expand under PRC President Xi Jinping and extend beyond his tenure. China's global economic outreach has been reenergized by President Xi's 2013 proclamations launching the Belt and Road Initiative and his subsequent follow-through efforts. Diplomatically, high-profile travel by senior leaders seems destined to continue apace, and China should remain actively engaged in sustaining bilateral partnerships around the globe, as well as participating in multilateral forums. Militarily, the PLA is likely to be increasingly active further afield, conducting more port visits, field exercises, arms sales, and peacetime operational employments in the Developing World. China could set up more military bases, although may not call them bases.

Chinese leaders perceive certain regions to be more important than others. Beijing appears to be far more concerned with those regions of the Developing World that abut China's borders and that are in its immediate neighborhood than those at a distance. Regions along its borders—Southeast Asia, Central Asia, and South Asia—China's second ring of security, are of greatest concern because instability there poses a direct and proximate threat to internal security, to China's first ring. These regions spill over into the third ring. Oceania, also in China's third ring, is a lower priority, but there is growing Chinese interest in this region. Outside of the Asia-Pacific, in the fourth ring, are the Middle East, Africa, and Latin America and the Caribbean. Although of lesser importance than those regions that occupy the second and third rings, the Middle East and Africa have loomed increasingly important for China during the past decade or so. The Middle East seems to garner greater attention because it is increasingly viewed as part of China's extended periphery—intertwined with China's first, second, and third rings of security. Meanwhile, Africa has become an ever more central Developing World arena for Chinese economic and political activity, while Latin America and the Caribbean is of lower priority but growing importance.

The United States and China: Partners in Parallel

Across the Developing World, the United States and China are neither in direct conflict nor working in close cooperation, although there is significant variation by region. In Southeast Asia, for example, Washington and Beijing are in confrontation mode over Chinese activities in the South China Sea and China's insistence that freedom of navigation does not extend to U.S. military vessels and aircraft traversing disputed waters claimed by China. But outside of Southeast Asia (and Northeast Asia, among developed regions), the United States and China appear to be "partners in parallel"—meaning that the two states work separately with no real collaboration in pursuit of similar ends but with no conflicts.

Two caveats are in order. First, the partners in parallel concept risks oversimplifying and mischaracterizing a complex reality. In some regions, notably Southeast Asia, the United States and China are at loggerheads. Second, this concept describes peacetime U.S.-China interactions. In wartime or during periods of escalating bilateral tensions, these parallel Chinese and American trajectories are likely to converge toward confrontation or diverge in estrangement. How China might act economically, diplomatically, and militarily in the Developing World vis-à-vis the United States in time of war or on the road to war remains unclear.

For now, the overriding trend is one in which both countries pursue their own ends, often similar, without conflict. There may even be some minimal coordination, such as in the Gulf of Aden anti-piracy missions or in post-2014 Afghanistan. These parallel efforts have tended to occur either within or at the fringes of existing frameworks, institutions, and regimes. More recently, the United States and China also appear to be acting as partners in parallel in separate universes as Beijing begins to operate in parallel institutions created by China.

Acknowledgments

The authors thank Major General Todd McCaffrey, Major General Gregory Bilton, Rodney Laszlo, and Colonel Newman Yang of U.S. Army Pacific for their invaluable input and guidance. Briefings at Pacific Command and Pacific Air Forces also resulted in valuable comments. This report has also benefited from the trenchant peer reviews of Andrew Erickson, Eric Heginbotham, and Troy Smith, and from research assistance by Samuel Berkowitz. All errors of fact and interpretation remain the responsibility of the authors. The authors thank Kenneth Todd Duft and Cynthia Lyons, the RAND production editors who guided the manuscript through publication; Kathi Anderson, who provided expert copy-editing; and Katherine Wu, who designed the cover.

Abbreviations

ACFTA	ASEAN-China Free Trade Area
ACJCC	ASEAN-China Joint Cooperation Committee
ACSOC	ASEAN-China Senior Officials Consultations
AIIB	Asian Infrastructure Investment Bank
ARF	ASEAN Regional Forum
ASEAN	Association of Southeast Asian Nations
BIT	bilateral investment treaty
BRIC	Brazil, Russia, and India
BRICS	Brazil, Russia, India, China, and South Africa
CABC	China-ASEAN Business Council
CASCF	China-Arab States Cooperation Forum
CASS	Chinese Academy of Social Sciences
CCP	Chinese Communist Party
CDB	China Development Bank
CELAC	Community of Latin American and Caribbean States
CICA	Conference for Interaction and Confidence-Building Measures in Asia

CMC	Central Military Commission
CNPC	China National Petroleum Corporation
CPEC	China-Pakistan Economic Corridor
CPIC	China-Pacific Island Countries Economic Development and Cooperation Forum
CSTO	Collective Security Treaty Organization
EAS	East Asian Summit
EXIM	Export-Import Bank of China
FARC	Revolutionary Armed Forces of Colombia
FDI	foreign direct investment
FTA	free trade agreement
FOCAC	Forum on China-Africa Cooperation
FONOP	Freedom of Navigation Operations
GCC	Gulf Cooperation Council
HADR	humanitarian assistance and disaster relief
IMF	International Monetary Fund
IRMB	intermediate-range ballistic missiles
LDC	Least Developed Countries
LSG	Leading Small Group
MINUSMA	United Nations Multidimensional Integrated Stabilization Mission in Mali
MOFA	Ministry of Foreign Affairs
MOOTW	military operations other than war
NDB	New Development Bank

OPIC	Overseas Private Investment Corporation
PKO	peacekeeping operation
PLA	People's Liberation Army
PLAAF	People's Liberation Army Air Force
PLAN	People's Liberation Army Navy
PME	professional military education
PRC	People's Republic of China
PRPs	pivotal regional partnerships
RCEP	Regional Comprehensive Economic Partnership
RMB	renminbi
SAARC	South Asian Association for Regional Cooperation
SABIC	Saudi Basic Industries Corporation
SALW	small arms and light weapons
SCO	Shanghai Cooperation Organization
SIPRI	Stockholm International Peace Research Institute
SOE	state-owned enterprise
TDA	Trade and Development Agency
TPP	Trans-Pacific Partnership
UAE	United Arab Emirates
UAV	unmanned aerial vehicle
UCAV	unmanned combat aerial vehicle
UN	United Nations
UNCTAD	United Nations Conference on Trade and Development

UNIFIL	United Nations Interim Force in Lebanon
UNITA	National Union for the Total Independence of Angola
UNMOGIP	United Nations Military Observer Group in India and Pakistan
UNPKO	United Nations Peacekeeping Operations
UNSC	United Nations Security Council
UNTAC	United Nations Transitional Authority in Cambodia
UNTSO	UN Truce Supervision Organization
WTO	World Trade Organization

CHAPTER ONE

Introduction

> China . . . [is] a large developing country . . . [that] faces multiple and complex security threats, as well as increasing external impediments and security challenges. . . . [T]he armed forces will actively participate in both regional and international security cooperation and effectively secure China's overseas interests.
>
> —PRC Defense White Paper, May 2015

Since its establishment in 1949, the People's Republic of China (PRC) has viewed itself as an underdeveloped country—economically backward, physically weak, and vulnerable to exploitation by much more powerful states. Indeed, the narrative of modern Chinese history is the story of an enfeebled great civilization victimized by 100 years of humiliation at the hands of industrialized and militarized imperialist powers.[1] Even as the PRC has grown stronger economically and militarily, especially since the launching of the reform and opening policy by the late Deng Xiaoping in 1978, PRC officials continue to insist that China is a developing country (see Chapter 2 for more discussion).

The legacy of Marxist-Leninist-Maoist ideology has tended to reinforce an enduring perception in Beijing that China has more in common with the poorer and less developed states of the world than it

[1] The so-called "Century of Humiliation" has been a central contextual feature of PRC foreign policy since 1949, and this continues in the twenty-first century. See Zheng Wang, *Never Forget National Humiliation: Historical Memory in Chinese Politics and Foreign Relations*, New York: Columbia University Press, 2012.

does with the economically developed and militarily powerful states of Europe and North America. At the same time, this also meant Beijing unambiguously differentiated the PRC from the two superpowers that emerged out of the Second World War—the United States and the Soviet Union. Even during the 1950s, when Beijing viewed Moscow as an ally and a successful model of a communist-ruled country that modernized itself, Mao Zedong's writings made clear that China saw itself as part of a vast "intermediate zone," an expansive middle ground located between the two superpowers.[2] In Mao's view, the rivalry between the two superpowers was being played out in this "intermediate zone," which Beijing eventually began to refer to as the "Developing World" or "Third World."[3] For Mao, this meant that China had emerged from the global periphery and moved to the center stage of geostrategic competition. From the perspective of Beijing, China was clearly the most important country in this zone and the natural leader of the group of weaker states and national liberation movements spread across Asia, Africa, and Latin America.

The Developing World has never been more important to China than it is today. In the twenty-first century, China needs the Developing World more than ever for a multitude of reasons. Ironically, in Mao's day, while the Developing World rhetoric made these regions seem like the centerpiece of Chinese foreign policy, they were not (except in the sense that China saw itself as located at the center of the Developing World).[4] Today the rhetoric has moderated, but in reality, China relies more on the Developing World than ever: for resources, markets, expansion of geostrategic influence, and for advantage in its global competition with the United States. During the Cold War, China was

[2] Chen Jian, *Mao's China and the Cold War*, Chapel Hill: University of North Carolina Press, 2001, p. 5.

[3] For some prominent articulations of Beijing's views of the Developing or Third World, see Lin Piao, "Long Live the Victory of People's War!" *Peking Review*, September 3, 1965, pp. 9–30, and "Chairman of Chinese Delegation Teng Hsiao-ping's Speech at the Special Session of the U.N. General Assembly," *Peking Review*, April 19, 1974, pp. 6–11.

[4] The reality was that Beijing was focused on the strategic triangle—dealing with two superpowers—evidenced by rapprochement with Washington in the early 1970s.

at least symbolically countering both superpowers and rhetorically promoting world revolution; in the post–Cold War era, China is actively engaged in competing with the United States for influence and promoting Chinese political, economic, and diplomatic interests.

China seemed to cement the importance of the Developing World for its future development in 2013 when new Chinese leader Xi Jinping announced his vision for what has become the Belt and Road Initiative. First in Kazakhstan and then in Indonesia, Xi presented a vision of land and sea corridors and linkages that would integrate Eurasia, involving Southeast Asia, Central Asia, the Middle East, and even Oceania, stretching to Europe.[5]

This renewed interest raises a number of questions. What are China's goals and interests, and do these run contrary to U.S. goals and interests? What is the scope and scale of China's economic, diplomatic, and military activities in the Developing World? For example, does trade follow the flag or does the flag follow trade? And what are the implications for the United States of Chinese activism in the Developing World?

Focus, Context, Methodology, Outline

This study is a comprehensive effort to analyze the range of Chinese involvements in developing regions. It focuses on China in the twenty-first century through late 2014, the early days of the Belt and Road Initiative. By doing so, it shows the trends that China was building on and can help explain how China might gain from Belt and Road. More important, it can show China's interests and activities well beyond its Belt and Road Initiative, which is only one aspect of China's policies, and one that remains not fully defined and, therefore, with uncertain prospects of success.

Only a small number of studies have comprehensively examined China's policy toward the Developing World during the past five decades. Three of them were edited volumes published in recent

[5] "Chronology of China's Belt and Road Initiative," *Xinhua News*, March 28, 2015.

years.[6] Somewhat surprising, few studies of China's Cold War era policy toward the Developing World have been published; the most well known is a study examining China's support for national liberation movements.[7] More studies focused on China's policy toward particular geographic regions, such as Africa and the Middle East, or on China's relations with specific developing countries, such as India or Iran.[8] These studies have been empirically rich but largely descriptive.

By contrast, this study concentrates on a more structured and quantitative approach. It is structured in that it analyzes China's relations with entire regions rather than just selected countries within a region. This study classifies regions of the world, rather than specific states, as developing. The developing regions examined in this report are all the areas of the world except Northeast Asia, Europe, and North America. Specifically, the following regions are the focus of this report: Southeast Asia, South Asia, Central Asia, Oceania, Middle East, Africa, and Latin America and the Caribbean. The study is quantitative in that it attempts to apply numerical information to measure China's interactions with different regions.

We do not ignore specific countries. In almost every developing region, we can identify one country that China considers the pivotal partner because of, in China's view, the combination of its crucial sig-

---

[6] Joshua Eisenman, Eric Heginbotham, and Derek Mitchell, *China and the Developing World: Beijing's Strategy of the Twenty-First Century*, Armonk, N.Y.: M.E. Sharpe, 2007; Lowell Dittmer and George T. Yu, eds., *China, the Developing World, and the New Global Dynamic*, Boulder, Colo.: Lynne Rienner Publishers, 2010.

[7] Joshua Eisenman and Eric Heginbotham, eds. *China Steps Out: Beijing's Major Power Engagement with the Developing World*, New York: Routledge, 2018. Peter Van Ness, *Revolution and Chinese Foreign Policy: Peking's Support of Wars of National Liberation*, Berkeley: University of California Press, 1971. For a more recent overview of China's approach to the Developing World, see Peter Van Ness, "China and the Third World: Patterns of Engagement and Indifference," in Samuel S. Kim, ed., *China and the World: Chinese Foreign Policy Faces the New Millennium*, 4th ed., Boulder, Colo.: Westview Press, 1998, pp. 151–170.

[8] See, for example, Philip Snow, *The Star Raft: China's Encounter with Africa*, Ithaca, N.Y.: Cornell University Press, 1988; Yitzhak Shichor, *The Middle East in China's Foreign Policy, 1949–1977*, New York: Cambridge University Press, 1979; John W. Garver, *Protracted Contest: China-India Rivalry in the Twentieth Century*, Seattle: University of Washington Press, 2000; John W. Garver, *China and Iran: Ancient Partners in a Post-Imperial World*, Seattle: University of Washington Press, 2006.

nificance to its particular neighborhood and to China's interests. Southeast Asia is the only region where there was no clear priority country, and we identify four key states rather than a single pivotal partner. For China, such pivotal countries and the four key states in Southeast Asia merit greater attention as partner states.

Data and Methodology

We examine China's engagement with each region in several different ways. We first highlight China's main interests in the region, and, in some regions, the actors involved in shaping Chinese policy. We then analyze China's political, economic, and military activities. Within the political engagement section, we examine China's foreign policy priorities and agenda, diplomatic relations with countries in the region, high-level leadership visits to the region, and its cultural influence in the region, and then identify the small set of countries China sees as its most important partners. In the economic sections, we dissect Chinese trade and investments in the region and economic agreements China has signed with local partners. We also discuss particular or special economic projects China has within the region. We then examine a range of ways China could be enhancing military or security cooperation with the region, including Chinese arms sales, high-level military visits, combined exercises, People's Liberation Army (PLA) naval port visits, and other military activities.

To be consistent across regions, we relied on several common sources of data. For political and military leadership visits, we referred to China Vitae's biographical database of reports of Chinese Communist Party officials' foreign travel and corroborated and supported this dataset with articles from the Chinese Ministry of Foreign Affairs (MOFA) website and *Xinhua Online*. For the officials tracked, we coded each visit by country, region, and date of travel; when possible, we identified counterparts visited and recorded whether the meeting took place as part of a summit, defined here as a meeting of counterparts from three or more countries.

Political, Economic, and Military Data

For our political sections, information on China's bilateral relations with each country (the particular terms used to define the relationship) were from official Chinese press statements, documents, and information from the Chinese Ministry of Foreign Affairs website. Data on Confucius Institutes was compiled from the lists of Confucius Institutes worldwide maintained at the University of Nebraska-Lincoln[9] and on the Confucius Institute Online website.[10] China started Confucius Institutes in 2004 as nonprofit institutions to promote Chinese language and culture in foreign countries.[11] Only university-level Confucius Institutes, not the far more numerous but far less influential and established Confucius Classrooms, are counted in our dataset. Data on ethnic Chinese populations across the Developing World were gathered from the *2013 Statistical Yearbook of the Overseas Community Affairs Council*, Republic of China (Taiwan).[12] However, our focus was on estimating the numbers of PRC citizens in regions around the world and there is no single authoritative or reliable source for these figures. We therefore used a range of different sources, as detailed in individual regional chapters.

Our economic data focus on several different forms of economic exchange, specifically trade, direct investment, and agreements. For each region, we present data on China's bilateral merchandise exports and imports drawn from the UN Comtrade Database.[13] Because of its availability, we provide data on trade from 2000 to 2013, in ten different categories[14] (with the term we use in subsequent charts in parentheses):

- Food and live animals (food)
- Beverages and tobacco (beverages and tobacco)
- Crude materials, inedible, except fuel (crude materials)

9 "Confucius Institutes Around the Globe," University of Nebraska-Lincoln.

10 "Worldwide Confucius Institutes," Confucius Institute Online.

11 Confucius Institute Headquarters, "About Confucius Institutes," Beijing, China, 2014.

12 *2013 Statistical Yearbook of the Overseas Community Affairs Council,* Republic of China (Taiwan), Overseas Community Affairs Council, Republic of China (Taiwan), September 2014.

13 United Nations, UN Comtrade Database, 2014.

14 These are the top-level categories of the Standard International Trade Classification, revision 3.

- Mineral fuels, lubricants, and related materials (mineral fuels)
- Animal and vegetable oils, fats, and waxes (animal and vegetable oils)
- Chemicals and related products (chemicals)
- Manufactured goods classified chiefly by material (manufactured goods; this is one of three categories of manufactured items, although "chemicals and related products" can also be considered a manufactured item)
- Machinery and transport equipment (machinery and transport; this is one of three categories of manufactured items)
- Miscellaneous manufactured articles (miscellaneous manufactured; this is one of three categories of manufactured items)
- Commodities and transactions not classified elsewhere (other).

We use the United Nations Conference on Trade and Development (UNCTAD) foreign direct investment (FDI) database to show the stock of China's outward FDI relations around the world. Direct investment is overseas investment for the purpose of controlling a company or owning real estate; it is different from portfolio investment, which is investment into debt or equity securities.[15] The stock is the cumulative amount, whereas the flow is the annual amount of investment. In this report, we focus on the stock. For agreements, we present data on bilateral investment treaties,[16] tax treaties,[17] free trade agreements,[18] and membership in the Asian Infrastructure Investment

---

[15] United Nations Conference on Trade and Development, *Bilateral FDI Statistics*, 2014.

[16] *Bilateral Investment Treaty*, Ministry of Commerce of the People's Republic of China, Department of Treaty and Law, 2011; *Investment Policy Hub: International Investment Agreements*, UNCTAD, 2013.

[17] United Nations Conference on Trade and Development, "China: Total Number of Double Taxation Agreements Concluded 1 June 2011," 2011; State Administration of Taxation of the People's Republic of China, "Zhongguo Shuishou Xieding Tanqian De Zongti Qingkuang" ["The Overall Situation of the Negotiation of China's Tax Treaty"], 2013; Dezan Shira and Associates, "Understanding China's Double Tax Agreements," *China Briefing*, February 12, 2014.

[18] Asian Development Bank, "Free Trade Agreements," Asia Regional Integration Center, 2015.

Bank (AIIB).[19] In terms of tax treaties, we focus specifically on treaties that deal with treatment of income from foreign investment or with treatment of income and capital related to foreign investment.

For our military indicators, we present a quantitative assessment of Chinese major conventional arms sales in each of the regions based on the Stockholm International Peace Research Institute (SIPRI) Arms Transfers Database (2000–2014), which measures the volume of arms transfers in millions of trend-indicator values.[20] Although the term "arms sales" in this report refers specifically to transfers of major conventional weapons, information on China's sales of small arms and light weapons (SALW), taken from UN Comtrade data, is discussed where relevant. Since 2000, Chinese sales of major conventional weapons to South Asia, Africa, Southeast Asia, and Latin America and the Caribbean have increased; sales to the Middle East have decreased during that time. Notably, China has not sold major conventional arms to Central Asia or Oceania. Perhaps most interesting, more than three-fifths of China's major conventional arms exports went to just three states: Pakistan, Bangladesh, and Myanmar. The data on PLA Navy (PLAN) port visits was compiled from several sources. We supplemented parts of a dataset compiled by Phil Baxter[21] with findings from the Chinese Ministry of Defense (MOD) website, *Xinhua Online*, *China Daily Online*, and an article by Andrew S. Erickson and Austin M. Strange.[22] The data on PLA military exercises is based on the list published in the Department of Defense's 2015 annual report

---

[19] "Prospective Founding Members," webpage, 2015a; Asian Infrastructure Investment Bank, "50 Countries Sign the Articles of Agreement for the Asian Infrastructure Investment Bank," June 29, 2015b.

[20] Trend-indicator values (TIV) are expressed in constant 1990 USD and are assigned based on standardized values of each type of weapon rather than the actual value of the financial transaction. For more information on how TIV is calculated, see http://www.sipri.org/reSoutheastAsiarch/armaments/transfers/measuring.

[21] Phil Baxter, "What Crunching the Data Tells Us About China's Naval Port Visits," *War Is Boring*, March 3, 2015.

[22] Andrew S. Erickson and Austin M. Strange, "China's Blue Soft Power: Antipiracy, Engagement, and Image Enhancement," *Naval War College Review*, Vol. 68, No. 1, Winter 2015, pp. 71–91.

on China's military; again, it is supplemented with data from the Chinese MOD website.

Caveats to the Data

It is important to note that the data we use have limitations. For example, in the realm of political data, Chinese press statements, documents, and information from the Chinese Ministry of Foreign Affairs website may be incomplete or incorrect. In the realm of economic data, China's recorded trade data often does not match the trade data of partner countries. For example, according to the UN Comtrade Database, China reported $325 billion worth of goods exports to the United States in 2011 and $352 worth of goods exports in 2012. In contrast, in the same database, the United States reported $417 billion worth of goods imports from China in 2011 and $444 billion worth of goods imports in 2012. Differences may arise from how the two countries treat trade through Hong Kong, but there may also be instances of overinvoicing or underinvoicing for a variety of purposes. For some of our other indicators, anything that relies on media reporting may miss information or be incorrect.

Our data on PLA Navy port visits provides an example. As noted, we initially relied on data compiled by one specialist and then built that out with government announcements, Chinese media reporting, and the findings of two other specialists. Yet, we have no doubt we missed some. In fact, at least in the case of Africa, other scholars have found somewhat more port visits.[23]

We chose to stay with our data as compiled for several reasons. First, due to time and budget constraints, we needed a reasonable cutoff for data collection. We have no doubt new sources are available that can help further strengthen the data. Second, we wanted to be consistent by region in our methods of data collection. Third, and most important, all data sources appear to have similar trends and magnitudes. Further data compilation is unlikely to change any findings. As a result, we are confident that our data can be used to give a reasonable

---

[23] Andrew S. Erickson and Austin M. Strange, *Six Years at Sea and Counting: Gulf of Aden Anti-Piracy and China's Maritime Commons Presence*, The Jamestown Foundation, June 2015.

indication of China's activities in the Developing World and be used to draw policy implications.

The Plan for the Report

This report proceeds as follows. In Chapter 2 it examines China's policy and strategy toward the Developing World and surveys the range and pattern of Chinese activities across different regions of the world. In Chapters 3 through 9, the study examines the seven regions into which we have divided the Developing World. Then in Chapter 10, it considers China's relations with pivotal states in each geographically distinct developing region of the world. Chapter 11 offers conclusions and implications of our research for the U.S. Army and the United States. Appendix A discusses the actors involved in shaping or influencing Chinese policy toward its most important region, Southeast Asia, and its least important region, Latin America and the Caribbean, to provide insight into how China manages its foreign policy priorities.

CHAPTER TWO

China in the Zone: The Cold War and After

Although the Developing World has never really been a strategic focus of the PRC, it has invariably figured significantly in China's official foreign policy schema. According to China scholar Peter Van Ness, "One of the most consistent themes in Beijing's foreign policy statements . . . is the identification of China with the Third World."[1] China's official pronouncements routinely insist that China "belongs" to the Developing World, China supports the Developing World and stands in solidarity with it, and China will maintain this stance even after it grows rich and strong, as Samuel Kim notes. On the basis of this official rhetoric, Kim observes, the developing states ought to be "central" to PRC foreign policy. And yet China has not demonstrated an enduring commitment to or engaged in close cooperation with states of the Developing World.[2] While the Developing World has long figured prominently in Beijing's foreign policy, it was never a true central focus except during the 1960s when China was racked by political turmoil at home and passionately committed to supporting liberation movements in Developing World countries.[3]

---

[1] Peter Van Ness, "China as a Third World State: Foreign Policy and Official National Identity," in Lowell Dittmer and Samuel S. Kim, eds., *China's Quest for National Identity*, Ithaca, N.Y.: Cornell University Press, 1993, p. 194.

[2] Samuel S. Kim, "China and the Third World: In Search of a Peace and Development Line," in Samuel S. Kim, ed., *China and the World: New Directions in Chinese Foreign Relations*, 2nd ed., Boulder, Colo.: Westview Press, 1989, p. 148. Kim actually uses the term "centrality of the Third World."

[3] Van Ness, 1993, pp. 202 (Table 2), 204.

PRC leaders have consistently identified China as a member of the Developing World, but they did not view China as merely another developing state. Rather, China holds a distinctive—if not unique—status within the Developing World.[4] In their eyes, as a former great power and natural leader, Beijing did not see itself merely as the champion of the nonaligned movement but also on a preordained trajectory to reclaim its rightful place at the center of the world stage. As such, the Developing World has served as a key arena for Chinese geostrategic and diplomatic activities and a location where China needed to build up hard and soft power to elevate itself to the status of a great power.[5] And especially since 1979, developing countries have become important in another dimension—economic.[6] But while the Developing World has always been a zone of competition for Beijing, China has never had a strategy specifically directed toward it. Rather, China's approach to the Developing World was always part of a broader strategy toward the superpowers and the larger world.[7]

Beijing's approach to the Developing World in PRC foreign policy can be divided into three periods: the Maoist era (1949–1977); the Dengist era (1978–1991), and the Globalist era (1992–present). Two of these periods span the Cold War, while the third corresponds to the post–Cold War period. The earlier periods correspond with the tenures of particular leaders and foreign policy orientations; the current period corresponds to a global orientation across the tenures of multiple paramount leaders. In this chapter, we analyze for each period PRC foreign

---

[4] Van Ness, 1993, p. 213.

[5] Of course, the term "soft power," coined by Joseph Nye in the 1990s, was not in use in the 1950s, 1960s, 1970s, or 1980s. However, since the 1990s, Chinese leaders have embraced the term and consider it just as important as hard power. See Andrew J. Nathan and Andrew Scobell, *China's Search for Security*, New York: Columbia University Press, 2012, Chapter 12.

[6] According to Peter Van Ness, China has had four "consistent patterns" of goals in its policy toward the Developing World since 1949. The first is to build fruitful trade relationships; the second is to support Beijing in the UN; the third is to contain Taipei diplomatically; and the fourth is to lure Third World states away from the superpowers. See Van Ness, "China and the Third World: Patterns of Engagement and Indifference," in Samuel S. Kim, ed. *China and the World: Chinese Foreign Policy Faces the New Millennium*, 4th ed., Boulder, Colo.: Westview Press, 1998, p. 155.

[7] Nathan and Scobell, 2012, p. 14.

policy strategy and how the Developing World factors in, through an examination of global trends, and then examine Beijing's views of the three key elements of strategy: ends, ways, and means.[8] Last, we outline how China prioritizes the globe, specifically the relative importance of different regions of the Developing World.

Maoist Foreign Policy Strategy and the Developing World, 1949–1977

China assessed the global environment as tumultuous and rife with revolution and the ever-present specter of major war. At home, this corresponded to conditions of social upheaval, economic mobilization, and political struggle. Mao stressed the need for continuous revolution domestically, which resulted in an internal situation of sustained turmoil in which Chinese Communist Party (CCP) leaders emphasized the threat of ideological enemies and traitors inside China being controlled or orchestrated by outside forces. This produced a mix of heightened social paranoia and political and economic chaos, which at times plunged the country into widespread famine (for example, the Great Leap Forward, 1959–1962) and at other times erupted into civil war-like violence (for example, the Cultural Revolution, especially 1966–1969). The toll in death and human suffering was substantial. The upheaval also stunted China's economic development and resulted in a rhetorically boisterous and ideologically charged foreign policy.

In this environment, China was shadowed by the prospect of major military conflict, specifically attack from one or both of the superpowers. This entailed a primary foreign policy focus on the Soviet Union and the United States as the best way to safeguard China's national security.[9] Initially, during the first decade of the PRC's existence, it involved an alliance with the Soviet Union to counter the United States

---

[8] For a discussion of these elements of strategy, see Harry R. Yarger, *Strategic Theory for the 21st Century: The Little Book on Big Strategy*, Publication 641, Strategic Studies Institute, U.S. Army War College, Carlisle, Pa., February 2006.

[9] For a review of Beijing's relations with Moscow since 1949, see Nathan and Scobell, 2012, Chapter 3.

(what Mao dubbed "leaning to one side"); then, during roughly the PRC's second decade, following a split with Moscow, Beijing pursued an uneasy course having tense relationships with both Moscow and Washington and, later in the subsequent decade, consummating a rapprochement with the United States to counter what China perceived as an escalating Soviet threat. By the time relations between Beijing and Moscow began to thaw in the late 1980s, the days of the Soviet Union were numbered.

In the overall context of the Cold War, the Developing World became important as an arena in which China could appear stronger and more influential than it really was. China's message was that Beijing was an authentic champion of the Developing World because, unlike Washington or Moscow, China was also a Developing World state. Beijing's message resonated with a Developing World audience, although there was recognition that China was not capable of supplying the armaments or economic support that the two superpowers could. Moreover, China's actions rarely lived up to the grandiosity of its rhetoric: spouting verbiage supporting global revolution was one thing, but backing this up with material goods and concrete acts was another matter.

Nevertheless, this high-decibel, militant rhetoric did grab attention and allowed China to project an image of being a major world player in the same league as the two superpowers. China's actual support for communist regimes and national liberation movements around the world was modest in practice. Its most tangible assistance was to insurgencies in the Asia-Pacific neighborhood, especially in Southeast Asia, with real success in a handful of countries, notably in Indochina. In the 1950s, in addition to China's pivotal role in the Korean War, Chinese support helped the Viet Minh emerge victorious against France, and China played a key role brokering an agreement by which the French withdrew from Indochina. In the 1960s, China helped North Vietnam wage an ultimately successful extended armed struggle against South Vietnam backed by the military might of the United States. Then, in the 1970s, China backed the victorious Khmer Rouge in Cambodia.[10]

---

[10] See, for example, Nayan Chanda, *Brother Enemy: The War After the War*, New York: Harcourt Brace and Jonvanovich, 1986.

While China also supported other revolutionary movements with at least modest levels of assistance and training, none of these elsewhere in Asia were as successful as those in Indochina.

China did maintain and cultivate relationships with a number of other regimes and movements around the globe. However, China was rarely the patron of choice since it was unable to provide the armaments and resources available to clients of Moscow or Washington.

The means China employed were a mix of hard and soft power instruments with a heavy emphasis on the latter. China's rhetoric was high powered and its revolution-for-export zeal was probably at its height during the 1960s, symbolized by Marshal Lin Biao's impassioned 1965 address titled "Long Live People's War!" At that time, China reportedly supported 24 insurgencies.[11] Such rhetorical support for the struggles of the peoples of the Developing World China identified as oppressed was a constant feature of Chinese foreign policy from the 1950s through the 1970s. The themes of Beijing's solidarity with the Developing World are evident in Premier Zhou Enlai's speech at the 1955 Bandung Conference and Vice Premier Deng Xiaoping's address to the UN in 1974.[12]

China's diplomatic clout and support for the countries of the Developing World was weak and limited until after Beijing was admitted to the UN in 1971. However, China played a weak hand very adeptly by making a considerable fuss over the rulers of small countries in Africa and Latin America. According to one of the first U.S. diplomats to be stationed in Beijing during the mid-1970s, "China's attention to . . . Third World countries is amazing. In how many big countries do they give such a great stylist [sic] welcome to chiefs of state from tiny African countries for example. The airport is bedecked, downtown is colored [with] banners all over and big signs of welcome in French or English."[13]

---

[11] Van Ness, 1971, Chapters 4 and 6.

[12] Lin Piao, "Long Live the Victory of People's War!" *Peking Review*, September 3, 1965; and "Chairman of Chinese Delegation Teng Hsiao-ping's Speech at the Special Session of the U.N. General Assembly," *Peking Review*, April 19, 1974.

[13] George H. W. Bush, *The China Diary of George H. W. Bush: The Making of a Global President*, Jeffrey Engel, ed., Princeton, N.J.: Princeton University Press, 2008, p. 341.

China's military support in terms of weapons, training, and manpower during the Cold War was generally humble but significant for the specific movements involved, especially those in Asia. Similarly, economic aid and assistance were quite modest with some notable exceptions such as the 1970s construction of the TanZam railway connecting landlocked Zambian copper mines to ports in Tanzania.[14] Nevertheless, such efforts earned Beijing much goodwill among developing countries, and this is still evident today, especially in Africa.

Dengist Foreign Policy Strategy and the Developing World, 1978–1991

Following the death of Mao Zedong in 1976, China was in a sorry condition, economically impoverished and with a populace weary of domestic political struggle.[15] Within two years, a leader who championed the priorities of economic development and opening up to the outside world came to power. Deng Xiaoping, although a protégé of Mao, was less of an ideologue and recognized the most logical way to modernize China was to rebuild its economy pragmatically and to reorient the country outward by engaging with the global economic system. Deng justified the logic of China focusing on economic reform by proclaiming that the world was entering a new era in which peace and development were the main trends of the times. While there would continue to be conflict and tensions in the world, notably persistent struggle between the two superpowers and real threats to China's security, mainly from the Soviet Union and its proxies, China now faced a period of strategic opportunity in which it could seize upon modernizing its backward economy. This external economic outreach focused on the developed world because this is where Deng and other Chinese leaders believed Beijing could find trading partners and investors who

---

[14] For an overview of Chinese aid projects of that period, see Snow, 1988, Chapter 5.

[15] For an excellent analysis of the political climate and conditions in China upon Mao's death in 1976, see Harry Harding, *China's Second Revolution: Reform After Mao*, Washington, D.C.: Brookings Institution Press, 1987, Chapter 2.

could help China grow through the official policy of "reform and opening to the outside world."[16]

A high priority was for China to catch up with global advances in science and technology, and to this end the United States, Japan, and the countries of Western Europe would be of most value. In prioritizing reform and opening, by 1980 China had "turned its back on the Developing World."[17] But this did not mean China completely ignored the Developing World. Indeed, the key prerequisite for economic development at home was peace and stability in the Asia-Pacific, especially in China's immediate neighborhood. Yet here China was largely focused on countering the Soviet Union and its "adventurism" in the region—from the Red Army in Afghanistan to Soviet forces along their extended common border (including the Soviet satellite of Mongolia) and the Soviet client state of Vietnam. China sought to manage these problems and keep tensions from escalating into all-out war through actions aimed to deter Moscow and any of its allies from stirring up too much trouble. Moreover, China sought to maintain its identity as a champion and member of the Developing World.

While China was focused on developed countries, it also sought to gain access and influence in developing countries. One of the most attractive aspects of China to some countries was the array of reasonably priced weaponry and difficult to obtain items Beijing was willing to sell. For some countries, like Iran and Iraq in the 1980s, China was a useful source of armaments as they waged war on each other.[18] China was also willing to sell missiles and missile technology that other countries, such as the United States, were unwilling to provide. China sold intermediate-range ballistic missiles (IRBMs) to Saudi Arabia. The reasons for this were not just to earn foreign exchange but also to help persuade Riyadh that it should switch diplomatic relations from Taipei to Beijing. China worked to win diplomatic allies by wooing them away

---

[16] Nathan and Scobell, 2012, Chapter 10.

[17] Van Ness, 1993, p. 206.

[18] On arms sales to the Developing World during the Deng era, see John W. Lewis, Hua Di, and Xue Litai, "Beijing's Defense Establishment: Solving the Arms Export Enigma," *International Security*, Vol. 15, No. 4, Spring 1991, pp. 87–109.

from Taiwan. Another reason China was engaged in the Developing World was to counter the Soviet Union. Beijing supported various anti-Soviet insurgent movements in Afghanistan and in various civil wars in Africa.[19]

China used various instruments of hard and soft power. These means included military support for anti-Soviet mujahedeen in Afghanistan and for the Khmer Rouge forces in Cambodia fighting against the Vietnamese troops that had invaded in late 1978. China also supported groups such as the National Union for the Total Independence of Angola (UNITA), which was fighting against Cuban troops and the Soviet-backed government in Luanda. But economically China tended to concentrate mostly on the developed world. Moreover, in terms of messaging and rhetoric, Beijing was rather low-key where the Developing World was concerned because its primary focus was on the superpowers and the developed world.

Beijing also waged a diplomatic struggle against Taipei. In the 1980s and early 1990s, many countries, mostly in the Middle East and Latin America, switched ties from Taiwan to China.

Globalization Strategy and the Developing World, 1992 to Present

After the Cold War, Beijing determined that peace and development remained the main trends of the times. Moreover, in the aftermath of the Tiananmen Square crackdown in 1989, sparking Western condemnation and sanctions, and of the collapse of the Soviet Bloc from 1989 to 1991, China revived its Developing World rhetoric and paid greater attention to developing regions.[20]

Feeling diplomatically isolated, politically shunned, and economically blocked by the United States and other countries in the developed world in the immediate aftermath of the Tiananmen Massacre, China

---

[19] For a survey of China's political and military involvement in Africa, see Snow, 1988, Chapter 4.

[20] Van Ness, 1993, pp. 213–214.

launched an initiative to reach out energetically to Developing World countries, including other countries blackballed by the West.[21] In the first months and years of the post-Tiananmen crackdown, Beijing retrenched economically. However, by 1992, Chinese leaders had regained their confidence and paramount leader Deng Xiaoping had given a green light for a reinvigoration of economic reforms. Along with this second wave of reform came a realization that China's industries needed to import more resources and raw materials for ramped-up production, and that further export-led growth required new markets beyond those in the developed world. In short, an economic logic prompted Beijing to focus far greater attention on the Developing World.[22]

China's goals were partly geostrategic in seeking to counter the United States in an era of a sole superpower. This meant looking for friends around the world and building Beijing's status as a rising great power and champion of the Developing World. Moreover, China's burgeoning economy put a high priority on acquiring new sources of raw materials resources and commodities for Chinese factories and new markets for Chinese products. This quest necessitated China broadening out from the developed states and the Soviet bloc and into the Developing World.

China took a far more activist stance than it had during the previous two periods, internationally and within the Developing World, in an unprecedented range of ways, both multilaterally and bilaterally. This activism was characterized by mostly conciliatory rhetoric and nonviolent actions. First, China was particularly active economically through expanded trade and investment, especially in the Asia-Pacific but also further afield in the Middle East, Africa, and Latin America and the Caribbean. Second, China participated actively in existing global and regional organizations, including but not limited to the United Nations (UN), the World Trade Organization (WTO), the Association for Southeast Asian Nations Regional Forum (ARF), the South

---

[21] Dittmer, "China's Rise, Global Identity, and the Developing World," in Dittmer and Yu, 2010, pp. 222–223.

[22] Evan S. Medeiros, *China's International Behavior: Activism, Opportunism, and Diversification*, Santa Monica, Calif.: RAND Corporation, MG-850-AF, 2009, p. 206.

Asia Association for Regional Cooperation (SAARC), and the Organization of American States. Third, the PRC also started creating an "alternative universe" of multilateral institutions and mechanisms that tended to be China-centric. These newly established entities included the Conference for Interaction and Confidence-Building Measures in Asia (CICA), the Forum on China-Africa Cooperation (FOCAC), the Shanghai Cooperation Organization (SCO), the China-Community of Latin American and Caribbean States (CELAC) forum, the Brazil, Russia, India, China, South Africa grouping (BRICS), and later, the Asian Infrastructure Investment Bank (AIIB) and the New Development Bank (NDB, also known as the BRICS bank), among others. Fourth, China has vigorously pursued an array of bilateral partnerships with states around the world. Many of these partnerships are comprehensive, involving not just economic, but diplomatic, cultural, and military components (see Chapter 10).

China wielded a dizzying array of hard and soft power instruments. The greatest emphasis was on economic levers. China offered many countries the chance to modernize, prosper, and improve their infrastructure without the conditions required by many developed countries.

Diplomatically—both bilaterally and multilaterally—China showed many countries attention and deferential treatment they had not experienced before. Senior Chinese leaders paid visits, making leaders of developing countries look and feel important. When these leaders visited China, Beijing rolled out the red carpet; when Chinese leaders visited their countries, they came bearing gifts and offering concrete deliverables for their hosts.[23]

China promoted rhetoric of China also being a Developing World country and emphasized that they stood for different principles than those of the United States and other developed states. China claimed it respected the principle of noninterference in the internal affairs of other countries and did not insist on criticizing human rights violations or insisting on democracy or rule of law.

---

[23] Medeiros, 2009, and Phillip C. Saunders, *China's Global Activism: Strategy, Drivers, Tools*, Institute for National Strategic Studies Occasional Paper No. 4, Washington, D.C.: National Defense University Press, October 2006.

Security-wise, China paid increasing attention to military-to-military relations; peacekeeping deployments in the Middle East, Africa, and Latin America; port visits; and military exercises—often very small in scale. China also invited military officers to attend professional military education (PME) institutions in China. Defense diplomacy was stressed more than it ever had been before.[24]

Contemporary Chinese Foreign Policy and the Developing World

According to one leading scholar of Chinese foreign policy, many in China continue to view their country as a "developing state" and believe that China has common cause with other "developing countries."[25] Although Beijing does not seem to have a specific strategy focused on the Developing World, China views the Developing World within a larger context of its relations with different types of international actors. China has long proclaimed a foreign policy mantra of "major powers are the key, surrounding countries are the first priority, developing countries are the foundation, and multilateral forums are the important stage."[26] Major powers have typically included the most important and powerful countries internationally, such as the United States, Russia, and the European Union. Neighbors include more than two dozen countries that China borders by land or water. Chinese definitions of developing countries correspond to UN definitions. These three categories are not mutually exclusive, and countries could fall under more than one category. China has typically viewed developing countries as less important than major

[24] For overviews of these activities and events, see the biannual PRC Defense White Papers.

[25] However, according to Shambaugh, this is only one of seven "global identities" that he has discerned among Chinese elites. According to Shambaugh, China "possesses multiple international identities and is a conflicted country in its international persona." See David Shambaugh, *China Goes Global: The Partial Power*, New York: Oxford University Press, 2012, p. 43.

[26] Since the 18th Party Congress in 2012, China has also begun to talk about public diplomacy as a fifth type of diplomacy. See "Shibada Zhi Hou De Zhongguo Waijiao Xin Jumian" ["China's New Foreign Policy After the 18th Party Congress"], *Sina News*, January 9, 2014.

powers and neighboring countries. Multilateral forums, the fourth category, are growing in importance and becoming a means by which China can partner with developing and developed countries alike.[27]

Increasing Chinese Prioritization of the Developing World

Since the Chinese Communist Party's 18th Party Congress in 2012 and, particularly after Chinese President Xi Jinping came to power, there has been increasing Chinese attention to neighboring countries (of which a majority are developing countries) and the Developing World. In October 2013, Xi headed the Peripheral Diplomacy Work Conference, the first major work conference on foreign policy since 2006. He emphasized the need for a more "proactive" peripheral diplomacy to create a stable and beneficial environment for China's development, protect China's core interests, and strengthen China's leadership role in the region.[28]

This meeting was followed by a November 2014 Central Conference on Work Relating to Foreign Affairs.[29] At the conference, Xi

---

[27] There was some discussion as to whether leaders in Beijing have placed neighboring countries as more important than major powers since the 18th Party Congress and particularly after the October 2013 Peripheral Diplomacy Work Conference headed by Xi. A public statement to the contrary should not be taken at face value. See "Waijiaobu Yazhousi Sizhang Luo Zhaohui Tan Zhongguo Zhoubian Waijiao Xin Zhengcheng" ["Chinese Ministry of Foreign Affairs' Department of Asian Affairs Director-General Luo Zhaohui Discusses New Directions in China's Neighboring Country Policy"], Ministry of Foreign Affairs of the People's Republic of China, December 27, 2013.

[28] Timothy Heath, "Diplomacy Work Forum: Xi Steps Up Efforts to Shape a China-Centered Regional Order," *Jamestown China Brief*, Vol. 13, No. 22, November 7, 2013, pp. 6–9; Michael D. Swaine, "Chinese Views and Commentary on Periphery Diplomacy," *China Leadership Monitor*, No. 44, July 2014.

[29] Premier Li Keqiang presided over the conference, and an unprecedented number of Chinese leaders involved in foreign affairs attended, indicating that Xi's remarks during the meeting represents the most authoritative statements by the current Chinese leadership on foreign policy. According to Michael Swaine, this meeting included "central and local Chinese civilian and military officials, nearly every Chinese ambassador and consul-general with ambassadorial rank posted overseas, and commissioners of the Foreign Ministry to the Hong Kong Special Administrative Region and the Macao Special Administrative Region." See Michael D. Swaine, "Xi Jinping's Address to the Central Conference on Work Relating to Foreign Affairs: Assessing and Advancing Major-Power Diplomacy with Chinese Characteristics," *China Leadership Monitor*, No. 46, Winter 2014, p. 1.

began by assessing how the changing and new international situation required that China alter, broaden, and expand its diplomatic strategy—issuing what amounted to a directive to PRC diplomats to become more ambitious and forward leaning. After his assessment, he immediately discussed the importance of neighborhood diplomacy, suggesting that periphery diplomacy is one of China's top foreign policy priorities. In sequence (and likely priority), he also highlighted several other major priorities for Chinese foreign policy:[30]

- Strengthen relations with major countries and expand cooperation with major developing countries
- Strengthen unity and cooperation with developing countries and closely integrate Chinese development with their development
- Advance multilateral diplomacy and reform the international system and global governance to increase the representation and say of China and other developing countries.

Xi's speech and subsequent official and nonofficial commentary clarified Beijing's current categorization of developing countries. Xi appears to divide developing countries into three different types. A first group is composed of neighboring countries. With greater Chinese power projection capabilities and more overseas citizens and assets, Beijing is increasingly thinking of extended neighborhoods (*da zhou bian*) and is more willing to identify countries that do not border China but reside in nearby regions as neighbors.[31] This more inclusive view of its neighborhood helps explain Xi's calls for "pursuing an Asia-Pacific dream" and for establishing a "new Asian security concept."[32]

A second group comprises developing countries that play significant global or regional roles and qualify as major powers. These include,

---

[30] "The Central Conference on Work Relating to Foreign Affairs Was Held in Beijing," Ministry of Foreign Affairs of the People's Republic of China, November 29, 2014.

[31] "Lizhu Zhoubian, Moupian Quanqiu" ["To Gain a Foothold on the Periphery, We Must Look for Opportunities around the Globe"], *Xinhua News*, March 2, 2015.

[32] "Full Text of Foreign Minister Wang Yi's Speech on China's Diplomacy in 2014," *Xinhua News*, December 26, 2014; "New Asian Security Concept for New Progress in Security Cooperation," Ministry of Foreign Affairs of the People's Republic of China, May 21, 2014.

for example, Brazil, India, and South Africa. These major developing countries are important countries for China to work with to build Xi's "global network of partnerships."[33] As Foreign Minister Wang Yi explains, Xi's vision of global partnerships represents China's attempt to step out of the Cold War mind-set of needing military alliances. Instead of allies, China can work with friends or close partners abroad.[34]

A third and final category of developing countries are those that are not in neighboring regions and do not qualify as major powers. China still views many of these countries as global partners and will continue to strengthen cooperation with these countries politically and economically. Politically, China wishes to work with these countries to increase China's and the Developing World's representation and say in global institutions and governance. Economically, Chinese views close cooperation with the Developing World as critical to its economic development.

China at the Center: Ringed by the Developing World

Chinese conceptualization of the Developing World gives special attention to the Asia-Pacific, and such attention stems from Beijing's insecurity about stability at home, around China's periphery, and in China's neighborhood. Indeed, according to two U.S. scholars, China conceives of its environment in terms for four concentric circles (Figure 2.1).[35] The first or inner ring encompasses China itself—any territory that Beijing currently controls or claims as Chinese territory (the most significant feature in the latter is the island of Taiwan). China's second ring contains the countries, territories, and bodies of water directly adjacent to China's land and maritime borders. The third ring includes China's entire Asia-Pacific neighborhood, while the fourth ring include everything beyond Asia—the rest of the globe.

There is only one country in the early twenty-first century that has the capability, from Beijing's perspective, to challenge China in all four of these rings, and that is the United States. China is most absorbed with the first three rings and most preoccupied with the innermost

---

33 "The Central Conference on Work Relating to Foreign Affairs Was Held in Beijing," 2014.

34 "Full Text of Foreign Minister Wang Yi's Speech."

35 Nathan and Scobell, 2012, pp. 3–7.

Figure 2.1
China's Four Rings of Insecurity

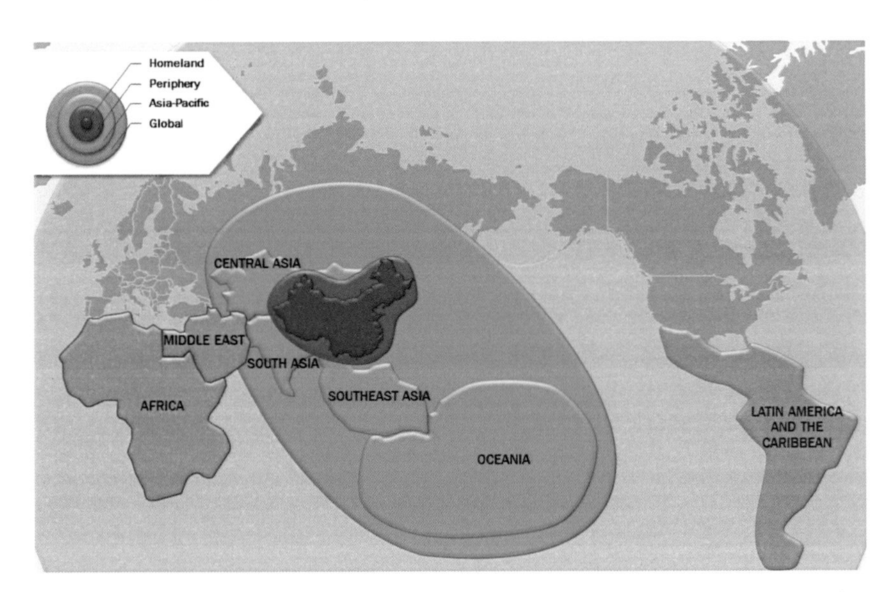

SOURCE: RAND, derived from Andrew J. Nathan and Andrew Scobell, *China's Search for Security*, New York: Columbia University Press, 2012, pp. 3–7.
RAND *RR2273A-2.1*

one. Chinese leaders were extremely fearful in the wake of the collapse of the Soviet bloc in 1989 and the disintegration of the Soviet Union two years later. More recently, the CCP has been alarmed by a series of upheavals in locations around the world: the color revolutions that swept Eastern Europe and Central Asia, the Arab Spring that began in 2011, and the umbrella movement of 2014 in Hong Kong. Despite heavy paranoia, closing China's borders and cutting China off from the world is not an option. Paradoxically, Beijing preoccupation with thinking locally drives China's global engagement, including vigorous involvement in the Developing World.[36]

But some regions are more important than others. The most important regions for Beijing are those inside the second ring. Less critical but still very important are those regions inside the third ring.

[36] Nathan and Scobell, 2012.

Table 2.1
The Geostrategy of China's Concentric Circles

Ring	Primary Strategy	Goal
First	Control	Continued CCP rule
Second	Buffer	Restrict the United States
Third	Sphere of influence	Limit access to the United States
Fourth	Competition	Balance against the United States

SOURCE: Derived from Figure 2.1.

And of lesser importance are those regions in the fourth ring. As noted, the most sensitive ring is the innermost one, in which the CCP desires to maintain stability through careful control of its domestic situation and, hence, ensure continued CCP rule (Table 2.1). In the second ring around China's periphery are the most proximate portions of three Developing World regions: Central Asia, South Asia, and Southeast Asia. In each of these regions Beijing has adopted a buffer strategy to keep countries and areas—both maritime and continental zones—friendly to China or at least neutral and pressed to expel outside powers and their armed forces, including the United States and its military. Next is the third ring, encompassing the more distant portions of Central Asia, South Asia, and Southeast Asia as well as Oceania, which is geographically well removed from China itself. In this ring, China's goal is to limit U.S. access to the Asia-Pacific and establish a Chinese sphere of influence.[37] Last, in the fourth ring, China is increasingly active and engaged but also weakest in terms of power and influence. In the wider world outside of the Asia-Pacific, China has adopted a strategy of nonmilitary competition in an effort to balance against the influence of the United States.

Nevertheless, China does not seek direct confrontation or conflict with the United States. In fact, at a minimum, Beijing desires cordial relations with Washington. Indeed, U.S.-China coordination is preferred, and U.S.-China cooperation is considered ideal. How-

[37] The Asia security analyst Phillip C. Saunders notes that, among other goals, China seeks to reduce U.S. influence in Asia (Saunders, 2006).

ever, coordination and cooperation are particularly difficult in rings 1, 2, and 3 because of Beijing's heightened national security sensitivities over what China considers core interests.

In terms of the ranked order of importance of developing regions to China, those that spill over from the second ring to the third ring are, primarily, Southeast Asia, Central Asia, and South Asia. Next, fully in the third ring is Oceania, following by the Middle East, which seems to be the one region ostensibly outside the Asia-Pacific that actually appears to straddle the third and fourth rings. Of growing importance but less vital are developing regions completely in the fourth ring: Africa and Latin America.

The Belt and Road Initiative: China's Flagship Initiative for the Developing World

Under President Xi Jinping, Beijing is working to solidify its presence in the second and third rings and to expand its involvement in the fourth ring. Since Chinese President Xi Jinping came to power, he has pushed for the realization of the "China dream" to rejuvenate the Chinese nation through constructing a "community of common destiny." The "Silk Road Economic Belt" and "21st Century Maritime Silk Road," known originally as One Belt, One Road but subsequently dubbed the Belt and Road Initiative, represents China's strategic path for achieving this community in the next thirty or more years.[38] This flagship foreign policy initiative was officially launched less than twelve months into Xi's tenure. The Belt and Road Initiative is a critical, longer-term objective as well as a near-term focus. As Chinese Foreign Minister Wang Yi noted in March 2015, China's foreign policy agenda in 2015 consisted of "one main focus," the Belt and Road Initiative, and "two themes," peace and development.[39]

The Belt refers to the new Silk Road Economic Belt; it consists of a series of overland networks through Central Asia to South Asia,

---

[38] "'Yi Dai Yi Lu' Jiang Shi Weilai 30 Nian Zhongguo Dui Wai De Da Zhan Lue" ["'One Belt, One Road' Will Be China's Grand Diplomatic Strategy for the 30 Years to Come"], *Guangming Daily*, February 26, 2015.

[39] "Foreign Minister Wang Yi Meets the Press," Ministry of Foreign Affairs of the People's Republic of China, March 8, 2015.

to the Middle East and onward to Africa and Europe (Figure 2.2). The Road refers to a 21st Century Maritime Silk Road stretching from China through the South China Sea to the India Ocean to South Asia, the Middle East, Africa, and Europe. It is an extremely ambitious and comprehensive effort to build a vast web of infrastructure—roads, railways, canals, and pipelines intended to link China to its neighborhood and the wider world. Xi also spelled out five types of "connectivity": policy or political coordination, transportation connectivity, trade and investment cooperation, financial integration and use of the renminbi (RMB, China's currency) as a currency, and stronger people-to-people connections.[40] Almost the only portion of the globe not explicitly part of this concept is the Western Hemisphere.[41]

While the Belt and Road Initiative constitutes a serious foreign policy concept, specific infrastructure projects may be overly ambitious and perhaps even unworkable. So how should one understand this heavily promoted initiative? Perhaps the prime value of the Belt and Road Initiative is that it presents China's rise in nonthreatening terms to its Asia-Pacific neighbors and countries in the wider world. Moreover, the initiative portrays a more powerful China as a force for global good focused on building a peaceful and prosperous common future. In this light, the Belt and Road Initiative is best viewed as Beijing's overarching rubric for positively framing contemporary Chinese foreign policy toward all regions of the world—developed and underdeveloped. Whether it will actually accomplish that is debatable.

Beijing is aiming for what it calls a "win-win situation" by financing a substantial part of the infrastructure construction needed to facilitate greater trade and transportation connectivity. China is establish-

---

40 "'Yi Dai Yi Lu' Zheng Gaixie Quanqiu Jingji Bantu" ["'One Belt, One Road' Is Remaking the Global Economic Map"], *People's Daily Overseas Edition*, December 29, 2014; See also China Institute of International Studies, "Tiujin 'Yidai Yilu' Nengyuan Ziyuan Hezuo De Waijiao Yunchou" ["Carry Forward 'One Belt One Road': A Diplomatic Plan for Cooperation on Energy and Natural Resources"], 2014.

41 *Vision and Actions on Jointly Building Silk Road Economic Belt and 21st Century Maritime Silk Road*, Beijing, March 28. 2015. Issued by the National Development and Reform Commission, the Ministry of Foreign Affairs, the Ministry of Commerce of the People's Republic of China with State Council authorization.

Figure 2.2
China's Belt and Road Initiative, 2015

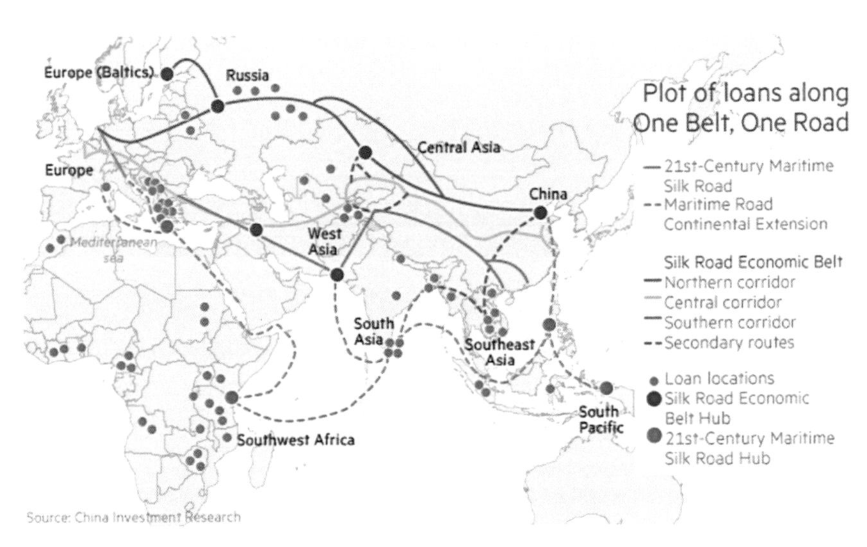

SOURCE: "Chinese Overseas Lending Dominated by One Belt, One Road Strategy," *Financial Times*, June 18, 2015. As of October 14, 2015: http://www.ft.com/intl/cms/s/3/e9dcd674-15d8-11e5-be54-00144feabdc0.html #axzz3oaGo0kiB
NOTE: There is no single official map of Belt and Road Initiative. Figure 2.2 displays one of several different maps, one of the few that includes Oceania.
RAND *RR2273A-2.2*

ing new international financial institutions to help fund the Belt and Road Initiative, including the Asian Infrastructure Investment Bank, the BRICS New Development Bank, and the Silk Road Fund. Notably, however, much of the financing will still come from purely Chinese institutions, such as China's Export-Import Bank and the Development Bank of China. In the new financial institutions, China seeks to play a leadership role or serve as a veto player. Beijing will also involve the China-ASEAN Interbank Association in financing Belt and Road Initiative activities.[42] In funding infrastructure initiatives, these new institutions will help internationalize the use of the RMB. China, for example, is encouraging the AIIB and Silk Road Fund to use the RMB

[42] Philippa Brant, "One Belt, One Road? China's Community of Common Destiny," *The Interpreter*, Lowry Institute for International Policy, March 31, 2015.

in the basket of currencies to denominate and settle loans.[43] Some Chinese experts, however, are critical of China's ability to fund and realize such an ambitious initiative.[44] While the fate of the Belt and Road Initiative in terms of building concrete infrastructure projects around the world remains to be seen, its effectiveness in portraying China as a positive and influential global player is already evident.

Drivers of Current Chinese Engagement with the Developing World

Several factors drive China's desire and need for more engagement with the Developing World. First, China seeks to sustain its domestic economic growth and sees the Developing World as offering significant economic potential. Second, China believes the international system is heading toward multipolarity and wishes to work with developing countries to increase China's global influence. Third, as China invests abroad and its citizens venture overseas, Beijing needs to increasingly work with or partner with developing countries to ensure their safety and security. Finally, China's increasing engagement with developing countries, mainly countries to its west, helps alleviate the pressure and tensions in Northeast Asia caused by the U.S. rebalancing to the Asia-Pacific and Chinese territorial disputes with Japan.

Sustaining Chinese Economic Growth

China sees partnering with the Developing World as critical to enabling Chinese economic development and growth. China's rapid growth over the past 30 years has been fueled first by the introduction of markets into its agricultural sector, which is massive in terms of employment, then by the expansion of low-skill manufacturing and assembly driven in large part by the movement of rural farmers to coastal cities; and

---

[43] "China Seeks Role for Yuan in AIIB to Extend Currency's Global Reach," *South China Morning Post*, April 27, 2015.

[44] Shi Yinhong, "Tuijin 'Yi Dai Yi Lu' Jianshe Yingyou Shenshen Xintai" ["In Advancing the Construction of 'One Belt, One Road,' We Must Be Prudent"], *People's Daily*, July 5, 2015.

more recently, by levels of investment far above those of other countries at its stage of development, including the East Asian economies that grew rapidly in the past. However, the investment- and export-led growth model is no longer delivering, and China is trying to make the difficult transition to an economy fueled by innovation and consumption. China views the Developing World as important to its transition. The Developing World is viewed as a site of increased Chinese investment for its firms that have difficulty expanding in China; as a growing market for Chinese goods; and as a location for Chinese construction and infrastructure activity, which is also declining in China. Regardless of China's growth path, it will continue to need resources, which the Developing World has in abundance.

The importance of the Developing World was elevated for China after the 2008 financial crisis. One of China's lessons from the 2008 financial crisis was that it is too risky for China to tie its development mainly to Western developed countries. Instead, China needed to increase its engagement with developing countries that are growing at a rapid pace and have significant market demand.[45]

Increasing China's International Influence in the Transition to a Multipolar World

China sees partnering with the Developing World as critical to increasing China's global influence as the international system becomes, in its view, more multipolar. Chinese leaders and strategists have repeatedly stated that "peace and development" are the "underlying trends" of the current times and the global march toward economic globalization and multipolarity cannot be stopped.[46] China has long advocated for a more dispersed international governance system where the interests of developing countries are more equitably reflected in international institutions and governing structures.

---

[45] Sun Zhiyuan, "'Yi Dai Yi Lu' Zhanlue Gouxiang De Sanzhong Neihan" ["The Three Major Details of the Strategic Concept of 'One Belt, One Road'"], Information Office of the State Council of the People's Republic of China, August 11, 2014.

[46] For example, see "The Central Conference on Work Relating to Foreign Affairs Was Held in Beijing," 2014; *The Diversified Employment of China's Armed Forces*, Information Office of the State Council of the People's Republic of China, April 2013.

After the 2008 financial crisis, Chinese experts have recognized the growing political and economic influence of the Developing World and the narrowing of the power gap between developed and developing countries. As then Chinese Foreign Minister Yang Jiechi remarked in 2011:

> Developing countries are gaining equal status in the G20 and other global economic governance mechanisms, with significantly increased representation and voice. At the same time, major developing countries have enhanced cooperation among themselves, and the BRICs, the BASIC and other cooperation mechanisms have moved into a new stage of development. The BRIC countries, in particular, have shown great promise. Their combined GDP makes up nearly one sixth of the world's total, and they are expected to enjoy faster growth than the developed countries in the medium and long term. The above-mentioned mechanisms carry not only considerable economic weight, but also increasing political influence.[47]

As China seeks to become a more important international player, Beijing will need to win the support of developing countries.

As a developing country itself, China also identifies with the concerns of fellow developing countries and views the United States, Japan, and other Western countries as dominating decisions in existing international institutions. Despite China's rapid economic growth in the past decades, its economic power has not translated into proportional vote shares in the International Monetary Fund (IMF), World Bank, or the Asian Development Bank. For example, while China's share of global GDP in 2014 was 13.3 percent, and the U.S. share was 22.4 percent, less than twice as much, the U.S. vote share of 16.74 percent in the IMF is more than four times China's vote share, 3.81 percent.[48] China and other major developing countries have repeatedly

---

[47] Yang Jiechi, "The Evolving International Pattern and China's Diplomacy," China Institute of International Studies, August 22, 2011.

[48] "IMF Members' Quotas and Voting Power, and IMF Board of Governors," International Monetary Fund, October 12, 2015; GDP shares are from World Bank, *World Development Indicators*, last updated November 12, 2015.

asked for more equitable representation, and there has been little progress to date.[49]

Protecting Chinese Citizens and Assets Abroad

Protecting Chinese citizens and assets abroad is also becoming an increasing focus and concern of the Chinese government. Currently, China has millions of citizens traveling or working abroad. Some estimate that there 5 million Chinese citizens abroad, including 2 million in Africa[50] In 2012, Chinese companies had invested almost $532 billion in direct investment abroad, up from only $33.2 billion in 2003.[51] Many Chinese abroad are traveling or working in unstable or unsafe developing countries. In 2011, China rescued 47,000 Chinese abroad, of which more than 35,000 were workers in Libya. This number is more than the total number of citizens it has had to rescue abroad since the founding of the People's Republic of China in 1949. Similarly, in 2015, China evacuated more than 600 of its citizens from Yemen. To ensure the safety and security of its citizens and investments abroad, China is becoming more proactive and is building stronger relationships with the local governments.[52]

Moreover, the PLA appears to be wrestling with the scope and scale of its impending roles and missions in support of Chinese activities in the Developing World. The impetus for this discourse is President Xi Jinping's formal launching of the Belt and Road Initiative in late 2013. Clearly, the PLA recognizes that it faces a daunting challenge to protect China's burgeoning "overseas interests."[53] According

---

[49] "BRICS Pour Cash into the IMF in Exchange for Bigger Say," *RT*, July 19, 2012; "China Leads Nations Costing IMF's Firewall to $456 Billion," *Bloomberg*, June 19, 2012; see also Ding Yifan, "China's IMF Contribution, a Move of Multiple-Layered Meaning," *China-US Focus*, July 13, 2012.

[50] Jonas Parello-Plesner and Mathieu Duchâtel, "How Chinese Nationals Abroad Are Transforming Beijing's Foreign Policy," *Caixin*, June 19, 2015.

[51] United Nations Conference on Trade and Development, *Bilateral FDI Statistics*, 2014.

[52] Parello-Plesner and Duchâtel, "How Chinese Nationals Abroad Are Transforming Beijing's Foreign Policy"; "Expanding Global Footprint Forces China to Rethink Its Policy of 'Noninterference,'" *Japan Times*, June 16, 2015.

[53] See, for example, *China's Military Strategy*, Information Office of the State Council of the People's Republic of China, May 2015.

to many Chinese civilian and military analysts, how the armed forces of the PRC are supposed to provide security for the Belt and Road Initiative has yet to be properly addressed. Conversations in late 2015 with an array of analysts at think tanks and universities in Beijing and Shanghai reveal that many experts do not believe the PLA is yet capable of protecting Chinese interests beyond the borders of the PRC.[54]

There is widespread recognition that considerable hurdles must be surmounted and that major reassessments of PRC foreign policy principles and defense policy tenets are required. China, for example, must enhance security cooperation with other states and probably establish overseas bases.[55] At the very least, logistical facilities, or "Southeast Asia posts"—such as that in Djibouti—are needed west of Singapore around the rim of the Indian Ocean.[56] It seems all but inevitable that the PLA will increase its global deployments and employments, but this growth is most likely to occur gradually, playing out over many years.[57] The barriers to a more expansive role for China's military are many, including hesitancy in Beijing and agreement by relevant capitals to have Chinese forces operate on or occupy portions of their sovereign territory.[58] It is possible that greater PLA activism overseas could be accelerated if unforeseen global tensions emerge or serious crises arise in the Developing World.

Several preliminary observations can be drawn from the ongoing discourse on the topic, especially the discussion among Chinese military analysts. First, no definitive policy decision or new doctrinal edict has been reached regarding PLA roles and missions in the Third World beyond a general commitment by President Xi, in an address to the United National General Assembly in September 2015 that the

---

[54] Author conversations, Beijing and Shanghai, September 2015.

[55] Andrea Ghiselli, "The Belt, the Road and the PLA," in *China Brief*, Vol. XV, No. 20, October 19, 2015, p. 16.

[56] Morgan Clemens, "The Maritime Silk Road and the PLA: Part One," *China Brief*, Vol. XV, No. 6, March 19, 2015, pp. 7–8; Morgan Clemens, "The Maritime Silk Road and the PLA: Part Two," *China Brief*, Vol. XV, No. 7, April 3, 2014, pp. 10–11.

[57] Clemens, 2014, p. 12.

[58] Ghiselli, 2015, pp. 15–16; Clemens, 2014, p. 10.

PRC will commit greater resources to UN peacekeeping.[59] If more specific decisions had been reached then almost certainly public discourse about the appropriate global roles and missions for China's armed forces would have been quashed or at least significantly dialed back.[60]

Second, the lively discourse has provided a window into the current state of military service rivalries. Analysts affiliated with the People's Liberation Army Navy (PLAN), for example, have emphasized the "Maritime Silk Road" and the importance of Southeast Asia power requirements.[61] Ground force-affiliated analysts, meanwhile, have stressed the "Silk Road Economic Belt," the land power requirements, and the importance of cooperation with the PLA Air Force to provide airlift to ground force units.[62] Looming major national security decisions or important changes in PLA doctrine provide the opportunity for different components of the Chinese armed forces to advocate for the particular service.[63]

Moving Westward to Circumvent Tensions in the East

Finally, and on its immediate periphery, China's greater emphasis on the Developing World is also reflective of the increasingly tense Northeast Asian strategic environment. In the recent years, as the United States rebalanced as the Asia-Pacific and the Sino-Japanese dispute over the Senkakus and Diaoyu islands escalated, Chinese academics and strategists have increasingly pushed Beijing to "move west" or

---

[59] Xi announced that the PRC would take the lead in creating an 8,000 man standby force for UN peacekeeping. Cited in Ghiselli, 2015, p. 14.

[60] See, for example, the high-profile article on the subject: "'Yi Dai Yi Lu' Huo You Li Yu Jiefangjun Gaige" ["'One Belt One Road' Might Benefit PLA Reforms"], *Huanqiu Shibao* [*Global Times*], October 21, 2015, p. 6. The article, which is a summary translation of the October 19, 2015, *China Brief* article by Andrea Ghiselli cited earlier, appears in a very prominent PRC media outlet, the *Global Times*.

[61] Ghiselli, 2015, pp. 14–17.

[62] Ghiselli, 2015, pp. 14–17.

[63] For prior PLA discourse on a contentious doctrinal issue, see Andrew Scobell, "Discourse in 3-D: The PLA's Evolving Doctrinal, Circa 2009," in Roy Kamphausen, David Lai, and Andrew Scobell, *The PLA at Home and Abroad: Assessing the Operational Capabilities of China's Military*, Carlisle Barracks, Pa.: U.S. Army War College, 2010, pp. 99–134.

adjust its strategy toward strengthening relations with countries to its west, which includes Southeast Asia, Central Asia, South Asia, and the Middle East. They argue that the relatively tense environment in Northeast Asia increases the potential that China may find itself in an unwanted military clash with Japan, which could drag in the United States, should Beijing continue to push east. Instead, countries to China's west and southwest largely welcome—or hedge against—greater Chinese engagement and most have less means to resist Chinese influence.[64] Implied in such assessments is that China should strengthen relations with countries to its west to prevent strategic encirclement.

Most of the countries to China's west are developing countries. China can use its strengths of increasing trade and investment and building infrastructure to win local support. Moving westward would also help China avoid the fact that it is still militarily weaker than the United States and its allies.[65]

Roadmap for Regional Chapters

The following chapters examine Chinese activities in the Developing World by region. We divide the Developing World into seven regions: Southeast Asia, Oceania, Central Asia, South Asia, Middle East, Africa, and Latin America and the Caribbean. We cover all developing countries within each region, although we excluded entities currently on the UN list of non-self-governing territories.[66] The exception is Oceania, where we also included more developed countries in the region (Australia and New Zealand), because it is a predominately developing region and strategically important to China.

---

[64] Yun Sun, "March West: China's Response to the U.S. Rebalancing," Brookings Institution, January 31, 2013.

[65] Lin Hongyu, "'Haishang Sichou Zhi Lu' Guoji Zhanlue Yiyi Touxi" ["In-Depth Analysis of the International Strategic Value of the 'Maritime Silk Road'"], *People's Tribune*, September 1, 2014.

[66] United Nations, *Non-Self-Governing Territories*, website, undated. As of October 10, 2015.

CHAPTER THREE

China in Southeast Asia

Southeast Asia is the most important developing region for China and a neighboring region that shares land and maritime borders. It is one of China's most significant trade partners (making up 17 percent of Chinese global trade in 2013),[1] in part because of production networks in which countries throughout the region trade both inputs and final goods with China. In addition to trade with the region, much of Chinese global trade transits the South China Sea and the Strait of Malacca, and China has significant interests to maintain secure maritime shipment and Southeast Asia lines of communication. China also has unresolved territorial disputes with Vietnam, the Philippines, Malaysia, and Brunei in the South China Sea.

Southeast Asia is a focal region for PRC initiatives. It is a critical link in the country's important Belt and Road Initiative, or the Silk Road Economic Belt and the 21st Century Maritime Silk Road, which aims to build "an interdependent economic and political community" between China and key trade partners. Beijing is also pushing for regional free trade agreements between China and the Association of Southeast Asian Nations (ASEAN) as well as China and the larger Asia-Pacific region. Beijing hopes that greater integration with the region will encourage regional actors to accept China's growing influence as well as its territorial claims. Maritime Southeast Asia, in particular, is becoming an arena of strategic competition and hedging between China, its neighbors, and, increasingly, the United States, Japan, and even India.

---

[1] UN Comtrade Database.

Key Chinese Activities in the Region

China is engaging in several different types of activities in the region. Politically and economically, Beijing seeks to increase cooperation with its neighbors and regional influence through greater connectivity and trade. Beijing's core agenda for the region and the larger Developing World is the Belt and Road Initiative. Beyond Belt and Road there are supporting initiatives that can increase China's involvement in the region, such as the Asian Infrastructure Investment Bank (AIIB), which will help finance infrastructure projects in ASEAN as well as greater Asia. China also supports the completion of the Regional Comprehensive Economic Partnership (RCEP) trade agreement with ASEAN and four other countries (16 total, including China) that was often portrayed as competing with the now defunct Trans-Pacific Partnership (TPP) trade agreement. RCEP includes China and excludes the United States (the TPP included the United States, excluded China, and also included four ASEAN countries as well as three non-ASEAN countries in RCEP).

Militarily, China has stepped up its regional involvement with more high-level exchanges, arm sales, combined exercises, and humanitarian and disaster relief operations. Beijing has provided substantial arms to Myanmar and is strengthening military ties with Thailand. In the South China Sea, China has been willing to use maritime militia, coast guard, and law enforcement agencies—all operating under the shadow of the Chinese People's Liberation Army—to stake out and defend its territorial claims. Beijing has also undertaken extensive and rapid land reclamation activities to strengthen its claims in the South China Sea. China is likely to further expand its maritime civilian and military presence in the region.

Beijing views four countries in Southeast Asia—Indonesia, Malaysia, Thailand, and Vietnam—as the most important states for its interests (Figure 3.1). Indonesia, Malaysia, and Thailand have not taken firm stances against Chinese territorial claims in the South China Sea, have friendly relations with China, and are among ASEAN's largest, most developed economies. Vietnam, on the other hand, still has strong ties to China given the two countries' shared communist political ideology, but it has also repeatedly challenged China's maritime claims. China

Figure 3.1
China's Relations with Countries in Southeast Asia, 2015

NOTE: Due to small scale of map, not all countries are displayed and color-coded.
RAND *RR2273A-3.1*

views most of continental Southeast Asia as major regional partners. In contrast, Beijing views Manila as a troublemaker in the region, and relations between the two countries have suffered.

Drivers of Chinese Engagement

Chinese Activities in the Region Prior to 2000

China has had extensive historical involvement in the region. It largely divides the region into continental and maritime Southeast Asia, although Vietnam falls into both categories. Continental Southeast Asia includes Cambodia, Laos, Myanmar, Thailand, and Vietnam. China has sought to exert more influence on these countries and has been willing to provide significant political, economic, and military assistance to create friendly or buffer states along its border. Under Mao, China also supported Communist insurgencies, both verbally and materially, in half a dozen Southeast Asia countries, and the insurgencies drew heavily from ethnic Chinese in the region.

Countries have not uniformly welcomed greater Chinese influence. Vietnam, for example, has consistently sought to maintain its autonomy from China by either aligning with external powers or attempting to dominate its smaller neighbors. China's land borders with continental Southeast Asia also continue to present it with ongoing problems of cross-border crime and illegal trafficking of drugs, goods, and people.[2]

China's relations with maritime Southeast Asia—Brunei, Indonesia, Malaysia, the Philippines, Singapore, and Vietnam—have largely centered on two goals: promoting trade and investment in the region and enhancing China's territorial claims in the South China Sea. In the 1970s, countries surrounding the South China Sea gained both the naval and commercial capability to stake claims and exploit resources. Since then, China has repeatedly clashed with its Southeast Asian neighbors, particularly the Philippines and Vietnam, over its claims to all four clusters of land features in the South China Sea—the Paracel Islands (called Xisha Islands by China), the Spratly Islands (called Nansha Islands by China), the Pratas Islands (called Dongsha Islands by China), and the Macclesfield Bank (Zhongsha Islands). China has been willing to use military force to protect its claims and used force against the Republic of Vietnam (then South Vietnam) over the Paracel Islands in 1974 and against the Socialist Republic of Vietnam over Johnson Reef in the Spratly Islands in 1988.[3] By the mid-1990s, after the Taiwan Strait Crisis, Beijing recognized that its assertive actions in North and Southeast Asia had damaged its image internationally and

---

[2] Nathan and Scobell, 2012, pp. 148–154.

[3] Nathan and Scobell, 2012, pp. 141–146.

its relations with its neighbors. China introduced a "new security concept," in which countries should "rise above one-sided security and seek common security through mutually beneficial cooperation" and began considering more cooperative approaches.[4] In 2002, Beijing signed the Declaration of Conduct of Parties in the South China Sea, but the declaration did not contain any specific provisions on how to resolve the sovereignty disputes.

Current Chinese Policy Toward the Region

Chinese Priorities and Policies

China has three overarching interests in Southeast Asia:

1. Promote and protect trade, investment, and other linkages to the region to support China's economic growth. This includes protecting China's sea lines of communication and developing the 21st Century Maritime Silk Road to further expand political and economic cooperation.
2. Protect Chinese sovereignty and territorial integrity, including upholding Chinese claims to features in the South China Sea, enlarging these features, and increasing China's maritime presence and capabilities.
3. Maintain regional stability and promote regional solidarity and cooperation with China by minimizing unwanted influence of external actors and increasing Chinese exchanges with the region.

China does not have a white paper focused on Southeast Asia, but many policy documents point to the importance of the region in Chinese strategic thinking. Among its top priorities in the region, China seeks to protect its territorial claims in the South China Sea. Beijing has labeled "protecting national sovereignty and territorial integrity" as one of China's most important national interests or "core national interests" (*hexin liyi*). While official Chinese documents discussing

---

[4] *China's Position Paper on the New Security Concept (July 31, 2002)*, Ministry of Foreign Affairs of the People's Republic of China," August 6, 2002.

territorial integrity as a core interest mention Taiwan, Xinjiang, and Tibet, senior Chinese leaders have yet to explicitly and uniformly identify features in the South China Sea as a core interest. There is, however, increasing quasi-official and nonofficial commentary linking the South China Sea to Chinese core interests.[5] China also released an official position paper on the South China Sea in late 2014 arguing for its "indisputable sovereignty over the South China Sea Islands . . . and the adjacent waters."[6]

Chinese strategists view the South China Sea as a critical body of water to be secured for Chinese development and protection. Economically, 21 of China's 39 maritime trade routes and 60 percent of Chinese trade pass by the Spratly Islands, a quarter of global maritime trade flows through the South China Sea annually, and over 85 percent of Chinese oil imports arrive via the South China Sea. The South China Sea also boasts vast, unexplored natural resources. Geopolitically, control over the South China Sea provides China with maritime and border security for a significant portion of southern China. Militarily, it helps China transition to a stronger naval power, including providing a secure location for the training and positioning of China's nuclear submarines and aircraft carriers. China has also invested in space launch facilities on Hainan Island, and the South China Sea area may be a critical region where China continues to invest in its space capabilities.[7]

China's 2015 Defense White Paper notes that some "offshore neighbors [are] tak[ing] provocative actions and reinforce their military presence on China's reefs and islands that they have illegally occupied" and "some external countries are also busy meddling in South

---

[5] "Zhongguo Hexin Liyi Bu Rong Tiaozhan" ["China's Core Interests Are Not to Be Challenged"], *Xinhua News*, May 25, 2015; "Zhongmei Zai Nanhai Wenti Shang Bu Ying Tiaozhan Duifang De Hexin Li Yi" ["China and America Should Not Challenge Each Other's Core Interests in the South Southeast Asia"], *CRI Online*, August 11, 2015; "Security Law Suggests a Broadening of China's 'Core Interests,'" *New York Times*, July 2, 2015.

[6] "China's Position Paper on South China Southeast Asia," December 7, 2014, *China Daily*.

[7] "Nanhai Zai Zhongguo Guofang Anquan Zhanlue Zhong Duju Zhongyao Diwei" ["The South China Sea Holds a Uniquely Important Position in China's National Defense and Security Strategy"], *CRI Online*, August 14, 2015.

China Sea affairs." The paper also mentions "a tiny few maintain close-in air and sea surveillance and reconnaissance against China."[8] Against these threats, Beijing seeks an active defense military strategy. Among other elements, this strategy includes the PLA Navy shifting from conducting only "offshore waters defense" to also engaging in "open sea protection."[9] China will be developing "modern maritime military force structure" to "safeguard its national sovereignty and maritime rights and interests, protect the security of strategic sea lines of communication and overseas interests, and participate in international maritime cooperation."[10] China has already established an Air Defense Identification Zone in the East China Sea—where it has similar maritime territorial disputes with Japan—and Beijing has not ruled out the possibility of establishing one in the South China Sea.[11]

China's desire to stake its claims in the South China Sea and protect its sea lines of communication is balanced by its interests in promoting trade, investment, and other forms of cooperation with Southeast Asia and maintaining a peaceful and stable external environment to facilitate China's continued political and economic growth. Senior Chinese leaders have stated that China will be more proactive in fostering a periphery policy that supports its growth and "will firmly prioritize ASEAN member countries in the country's peripheral diplomacy."[12] Southeast Asia also features prominently in China's Belt and Road Initiative, and some have characterized Southeast Asia as the most important region for Belt and Road.[13] While official Chinese

---

8 *China's Military Strategy*, 2015.

9 "China Rolls Out Military Roadmap of 'Active Defense' Strategy,'" Ministry of National Defense of the People's Republic of China, May 26, 2015.

10 *China's Military Strategy*, 2015.

11 "Foreign Ministry Spokesperson Hua Chunying's Regular Press Conference on May 7, 2015," Ministry of Foreign Affairs of the People's Republic of China, May 7, 2015.

12 "Premier Li Keqiang's Keynote Speech at 10th China-ASEAN Expo," September 4, 2013, *Xinhua News*.

13 "Dongnanya Zai 'Yi Dai Yi Lu' Jianshe Zhong Jiang Fahui Zhongyao Zuoyong" ["Southeast Asia Will Play an Important Role in the Construction of 'One Belt, One Road'"], Information Office of the State Council of the People's Republic of China, July 6, 2015.

policy does not seek to exclude the United States or other external actors from involvement in Southeast Asia, some regional initiatives China supports—such as Belt and Road and RCEP—will significantly increase China's relative connectivity to the region.

Overall, Chinese strategists recognize that China needs to address a number of challenges in Southeast Asia. These include anxiety among Southeast Asian countries over China's growing military power, intensification of territorial disputes in the South China Sea, and involvement of external powers in Southeast Asia that negatively impact and complicate the strategic situation. Chinese experts are also concerned with the domestic situations in Southeast Asian countries, such as Myanmar's political transition and internal stability.[14]

To advance its interests in Southeast Asia, China engages with the region on a bilateral and multilateral basis. Since the early 1990s, China has viewed ASEAN as a preferred multilateral vehicle for reaching out to Southeast Asia. Beijing established relations with ASEAN in 1991. China has participated in several additional political, security, and economic groupings with ASEAN serving a leading role, including ASEAN+1, ASEAN+3, East Asian Summit (EAS), and ASEAN Regional Forum (ARF). In 2010, China also signed the ASEAN-China Free Trade Area (ACFTA). Appendix A discusses the various actors in China involved in shaping policy toward Southeast Asia.

Political Engagement

China has multiple and competing political interests in Southeast Asia. It seeks to safeguard its territorial claims in the South China Sea against rival regional claimants, increase the region's political and economic linkages with China, minimize external powers from interfering in the region to China's detriment, and maintain peace and stability in Southeast Asia. While China has typically sought to balance these competing objectives, there are more recent indications that it will not

---

[14] He Shengda, "Dongnanya Diqu Zhanlue Geju Yu Zhongguo—Dongmeng Guanxi" ["The Strategic Situation in the Southeast Asian Region and China-ASEAN Relations"], *Southeast Asia and South Asia Studies*, No. 1, 2014.

back down on its territorial claims, even when Chinese actions come at the cost of worsening relations with particular regional claimants.

Recent Chinese political engagement with Southeast Asia has been defined by initiatives announced by Chinese leaders during their visits to the region. The most important of these visits occurred in October 2013, when both President Xi Jinping and Premier Li Keqiang made their first visits to Southeast Asia as new leaders of China and to celebrate the ten-year anniversary of the establishing of strategic relations between China and ASEAN. Xi visited Indonesia and Malaysia and attended the twenty-first APEC Economic Leaders Summit, where he met with Asian leaders on the side, including Thai Prime Minister Yingluck Shinawatra.[15] Li commenced his first visit to Southeast Asia soon afterward. Following the APEC summit, Xi traveled to Brunei, Thailand, and Vietnam.[16]

In his speech to the Indonesian Parliament on October 3, Xi listed key Chinese objectives for the region for the coming years:

- Develop maritime cooperation and build a 21st Century Maritime Silk Road that puts the China-ASEAN Maritime Cooperation Fund to use.
- Establish an Asian Infrastructure Investment Bank that would give priority to ASEAN countries' needs.
- Upgrade the China-ASEAN Free Trade Area and strive to expand two-way trade to one trillion U.S. dollars by 2020.
- Provide ASEAN countries with 15,000 government scholarships for cultural exchanges in the next three to five years.

All those efforts would help "build a more closely-knit China-ASEAN community of common destiny."[17]

---

[15] Wang Yi, "Creating a New Landscape for the Diplomacy with Neighboring Countries and Boosting the Asia-Pacific Regional Cooperation," Ministry of Foreign Affairs of the People's Republic of China, October 9, 2013.

[16] "Li Keqiang Starts First Southeast Asia Visit," *Global Times*, October 9, 2013.

[17] Xi Jinping, "Speech by Chinese President Xi Jinping to Indonesian Parliament," Jakarta, Indonesia, October 3, 2013.

Premier Li echoed all of Xi's points during his trip and coined the Chinese strategy toward ASEAN as following a "2+7 cooperation framework." The "2" refers to China trying to achieve political consensus on two issues: deepening mutual trust and good neighborly relations to promote cooperation and focusing on economic development as a driver of cooperation. The "7" includes all the proposals in the previous bullet points as well as increasing regional financial cooperation via more bilateral currency swaps, full leveraging of the China-ASEAN Inter-Bank Association, strengthening cooperation on the Chiang Mai Initiative Multilateralization. Li also included increasing security ties as one of the seven proposed areas of cooperation, and he pushed for hosting a formal China-ASEAN defense ministers meeting and increasing cooperation on humanitarian assistance and disaster relief.[18] This could be an attempt by China to develop an alternative security forum to the ARF and one in which the United States would be excluded.[19] Along with region-wide agreements, Xi's and Li's trips led to the strengthening of China's relationship with all five visited countries, including the elevation of China's relationship with Malaysia and Indonesia to "comprehensive strategic partnerships" and agreements to exploit energy resources with Brunei, invest in high-speed rail technology with Thailand, and engage in potential maritime exploration with Vietnam.[20]

Maritime Cooperation and the 21st Century Maritime Silk Road

Since signing the Declaration of Conduct in 2002, China has engaged in continuous diplomatic and political measures to resolve its territorial disputes in the South China Sea and to strengthen relations with ASEAN countries. Chief among these are efforts to set aside the dispute and engage in joint economic development and extraction of

---

[18] Li Keqiang, "Remarks by H. E. Li Keqiang Premier of the State Council of the People's Republic of China at the 16th ASEAN-China Summit," Bandar Seri Begawan, Brunei, October 9, 2013.

[19] The authors thank Andrew Erickson for this observation.

[20] Prashanth Parameswaran, "Beijing Unveils New Strategy for ASEAN–China Relations," *Jamestown China Brief*, Vol. 13, No. 21, October 24, 2013.

resources from the South China Sea.[21] In practice, this has mainly translated into Chinese use of bilateral negotiations with individual dispute claimants despite the fact that multiple actors claim the same territory. Not surprising, Chinese bilateral efforts have been met with little success, as Southeast Asian countries are afraid of being left with the short end of the stick in any bilateral agreement and see that they have more bargaining power against China in a multilateral or international setting.[22]

In 2011, China further established a China-ASEAN Maritime Cooperation Fund that had an initial capital of RMB 3 billion (approximately $500 million). The fund promotes maritime partnership through increased maritime economy, greater connectivity, more scientific research and environmental protection, and cooperation on navigation safety and search and rescue. In 2013, Xi announced that the fund would also support the construction of the 21st Century Maritime Silk Road.[23]

Although the 21st Century Maritime Silk Road extends beyond Southeast Asia, Chinese strategists view the region as crucial to the success of the initiative.[24] The Silk Road envisions increasing Chinese trade via merchant vessels traveling through the South China Sea and potentially stopping at several key ports. These ports are also connected to critical rail and road transportation routes. An early blueprint of Belt and Road suggests that China may be considering ports in Vietnam,

---

[21] "Set Aside Dispute and Pursue Joint Development," Ministry of Foreign Affairs of the People's Republic of China.

[22] For examples of limited bilateral agreements China concluded with Southeast Asia countries, see *Joint Statement Between the People's Republic of China and Brunei Darussalam*, Ministry of Foreign Affairs of the People's Republic of China, April 6, 2013; Carl Thayer, "China-ASEAN Joint Development Overshadowed by South China Southeast Asia," *The Diplomat*, October 25, 2013.

[23] In 2014, the fund announced supporting a second round of projects, including projects on disaster relief and environmental protection. See Bao Haibin, "China-ASEAN Maritime Cooperation Fund," Ministry of Foreign Affairs of the People's Republic of China, March 2014.

[24] "Dongnanya Zai 'Yi Dai Yi Lu' Jianshe Zhong Jiang Fahui Zhongyao Zuoyong," 2015.

Malaysia, and Indonesia.[25] Both Malaysia and Indonesia welcome Chinese investment in port and railway infrastructure.[26] Chinese policymakers are also portraying the Silk Road as part of a larger effort for China to move up the production value chain, shifting less competitive and labor-intensive Chinese industries in Southeast Asia, where labor is still relatively cost effective in at least some countries.[27]

Chinese experts argue that Southeast Asia is a testing ground for using infrastructure connectivity to achieve a community of common destiny. Southeast Asia is geographically close to China and is one of the anchoring regions on which other portions of the Maritime Silk Road will depend. It is also a region with some of the most favorable conditions for forming a community of common destiny. It is one of the more advanced developing regions with significant trade with China and the region that is more culturally similar to China and has the most overseas ethnic Chinese. At the same time, Chinese experts recognize that Beijing's ability to manage territorial disputes in the South China Sea is crucial to realizing the Maritime Silk Road and ensuring China's peripheral security.[28]

Chinese Activities in the South China Sea

Along with political and diplomatic measures to increase maritime cooperation, China continues to strengthen its territorial claims in the South China Sea. China currently holds eight outposts in the Spratly Islands, the most disputed area of the South China Sea. Vietnam has 48 outposts, the Philippines has eight, Malaysia has five, and Taiwan holds one. All the claimants have engaged in various degrees of outpost upgrade and land reclamation, but Vietnam was the most active from 2009 to 2014, reclaiming approximately 60 acres

---

[25] "New Silk Road, New Dreams," *Xinhua News*, website, undated. As of October 10, 2015.

[26] "Indonesia, China Committed to Infrastructure Co-Op: Indonesian Spokesman," *Xinhua News*, April 24, 2015. As of October 10, 2015; Vincent Wee, "Malaysia Hoping to Tap on Chinese for New Port Investment," *Seatrade Maritime News*, June 12, 2015.

[27] Sun Zhiyuan, 2014.

[28] "Dongnanya Zai 'Yi Dai Yi Lu' Jianshe Zhong Jiang Fahui Zhongyao Zuoyong," 2015.

of land.[29] Several Southeast Asian claimants have also built airstrips and other installations.[30] In December 2013, China began land reclamation on its outposts. As of June 2015, Chinese reclamation has proceeded at a rapid pace and China has reclaimed approximately 2,900 acres (1,700 hectares) of land, or 17 times more land than all the other claimants combined. China's recent reclamation efforts in the South China Sea are different in nature and scope than the actions by other actors; its activities can enable the PRC to have a more robust power projection capability in the South China Sea. China is constructing significantly larger airstrips for deployment of various types of aircraft and excavating deeper channels and berthing areas for larger ships.[31] As an example, while five countries have built airstrips in the South China Sea, China's 3,000 meter airstrip on Fiery Cross Reef was, in late summer 2015, more than twice as large as the next largest and was the only one that could accommodate bombers.[32] Figure 3.2 displays the location of China's reclamation efforts on the Spratly Islands.

China's strategy in the South China Sea is largely one of divide and conquer: encourage ASEAN countries with no disputes with China to stay on the sidelines and deal with dispute claimants on a bilateral basis. China is proceeding cautiously to prevent ASEAN countries from uniting against China. To dampen regional concerns of Chinese military strength, Beijing has opted to use its coast guard, not the PLA Navy, as the frontline actor in preserving Chinese territorial claims. Beijing has also engaged in a media campaign to portray its actions in the South China Sea as defensive and the other claimants—particularly the Philippines and Vietnam—as instigating problems in

---

[29] David Shear, "Statement of David Shear Assistant Secretary of Defense for Asian and Pacific Security Affairs," Senate Committee on Foreign Relations, May 13, 2015.

[30] Vietnam, Philippines, Taiwan, and Malaysia all have airstrips in the disputed territories. China is building its third airstrip. See *CNN*, "Satellite Images Suggest China 'Building Third Airstrip' in South China Southeast Asia," September 15, 2015.

[31] Department of Defense, *Asia-Pacific Maritime Security Strategy*, August 2015, pp. 16–17.

[32] Asia Maritime Transparency Initiative, "Airpower in the South China Sea," Center for Strategic and International Studies, July 29, 2015.

Figure 3.2
Chinese Maritime Claims in the South China Sea and Land Reclamation, June 2015

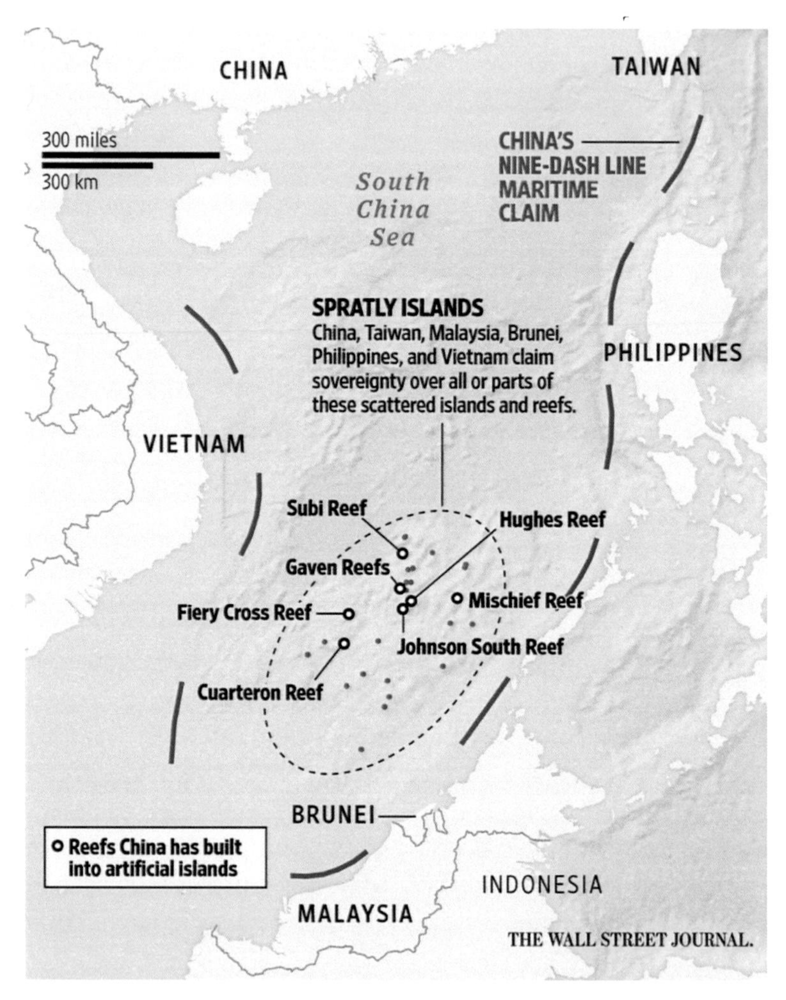

SOURCE: "Pentagon Says China Has Stepped Up Land Reclamation in South China Sea," *Wall Street Journal*, August 20, 2015. As of September 19, 2015: http://www.wsj.com/articles/pentagon-says-china-has-stepped-up-land-reclamation-in-south-china-sea-1440120837

RAND *RR2273A-3.2*

the region.[33] Beijing has repeatedly assured the United States and other actors that its claims and activities in the South China Sea will not affect the freedom of navigation. While there has been little progress settling conflicting claims, China and ASEAN are negotiating a code of conduct in the South China Sea and seek to set up a China-ASEAN hotline for maritime search and rescue and a China-ASEAN senior foreign officials hotline for emergencies. China also held the first special meeting of China-ASEAN defense ministers in Beijing in October 2015.[34] Beijing offered to hold joint military drills with ASEAN countries in the disputed South China Sea to increase military ties between the PLA and Southeast Asian militaries and to diminish mutual suspicion.[35] These measures aim to decrease the potential for clashes in the South China Sea.

Beijing, however, has demonstrated willingness to press its territorial claims at the cost of worsening some bilateral relationships. This includes China's relocation of an oilrig close to the Vietnamese coast in May 2014 that sparked massive and deadly anti-Chinese riots in Vietnam and a significant dip in bilateral relations between the communist neighbors.[36] It also includes China's continued assertion of its Nine-Dash Line claim that covers almost the entirety of the South China Sea, efforts to interfere with the Philippines resupply of its outpost at the Second Thomas Shoal, and its efforts to restrict the access of fishermen from ASEAN states to disputed fishing zones.[37] Since mid-2014,

---

[33] For example, see "Waijiaobu Jie Feibin Yuenan Nanhai Feifa Qinquan Huodong: Yaoqiu Liji Tingzhi" ["Foreign Ministry Exposes Philippines and Vietnams Illegal Activities Infringing on Sovereignty in the South Southeast Asia, Demands Immediate End"], *Xinhua News*, April 29, 2015; "Yuenan Deng Guo Zai Nai Hai Fengkuang Tianhai Xifang Shi Er Bu Jian Zhi Pi Zhongguo" ["Vietnam and Other Countries Reclaim Land Like Mad in the South Southeast Asia, West Ignores and Criticizes Only China"], *Sina News*, June 21, 2015.

[34] Zhou Bo, "China-ASEAN Hotlines: The Best Fruits in an 'Early Harvest,'" *China-US Focus*, August 20, 2015; Prashanth Parameswaran, "China to Hold First Meeting with ASEAN Defense Ministers in Beijing," *The Diplomat*, June 3, 2015.

[35] Kristine Kwok, "China Offers Joint Drills with ASEAN in South China Southeast Asia to Check US Plan to Send Warships Near Spratly Islands," *South China Morning Post*, October 16, 2015.

[36] "How an Oil Rig Sparked Anti-China Riots in Vietnam," *CNN*, May 19, 2014.

[37] David Shear, May 13, 2015.

Vietnamese fishermen have reported increasing confrontations with Chinese Coast Guard and civilian ships.[38]

Diplomatic Relations and Presence

China has diplomatic relations with all of Southeast Asia. China has close political relations and signed comprehensive strategic cooperative partnerships with Cambodia, Laos, Myanmar, Thailand, and Vietnam. These agreements do not necessarily result in strong partnerships. China and Vietnam signed their agreement in 2008, but Beijing's relations with Hanoi have deteriorated in recent years due to territorial disputes in the South China Sea. Similarly, China and Myanmar signed their agreement in 2011, but domestic economic and political reforms in Myanmar have complicated recent bilateral relations. China has comprehensive strategic partnerships with Malaysia and Indonesia, two countries that are friendly to China and have not taken sides or significantly opposed Chinese territorial claims in the region. China also has some form of partnership agreement with Timor-Leste, ASEAN, Brunei, and the Philippines.

Pivotal Partners, Key States, and Major Partners

Unlike in other regions, there is no single pivotal state for China in Southeast Asia. Among these relationships, four are especially important and can be categorized as key states—those with Indonesia, Malaysia, Thailand, and Vietnam. Beijing views these four Southeast Asian states as capable of either significantly helping or hindering attempts to consolidate and extend Chinese influence throughout the region. In summarizing President Xi Jinping's trip to Southeast Asia in 2013, Chinese Foreign Minister Wang Yi explicitly stated that Indonesia and Malaysia have "always ranked at the top of China's relationships with other ASEAN countries."[39] Between these two countries, Chinese leaders typically mention Indonesia first, signifying that it is most important. Geographically and economically, Indonesia is the largest state in Southeast Asia and an important emerging market and large

[38] "Report: Chinese Navy Warship Rammed Two Vietnamese Fishing Vessels," *USNI News*, August 7, 2015.

[39] Wang Yi, 2013.

developing country. It is politically stable, undertaking naval modernization under the new administration of President Jokowi, and pursues a moderate foreign policy that has earned it regional and global respect. Some Chinese experts point to Indonesia as the most critical state in its Maritime Silk Road project and as a priority target for engagement.[40] Similarly, Malaysia is China's largest trading partner in ASEAN and has largely remained on the sidelines in China's territorial disputes in the South China Sea. China has also increased outreach to Thailand, and the two countries enjoy strong relations despite the fact that Bangkok is a U.S. treaty ally. Vietnam, on the other hand, is pivotal but not a potential partner for China. Although both countries embrace communist ideology, Beijing increasingly views Hanoi as a troublemaker in the region because of its stance on the South China Sea territorial disputes and the resulting confrontations between the two countries.

High-Level Exchanges

China engages in significant high-level exchanges with Southeast Asian countries, and such exchanges have been increasing. From 2003–2014, there were 94 Chinese leadership visits to ASEAN countries.[41] Most of these visits (62 visits) occurred from 2009 onward. Chinese leaders were in the region to attend bilateral and multilateral meetings, including ASEAN, APEC, Greater Mekong Subregion, and East Asian Summits.

The countries most visited by Chinese leaders were Indonesia, Thailand, and Vietnam. Among ASEAN countries, Myanmar was the only country Chinese presidents did not visit during this period, although Chinese premiers and other high-level officials did visit the country. Not surprising given the tensions in Sino-Philippines relations in the recent years, there has not been a single high-level Chinese visit to the Philippines since 2007 through 2014. There were no high-level visits to Timor-Leste.

---

[40] "Zhiku Luntan: Yi Dai Yi Lu Tiaozhan Yu Jiyu Dongnanya Zhongyao" ["Think Tank Forum: The Challenges and Opportunities of One Belt, One Road, Southeast Asia Is Important"], *CRNTT News*, June 23, 2015.

[41] Chinese political leaders include the president, premier, vice president, minister of foreign affairs, and state councilor in charge of foreign affairs.

Cultural Influence

Chinese experts perceive that China can exert significant cultural influence on Southeast Asia given the region's close historical ties to China, geographical proximity, and large numbers of ethnic Chinese. China has 25 Confucius Institutes in Southeast Asia. Most countries—except for Brunei, Timor-Leste, Myanmar, and Vietnam—have one or more institutes. Thailand (12 institutes), Indonesia (six institutes), and the Philippines (three institutes) each have more than one Confucius Institute.

Across the Developing World, Southeast Asia is the region with the most ethnic Chinese. According to Taiwanese government statistics, approximately 69 percent of all overseas ethnic Chinese (or nearly 29 million people) were in Southeast Asia in 2012.[42] There are significant numbers of ethnic Chinese in most of the countries in the region. They make up over half the population in Singapore, over a fifth of the population in Malaysia, and approximately a tenth of the population in Thailand and Brunei. In the remaining countries, ethnic Chinese are less than 5 percent of the local population.

The entire Chinese ethnic diaspora is well assimilated into Southeast Asian states in which they reside and hold citizenship, but there are variations as to how they are viewed and treated in each. Ethnic Chinese in region are a diverse group and do not share any special bond with the PRC beyond cultural affinity. Virtually none would compromise their status to help the PRC. Indeed the Chinese diaspora tends to be vulnerable to scapegoating and racial discrimination in their respective Southeast Asian states. They are not willing to lose their political and economic privileges to serve Chinese interests.[43]

Notably, the flows of Chinese citizens have been large. One scholar estimates that from the 1980s through about 2009, Southeast

---

[42] For Taiwanese statistics, see *2013 Statistical Yearbook of the Overseas Community Affairs Council*, Republic of China (Taiwan). Taiwanese statistics correspond to but are lower than official Chinese figures of approximately 30 million to 40 million ethnic Chinese in Southeast Asia. See "Dongna nya Zai 'Yi Dai Yi Lu' Jianshe Zhong Jiang Fahui Zhongyao Zuoyong," 2015.

[43] Amy Chang, "Beijing and the Chinese Diaspora in Southeast Asia: To Serve the People," *NBR Special Report*, No. 43, June 2013.

Asia received more than 2.5 million migrants from China. This does not indicate the number that have returned to China.[44]

Economic Engagement

China economic engagement with Southeast Asia has accelerated in the past decade and has been greater than with any other region of the Developing World. Not only has it been greater, it also has been qualitatively different. This is due in part to its economic potential. ASEAN as a bloc, for example, is the second fastest growing economy in Asia,[45] with GDP growth of 5 percent in 2013.[46] However, it also stems from the fact that ASEAN is more developed than other developing regions and has a strong consumer market, a strong manufacturing base, and the ability to use Chinese inputs or provide Chinese manufacturers with intermediate inputs; intra-Asian production networks that rely on trade in intermediate products have developed over the last 30 years. As a result, China's trade with ASEAN is weighted much more heavily toward imports and exports of manufactured items rather than raw materials, as it is with other developing regions. And although this is changing, these production networks have tended to be controlled by companies from developed countries and regions.[47]

Today, China is not only ASEAN's most important trade partner but also competes with the region for market share, manufacturing, and foreign direct investment. In 2009, China surpassed both the United States and Japan to become ASEAN's largest trade partner,

---

[44] Zhuang Guotu, "Dongnanya Huaqiao Renshuliang De Xin Gusuan" ["A New Estimate of the Ethnic Chinese Population in Southeast Asia"], *Journal of Xiamen University (Arts & Social Sciences)*, General Serial No. 193, No. 3, 2009, pp. 62–69.

[45] "ASEAN GDP and GDP per Capita," *ASEAN Matters for America*, East-West Center, 2013.

[46] "Global Recovery Should Carry ASEAN Through the Economic Headwinds," *Forbes*, January 19, 2014.

[47] Organization for Economic Cooperation and Development, World Trade Organization, and World Bank Group, *Global Value Chains: Challenges, Opportunities, and Implications for Policy*, report prepared for submission to the G20 Trade Ministers Meeting, Sydney, Australia, July 19, 2014.

Figure 3.3
U.S. and Chinese Trade with ASEAN, 2000–2013

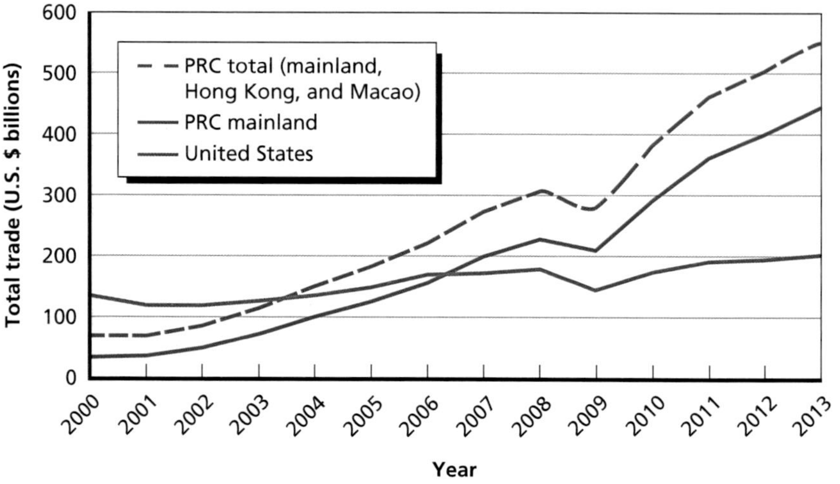

SOURCE: UN Comtrade Database.
RAND *RR2273A-3.3*

and ASEAN has been China's third largest external trade partner since 2011 (Figure 3.3).[48] A China-ASEAN free trade agreement (FTA) for goods entered into force in July 2005, and one for services entered into force in 2007.[49] Currently, approximately half of the Southeast Asian countries have bilateral investment treaties with China and roughly 40 percent have tax treaties.

Trade

Southeast Asia is China's largest source of imports and largest destination for exports. As part of the ASEAN-China Free Trade Area (which includes all Southeast Asian countries except East Timor), the countries have signed agreements on goods, services, and investment. In

---

[48] Meredith Miller, "China's Relations with Southeast Asia," testimony for the U.S.-China Economic and Security Review Commission, May 13, 2015.

[49] "China-ASEAN FTA," *China FTA Network*, Ministry of Commerce of the People's Republic of China, undated; see also "Overview of ASEAN-China (ACFTA)," Singapore Government, 2014.

2013, Chinese Premier Li Keqiang called for upgrading the free trade area, and China hoped to wrap up talks upgrading the agreement by the end of 2015. In 2014, ASEAN and China further agreed to expand two-way trade to $1 trillion in 2020, a roughly 60 percent increase over 2013 trade levels, and achieve two-way investment of $150 billion by 2020. There is no guarantee trade or investment figures will reach these levels.

In 2013, Chinese trade with Southeast Asia made up 15 percent of China's total global trade. China's imports grew from $22.2 billion in 2000 to $199.6 billion in 2013 with growth in every sector. Roughly 55 percent of imports have been manufactured goods and machinery throughout the entire time, although there was an increase in machinery imports in the mid-2000s, with corresponding decreases in manufactured goods and mineral fuels that have since reversed course (Figure 3.4).

Figure 3.4
Composition of Imports from Southeast Asia

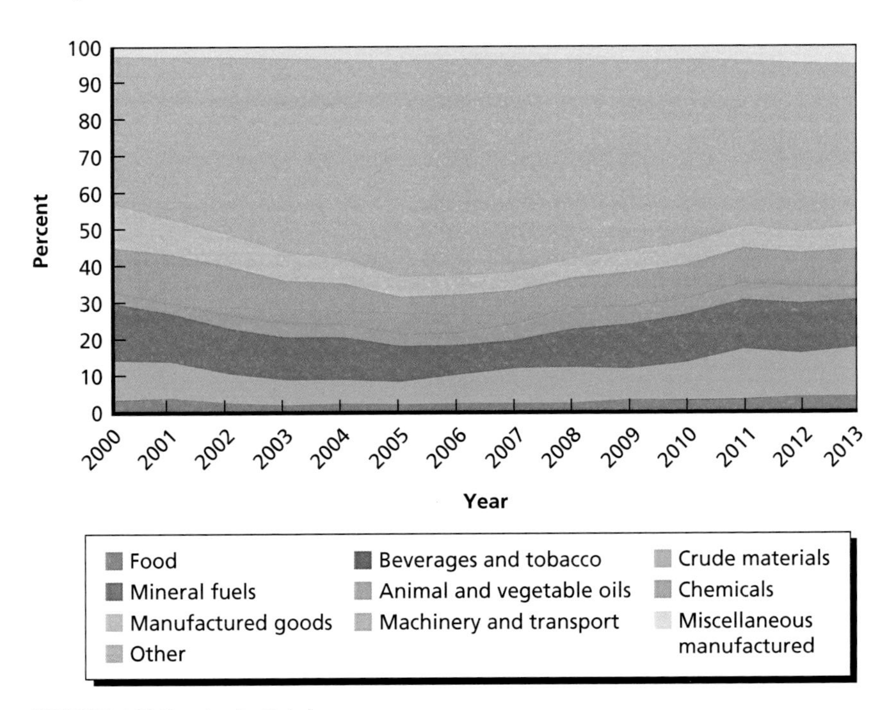

SOURCE: UN Comtrade Database.

RAND *RR2273A-3.4*

Exports from China to Southeast Asia have grown from $17.3 billion in 2000 to $244.0 billion in 2013, with growth in every sector. Manufactured goods and machinery were roughly 75 percent of all exports to Southeast Asia in 2000 and roughly 83 percent in 2013 (Figure 3.5). In contrast, the share of food and mineral fuel exports has fallen even though there has been a more then eightfold increase in the level of food and mineral fuels exports from 2000 to 2013.

Southeast Asia has had a small trade surplus for much of the 2000 to 2013 period, although this has reversed in 2012 and 2013 (Figure 3.6). China's largest trade surplus is with Vietnam, at almost $32 billion in 2013, and the largest trade deficit is with Malaysia, at $14.2 billion in 2013. The largest trading partners are Malaysia, Singapore, Thailand, Indonesia, and Vietnam.

Figure 3.5
Composition of Exports to Southeast Asia

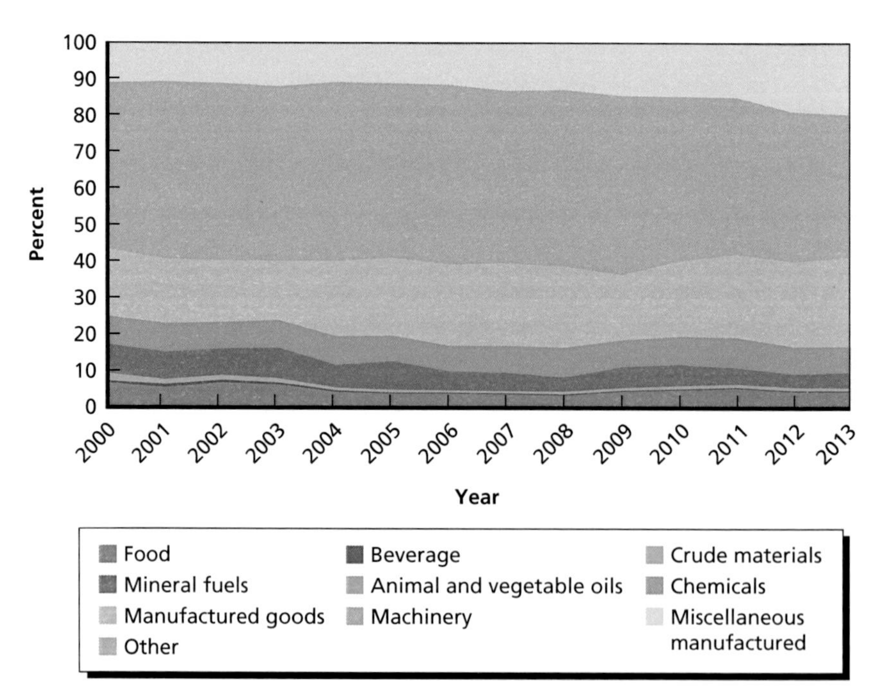

SOURCE: UN Comtrade Database.
RAND *RR2273A-3.5*

Figure 3.6
Level of Exports to and Imports from Southeast Asia

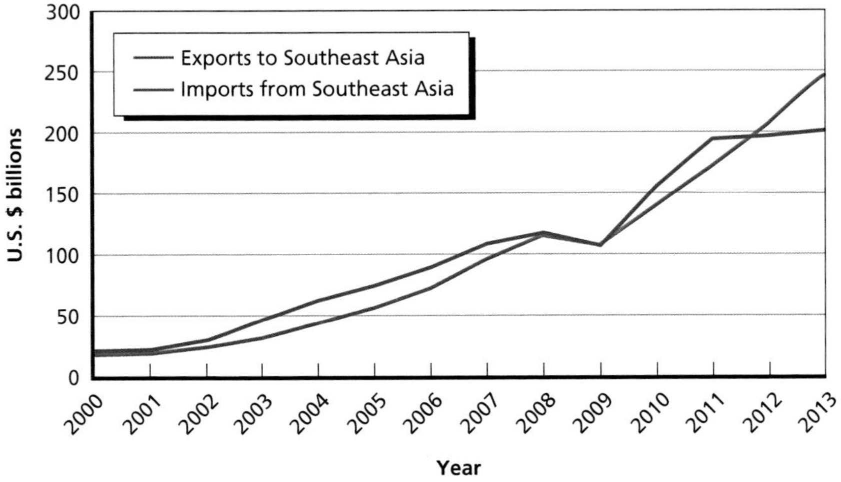

SOURCE: UN Comtrade Database.
RAND *RR2273A-3.6*

Foreign Direct Investment and Lending

Singapore is the largest recipient of China's FDI (Figure 3.7), with over 40 percent of the regional FDI stock in 2013 ($14.7 billion). All other countries are minor by comparison. Only Brunei, Philippines, and East Timor did not have at least $1 billion in FDI stock from China. Singapore has long been a site of inward FDI from around the world, instituting its first tax incentives to attract FDI in the 1960s. As it developed, it became the site not only of manufacturing facilities but also of regional headquarters and of its own major companies, the latter two of which conduct their own FDI activities. In 2010, it received half of all FDI flows into ASEAN from all sources worldwide.[50]

Agreements and Other Issues

China has long engaged in economic diplomacy with Southeast Asia. For example, China has signed bilateral investment treaties (BITs) with

[50] Locknie Hsu, "Inward FDI in Singapore and Its Policy Context," Columbia FDI Profiles, Vale Columbia Center on Sustainable International Investment, Columbia University, 2012.

Figure 3.7
Chinese FDI Stock in Southeast Asia by Receiving Country, 2013

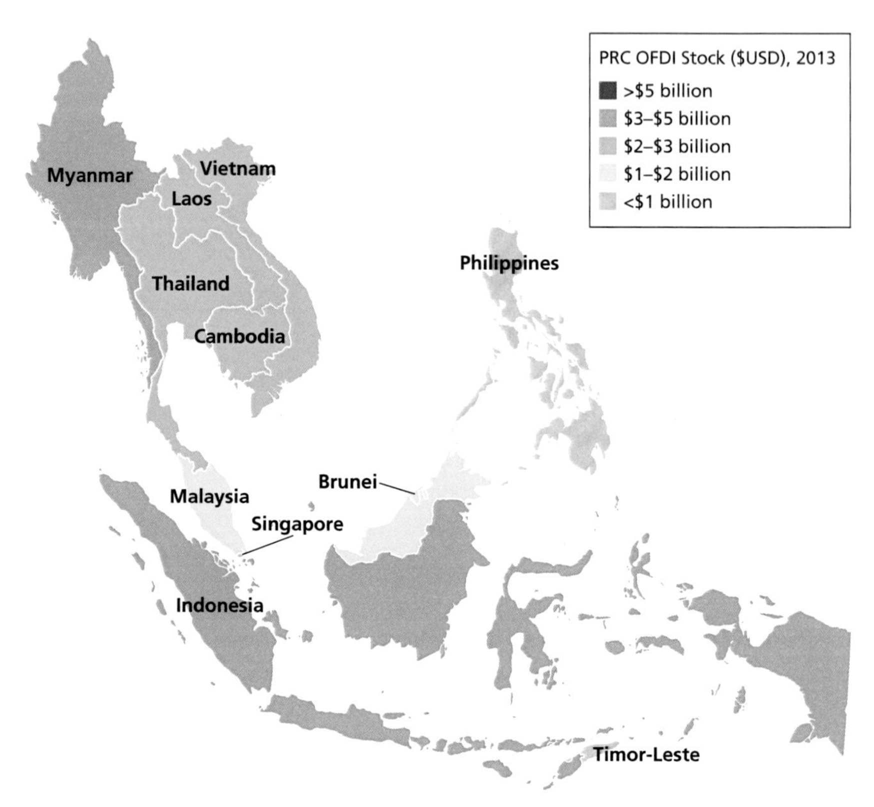

SOURCE: UNCTAD.
NOTE: Due to small scale of map, not all countries are displayed and color-coded. Singapore and Brunei, not visible on the map, received $14.7 billion in Chinese FDI stock and less than $1 billion in Chinese FDI stock, respectively.
RAND *RR2273A-3.7*

all ten ASEAN countries, of which nine are in force. It signed its first BITs with Thailand and Singapore, both in 1985, had signed seven by 1995, and had signed all ten by 2001. Likewise, China has income or income and capital tax treaties with eight of the ten ASEAN members. The first of these were completed in 1985 with Malaysia and 1986 with Thailand.

China's involvement with Southeast Asia goes well beyond simple trade, investment, and legal agreements. Unlike China's trade with other regions, China's trade with Southeast Asia involves numerous production sharing networks. These networks include affiliated and unaffiliated companies that sell parts and components from multiple destinations for assembly in a different destination and then for sale globally. Southeast Asia's role in these networks started in 1968 when two U.S. electronics companies established component-manufacturing plants in Singapore.[51] One recent estimate of network trade—defined as parts, components, and final assembly within production networks—finds that 64 percent of all ASEAN exports to China in 2007–2008 were parts and components, as were 40 percent of ASEAN imports from China.[52] An estimate by country from 2005–2006 found that more than 75 percent of all Philippines exports to China were parts and components, as were almost 70 percent of Malaysian exports. Import proportions were much lower, but almost 22 percent for all of ASEAN.[53]

Just as Southeast Asia is closely linked with China in economic exchange, it is closely linked with China's recent institutional initiatives, and Chinese leaders and commentators have consistently emphasized how critical the region is to trade routes and to the success of projects aimed at reviving both the land and maritime silk road. All ten ASEAN members were among the 57 prospective founding members of the China-led Asian Infrastructure Investment Bank, widely seen as a vehicle for helping fund Belt and Road. Notably, when the articles of incorporation were signed on June 29, 2015, seven of the ASEAN countries were among the 50 signing founding members: Brunei, Cambodia, Indonesia, Laos, Myanmar, Singapore, and Vietnam. Malaysia

---

[51] Prema-chandra Athukorala, "Global Production Sharing and Trade Patterns in East Asia," Working Paper No. 2013/10, Working Papers in Trade and Development, Arndt-Corden Department of Economics Crawford School of Public Policy, ANU College of Asia and the Pacific, June 2013.

[52] Athukorala, 2013, p. 28 (Table 5).

[53] Prema-Chandra Athukorala and Jayant Menon, "Global Production Sharing, Trade Patterns, and Determinants of Trade Flows in East Asia," Working Paper No. 41, ADB Working Paper Series on Regional Economic Integration, Asian Development Bank, January 2010.

signed on August 21, and Thailand signed in late September. As of early October 2015, Philippines had not yet signed.[54]

These developments mean that Southeast Asia will continue to be strongly intertwined with China. Proximity, existing trade relations, and ongoing negotiations about region-wide free trade all argue for deepening economic relations. This may not necessarily translate into political or military influence, however, as the overall relationships remain complicated. Moreover, major external powers, notably the United States, Japan, and India, continue to conduct significant trade with and invest in Southeast Asia too.

Military and Security Engagement

China has significantly increased its military and security engagement with Southeast Asia. Chinese arms sales to the region have increased, and Myanmar is China's top customer in the region. Compared to other developing regions, Chinese military leaders have paid the most visits to Southeast Asia and have particularly focused on increasing ties with the Thai military. The PLA also engages in a number of combined exercises, port visits, and military operations other than war in Southeast Asia. Increasing maritime cooperation, counterterrorism, and humanitarian assistance and disaster relief are the drivers for many of these activities, although the PLA does appear to be expanding cooperation and exercises beyond such, particularly with Thailand.

PRC Arms Sales

Chinese arms sales to countries in Southeast Asia are increasing but have remained lower than those from the United States over the past

---

[54] For the 57 prospective founding members, see Asian Infrastructure Investment Bank, "Prospective Founding Members," webpage, undated; for the 50 original signing members, see Asian Infrastructure Investment Bank, "Fifty Countries Sign the Articles of Agreement for the Asian Infrastructure Investment Bank," June 29, 2015; for the date of signing for Malaysia, see "Malaysia Backs China over AIIB," *The Star Online*, August 28, 2015; for the date of signing for Thailand, see "Thailand's Ambassador to China Signed Articles of Agreement of the Asian Infrastructure Bank," Asian Infrastructure Investment Bank, September 29, 2015.

15 years, according to the SIPRI Arms Transfers Database. Myanmar is China's key customer in the region, and the third-largest recipient of Chinese arms worldwide in the five years through 2014, after Pakistan and Bangladesh.[55] Sales to Myanmar have included items such as frigates, tanks, and infantry fighting vehicles.[56] Beijing also appears to be interested in increasing its arms sales to Thailand, which has purchased items such as multiple rocket launch systems and anti-ship missiles from Beijing in recent years. Regional media reports indicate China is one of a small number of countries Thailand is considering as a potential supplier of submarines.[57]

PLA Military Diplomacy

Chinese military diplomacy, particularly exchanges of high-level visits, is an important feature of Chinese military engagement with countries in Southeast Asia. Notably, China has conducted at least 38 high-level military visits to the region from 2003 to 2014, with 28 from the 2009–2014 period, making Southeast Asia by far the most frequently visited region under consideration as part of this study. Some of the key destinations have included Brunei, Cambodia, Indonesia, Laos, Myanmar, Singapore, Vietnam, and Thailand. Indeed, one of the most notable aspects of China's military diplomacy in Southeast Asia involves high-level exchanges and other military engagement events with Thailand, which is one of the five U.S. treaty allies in Asia but also enjoys a strong and growing relationship with the PRC.[58]

Since the May 2014 coup in Thailand, China appears to be concentrating on increasing its ties to the new leadership in Bangkok, with security cooperation a prominent item on the agenda, in addition

---

[55] According to SIPRI, Myanmar accounted for 12 percent of Chinese arms sales from 2010–2014.

[56] Kyle Mizokami, "A Look at China's Growing International Arms Trade," *USNI News*, May 7, 2015; H. Shivananda, "Sino-Myanmar Military Cooperation and Its Implications for India," *Journal of Defence Studies*, Vol. 5, No. 3, July 2011.

[57] Wassana Nanuam, "Submarine Plan Resurfaces with Backing from Prawit," *Bangkok Post*, March 25, 2015.

[58] See, for example, Prashanth Parameswaran, "Thailand Turns to China," *The Diplomat*, December 20, 2014.

to boosting economic ties and infrastructure investments. Demonstrating the importance Beijing appears to attach to cultivating its ties with Bangkok, there have been several high-level military visits there recently. In February 2015, PRC Defense Minister Chang Wanquan met with Thai Prime Minister Prayuth Chan-ocha and Thai Defense Minister Prawit Wongsuwan in Thailand. During these meetings, Chang reportedly highlighted strategic communication between the two sides as well as strengthening joint training and cooperation related to multilateral security and defense industry issues.[59] In early April 2015, Thai Defense Minister Prawit traveled to Beijing for meetings with PLA leaders, and just a few weeks later, Central Military Commission (CMC) Vice Chair Xu Qiliang visited Bangkok, where he met with Prawit and Prime Minister Prayuth. Official media reports on Xu's meetings in Bangkok highlighted infrastructure projects, economic cooperation, and security cooperation. PLA media reports stated the two sides would enhance their comprehensive strategic cooperative partnership and noted that Xu and his hosts discussed subjects such as strengthening "exchange and cooperation in the sectors of joint military exercises and joint training, military medicine, arms equipment and technology, multilateral security and fighting against terrorism."[60] Media reports from Thailand also highlighted other areas of cooperation, such as intelligence exchanges, and a proposal to establish a defense hotline between the PLA and Thailand's armed forces.[61]

The PLA has also conducted a number of other lower-level engagement events with the Thai military. For example, in February 2015, Royal Thai Navy ships visited the PLAN South Sea Fleet, arriving at Zhanjiang in Guangdong province for a four-day goodwill visit.[62] In

---

59 "Thai PM Meets with Chang Wanquan," *China Military Online*, February 9, 2015; this trip also included South Korea.

60 "Thailand, China Agree to Deepen Military Ties," *China Military Online*, April 24, 2015.

61 See Patsara Jikkham and Wassana Nanuam, "Thailand, China Deepen Defence Ties," *Bangkok Post*, April 24, 2015.

62 The Royal Thai Navy taskforce consisted of three ships led by Telist Panst, vice president of the Royal Thai Naval Academy. See "Thai Warships Visit South China Southeast Asia Fleet," *China Military Online*, February 10, 2015.

addition, following its four "air ballet" performances at the Langkawi Air Show in Malaysia in March 2015, the People's Liberation Army Air Force (PLAAF) Bayi Aerobatics Team stopped at Don Mueang Royal Thai Air Force Base in Thailand on the way back to China for a military exchange program. The Bayi Aerobatics Team's J-10s and one of its IL-76 transports flew alongside two Royal Thai Air Force Gripen fighter jets as part of a welcoming ceremony,[63] and the exchange also featured a meeting between PLAAF Major General Feng Aiwang, deputy chief of staff of the Beijing Military Region Air Force and commanding officer of the Bayi Aerobatics Team, and a senior Royal Thai Air Force officer.[64]

As the example of the Bayi Aerobatics Team's visit to Thailand illustrates, China has started employing the team as an instrument of military diplomacy.[65] In addition to exchanges with other countries' air forces, China has also sent it to participate in international air shows, with its most recent international performances taking place in March 2015 at the Langkawi International Maritime and Aerospace Exhibition in Malaysia. The PLAAF sent seven J-10 fighters as well as two IL-76 transport aircraft responsible for carrying the team's equipment, supplies, and members of its support crew.[66]

---

[63] Jeffrey Lin and P. W. Singer, "Chinese Fighter Jets Fly South for Spring Break," *Popular Science*, March 25, 2015.

[64] PLA media and the Ministry of National Defense of the People's Republic of China website published a number of photos from this stopover, emphasizing China's growing military ties with Thailand. See Guo Renjie, "PLAAF Aerobatics Team Stops Over in Thailand," *China Military Online*, March 25, 2015.

[65] The Bayi Aerobatics Team's first international performance was at the 2013 Moscow Air Show. See "Chinese Air Force Bayi Aerobatics Team Arrives in Russia with Seven J-10 Fighters," *People's Daily Online*, August 29, 2013; and Yan Meng and Zhang Qian, "China's J-10 Presence at Russian Air Show Shows Good Relationship Between the Two Militaries," *People's Daily Online*, August 28, 2013.

[66] According to a PLA media report, the PLAAF aircraft departed from a PLAAF base in Southwest China on March 11, 2015, and they made a stopover in Thailand for refueling before their arrival at Langkawi Airport in Malaysia, where they performed in the air show from March 17–21. See "PLAAF Aerobatic Team Arrives in Malaysia for Stunt Shows," *China Military Online*, March 12, 2015.

Combined Exercises

As in other regions, PLA participation in combined exercises in Southeast Asia is another important means of strengthening its military ties with countries that China sees as important diplomatic, economic, and security partners. The PLA has participated in more than two dozen combined exercises in Southeast Asia from 2002 through 2014. Among the countries China has conducted exercises with most often in the region are Thailand, Vietnam, Indonesia, and Singapore. These combined exercises have focused mainly on topics such as counterterrorism, special operations, and various types of military operations other than war (MOOTW) (Table 3.1).

Table 3.1
Selected Chinese Combined Exercises in Southeast Asia, 2002–2014

Year	Name of Exercise	Partner(s)	Exercise Content
2005	China-Thailand Friendship	Thailand	Search and rescue
2007	Strike 2007	Thailand	Special operations
2007	WPNS Forum Singapore	ASEAN; Others	Maritime exercises
2008	Strike 2008	Thailand	Special operations
2009	Cooperation 2009	Singapore	MOOTW
2010	Blue Strike/Blue Assault 2010	Thailand	Counterterrorism
2010	Cooperation 2010	Singapore	MOOTW
2010	Strike 2010	Thailand	Counterterrorism
2010	[Unknown]	Vietnam	Search and rescue
2011	Sharp Knife 2011	Indonesia	Special operations
2011	[Unknown]	Vietnam	Maritime
2012	Blue Strike 2012	Thailand	Marine training
2012	Sharp Knife 2012	Indonesia	Counterterrorism
2012	[Unknown]	Vietnam	Maritime search and rescue
2013	Sino-Singaporean Maritime Exercise	Singapore	Maritime exercise

Table 3.1—Continued

Year	Name of Exercise	Partner(s)	Exercise Content
2013	ADMM+ Exercise in Brunei 2013	ASEAN; Others	Maritime search and rescue; HADR (humanitarian assistance and disaster relief)
2013	ADMM+ Exercise in Indonesia 2013	ASEAN; Others	Counterterrorism
2013	ADMM+ Exercise in Australia 2013	ASEAN; Others	Maritime security
2013	Sharp Knife 2013	Indonesia	Counterterrorism
2013	Strike 2013	Thailand	Counterterrorism
2014	Cobra Gold 2014	United States; Thailand; Others	Humanitarian civil assistance portion of exercise only
2014	Komodo	Indonesia; Others	Humanitarian rescue
2014	Cooperation 2014	Singapore	Combat in mountainous environment
2014	WPNS Maritime Cooperation 2014	ASEAN; Others	Maritime exercise
2014	Sharp Knife 2014	Indonesia	Counterterrorism
2014	Peace and Friendship-2014	Malaysia	HADR

SOURCE: Department of Defense China Military Power Report and Chinese Ministry of Defense website.

NOTE: China did not begin engaging in combined exercises with foreign militaries until 2002.

Two large bilateral PRC exercises with Southeast Asian countries in 2015 are particularly noteworthy. In September, the PLA conducted its first joint naval exercise with Malaysia and its largest exercise to date with an ASEAN country. The exercise involved more than 1,000 PLA personnel and took place around the Strait of Malacca. The Chinese Air Force was planning to hold a three-week long joint drill in late November with the Thai Air Force.[67]

---

[67] Minnie Chan, "PLA Air Force Joins Thai Military for Joint Drills," *South China Morning Post*, November 12, 2015.

PLAN Port Visits

From 2000 to 2014, the PLA Navy conducted 33 port visits to Southeast Asia. Since 2009, the PLAN has visited 23 ports in Southeast Asia; 11 of these visits were associated with the PLAN's anti-piracy mission in the Gulf of Aden. With ten PLAN port visits from 2000 to 2008, Southeast Asia was the most frequently visited region prior to the PLAN's involvement in the anti-piracy mission. Several ports across the region have been visited at least twice since 2009: Changi, Singapore (four), and Sattahip, Thailand (three), were the two most frequently visited ports in the region. Port Klang, Malaysia; Port Muara, Brunei; Yangon, Myanmar; and Ho Chi Minh City, Vietnam, have each been visited twice over the same time period. In 2013, the PLAN *Peace Ark* hospital ship made four port visits to the region, stopping in Brunei,[68] Myanmar,[69] Indonesia,[70] and Cambodia[71] to provide free medical treatment to local residents. As noted under the later section describing Chinese MOOTW in the region, the *Peace Ark* also traveled to the Philippines in November 2013 to provide humanitarian relief and medical attention, and to carry out epidemic prevention in areas affected by the Typhoon Haiyan disaster.[72]

UN Peacekeeping Operations

Chinese participation in UN Peacekeeping Operations (PKO) is an important aspect of PRC engagement with the Developing World,

---

[68] "Chinese Hospital Ship 'Peace Ark' Provides Free Medical Checkups for Brunei Residents," Ministry of National Defense of the People's Republic of China, *Xinhua News*, June 17, 2013.

[69] "Chinese Hospital Ship 'Ark Peace' [sic] Arrives in Yangon," Ministry of National Defense of the People's Republic of China, *Xinhua News*, August 29, 2013.

[70] "'Peace Ark' Hospital Ship Participates in Joint Medical Tour in Indonesia," Ministry of National Defense of the People's Republic of China, *China Military Online*, September 12, 2013.

[71] "Chinese Hospital Ship Arrives in Cambodia for Goodwill Visit," *CNTV*, September 24, 2013.

[72] Peng Yining, "Medics Soon at Work as Peace Ark Sails In," *China Daily*, November 26, 2013; "'Peace Ark' Hospital Ship Carries Out Remote Consultation for Philippine Patients," Ministry of National Defense of the People's Republic of China, *China Military Online*, December 9, 2013.

but there are no current UN peacekeeping missions in Southeast Asia. Nevertheless, Southeast Asia has an important place in the history of Chinese participation in UNPKOs. In 1992, Beijing sent a unit of engineering troops to participate in the United Nations Transitional Authority in Cambodia (UNTAC), the UNPKO that was active in Cambodia from 1991 to 1993. This marked the first time China dispatched a military unit to participate in a UNPKO. According to one scholar, the involvement of the Chinese engineering troops in the mission helped improve Beijing's image in Cambodia.[73] China also sent a small number of observers to participate in UN mission in Timor-Leste, which was active from 2006 to 2012.

Military Operations Other than War

Participation in MOOTW is another important component of PLA engagement with Southeast Asia. As in other regions, it has the potential to help China develop its image as a responsible major power and to bolster China's relationships with key countries. At the same time, however, having the capacity to conduct such operations may raise questions when China does less than other countries expect of it given its growing capabilities, as was demonstrated by the criticism Beijing endured as a result of its limited offer of disaster relief assistance to the Philippines immediately following Super Typhoon Haiyan in November 2013.[74] After a slow response that many observers interpreted as a consequence of a tense diplomatic relationship stemming from China's territorial dispute with the Philippines in the South China Southeast Asia, Beijing eventually sent its hospital ship to assist the victims of the typhoon.[75]

---

[73] Miwa Hirono, "China's Charm Offensive and Peacekeeping: The Lessons of Cambodia—What Now for Sudan?" *International Peacekeeping*, Vol. 18, No. 3, 2011, pp. 328–343.

[74] Some commentators lambasted China for providing less assistance at first than the furniture company Ikea. See, for example, Will Oremus, "China Is Finally Sending Its 'Peace Ark' to the Philippines," *Slate*, November 20, 2013.

[75] See, for example, "Chinese Hospital Ship Peace Ark Arrives in the Philippines," *Xinhua News*, November 25, 2013; Jane Perlez, "China Offers Hospital Ship to the Philippines," *New York Times*, November 19, 2013.

Conclusion

Southeast Asia is the most challenging but also possibly the most important developing region for China. In the past decade, Beijing has steadily increased its involvement in the region through a range of political, economic, and military means. Politically, China has continued to press its territorial claims while increasing linkages to the region to reassure the region that China's growing influence and territorial claims do not threaten regional stability. From 2003 through 2014, Chinese political leaders visited ASEAN 94 times, making countries in the region among the most visited across the Developing World. Economically, China is advancing large trade and connectivity initiatives and has become ASEAN's most important trade partner. Southeast Asia is particularly crucial for realizing China's vision for a 21st Century Maritime Silk Road. Militarily, China is selling arms to the region and has engaged in more than two dozen exercises with ASEAN countries from 2002 to 2014, 33 port visits from 2000 to 2014, and 66 high-level military visits to the region from 2003 to 2014. All of this has occurred as Beijing began engaging in significant land reclamation activities in the South China Sea in late 2013.

Looking forward, Beijing is likely to continue to deepen economic and political engagement with the region as a whole and with particular friendly countries on a bilateral basis. At the same time, Beijing is likely to continue to use all necessary means to advance and secure its territorial claims in the South China Sea. Although Chinese public statements emphasize that the region is large enough to accommodate a growing China and the United States, there is significant Chinese concern that activities in the region are becoming more complex, zero-sum, and competitive between China, select Southeast Asian countries, the United States, and other external actors. There is also a clear recognition that China needs to be firm but very cautious; how China deals with South China Sea disputes and relations with its southeastern neighbors will be crucial to its ability to peacefully develop and transform internally and internationally.

Within the region, China has mixed success in achieving its political objectives of decreasing regional anxiety over China's growing influence and strengthening its territorial claims in the South China

Sea. Most ASEAN countries are hedging against China, wary of Beijing, and not willing to accept China's territorial claims in the South China Sea. Countries are avoiding clear alignments against China and are cautious of appearing too close to other countries involved in the region, such as the United States. They recognize that it is difficult to balance against China given their high levels of political and economic linkages to China. They also wish to avoid being potential pawns in any U.S.-China competition. Chinese military and economic power dwarfs most of its southeastern neighbors, and being the frontline state in a crisis against China could have significant negative consequences. With regard to the South China Sea, most countries have not been willing to challenge Chinese claims directly and openly. Instead, most countries urge regional stability and rule of law and may support lower-key and less public means to pushback against Chinese claims.

Regional responses to the United States' sending of the USS *Lassen* to engage in Freedom of Navigation Operations (FONOP) in the South China Sea in October 2015 are examples of the hedging behavior ASEAN countries engage in. Philippines and Malaysia welcomed the U.S. Navy patrol.[76] Vietnam did not immediately release a statement and provided only a relatively noncommittal response to U.S. actions when pressed.[77] Singapore, a close U.S. partner in the region, released a statement supporting the right of freedom of navigation and overflight, but also urged all parties to manage their differences calmly and peacefully.[78] Indonesian President Joko Widodo similarly supported freedom of navigation but also called for restraint in the South China Sea.[79] Soon after the FONOP, both Vietnam and Singapore hosted President Xi Jinping for a visit and Xi stated in Singapore that "there has been

[76] Matthew Southerland, "U.S. Freedom of Navigation Patrol in the South China Southeast Asia: What Happened, What It Means, and What's Next," U.S.-China Economic and Security Review Commission, Issue Brief, November 5, 2015.

[77] "Vietnam Gives Noncommittal Response to US Patrol in S. China Southeast Asia," *Voice of America*, October 29, 2015.

[78] "MFA Press Statement: Introductory Calls on Minister for Foreign Affairs Minister Dr. Vivian Balakrishnan," Ministry of Foreign Affairs of Singapore, October 28, 2015.

[79] Prashanth Parameswaran, "Indonesia Calls for South China Southeast Asia Restraint Amid US-China Tensions," *The Diplomat*, October 28, 2015.

no problem with maritime navigation or overland flights [in the South China Sea], nor will there ever be in the future."[80]

Implications for the United States

The United States should act judiciously and deliberately in Southeast Asia. Although Beijing's use of paramilitary assets in the South China Sea in territorial disputes inhibits immediate escalation to the use of military assets, China is not backing down from its sovereignty claims. U.S. allies and partners in the region, on the other hand, are actively contesting Chinese territorial claims and have engaged in similar land reclamation activities, albeit at a much smaller scale. The United States does not take a position or stance on South China Sea disputes and has urged for a peaceful resolution of maritime disputes. The United States, however, is obligated to support—and, if needed, restrain—its allies and partners.

While current and past Chinese actions in the region have not affected the free transit of maritime goods through the South China Sea, there is considerable uncertainty over the long-term Chinese agenda for the region. Does China, for example, seek to control all of the maritime territory within its self-proclaimed Nine-Dash Line in the South China Sea? China's growing military capabilities and its activities in the South China Sea—including building military infrastructure on its outposts that will enhance its power projection capabilities—are also changing the regional balance of power and providing China with more options and capability to impact freedom of navigation in the future should it choose to do so.

Current trends put ASEAN countries at a disadvantage if China has more expansive ambitions in Southeast Asia. Greater Chinese trade and economic development benefits ASEAN countries economically but also makes them increasingly vulnerable to Chinese coercion. Countries may be more willing to disregard provocative Chinese behavior in the region as long as PRC actions do not affect them directly or they continue benefiting from positive interactions with China. Most

---

[80] Rachel Chang, "There Will Never Be a Problem with Freedom of Navigation in South China Southeast Asia: Xi Jinping," *Strait Times*, November 7, 2015.

Southeast Asian countries are, thus, hesitant or incapable of contesting Chinese influence individually and have sufficiently different interests that prevent them from working together. In their attempt to hedge against China, most ASEAN countries are also reluctant to be seen as too close to the United States and may only provide lukewarm public support for—and may even openly criticize—U.S. efforts to promote regional stability and ensure freedom of navigation.

CHAPTER FOUR

China in Oceania

Oceania is a Developing World region important to China despite the small size of the region's economy and population. Stretching thousands of miles, the region contains dozens of Pacific Ocean islands scattered along key Chinese maritime trade routes. It includes the developed countries of Australia and New Zealand, as well as many developing ones, such as Papua New Guinea, 13 independent, self-governing states,[1] and a number of non-sovereign territories and dependent territories such as Guam.[2]

In the last decade, Beijing has paid more attention to Oceania and has increased political and economic engagement. President Xi Jinping became the first Chinese president to visit a country in the region other than Australia and New Zealand. Chinese goods trade with the region increased by over 14 times, from approximately $10 billion in 2000 to more than $153 billion in 2013.[3] Xi also seeks to involve the region in Beijing's Belt and Road Initiative and the Asian Infrastructure Investment Bank.[4] China currently has limited military engagement with the region.

---

[1] These 13 Pacific Island countries include: Cook Islands, Federated States of Micronesia, Fiji, Kiribati, Republic of Marshall Islands, Nauru, Niue, Palau, Samoa, Solomon Islands, Tonga, Tuvalu, and Vanuatu.

[2] Although Australia and New Zealand are developed countries, we have included them in this analysis because they are located in a developing region.

[3] UN Comtrade Database.

[4] "China, Pacific Island Countries Announce Strategic Partnership," *Xinhua News*, November 23, 2014.

Drivers of Chinese Engagement

Several factors drive China's engagement with the region. Politically, China seeks to win international support, facilitate political and economic cooperation, and isolate Taiwan. As China continues to press its territorial claims in the East and South China Seas, Beijing seeks to reassure Oceania that China is not a regional threat and discourage regional countries from taking sides in territorial disputes against Chinese interests. This has become even more important with the U.S. rebalance to the Asia-Pacific and U.S. movement of military assets to the region. Key Chinese maritime trade routes also pass through Oceania and there are Chinese concerns that islands in the region can serve as part of a second island chain around; such a chain is a flexible concept in Chinese strategic doctrine but that includes the idea of a barrier to contain China, a springboard from which to use force against China, and as a benchmark for marking China's progress in power projection.[5] Economically, Beijing is interested in Oceania for its natural resources, such as iron ore from Australia and natural gas and minerals from Papua New Guinea.[6]

Chinese policy toward the region has been largely centered on economic cooperation and development, with the hope that greater economic linkages would bind the region toward China. Beijing has repeatedly emphasized the need to deepen cooperation with the region on a number of areas, including trade, agriculture and fisheries, energy and resources, marine industry, and infrastructure construction. President Xi Jinping has further pledged to increase high-level interactions, people-to-people exchanges, and contributions to the region's economic development. To facilitate greater linkages to the region, Beijing's Belt and Road Initiative is likely to include an eastern leg of its 21st Century Maritime Silk Road that connects Oceania to the rest of its trade

---

[5] Andrew S. Erickson and Joel Wuthnow, "Barriers, Springboards and Benchmarks: China Conceptualizes the Pacific 'Island Chains,'" *China Quarterly*, Vol. 225, March 2016, pp. 1–22; Yu Chang Sen, "The Pacific Islands in Chinese Geo-Strategic Thinking," paper presented to the "China and the Pacific: The View from Oceania" conference, National University of Samao, Apia, Samoa, February 25–27, 2015.

[6] Terence Wesley-Smith, *China in Oceania: New Forces in Pacific Politics,* East-West Center, Pacific Islands Policy, No. 2, 2007.

routes. Beijing also aims to involve the region in its Asian Infrastructure Investment Bank.[7]

Unlike its policy toward Africa or Latin America (Chapters 8 and 9, respectively), Beijing does not have a policy paper on its relations with Oceania. China also does not have a dedicated ambassador or special envoy to the region, although it does send special envoys to attend key regional meetings. Like most other regions, China engages with the countries bilaterally and multilaterally. In 2006, China established the China-Pacific Island Countries Economic Development and Cooperation (CPIC) Forum to provide a multilateral forum for high-level dialogue and cooperation between China and Oceania. There have been only two high-level Forum meetings as of 2015.

Political Engagement

Unlike neighboring Southeast Asia, where China enjoys diplomatic relations with all of ASEAN, China has diplomatic relations with ten of the 16 states in Oceania.[8] These include the most populous and largest regional economies of Australia, New Zealand, and Papua New Guinea. Six states (Kiribati, Marshall Islands, Nauru, Palau, Solomon Islands, and Tuvalu) continue to recognize Taiwan. Despite the lack of diplomatic relations with these six states, all 16 states are part of the Pacific Islands Forum Secretariat, and China is a dialogue partner to the forum.[9]

As in other regions, China has been willing to engage with authoritarian regimes sanctioned by the West. In Oceania, the most notable case of this is China's close relationship with Fiji after the country underwent a military coup in 2006. Some have criticized China for providing support and development funding to sustain the authoritarian government while others have pointed to the fact

---

[7] "China, Pacific Island Countries Announce Strategic Partnership," *Xinhua News*, November 23, 2014.

[8] These ten are: Australia, the Cook Islands, Federated States of Micronesia, Fiji, New Zealand, Niue, Papua New Guinea, Samoa, Tonga, and Vanuatu.

[9] See Pacific Islands Forum Secretariat, "About Us," webpage, undated.

that China contributed $780,000 to support elections in Fiji in September 2014.[10]

During President Xi Jinping's November 2014 visit to Australia, New Zealand, and Fiji, China sought to strengthen relations with Oceania countries. China upgraded relations with Australia and New Zealand to comprehensive strategic partnerships, and China and Australia signed a bilateral FTA in June 2015. With New Zealand, China agreed to strengthen and increase existing economic ties and expand bilateral trade to 30 billion New Zealand dollars by 2020. China also signed Antarctic Cooperation agreements with Australia and New Zealand.[11]

Within the region, China prioritizes Australia and New Zealand because these two countries are the largest geopolitical and economic actors in the region. Australia and New Zealand are also the only two countries in the region with which China has signed comprehensive strategic partnerships, and neither has taken a stance on the South China or East China Seas disputes. Between the two countries, China views Australia as more important. Chinese strategists are aware of Australia's important role as a U.S. ally in the Asia-Pacific and in supporting U.S. rebalancing to the Asia-Pacific. Beijing, however, believes there are factors that could diminish Australia's willingness to cooperate with the United States. Greater Chinese political and economic exchanges with Australia could show Canberra the benefits of a healthy relationship with China and discourage Australia from engaging in measures to contain China's growth or counter China's claims in the South or East China Seas.[12] In contrast, China has lesser forms of stra-

---

[10] "Big Fish in a Big Pond," *The Economist*, March 25, 2015; Lucy Craymer, "Fiji Attracts Old Friends as China's Clout Grows," *Wall Street Journal*, October 30, 2014.

[11] Wang Yi, "Foreign Minister Wang Yi Talks About President Xi Jinping's Attendance at the G20 Summit and Visits to Three Countries Including Australia," Ministry of Foreign Affairs of the People's Republic of China, November 23, 2014.

[12] Sun Junjian, "Aodaliya Dui Meiguo 'Chongfan Yatai' Zhanlue De Fanying" ["Australia's Response to the United States' 'Pivot to Asia' Strategy"], *Contemporary International Relations*, No. 8, 2014; "Zihuo Xieding Li Zhongao Xingfen Meimei Danyou 'Yatai Zhanlue Luokong'" ["Free Trade Agreement Excites China, Australia, U.S. Media Worries About 'Asia-Pacific Strategic Failure'"], *Global Times*, June 19, 2015.

tegic partnership deals with the remaining eight countries it has diplomatic relations with in Oceania.

Overall, Chinese leaders visit Oceania relatively infrequently. From 2003 to 2014, there were 18 visits to the region by Chinese leaders, of which ten occurred from 2003 to 2008 and eight occurred from 2009 to 2014.[13] In the last decade, Chinese presidents and premiers have visited only three countries in Oceania: Australia, New Zealand, and Fiji. President Xi Jinping's visit to Fiji in November 2014 was the first time a Chinese president had visited Fiji.

China has limited cultural presence and influence in the region. China currently has 16 Confucius Institutes in three countries in the region, with 12 in Australia, three in New Zealand, and one in Fiji. There are also low numbers of ethnic Chinese in the region. According to Taiwanese government statistics, approximately 3 percent of all overseas ethnic Chinese (or nearly 1 million people) lived in Oceania in 2012.[14] Australia has the most ethnic Chinese—approximately 900,000 ethnic Chinese, or 4 percent of the country's total population. Approximately 4 percent of New Zealand's population (170,000 people) is ethnic Chinese. Ethnic Chinese account for 0.3 percent (20,000 people) of the population of Papua New Guinea. China is Australia and New Zealand's largest source of foreign students.[15]

In terms of people actually from China, one source notes that, as of 2017, about 500,000 residents of Australia were born in China.[16] As of 2013, 89,000 residents of New Zealand were born in China.[17]

---

[13] Chinese political leaders include the president, premier, vice president, minister of foreign affairs, and state councilor in charge of foreign affairs.

[14] For Taiwanese statistics, see *2013 Statistical Yearbook of the Overseas Community Affairs Council*, Republic of China (Taiwan).

[15] Wang Yi, 2014.

[16] Helen Clark, "Should Australia Fear an Influx of Chinese?" *South China Morning Post*, June 30, 2017.

[17] Stats New Zealand—Taturanga Aotearoa, "2013 Census QuickStats About Culture and Identity," Wellington, April 15, 2014.

Economic Engagement

China has been increasing its economic engagement with the region, particularly in the last decade. Two high-level CPIC forums took place in 2006 and 2013 and China has used them to increase economic cooperation and announce economic commitments to the region. In the 2006 forum, China promised RMB 3 billion in preferential loans, a zero-tariff policy to the majority of exports from Least Developed Countries (LDC) in the region that have diplomatic ties to China, anti-malaria medicine, training and scholarships, increased tourism, and disaster assistance.[18] By 2013, China had set up 150 enterprises in the region.[19] In the most recent November 2013 forum, China promised $1 billion in concessional loans over a four-year period, with most of the loans to be used in infrastructure-related projects.[20]

Aside from the previously noted China-Australia FTA, which entered into force on December 20, 2015, Australia and New Zealand are also negotiating partners in the Regional Comprehensive Economic Partnership trade deal, of which the United States is not a partner. Both are also partners in the recently completed Trans-Pacific Partnership (TPP) trade deal, in which the United States was a partner.

Trade

China's trade with Oceania is dominated by trade with Australia and, to a lesser extent with New Zealand. All the other countries are minor by comparison. China is Australia's largest trade partner, and it buys approximately a third of all Australian exports. The commodity composition of goods trade between China and Oceania is similar to that of China with most developing regions except for Southeast Asia.

---

[18] "Wen's Speech at the China-Pacific Island Countries Forum," *China Daily*, April 5, 2006.

[19] "Address of Wang Yang at the 2nd China-Pacific Island Countries Economic Development and Cooperation Forum and the Opening Ceremony of 2013 China International Show on Green Innovative Products and Technologies," Ministry of Commerce of the People's Republic of China, November 12, 2013.

[20] "Chinese Development Aid in Pacific Island Countries and Opportunities for Cooperation," United Nations Development Programme, China, Issue Brief No. 7, December 2014.

The majority of Chinese imports from Oceania are crude minerals and mineral fuels (Figure 4.1). Imports in those two categories made up more than 50 percent of total imports and almost 10 percent of total imports from the region, respectively, in 2000 and grew to nearly 70 percent and 13 percent, respectively, in 2013. China imported more than $70 billion in crude minerals alone from Australia.

Chinese exports to Oceania are in the form of manufactured goods and machinery, with machinery taking an increasing role over the past decade (Figure 4.2).

As with other regions that China imports raw materials from, such as the Middle East, Oceania has a significant trade surplus with China (Figure 4.3).

Figure 4.1
Composition of Imports from Oceania

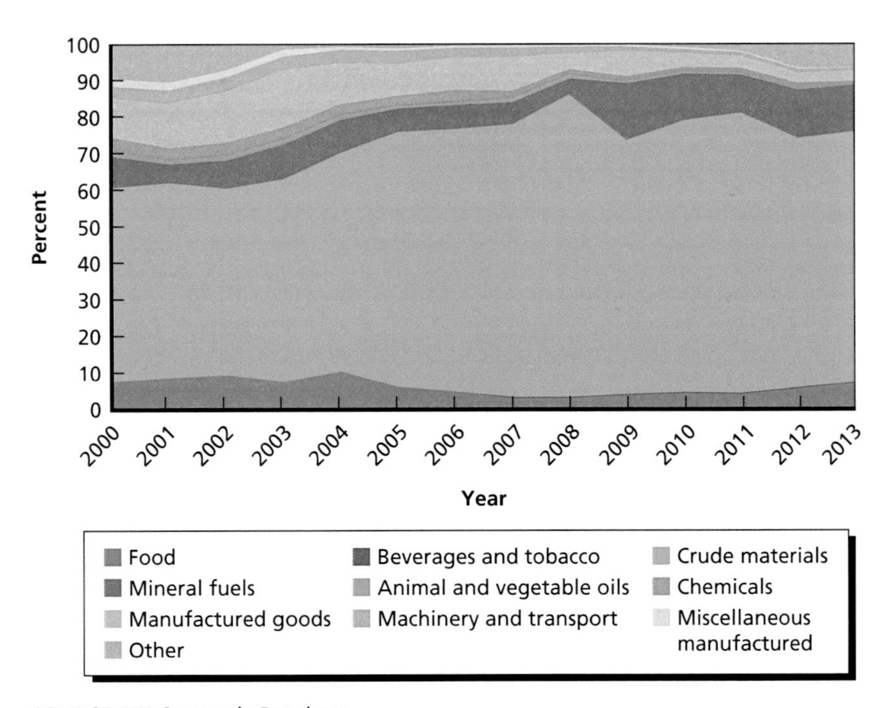

SOURCE: UN Comtrade Database.

RAND *RR2273A-4.1*

Figure 4.2
Composition of Exports to Oceania

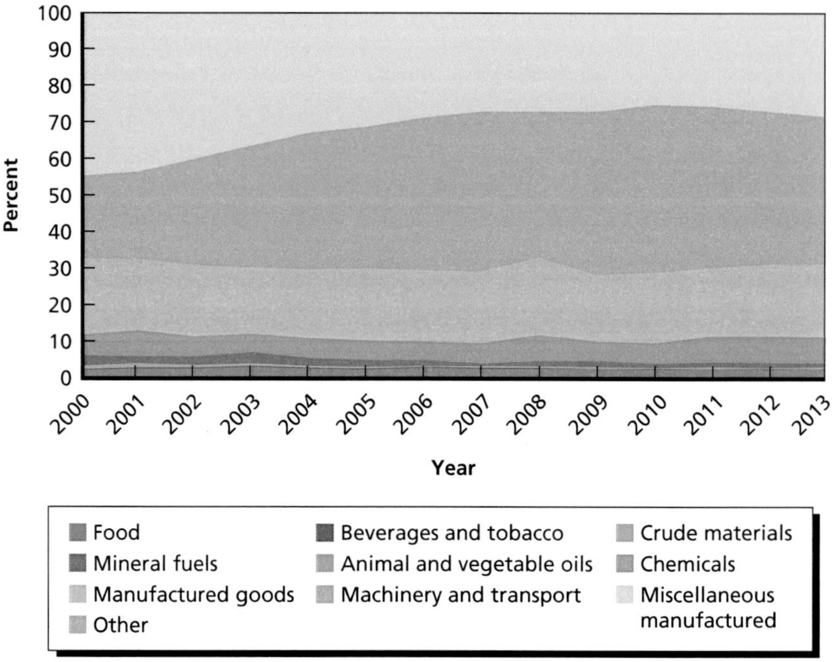

Percent: 0, 10, 20, 30, 40, 50, 60, 70, 80, 90, 100

Year: 2000, 2001, 2002, 2003, 2004, 2005, 2006, 2007, 2008, 2009, 2010, 2011, 2012, 2013

Food; Beverages and tobacco; Crude materials; Mineral fuels; Animal and vegetable oils; Chemicals; Manufactured goods; Machinery and transport; Miscellaneous manufactured; Other

SOURCE: UN Comtrade Database.
RAND *RR2273A-4.2*

Foreign Direct Investment and Lending

Chinese investments in Oceania are mainly concentrated in Australia. In 2013, China's stock of FDI in Australia reached $13.8 billion (Figure 4.4). In 2015, China became the largest investor in Australia, overtaking the United States. Most of this investment has been in real estate and is driven in part by the decline in the Australian dollar, making real estate investment in Australia relatively attractive.[21] In contrast, none of the other countries in Oceania have more than $1 billion in Chinese FDI.

[21] "Zhongguo Qudai Meiguo Chengwei Aodaliya Zui Da Waizi Laiyuan" ["China Replaces the U.S. as Australia's Largest Source of Foreign Investment"], *Sina News*, April 30, 2015.

Figure 4.3
Level of Exports to and Imports from Oceania

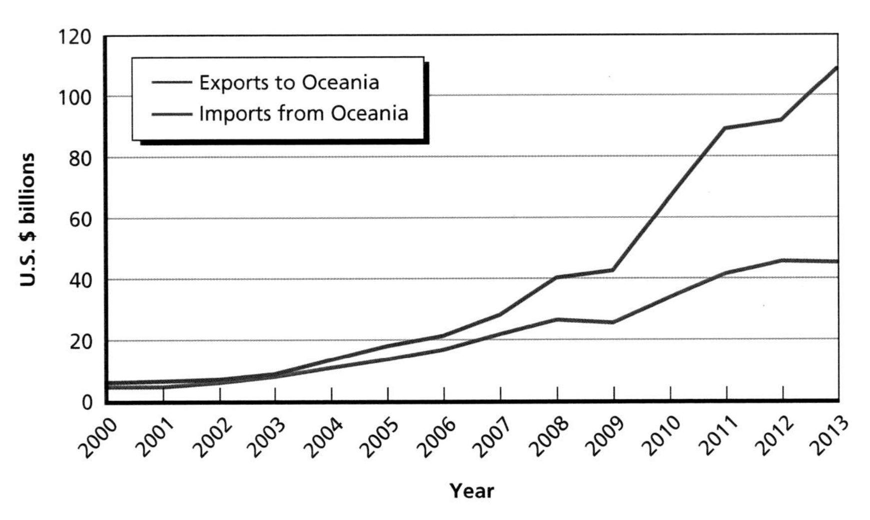

SOURCE: UN Comtrade.
RAND *RR2273A-4.3*

Figure 4.4
Chinese FDI Stock in Oceania by Receiving Country

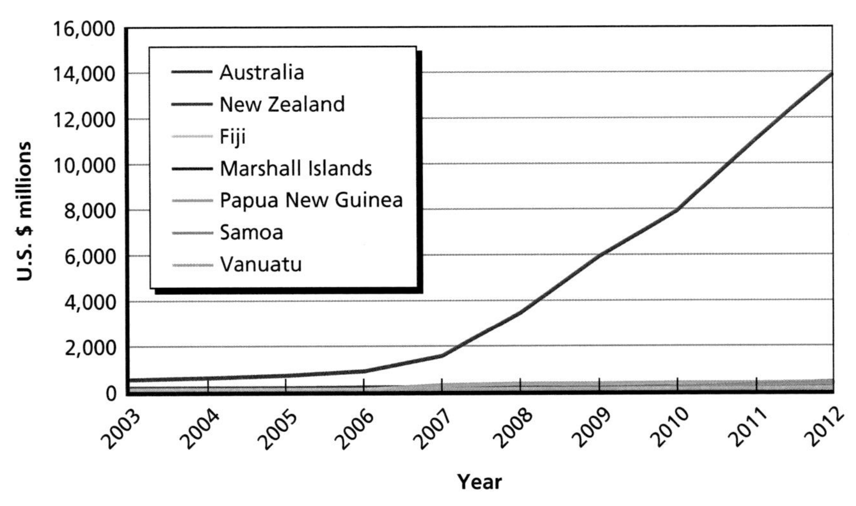

SOURCE: UNCTAD.
RAND *RR2273A-4.4*

In addition to FDI, China provides significant aid to the region. From 2006 to 2013, China provided $1.5 billion to nine states, with the most ($440 million) to Papua New Guinea, followed by Fiji ($339 million), Vanuatu ($224 million), and Samoa ($208 million). Beijing provided aid in the form of concessional loans and grants, and the aid packages and much of the other aid went to infrastructure-related projects. Although Chinese aid to the region during this period exceeded Japanese aid, it is still less than U.S. aid to the region ($1.8 billion) and less than a fifth of Australian aid to its neighbors ($6.8 billion).[22]

Agreements and Other Issues

China has bilateral investment treaties in force with Australia, New Zealand, and Papua New Guinea and a signed treaty that is not in force with Vanuatu. It has income and capital tax treaties with the same three countries with which it has BITs. Australia and New Zealand are also among the 50 founding members of the Asian Infrastructure Investment Bank.

Similar to its activities elsewhere, there is some local wariness over China's growing economic clout. Tonga exemplifies the mixed feelings people have regarding increased Chinese economic engagement and readily available Chinese funding. As of 2015, Tonga's debt was approximately half of its GDP, and two-thirds of that debt was owed to the Export-Import Bank of China and denominated in Chinese yuan. Many had mistakenly assumed that Beijing would convert the loans to grants, but it has not done so. Instead, the Pacific nation welcomed available finance and became severely indebted to China. Its leadership now worries about China's growing influence on the country given the amount of debt Tonga owns. Aside from growing government debt, some have also criticized China for bringing its own workers to Tonga to engage in infrastructure and other construction activities.[23]

---

[22] Philippa Brant, "Chinese Aid in the Pacific," Lowy Institute for International Policy, March 9, 2015.

[23] Michael Field, "China's 'Gift' Troubles New Prime Minister," *Nikkei Asian Review*, March 28, 2015.

Military and Security Engagement

China has limited military engagement with Oceania as a region. Since 2000, China has not sold major conventional arms to the region. It has engaged in some combined exercises with countries in the region and mainly with Australia and New Zealand (Table 4.1). From 2003 to 2014, China conducted nearly a dozen port visits to three countries in Oceania: Australia, New Zealand, and Papua New Guinea. In 2014, the *Peace Ark* engaged in Mission Harmony-2014, where it provided free medical assistance to Tonga, Fiji, Vanuatu, and Papua New Guinea.[24] In 2015, it paid its first-ever port visit to Australia.[25] Along with exercises and port visits, Chinese military leaders have been making more trips to the region in recent years. From 2003 to 2008, no CMC member traveled to Oceania. In contrast, CMC members made eight visits to Oceania from 2009 to 2014.

Table 4.1
Selected Chinese Combined Exercises in Oceania, 2002–2014

Year	Name of Exercise	Partner(s)	Exercise Content
2004	[Unknown]	Australia	Search and rescue
2007	Joint Maritime Search and Rescue	Australia; New Zealand	Maritime search and rescue
2010	Joint Maritime Maneuver; Joint Maritime Maneuver and Exercise	New Zealand; Australia	Maritime exercises
2011	Cooperative Spirit 2011	Australia	HADR
2012	Cooperative Spirit 2012	Australia; New Zealand	HADR
2014	Exercise Kowari-14	Australia; United States	Survival training

SOURCE: Department of Defense China Military Power Report and Chinese Ministry of Defense website.

NOTE: China did not begin engaging in combined exercises with foreign militaries until 2002.

---

[24] "Peace Ark Hospital Ship Returns to Zhoushan," *CCTV*, September 29, 2014.

[25] Prashanth Parameswaran, "China's Peace Ark Completes First-Ever Australia Visit," *The Diplomat*, October 16, 2015.

Within the region, China has particularly sought to strengthen defense ties with Australia. Australia is the only Western country that has engaged in live-fire exercises with the Chinese military.[26] In 2014, China and Australia engaged in 45 events of military cooperation or exchanges, and these activities accounted for a significant portion of the Australian armed forces' activities with foreign militaries. In December of the same year, the two countries agreed to further boost their military relations.[27] In November 2015, both countries again affirmed their desire to boost military relations, and China sought to improve communication and cooperation between the two militaries in areas like "peacekeeping, army training, humanitarian rescue and relief, strengthen personnel exchanges like communication between middle and young age officers, and two-way visit and learning between students." Australian Defense Minister Marise Payne also stated that Australia does not hold a position or take a side in the South China Sea disputes.[28]

Conclusion

China has been increasing political and economic engagement with Oceania in the past decade. Chinese trade and investment in the region has grown significantly, and Beijing aims to increase such linkages by extending the 21st Century Maritime Silk Road to the region. There is limited but growing PRC military engagement, mainly with Australia and New Zealand. Beijing hopes that greater economic and political ties with the region will prevent regional actors from taking a stance on territorial disputes in the South and East China Seas against China's interests. These ties, as well as more military-to-military exchanges, are part of Beijing's efforts to assure regional actors that China is not a

---

[26] "South China Southeast Asia: Australia's Live Fire Exercise with China's Navy Could Be 'PR Disaster,' Expert Warns," *ABC News*, November 2, 2015.

[27] "China, Australia Agreed to Boost Military Ties," *Xinhua News*, December 2, 2014.

[28] "China, Australia Vow to Promote Bilateral Defense Cooperation," *Xinhua News*, November 4, 2015.

threat and there is no need for Pacific nations to form a second island chain containing or threatening China.

While Oceania is within China's third ring, China has not afforded the region as a whole the same level of attention as those in the same ring or regions in the fourth ring further away from China. Beijing, for example, has not designated a special envoy or ambassador for Oceania and has yet to issue a policy paper spelling out its regional goals and activities. Similarly, whereas there have been only two high-level CPIC Forum summits in 2006 and 2013, its equivalent organization in Africa (which is in the fourth ring), the Forum on China-Africa Cooperation, was scheduled to hold its sixth ministerial meeting in South Africa in December 2015.

A number of circumstances explain Beijing's relatively lower prioritization of the region as a whole. China has selected to focus on particular countries, such as Australia and New Zealand. In addition, the smaller Pacific Island nations are not as resource rich as geographically large developing countries elsewhere. Given their smaller size and economic weight, Beijing does not view most countries in the region as actors with substantial international influence. Instead, China is likely to continue to steadily increase its influence in the region and prioritize relations with Australia and New Zealand.

With respect to its goals in the region, China's outreach and activities have had some success; it is encouraging countries to hedge instead of taking a clear stance against China. A recent example of such behavior is Australia's reactions to the United States' FONOP in the South China Sea in October 2015. The Australian Ministry of Defense issued a statement that simultaneously supported U.S. activities and also spelled out that Australia did not participate.[29] A week later, Australia also engaged in a live-fire exercise with China in the South China Sea, causing some to question the extent to which Canberra supports Washington's efforts to ensure freedom of navigation in the region.[30] While Australian defense planners are reportedly looking

---

[29] Australian Department of Defence, "Minister for Defence—Statement—Freedom of Navigation in the South China Southeast Asia," October 27, 2015.

[30] "South China Southeast Asia," 2015.

into the possibility of engaging in their own sail-through or fly-by (but have not publicly stated that they will do so),[31] there has been a significant divide in public commentary on what Australia should do. Some Australian defense and security analysts argue that it is not in Australia's best interests to engage in such an activity.[32] Instead, they contend Australia should use diplomacy to maintain regional stability.

Implications for the United States

Overall, China is not changing the balance of power in Oceania contrary to U.S. interests. Politically, China is not exerting the same coercive influence vis-à-vis U.S. allies and partners in Oceania as it is doing in Southeast Asia. Economically, China's efforts to promote economic development are mostly welcome, and increasing trade via its Belt and Road Initiative is also a positive for the region. Though China is providing significant aid to the region, the amount that China is providing is still less than what the United States provides and only a fifth of what Australia is giving to its neighbors. Militarily, China's engagement with Australia and New Zealand is unlikely to diminish the importance of their relationships with the United States.

Looking forward, one area that the United States does need to pay attention to is that increased Chinese engagement with Oceania may diminish the willingness of regional actors to counter more assertive Chinese moves in the South China Sea or other regions. China is building relations with Oceania, not only to exert influence in the Pacific but also to buy influence—or buy acquiescence—elsewhere.

---

[31] Rob Taylor, "Australia Prepares Option of Sail-Through to Test China," *Wall Street Journal*, October 28, 2015.

[32] For example, see Bob Carr, "South China Southeast Asia Would Be a Lonely Patrol for Australia," *Financial Review*, November 11, 2015; Sam Bateman, "Australia and the US: Great Allies but Different Agendas in the South China Southeast Asia," *The Lowy Interpreter*, November 12, 2015.

CHAPTER FIVE

China in Central Asia

In the broad sweep of thousands of years of history, Central Asia—on China's northern and western frontiers—has consistently posed the country's greatest geostrategic threats. The nomadic peoples of the steppe constituted perennial challenges as raiders and, sometimes, invaders. The Mongols were particularly troublesome—in the thirteenth century, these horsemen conquered China, establishing the Yuan dynasty (1271–1368) and ruling the country for almost one 100 years. In modern history, the main geostrategic challenge to China from Central Asia has come from Russia—first under the tsars and then under the Bolsheviks. These threats came both in the form of the strength of imperial Russia and, subsequently, the Soviet Union, and then in the form of weakness and collapse of successive regimes. The disintegration of the Soviet Union in 1991 created China's most immediate post–Cold War national security challenge.

Beijing's response to the new realities in Central Asia evolved from purely security cooperation to a ramping up of economic interactions. Cognizant of Russia's interests, China sought to tread lightly in the region militarily while playing to its strength and offering economic opportunities to its new neighbors. Certainly China did not ignore the security dimension, resolving territorial disputes and demilitarizing frontiers. Moreover, China has conducted near-annual field exercises since 2002 with other member states of the Shanghai Cooperation Organization (SCO), but these were quite modest displays. The result was that none of the Central Asian states—with the possible exception of Mongolia—see China as a threat; to the contrary, Central Asian capitals mostly consider Beijing to be an economic windfall. In fact, the precursor for the Belt and Road foreign policy initiative formally announced by President Xi Jinping in September 2013 in Kazakhstan appears to be a continuation of the economic relationship launched by Xi's two predecessors to develop economic cooperation with, and major infrastructure projects in, Central Asia in the 1990s and 2000s.[1] Even Mongolia has created important links with China, including its first joint military exercise in the field of special operations, Hunting Eagle 2015, focused solely on operations against terrorism.[2]

Key Chinese Activities in the Region

China is engaging in several different types of activities in the region. Politically and economically, Beijing seeks to increase cooperation with its neighbors and regional influence through greater connectivity and trade. Its most important new initiative is Belt and Road. Not only is Central Asia to have better connections to facilitate resource flow, but Central Asia also serves as the land bridge to West Asia and Europe as it has for millennia. As of fall 2015, rail routes from China through Central Asia went to Madrid (through Kazakhstan and Russia); Duisburg and Hamburg in Germany, and Warsaw (different routes through Kazakhstan, Mongolia, and Russia); and Azerbaijan (through Kazakhstan) with continuation expected through to Turkey. The rail route shortens the time to ship goods from China to Europe from four to six weeks by Southeast Asia routes to 14 days by rail.[3] However, rail shipping remains more expensive than ocean shipping.

Beyond the Belt and Road effort, there are supporting initiatives that can increase China's involvement in the region, such as the AIIB, which will help finance infrastructure projects in Central Asia; the New Development Bank, also known as the BRICS bank, established with BRICS partner Russia; and China's own Silk Road Fund, a $40 billion fund, open to other investors and focused on infrastructure in Asia.

---

[1] Author conversations with Chinese civilian and military analysts in Beijing and Shanghai, September 2015.

[2] B. Amarsaikhan, "Two Countries' Servicemen Join in Military Exercises Against Terrorism," *Montsame National News Agency*, October 12, 2015.

[3] "Mapping China's New Silk Road Initiative" *Forbes*, April 8, 2015.

Militarily, China increased the number of joint exercises in 2013, from one or two most years to five that year. High-level visits also increased as of about 2010. Much of this cooperation has focused on counterterrorism and anti-trafficking. Arms sales have not played a major role in China's military engagement with the region.

Beijing views Russia as its most important regional partner, although the two are also regional competitors (see Chapter 10). Note that we do not consider Russia to be part of the Central Asia region; rather, given its size and interests, it is the most important country for the region, possibly even including China. Kazakhstan and Mongolia are viewed as major regional partners (Figure 5.1). China does not have conflictual relations with any of the Central Asian countries.

Drivers of Chinese Engagement

Chinese Activities in the Region Prior to 2000

China confronted six new and unattached Central Asian neighbors in the 1990s with the collapse of the Soviet bloc and disintegration of the Soviet Union. Mongolia became a nonaligned state in 1989, while

Figure 5.1
China's Relations with Countries in Central Asia, 2015

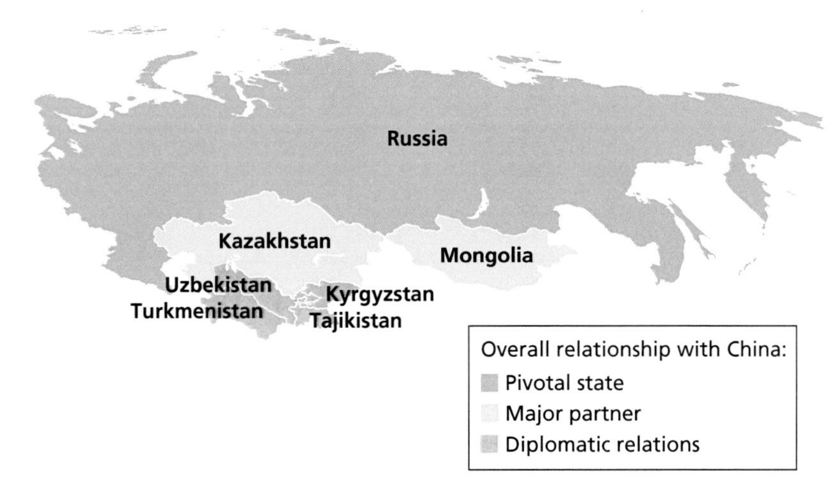

RAND *RR2273A-5.1*

Kazakhstan, Kyrgyzstan, Tajikistan, Uzbekistan, and Turkmenistan all became independent states in 1991. All six continued to have substantial Russian influence, yet all moved slowly but seemingly inexorably into China's orbit. While Russia's economy was in crisis in the early 1990s, the Chinese economy boomed. China was thirsty for energy resources and commodities, and the peoples of the six landlocked Central Asian states were hungry for inexpensive consumer goods.

But China's immediate motivation for engaging with its new neighbors was to establish a predictable and stable security framework on its Central Asian borders. Beijing worked hard to resolve border disputes with Kazakhstan, Kyrgyzstan, and Tajikistan. The negotiations were completed in a matter of years, but the actual demarcations took a decade or more to resolve. In addition, China cooperated to demilitarize the border regions and develop confidence-building measures. These efforts led to the formation of an informal grouping dubbed the "Shanghai Five" in 1996—China, the three Central Asian states, and Russia. In 2001, this bloc of five states formalized their association in the establishment of the Shanghai Cooperation Organization (SCO). The organization as of late 2015 also included Uzbekistan as a member; Afghanistan, India, Iran, Mongolia, and Pakistan as observer states; and Belarus, Sri Lanka, and Turkey as dialogue partners.[4]

Current Chinese Policy Toward the Region

Behind the aforementioned activism was an underlying sense of vulnerability and weakness. China's response to the complex challenges it confronts to the west during the past two decades has been to adopt an "Empty Fortress" strategy.[5] The Empty Fortress strategy is an ancient strategic ruse to trick an adversary into believing one is powerful when, in fact, one is weak. China's leaders recognize the country's westernmost regions are poorly defended and vulnerable to internal dissent and external threats. China's defense posture is heavily skewed

---

4 "Brief Introduction to the Shanghai Cooperation Organization," webpage, 2015. India and Pakistan were admitted as full members in 2017.

5 For more on this strategy, see Andrew Scobell, Ely Ratner, and Michael Beckley, *China's Strategy Toward South and Central Asia: An Empty Fortress*, Santa Monica, Calif.: RAND Corporation, RR-525-AF, 2014.

toward the east, where the most prosperous and densely populated areas are located. But Beijing refuses to accept its weaknesses. China will not abandon western areas, grant independence to the non-Han inhabitants, or cede tracts of territory to its neighbors. On the contrary, China has boldly projected an image of proactive strength in Central Asia.

Chinese Priorities and Policies

Where Central Asia is concerned, Beijing has had four overriding interests:

1. Ensure domestic stability and China's national unity
2. Maintain peace, predictability, and secularism in the region
3. Increase Chinese influence and limiting the influence of other outside powers
4. Promote and protect Chinese economic interests in the region and beyond.

1. Ensure Domestic Stability and National Unity. Beijing's paramount concern is internal security. Chinese leaders are most absorbed with stability in the ethnic Han heartland in eastern and coastal China, where the bulk of China's populace is concentrated. However, Beijing has become increasingly alarmed over a rise in disaffection among ethnic minorities, notably the Tibetans and Uighurs, who tend to be concentrated inland in westernmost China, often in remote but strategically important frontier areas, and spill across national borders. This disaffection is manifest in subtle and not-so-subtle ways and in peaceful as well as violent acts of resistance and defiance.

In the twenty-first century, Chinese leaders have tended to view the Central Asia challenge first and foremost as "an unpredictable zone from which Turkic nationalism and Islamic ideologies could radiate into Xinjiang."[6] This threat is "most directly and concretely manifest

---

6 Lena Jonson, "Russia and Central Asia," in Lena Jonson and Roy Allison, eds., *Central Asian Security: The New International Context*, Washington, D.C.: Brookings Institution Press, 2001, p. 22.

in Uighurs."[7] Indeed, there has been a dramatic rise in radicalism and activism among the Turkic Uighurs, who are geographically concentrated in the Xinjiang Uighur Autonomous Region. The protests and acts of violence in recent years are especially alarming for Chinese leaders because they have occurred not only in the Xinjiang Uighur Autonomous Region but also in major eastern cities, including Beijing and Guangzhou. China has worked to gain the cooperation of Central Asian states, notably the members of the SCO, to combat transnational Uighur activism and terrorist activity.

2. Maintain Peace, Predictability, and Secularism. Although Beijing is focused most on internal security, its worst nightmare is the linkage of domestic enemies with what it considers to be foreign troublemakers.[8] Thus, Chinese leaders consider that the country must be vigilant on its borders and do its utmost to develop and maintain a buffer of stability all the way around China. In short, peace on China's periphery is considered essential to domestic harmony. This presumes significant Chinese influence in these regions and limited influence by outside powers.

In the aftermath of the Soviet collapse of 1991, China sought to adjust to the new realities just beyond its borders. Internally, strengthening the CCP's grip on power was considered key, while externally, affirming the precise boundaries of its expansive land borders to the north and west was the highest priority.[9] Beijing worked hard to establish relations with these new states as well as the post-communist governments in Russia and Mongolia. By the mid-1990s, these efforts began to bear fruit, with the resolution of territorial disputes and confidence-building measures resulting in demilitarized borders. Beijing also worked to manage the threat posed by ethnic minorities inside China, who spilled across borders, through a combination of repression, economic development, and cooperation with its Central Asian neighbors.

---

[7] Zhao Huasheng, *Zhongguo De Zhongya Waijiao* [*China's Central Asian Diplomacy*], Beijing: Shishi Chubanshe, 2008, p. 61.

[8] This section draws upon Scobell, Ratner, and Beckley, 2014, pp. 18–19.

[9] Zhao Huasheng, 2008, p. 38.

The five former Soviet republics in Central Asia all have authoritarian and secular regimes. Each seeks to stay in power by suppressing religious extremism and ruling populations that are ethnically mixed and flow over borders. Major ethnic groups in the region include Afghans (who are themselves of multiple ethnicities) and Tajiks (who are related to Iranians or Persians), Kazakhs, Turkmens, and Uzbeks (a Turkic people), and sizable Russian populations. Only Mongolia could be properly described as a democracy.

Beijing quickly recognized all the post-Soviet states (setting aside its discomfort with these new entities) and, on the basis of its usual principles of noninterference, established good relations with whomever was in charge. There has been active diplomacy, including frequent high-level Chinese visits to these capitals. As noted, China settled all its border disputes with the post-Soviet states, but this took considerable time and effort to accomplish. China and Kazakhstan reached general agreement in 1994, with supplemental accords in 1997 and 1998, and demarcation was eventually concluded in 2002. The border with Kyrgyzstan was addressed by two accords, in 1996 and 1999; demarcation work began in 2001, and a boundary protocol was penned in 2004. The border with Tajikistan was settled in 2002, although the actual process of demarcation did not begin until 2006, and the process was not officially concluded until the Tajik parliament ratified the protocol in January 2011.[10]

3. Increase China's Influence and Limiting That of Other States. China also works to maintain a gentle but pervasive influence in Central Asia and deny or at least strictly limit the influence of other outside powers, notably Russia and the United States.[11]

Central Asia is geographically surrounded by three major powers: Russia to the north and west, China to the east, and Iran to the southwest. Other major powers are more distant but still have influence and interests in the region. These include Turkey, India, and the United

[10] See, for example, Fravel, *Strong Borders, Secure Nation: Cooperation and Conflict in China's Territorial Disputes*, Princeton, N.J.: Princeton University Press, 2008, pp. 161–167 (for Kazakhstan), p. 164 (for Kyrgyzstan), and p. 166 (for Tajikistan).

[11] These paragraphs draw upon Scobell, Ratner, and Beckley, 2014, pp. 34–35.

States. Other lesser powers have interests and influence in Central Asia, notably Afghanistan and Pakistan. All these outsiders—especially Russia and the United States—compete for influence in varying degrees, diplomatically, economically, and militarily. Beijing seeks to increase its influence in Central Asia and at the same time limit that of other powers.[12]

The SCO is particularly important because it enhances China's stature and provides Beijing with a vehicle to achieve greater influence in the region. It is the first multilateral organization to be established by China and be headquartered in China. With a Chinese city in the name, Beijing is proud of its central role. Moreover, rhetorically at least, SCO member states support Chinese stands on a variety of issues. Most obviously, this verbal support comes on the matter of the so called "three evils" of terrorism, separatism, and extremism but also on other matters of importance to Beijing.

China has played the leading role in the SCO. The SCO eased China's way into regional influence, providing a way to get involved without overtly challenging Russia. Although the organization diminishes Russian influence in the region, Russia's participation in the SCO also helps dilute Chinese influence in Central Asia. Russia continues to see other benefits in its SCO involvement, even if China's role is growing. In the absence of other comparable strong organizations, including the limited role of the Russian-led Collective Security Treaty Organization (CSTO), the SCO is a means for Russia to engage Central Asian states and China.[13] According to some, there is a division of labor in the SCO, with Russia focusing on security issues and China on economic issues.[14]

4. Promote and Protect Chinese Economic Interests. China has worked hard to tap the energy resources of Central Asia as well

---

[12] For more on great power competition in Central Asia, see Alexander Cooley, *Great Games, Local Rules*, New York: Oxford University Press, 2012.

[13] Of course Moscow would prefer a higher profile for the CSTO but is willing to utilize the SCO to exert Russian influence. Cooley, 2012, pp. 70–71.

[14] Nicola P. Contessi, "China, Russia and the Leadership of the SCO," *China & Eurasia Forum Quarterly*, Vol. 8, No. 4, 2010, pp. 101–123.

as the markets. It has facilitated both through the construction of infrastructure—including roads, railways, and pipelines. For example, the Central Asia-China Gas Pipeline runs 1,830 kilometers from the Turkmenistan-Uzbekistan border, through Kazakhstan, to Horgos in the Xinjiang Uighur Autonomous Region. A multiline pipeline, the first line became operational in 2009, the second in 2010, and the third in 2014. Overall capacity was expected to hit 55 billion cubic meters per year by the end of 2015.[15] In 2014, China and Tajikistan agreed to build a fourth line that would run from Turkmenistan through Uzbekistan, Tajikistan, and Kazakhstan before reaching China, with the expectation that the four lines together would be able to supply 80 billion cubic meters per year by 2020.[16]

Political Engagement

In recent years, Central Asia and the surrounding countries have been important destinations for China's leaders.[17] In June 2011, for example, President Hu Jintao undertook a nine-day trip and "conducted intensive diplomatic activities, visited three countries (Kazakhstan, Russia, and Ukraine) and five cities (Astana, St. Petersburg, Moscow, Kiev, Yalta), attended two international conferences (the annual SCO heads of state summit and 15th St. Petersburg International Economic Forum), and participated in more than 50 bilateral and multilateral activities."[18]

More recently, in September 2013, Hu's successor, President Xi Jinping, undertook an extended excursion in Central Asia. In doing

---

[15] China National Petroleum Corporation, "Flow of Natural Gas from Central Asia," webpage, 2015.

[16] Yen Ling Song, "Fourth Line of Central Asia-China Gas Pipeline to Start Construction This Year," *Platts*, March 10, 2014.

[17] This section draws upon Scobell, Ratner, and Beckley, 2014, pp. 28–29.

[18] "China, Ukraine Set Up Strategic Partnership," *Xinhua News*, June 20, 2011; "Building and Enhancing the Strategic Partnership and Writing a New Chapter of Friendly Cooperation—Foreign Minister Yang Jiechi Talks About the Outcome of President Hu Jintao's Visits," Ministry of Foreign Affairs of the People's Republic of China, June 21, 2011.

so, he became the third consecutive PRC head of state to pay such concerted attention to the region. Xi began his tour with a two-day visit to Turkmenistan, where the focus was on expanded energy cooperation. The Chinese president ceremonially opened a new gas field at Galkynysh and committed to the construction of a new multibillion-dollar natural gas pipeline as part of the Central Asia-China Gas Pipeline. Known as Route D, this pipeline will become the second route and reaffirm China's status as the number one customer for Turkmenistan's gas. From there, Xi flew to Russia, where he attended the G-20 Summit meeting in St. Petersburg. Following this high-profile meeting, President Xi visited Kazakhstan. There he gave a major speech focusing on PRC policy toward Central Asia at Nazarbayev University. It was in that speech that Xi first promoted the idea of a "Silk Road economic belt," one part of the Belt and Road Initiative, and announced a number of new Chinese initiatives, including a ten-year program to fund scholarships for 30,000 students from SCO countries and another to pay for 10,000 teachers and students from SCO member state Confucius Institutes to visit China. Xi's next stop was Uzbekistan, where the Chinese leader signed deals on oil, gas, and gold reportedly worth $15 billion. The PRC president's final stop was in Kyrgyzstan, where he participated in his first annual SCO heads of state summit in Bishkek and signed deals with his Kyrgyz counterpart worth $3 billion, including funding for a gas pipeline from Turkmenistan to China and an oil refinery.[19]

Diplomatic Relations and Presence

China has diplomatic relations with all Central Asian countries. This facilitates Beijing's ability to engage multilaterally with the region, and Chinese policy has concentrated on creating a stable condominium-like arrangement that is attentive to Chinese interests and constrains

---

[19] This paragraph draws on the following sources: Wu Jiao and Zhang Yunbi, "Xi Proposes a 'New Silk Road' with Central Asia," *China Daily* (US Edition), September 8, 2013; Martha Brill Olcott, "China's Unmatched Influence in Central Asia," Carnegie Endowment for International Peace, September 18, 2013; "China in Central Asia: Rising China, Sinking Russia," *The Economist*, September 14, 2013; "China to Allocate $3Bln to Kyrgyzstan—Reports" *RIA Novosti* (Moscow), September 11, 2013; Simon Denyer, "China Bypasses American 'New Silk Road' with Two of Its Own," *Washington Post*, October 14, 2013.

the future growth of Russian power. Meanwhile, Russia has found the SCO to be not just a worthwhile venue for basic Sino-Russian cooperation but also a way for Moscow to mitigate Beijing's influence in the region.[20] Moreover, China uses the organization to limit the influence of outside powers, such as the United States. In short, the SCO is a key management mechanism that Beijing uses to demonstrate growing influence in Central Asia.

Pivotal State and Major Partners

In designing their outreach strategy for this region, Chinese leaders must take into account a pivotal state that, in fact, exists outside of it. Five of the six states of Central Asia have for centuries been under Russian domination—first as territories fully incorporated into the Russian Empire and then as nominally sovereign republics within the Soviet Union.

The remaining state, Mongolia, was a Soviet client throughout the Cold War. The Mongolian People's Republic acted as a buffer against China, and in return, the USSR shielded it from Mao Zedong's revanchist claims to "Outer Mongolia." In the view of a leading Chinese expert, these states are "deeply Russified."[21] Today, the five former Soviet republics remain part of Russia's near abroad and are members of various Russia-led regional organizations, including the Commonwealth of Independent States, the Collective Security Treaty Organization, and for some, the Eurasian Economic Union, which was upgraded from the previous Eurasian Economic Community in response to Ukraine's attempt in 2014 to sign an association agreement with the European Union.

That being said, China has made significant inroads into Central Asia. It currently has a range of bilateral partnership agreements with all countries in this region. For example, Kyrgyzstan, Tajikistan,

---

[20] Mohan Malik, "The Shanghai Cooperation Organization," in Sumit Ganguly, Joseph Liow, and Andrew Scobell, eds., *The Routledge Handbook of Asian Security Studies*, New York: Routledge, 2010, pp. 74, 81.

[21] Zhao Huasheng, *Zhongguo De Zhongya Waijiao* [*China's Central Asian Diplomacy*], pp. 141, 142.

Turkmenistan, and Uzbekistan are all strategic partners. Both Kazakhstan and Mongolia are comprehensive strategic partners. Kazakhstan is the most significant of these six states, with the largest population—more than 17 million inhabitants—the largest area, the most sizeable economy, and largest number of men and women in its armed forces. Moreover, the overwhelming majority of China's trade with Central Asia is conducted with Kazakhstan.

China's key multilateral vehicle for inserting itself into the region has been the Shanghai Cooperation Organization. Of these Central Asian states, only Turkmenistan and Mongolia are not members, although Mongolia has observer status in the organization and routinely attends SCO summits. The organization does not restrict membership to the immediate region—in 2017 the SCO welcomed India and Pakistan as full members.

High-Level Exchanges

In the three years through 2014, senior Chinese leaders made 23 visits to Central Asia at the level of head of state or head of government. The most frequent destination was Kazakhstan, which received six such visits. Kyrgyzstan and Uzbekistan came next, at four visits each. Finally, Mongolia, Tajikistan, and Turkmenistan each received three visits.[22] Chinese leaders also regularly meet with Russian leaders either in Moscow or annually in China or Central Asia at SCO summits.

Cultural Influence

Beyond these very visible manifestations of China's growing hard power, less noticeable soft power aspects have also expanded in the region. The Chinese model of economic development and its education system have increasing appeal. For example, as of 2010, reportedly more Central Asian students study in China than in Russia.[23]

China currently has 11 Confucius Institutes across five of the six countries of Central Asia. Kazakhstan has the most, with four institutes. Kyrgyzstan has three. Uzbekistan has two. Mongolia and Tajiki-

---

[22] Compiled from RAND databases.

[23] Scobell, Ratner, and Beckley, 2014, pp. 45–46.

stan have one each. Turkmenistan, however, has no institutes. Russia has 22.[24]

There is no definitive measure of Chinese citizens in Central Asia. Alternate measures at various times in the late 2000s and early 2010s suggest anywhere from 40,000 to 450,000 Chinese citizens in the five former Soviet Central Asian republics. These include up to 200,000 in the capital of Kazakhstan and up to 100,000 in Kyrgyzstan, although official sources put the numbers much lower, such as citing only 9,500 legal workers in Kazakhstan.[25]

Economic Engagement

China's economic footprint in Central Asia has grown significantly in the twenty-first century, both in terms of trade and investments.[26] China is particularly dominant as a trade partner with the countries of the region and by 2012 appeared to have surpassed Russia as Central Asia's top trader. In terms of FDI in the region, while China's share has been growing, it has never exceeded 10 percent of the region's total. FDI in Central Asia tends to be dominated by the United States and Europe, and the lion's share of this investment is focused on Kazakhstan (80 percent to 90 percent of all FDI flowing into the entire region in each year from 1999 to 2008 has gone to Kazakhstan).[27] According to the IMF, in 2009, the United States and the Netherlands together accounted for just over 50 percent of the total foreign investment in

---

[24] Data from Russia are from Confucius Institute Online, "Worldwide Confucius Institutes," webpage, 2014.

[25] Zhu Yongbiao, "Zai Zhongya Zhongguo Laodong Quanyi Mianlin De Fengxian" ["The Risks Facing Chinese Labor Rights in Central Asia"], *Journal of Xinjiang Normal University*, No. 4, 2017.

[26] This section draws upon Scobell, Ratner, and Beckley, 2014, p. 42.

[27] According to United Nations Conference on Trade and Development (UNCTAD) data analyzed by RAND.

Kazakhstan.[28] By contrast, China and Russia were more significant foreign investors in Kyrgyzstan, although the total FDI in Kyrgyzstan was a fraction of the FDI in Kazakhstan.[29]

Although Russian results have proved disappointing, Chinese success in Central Asia has come, slowly but surely; in particular China's efforts at tapping petroleum in Kazakhstan and natural gas in Turkmenistan. The China National Petroleum Corporation (CNPC) bought a majority stake in the Aktyubinsk and PetroKazakhstan oilfields. In June 1997, CNPC and the governments of China and Kazakhstan agreed to build an oil pipeline. But construction did not begin until September 2004, and the Chinese-financed pipeline did not begin delivering crude oil from central Kazakhstan to western China along its 650-mile length until May 2006. Then, in December 2009, the Central Asia-China Natural Gas Pipeline began pumping natural gas from Turkmenistan to Xinjiang through more than 1,000 miles of rugged terrain across Uzbekistan and Kazakhstan into China. The official opening ceremony was attended by then PRC president Hu Jintao and his Turkmenistan, Uzbekistan, and Kazakhstan counterpart heads of state.[30] In September 2013, recently elected PRC President Xi Jinping and his Turkmen counterpart signed agreements to expand energy cooperation between their two countries, including a contract to construct a new gas pipeline, informally known as Route D. When finished, the pipeline will stretch some 850 kilometers through Turkmenistan, Uzbekistan, and Kyrgyzstan.[31]

---

[28] Reliable data are hard to find. The IMF data conflict with data provided by the Kazakh National Bank. According to the bank, the United States and the Netherlands do not make up 50 percent of total FDI. See National Bank of the Republic of Kazakhstan, "Gross Domestic Investment from Abroad: Inflows by Country."

[29] U.S. Department of State, "2010 Investment Climate Statement—Kyrgyz Republic," webpage, March 2010.

[30] On Chinese energy interests, see Kevin Scheives, "China Turns West: Beijing's Contemporary Strategy Toward Central Asia," *Pacific Affairs*, Vol. 79, No. 2, Summer 2006, pp. 215–217. On the oil pipeline completion, see Medeiros, 2009, p. 138, and "Xinjiang Pipeline Oils Wheels," *The Standard*, December 14, 2009.

[31] Tavus Rejepova, "Turkmenistan, China Reach New Energy Deals," *The Central Asia-Caucasus Analyst*, October 16, 2013.

Trade

Trade between Central Asia and China has changed considerably between 2000 and 2013. In 2000, roughly 50 percent of imports from Central Asia were mineral products and 10 percent were oil and gas. The remainder consisted of manufactured goods. By 2013, this had completely changed. More than 70 percent of imports consisted of oil and gas, 13 percent were mineral products, and only 9 percent were manufactured items (Figure 5.2). These large increases in imports of oil and gas were driven by trade with Kazakhstan. China's main imports from Kazakhstan, on a more disaggregated basis, for example, are metals and minerals such as steel, copper, and aluminum, as well

Figure 5.2
Composition of Imports from Central Asia

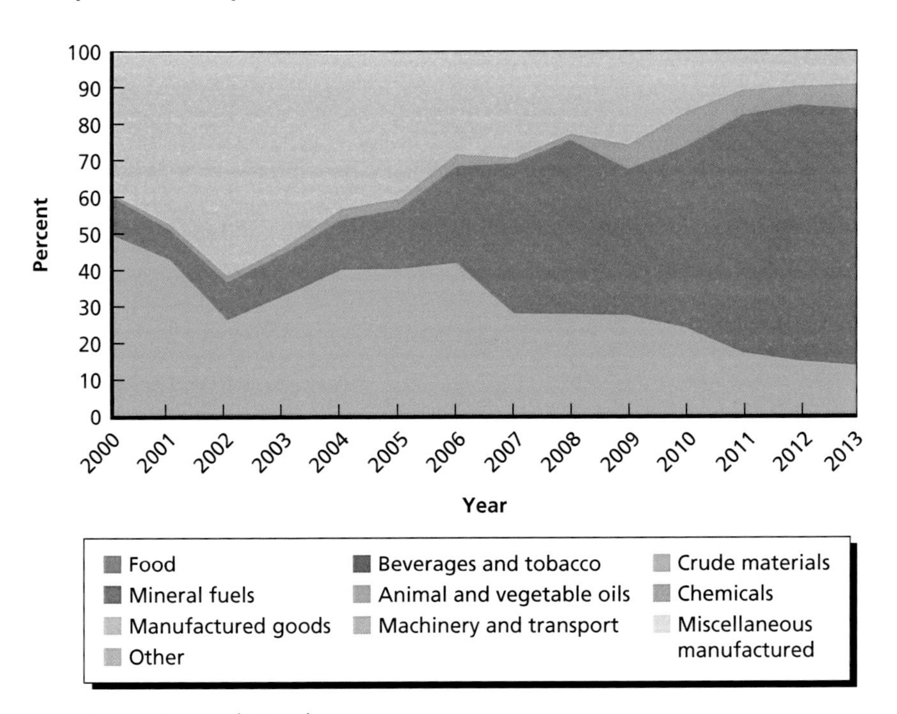

SOURCE: UN Comtrade Database.
RAND *RR2273A-5.2*

Figure 5.3
Composition of Exports to Central Asia

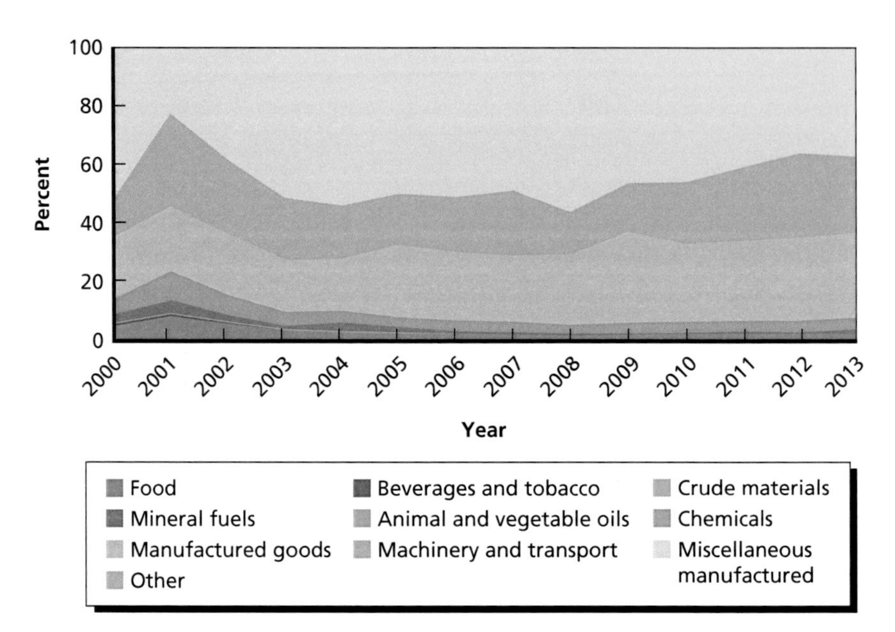

SOURCE: UN Comtrade Database.
RAND *RR2273A-5.3*

as crude oil; meanwhile China's main exports are clothing, electronics, and household appliances.[32]

The composition of exports to Central Asia has remained relatively constant since 2003, mainly the three categories of manufactured items (Figure 5.3).

The region as a whole had a large trade deficit during the mid-2000s. That has reversed as China's gas imports have increased (Figure 5.4). Kazakhstan, Mongolia, and Turkmenistan had trade surpluses in 2013, driven by Chinese resource imports from these three countries. Kazakhstan and Turkmenistan have always had a trade surplus.

---

[32] On trade, see Calla Wiemer, "The Economy of Xinjiang," in S. Frederick Starr, ed., *Xinjiang: China's Muslim Borderland*, Armonk, N.Y.: M.E. Sharpe, Inc., 2004, p. 185, and Edward Wong, "China Quietly Extends Its Footprints Deep into Central Asia," *New York Times* (Washington edition), January 3, 2011, pp. A4, A10.

Figure 5.4
Level of Exports to and Imports from Central Asia

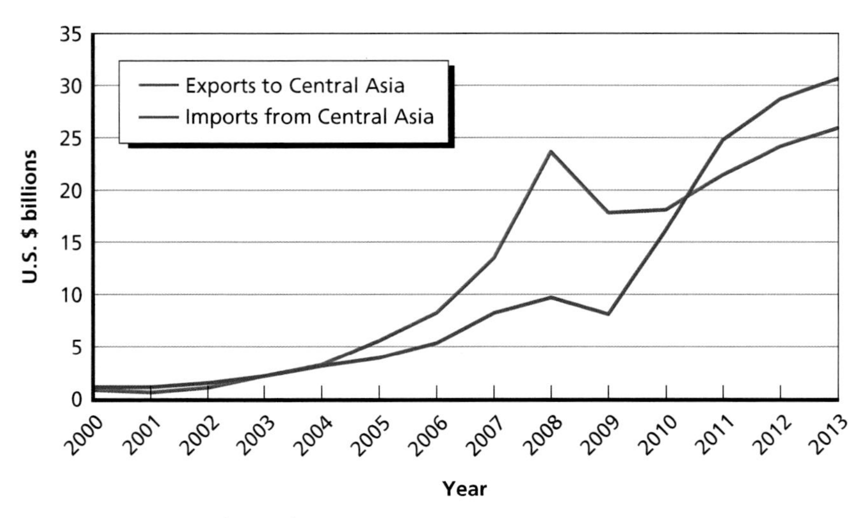

SOURCE: UN Comtrade Database.
RAND *RR2273A-5.4*

Foreign Direct Investment and Lending

There has been considerable buildup of the stock of FDI in Central Asia since 2003, again driven largely by resources (Figure 5.5). In 2003, China had only $44 million in FDI stock in Central Asia compared to about $7.5 billion in 2012. Much of this increase in investment has been to Kazakhstan, which in 2012 had more than $6 billion in Chinese FDI stock. Most recently, on December 14, 2014, Kazakhstan and China signed 30 agreements totaling at least $14 billion.

Chinese FDI stock has outstripped that of Russia in Central Asia, although for both, Kazakhstan has been the major recipient (Figure 5.6). Russian FDI in Central Asia totaled $4.1 billion in 2012, up from $2.9 billion in 2009.

Agreements and Other Issues

China moved to enable a well-regulated investment environment in Central Asia soon after the end of the Soviet Union. It now has BITs with all six countries in the region. The original BITs were all signed by 1993 and in force by 1995, but the BIT with Uzbekistan was

Figure 5.5
China's FDI Stock in Central Asia by Receiving Country

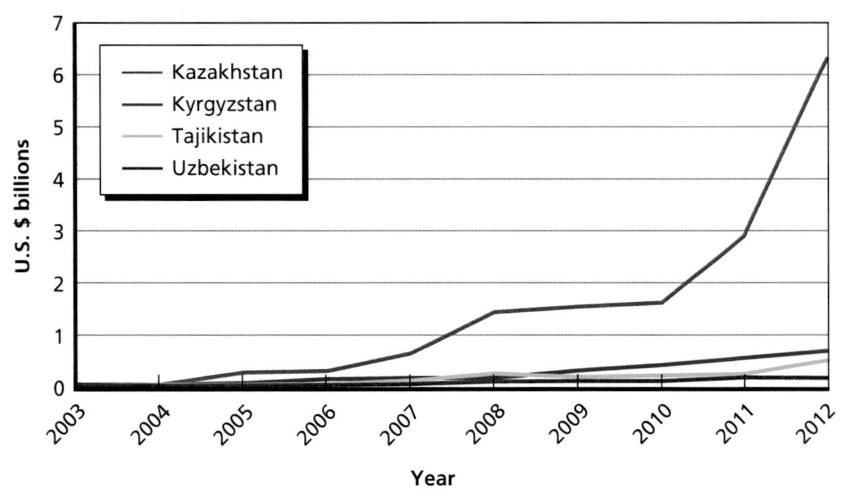

SOURCE: UNCTAD.
RAND *RR2273A-5.5*

Figure 5.6
Russia's FDI Stock in Central Asia by Receiving Country

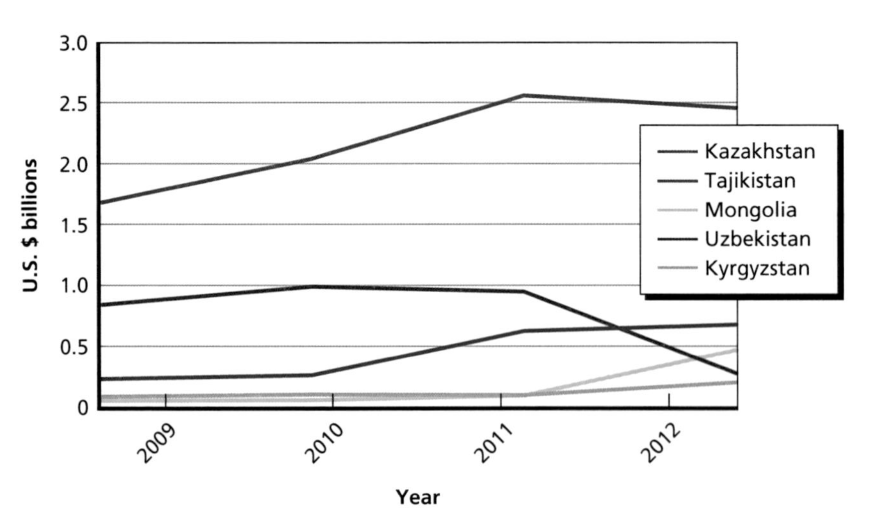

SOURCE: UNCTAD.
RAND *RR2273A-5.6*

terminated in 1994. A new BIT was signed and entered into force in 2011. China also has double tax treaties with all six countries, the first of which was signed with Mongolia in 1991 and entered into force in 1993. Uzbekistan was signed in 1996, and the rest were signed in the 2000s.

Almost all Central Asian countries are participants in the Asian Infrastructure Investment Bank. Only Turkmenistan did not sign the articles of incorporation as a founding member at the end of June 2015.

Military and Security Engagement

This section presents a brief overview of Chinese military engagement activities as an instrument of Chinese foreign and security policy in Central Asia. It addresses Chinese arms sales, military diplomacy, joint exercises, and port visits, as well as Chinese participation in UNPKOs and PLA MOOTW activities.

PRC Arms Sales

Since 2000, China has not sold any major conventional weapons to Central Asian countries. China has sought to increase its military influence with its neighbors in the region by providing modest military aid, especially to its primary regional trade partner Kazakhstan, which also has received free transfers of decommissioned military equipment from China. Support to other countries in the region has come in the form of equipment and training to border services, a trend that conforms to the overarching counterterrorism and anti-trafficking aims of China's security cooperation with Central Asia.[33] However, China is careful not to take actions that would create friction with Russia, which still views Central Asia as its sphere of influence and which has continued to be the primary supplier (and donor) of major conventional weapons

---

[33] Sébastien Peyrouse, "Military Cooperation Between China and Central Asia: Breakthrough, Limits, and Prospects," *China Brief*, Vol. 10, No. 5, March 5, 2010.

to Kazakhstan, Kyrgyzstan, Tajikistan, Turkmenistan, Uzbekistan, and Mongolia.[34]

China provides modest amounts of light weaponry and security equipment to at least several of the five Central Asian states, although not formally under the auspices of the SCO. Moreover, these deals are all bilateral agreements. China reportedly provided some $4.5 million worth of military assistance to Kazakhstan between 1997 and 2003. The aid consisted of communication equipment and vehicles. Between 1993 and 2008 China provided $15 million worth of military aid to Tajikistan, and in 2009 Beijing promised $1.5 million more. In 2000, China shipped sniper rifles to Uzbekistan and nine years later agreed to provide mobile scanning equipment to monitor border crossings. In 2007, China also provided a $3 million loan to allow Turkmenistan to purchase unspecified "military hardware" and uniforms for soldiers. Under the terms of an agreement signed in 2002, China promised to provide Turkmenistan with $1.2 million in "technical military assistance." In 2008, China's Ministry of Public Security reportedly provided computers and motor vehicles to the Kyrgyz agency in charge of border security.[35] These military packages are miniscule compared with the size and volume of weapons systems transferred to Pakistan (see Chapter 10).

PLA Military Diplomacy

With 17 trips of CMC members to Central Asia from 2005 to 2014, including 12 since 2010 alone, the region is clearly a very high priority for China's military diplomacy in the Developing World (Table 5.1). Six of these visits were for SCO-related events (SCO defense ministers meetings in 2007, 2008, 2011, 2013, and 2014, and an SCO chiefs of

---

[34] International Crisis Group, "China's Central Asia Problem," Asia Report No. 244, February 27, 2013.

[35] On Chinese military transfer to Central Asia generally, see Peyrouse, 2010, pp. 11–12. On Turkmenistan, see Viktoriya Panfilova, "China Will Dress Turkmenistani Army—Pekin Generously Credits Central Asian Countries," *Nezavisimaya Gazeta*, November 29, 2007b, Moscow (in Russian), translated by World News Connection, CEP20071129380002. On Kyrgyzstan, see Viktoriya Panfilova, "Kyrgyzstan to Get 0.5 m Dollars of Chinese Military Aid," *Kabar News Agency*, November 12, 2007a, Bishkek (in Russian), translated by World News Connection, CEP20071112950147.

Table 5.1
Chinese High-Level Military Visits to Central Asia, 2003–2014

Year of Visit	Country Visited	CMC Member	Foreign Counterparts	Summits
2005	Tajikistan	Cao Gangchuan, CMC Vice Chair/Defense Minister (DM)	DM Sherali Khairullaev	
2005	Kazakhstan	Cao Gangchuan, CMC Vice Chair/DM	DM Mukhtar Altynbayev	
2007	Mongolia	Liang Guanglie, CGS	Pres. Nambaryn Enkhbayar; DM Ts. Togoo	
2007	Kyrgyzstan	Cao Gangchuan, CMC Vice Chair/DM	DM Rustam Niyazov (Uzbekistan)	SCO DM meeting
2008	Tajikistan	Liang Guanglie, DM	Pres. Emomali Rakhmon	SCO DM meeting
2010	Turkmenistan	Liang Guanglie, DM	Pres. Gurbanguly Berdymukhamedov; DM Yaylym Berdiyev; NSM Carymyrat Amanov	
2010	Kazakhstan	Liang Guanglie, DM	Pres. Nursultan Nazarbayev; DM Adilbek Dzhaksybekov	
2010	Kazakhstan	Chen Bingde	Dep. DM and Chief of Staff of Armed Forces Saken Zhasuzakov	
2011	Kazakhstan	Liang Guanglie	DM Adilbek Dzhaksybekov	SCO DM meeting
2011	Uzbekistan	Liang Guanglie	Pres. Islam Karimov; DM Kabul Berdiev	
2012	Uzbekistan	Chen Bingde	DM Kabul Berdiev	
2012	Mongolia	Xu Caihou, CMC Vice Chair	Pres. Tsakhia Elbegdorj; DM Jadambaa Enkhbayar	
2012	Turkmenistan	Chen Bingde, CGS	Pres. Gurbanguly Berdymukhamedov; DM Begenc Gundogdiyev; Chief of Staff of Army Ismail Ismailov	
2012	Tajikistan	Chen Bingde, CGS	PM Oqil Oqilov	SCO Chief of Staff meeting
2013	Kyrgyzstan	Chang Wanquan, DM	Pres. Almazbek Atambayev; DM Taalaibek Omuraliev	SCO DM meeting
2013	Kazakhstan	Fan Changlong, Vice Chair CMC	PM Serik Akhmetov; DM Adilbek Dzhaksybekov	
2014	Tajikistan	Chang Wanquan, DM	Pres. Emomali Rakhmon; DM Sherali Mirzo	SCO DM meeting

staff meeting in 2012). The most frequently visited countries during this time were Kazakhstan with five visits and Tajikistan with four visits. Other destinations for such high-level visits included Uzbekistan and Turkmenistan.

China is also active in military-to-military exchanges with the Central Asian states, but language is a significant hurdle. High-level visits by defense officials routinely utilize skilled interpreters, but training courses in China for officers from Central Asia present more of a challenge. All courses for Central Asian officers at Chinese institutions of professional military education are conducted in Russian. Central Asian soldiers generally do not speak Chinese, and their Chinese counterparts generally cannot speak the various indigenous languages of the region. The number of Central Asia officers sent to study in China is modest but seems to be increasing. For example, while the first wave of Kazakh officers sent to China (starting in the 1990s) comprised just over a dozen, the second wave (since the mid-2000s) numbered more than 60. Smaller batches of officers from Kyrgyzstan and Tajikistan were sent to China in the 2000s.[36]

Combined Exercises

China has expanded its participation in combined exercises with partners in Central Asia over the years, with many of the drills taking place under the auspices of the SCO. According to Chinese media, the China-Kyrgyzstan combined Exercise 01 was the first PLA joint military maneuver with a foreign army and the first bilateral counterterrorism exercise conducted by SCO members. The first time the PLA participated in a multilateral joint military maneuver under SCO auspices was during the Coalition 2003 exercise, which also involved troops from Russia, Kazakhstan, Kyrgyzstan, and Tajikistan. About 1,300 troops participated in the Coalition 2003 exercise, according to Chinese media reports.[37]

The Peace Mission series of exercises began in August 2005, with a China-Russia joint exercise that took place over a period of one week

---

[36] Peyrouse, 2010, p. 12.

[37] Lin Zhi, "Backgrounder: SCO Anti-Terror Military Drills," *Xinhua News*, September 9, 2010.

in Vladivostok and the Shandong Peninsula and reportedly focused on counterterrorism operations. The second Peace Mission exercise, which was held in 2007, expanded participation to all six of the SCO countries (China, Kazakhstan, Kyrgyzstan, Russia, Tajikistan, and Uzbekistan), and involved more than 4,000 troops. Subsequent Peace Mission exercises have involved China and Russia (Peace Mission 2009) or China and multiple SCO members (Peace Mission 2010, Peace Mission 2012, Peace Mission 2013, and Peace Mission 2014).

Through 2014, the most recent, and in some ways the most notable, exercise in this series was Peace Mission 2014, which was held in August 2014 at Zhurihe in Inner Mongolia. The exercise, which reportedly focused on antiterrorism operations, included a total of approximately 7,000 troops from China, Russia, Kazakhstan, Kyrgyzstan, and Tajikistan (about 5,000 of the troops were from China). This made it the largest Peace Mission exercise to date, according to the PRC Ministry of National Defense.

A senior PLA officer said the exercise was intended to play an important role in deterring the "three evil forces" of terrorism, separatism, and extremism and in safeguarding regional peace and stability. "The drill focuses on joint multilateral decision making and action, with exchanges of anti-terror intelligence among the SCO members to effectively boost the troops' coordinated ability to fight terrorism," then Deputy Chief of General Staff Department Wang Ning said.[38] *Xinhua* reported that the exercise scenario involved "a separatist organization, supported by an international terrorist organization, plotting terrorist incidents and hatching a coup plot to divide the country. The SCO dispatches military forces to put down the insurrection and restore stability at the request of the country's government."

---

[38] See Mu Xuequan, "China's Drone Blasts Off Missile in SCO Anti-Terror Drill," *Xinhua News*, August 26, 2014; Xiang Bo, "'Peace Mission-2014' Scale: More than Ever," *Xinhua News*, August 28, 2014; Fu Peng, "China Focus: SCO Anti-Terror Drill Kicks Off in China," *Xinhua News*, August 24, 2014; "Defense Ministry's Regular Press Conference on August 28, 2014," Ministry of National Defense of the People's Republic of China, August 28, 2014; and Jeffrey Lin and P. W. Singer, "Biggest Anti-Terrorist Exercise in the World Stars Chinese Drones, Russian Troops and a Ukraine-Inspired Wargame," *Popular Science*, September 2, 2014.

Another notable aspect of Peace Mission 2014 involved the types of PLA forces that participated in the exercise. Peace Mission 2014 was the first time PLAAF unmanned combat aerial vehicles (UCAVs) took part in an international exercise, according to Chinese official media. *Xinhua* reported that an unidentified model UCAV fired several missiles during the exercise. PLAAF spokesperson Shen Jinke stated, "The drone, tasked with surveillance, reconnaissance and ground attacks, will play a vital role in fighting against terrorism." Additional Chinese forces participating in the exercise, included PLAAF fighter planes, early warning aircraft, and airborne troops, and Chinese tanks, armored vehicles, ground forces from the PLA's 38th Group Army, and WZ-10 and WZ-19 armed helicopters.

In addition to exercises held under the auspices of the SCO, China has held other combined exercises in Central Asia in recent years (Table 5.2). For example, it has participated in the U.S.-Mongolian

Table 5.2
Selected Chinese Combined Exercises in Central Asia, 2002–2014

Year	Name of Exercise	Partner(s)	Exercise Content
2002	Exercise 01	Kyrgyzstan	Counterterrorism
2003	[Unknown]	Russia	Illegal border crossing
2003	Coalition 2003	Russia; Kazakhstan; Kyrgyzstan; Tajikistan	Counterterrorism
2005	Peace Mission 2005	Russia	Counterterrorism
2006	Tianshan I	Kazakhstan	Counterterrorism
2006	Coordination 2006	Tajikistan	Counterterrorism
2007	Cooperation 2007	Russia	Counterterrorism
2007	Peace Mission 2007	Russia; Kazakhstan; Kyrgyzstan; Tajikistan; Uzbekistan	Counterterrorism
2009	Peace Mission 2009	Russia	Counterterrorism
2009	Peace Shield 2009	Russia	Maritime security (in the Gulf of Aden)
2009	Country-Gate Sharp Sword	Russia	Counterterrorism

Table 5.2—Continued

Year	Name of Exercise	Partner(s)	Exercise Content
2009	Peacekeeping 2009	Mongolia	Peacekeeping operations
2010	Peace Mission 2010	Russia; Kazakhstan; Kyrgyzstan; Tajikistan; Uzbekistan	Counterterrorism
2011	Khan Quest-11	Mongolia	Peacekeeping operations
2011	[Unknown]	Kazakhstan	Joint border patrol
2011	Tianshan II	Russia; Kazakhstan; Kyrgyzstan; Tajikistan; Uzbekistan	Counterterrorism
2012	Peace Mission 2012	Russia; Kazakhstan; Kyrgyzstan; Tajikistan; Uzbekistan	Counterterrorism
2012	Joint Sea 2012	Russia	Anti-submarine operations; maritime search and rescue
2013	Cooperation 2013	Russia	Counterterrorism
2013	Joint Sea 2013; Maritime Joint Exercise 2013	Russia	Maritime search and rescue
2013	Peace Mission 2013	Russia; Kazakhstan; Kyrgyzstan; Tajikistan; Uzbekistan	Counterterrorism
2013	Frontier Defense Joint Determination 2013	Kyrgyzstan	Counterterrorism
2013	Prairie Pioneer 2013	Mongolia	Disaster relief
2014	Peace Mission 2014	Russia; Kazakhstan; Kyrgyzstan; Tajikistan	Counterterrorism
2014	[Unknown]	Russia	Counterterrorism
2014	Joint Sea 2014	Russia	Maritime security
2014	Border Defense Cooperation 2014	Russia	Illegal border crossing

SOURCE: Department of Defense China Military Power Report and Chinese Ministry of Defense website.

NOTE: China did not begin engaging in combined exercises with foreign militaries until 2002.

Khaan Quest series of exercises in Mongolia, which focuses on peace-keeping operations.

Conclusion

Beijing has executed its Empty Fortress strategy since 1991 through sustained diplomatic efforts in Central Asia. These efforts have been combined with very modest security cooperation. These include high-profile displays of military power—small-scale exercises conducted with security forces from other SCO member states. These initiatives, which have been undertaken under the umbrella of the SCO, have enabled China to project the image of a mighty and influential power.

China's influence in Central Asia has grown significantly in the past decade in diplomatic, economic, and even military spheres, albeit starting from a very low level in each case.[39] The Central Asian states will likely continue to work to maintain good relations with China, in part out of a desire to avoid antagonizing Beijing and in part out of an interest in balancing against Moscow. Just as important are the economic opportunities that China provides. Nevertheless, Central Asian countries continue to look to Russia to balance against the prospect of Chinese domination in the realms of the economy, diplomacy, and defense, and some appear to see Russia as a more reliable partner and less of a threat to their sovereignty than China.[40]

Despite this, China's management of its relations with neighbors to the west in the twenty-first century has been quite impressive. Beijing's response to the daunting problems it confronts in Central Asia and western China has been to skillfully project an image of great strength and outward confidence to mask extreme weakness and inner insecurity: an Empty Fortress strategy. Through deft use of high-profile diplomacy and modest military exercises, combined with growing economic clout, Beijing has promoted the image of a powerful and

---

[39] These paragraphs draw upon Scobell, Ratner, and Beckley, 2014, p. 48.

[40] The adeptness of Central Asian states at balancing the influence of great powers is a key finding of Alexander Cooley. See his *Great Games, Local Rules.*

benevolent China. This is in spite of a defense posture in the west that is Spartan and stretched; the Western Theater Command—formerly the Lanzhou Military Region—is vast, and major military units are deployed well away from its borders with Central Asia.[41]

Moreover, SCO multilateralism and China's bilateral military engagement activities allow Beijing to project the image of a military great power in a manner that is nonthreatening to China's partners and neighbors. By planning cooperative small-scale activities with the security forces of other SCO member states and targeting nontraditional security threats, Beijing's military power does not loom too large in Moscow, Astana, Bishkek, Dushanbe, Tashkent, or other capitals.

But all China's security efforts pale in comparison to Russia's much greater military footprint and extensive program of military engagement with the armed forces of the region. In addition to the military bases mentioned, under the auspices of the CSTO, Russia conducts regular military exercises with a higher level of interoperability than is evident in SCO exercises. Moreover, Russia provides a significant amount of the weaponry and equipment used by the armed forces of the Central Asian states. The CSTO functions much more like a traditional military alliance than the SCO, with Russia very much in the center.[42]

Implications for the United States

The centerpiece of China's Empty Fortress strategy in Central Asia is the SCO, which has evolved over the past 15 years from a focus on border security to counterterrorism into a multifaceted, multilateral organization involved not only with security issues but also with energy and economic cooperation.[43] More recently, it has been joined on the economic side by Belt and Road.

---

[41] Scobell, Ratner, and Beckley, 2014, pp. 12–14.

[42] Alexander Frost, "The Collective Security Treaty Organization, the Shanghai Cooperation Organization, and Russia's Strategic Goals in Central Asia," *China and Eurasia Forum Quarterly*, Vol. 7, No. 3, 2008, pp. 83–102.

[43] These paragraphs draw upon Scobell, Ratner, and Beckley, 2014, pp. 30–31.

The SCO has been institutionalized with regular summit meetings and military exercises. Measured by the yardstick of Beijing's Empty Fortress strategy, the SCO has proved to be a success promoting the image of a strong and secure China in a region where the PRC is actually very weak and insecure. Especially considering that three months after its birth the attacks of September 11, 2001, paved the way for U.S. military intervention in Afghanistan and expanded U.S. security cooperation with Central Asian states, the SCO has survived, demonstrated its staying power, and it appears durable for the foreseeable future. What would constitute failure in China's Empty Fortress strategy? Probably the only development that would be viewed as such by Beijing would be the disintegration of the SCO. Thus, the bar for success is very low.

By another yardstick, the SCO bears up less impressively—whether the organization is "relevant." In other words, can the SCO address the real problems of the region in practical and meaningful ways? In terms of practical effects, the SCO's performance to date has proved disappointing—the organization has been disengaged from the domestic political crises of member countries and been little more than a bystander on Afghanistan. Indeed, the organization seemed strangely aloof from the U.S.-led Global War on Terrorism and in danger of disappearing into oblivion.[44] Some Chinese analysts openly express their frustration with the SCO's limited progress.[45] There are built-in limitations on its capabilities and potential because of loose organizational structure and cohesion and little economic and military compatibility. Moreover, other members are wary of Chinese hegemony.

The United States has found itself excluded from the SCO, but not necessarily by Chinese design.[46] The responses to feelers by Washington on the possibility of establishing some formal affiliation with

---

[44] Marc Lanteigne, "In Medias Res: The Development of the Shanghai Cooperation Organization as a Security Community," *Pacific Affairs*, Vol. 79, No. 4, Winter 2006–2007, p. 612.

[45] See, for example, Sun Zhuangzhi, "SCO Summit in Tashkent Opens 'New Chapter,'" *People's Daily Online* (in English), June 12, 2010; author conversations with Chinese analysts, spring 2011.

[46] These paragraphs draw upon Scobell, Ratner, and Beckley, 2014, pp. 30–31.

SCO have been cool. Since the organization operates on the basis of consensus, an invitation to the United States would require the unanimous consent of the member states—something that is difficult to obtain. While China is wary of Washington's involvement in Central Asia, Beijing also seeks to exploit the U.S.-led counterterrorism campaign to justify suppressing Uighur unrest in the name of contributing to a worldwide counterterrorism struggle. And while China works to mitigate U.S. influence in the region, it also treads cautiously so as not to unnecessarily antagonize the United States.[47] Indeed, as one Western analyst noted, "the SCO has pursued a policy of accommodation with the United States on Central Asia policy."[48]

Although the SCO is a potential instrument for checking U.S. influence in the region, China and other SCO members are not adamantly opposed to a temporary U.S. presence. However, Beijing does not desire a permanent U.S. military footprint in Central Asia and is wary of perceived U.S. efforts to constrain China. Yet no single country totally dominates the SCO. While some have interpreted Beijing's stance on U.S. involvement in the region as hostile, it can also be viewed as a low-key effort by China to guard against a permanent U.S. military presence in the region. At the conclusion of the July 2005 SCO heads of state summit in Astana, Kazakhstan, the six countries issued a statement urging the U.S.-led coalition forces to "determine a deadline" for withdrawal of its forces from SCO member countries. In July 2005, the United States was forced to close down its airfield at Karshi-Khanabad in Uzbekistan. But the pressure had come from individual countries and not the SCO itself. Indeed, the 2005 statement appears to have been prompted by states other than China, notably Uzbekistan.[49] In short, China has not spearheaded SCO efforts to expel U.S. military forces from Central Asia.

---

[47] Scheives, 2006, pp. 219–222; Hasan H. Karrar, *The New Silk Road Diplomacy: China's Central Asian Foreign Policy Since the Cold War*, Vancouver: University of British Columbia Press, 2009, pp. 58–66.

[48] Lanteigne, 2006–2007, p. 613.

[49] It appears Uzbekistan was a driving force behind the statement. See, for example, Scheives, 2006, p. 221, and Cooley, 2012, p. 52.

The SCO is an enigmatic organization that defies easy categorization.[50] It has a diplomatic component, with annual meetings of heads of state, heads of governments, and other multilateral governmental meetings. Although the SCO has a key military component, it is not a military alliance; certainly it is no "Asian NATO."[51] It may be akin to the Association of Southeast Asian Nations in the sense of being a regional organization that is often derided as little more than a "talk shop."[52] And even though it is billed as a regional organization, it is clearly a Chinese creature in the sense that it would not exist without Beijing's initiative and funding. But the SCO is not Beijing's lapdog, nor is it Beijing's attack dog. Moreover, the SCO is by no means anti-American, but neither is the SCO by any stretch of the imagination a pro-American entity. The SCO is a useful multilateral mechanism by which Beijing can maintain Central Asia as a de facto Chinese sphere of influence without appearing overbearing or heavy-handed. Therefore, the United States should not have undue alarm regarding the organization. The fact that the SCO has raised concerns in the United States is testament to China's successful implementation of the Empty Fortress strategy.

The effect of Belt and Road on China, Central Asia, and the United States is much harder to judge. This is largely because it is new. On the one hand, it gathers together under one umbrella a number of disparate projects that are already occurring, such as railway lines to Europe and pipelines to China. On the other hand, its inspirational vision combined with new financing vehicles and existing Chinese financing institutions could result in increased investment and greater links with China. The fact that the United States does not participate in these financing vehicles may make it more difficult for U.S. companies

---

[50] Malik, 2010, pp. 72–86.

[51] See, for example, "SCO's Purpose Is Not to Challenge NATO," *Global Times*, June 7, 2012.

[52] Michael J. Green and Bates Gill, "Unbundling Asia's New Multilateralism," in Green and Gill, eds., *Asia's New Multilateralism: Cooperation, Competition, and the Southeast Asiarch for Community*, New York: Columbia University Press, 2009, p. 3. Green and Gill note that is a common criticism leveled at many Asian multilateral forums.

to participate directly in any economic advances in the region. However, this negative effect is far from certain and may even be unlikely.

Just as the Central Asian countries do not want to be dominated by China militarily, they do not want to be dominated by it economically. They have found value historically to playing great powers off against each other. And the great powers have been willing to join in this playing off. In 2015, China and Kazakhstan signed 33 deals, worth $23.6 billion, in March, followed by India and Kazakhstan signing five key agreements in July and agreeing to expand bilateral trade, followed by Pakistan and Kazakhstan signing memoranda of understanding in August to strengthen trade.[53] Second, as suggested by these many agreements, once most infrastructure is built, anyone can use it. Finally, any lending for projects in Central Asia must earn a return. With China's growth slowing and its demand for commodities slowing as well, it is not clear yet as to what types of investment opportunities are actually available. Belt and Road may offer tremendous opportunities to China, or it may be a case of "loud thunder and small raindrops."[54]

U.S. Strategy in the Absence of a "Great Game"

While the "Great Game" may have been an apt characterization of contestations over Central Asia in an earlier age of empires, this is no longer an appropriate metaphor to use for the region today.[55] In the early twenty-first century, there is no great power rivalry. The United States does have security interests in the region, but it is not engaged in a zero-sum contest with other great powers. Rather, America's adversaries are nonstate actors. That said, the absence of a "great game" does not mean the United States concedes the region to a Chinese (or

[53] Ben Blanchard, "China, Kazakhstan Sign $23.6 Billion in Deals," *Reuters*, March 27, 2015; Press Trust of India, "India, Kazakhstan Sign Five Key Agreements," *The Hindu*, July 8, 2015; APP, "Pakistan, Kazakhstan Sign MOUs to Strengthen Trade Ties," *The Nation*, August 25, 2015.

[54] George Magnus, "China, the New Silk Road, Loud Thunder and Small Raindrops," May 15, 2015.

[55] These paragraphs draw upon Scobell, Ratner, and Beckley, 2014, pp. 80–81.

Russian) sphere of influence. Moreover, countries of the region have proven quite adept at managing the influence of powerful states on their periphery. While the states of the region are weak, especially compared with the major powers that seek influence in the region, none of them are powerless.

China, along with Russia and other great powers, will continue to play key roles in shaping the security environment in Central Asia. Chinese activities and aspirations also directly impact U.S. interests and initiatives in the region. But China is not currently a major threat to U.S. interests in Central Asia and is unlikely to pose one in the near future. Therefore, at present, China is not a decisive factor in determining U.S. policy, military strategy, or posture in this region.

CHAPTER SIX

China in South Asia

Although South Asia is geographically and topographically removed from China, in the twenty-first century distances have shortened because of technological developments, and mountain ranges have effectively shrunk because improvements in communication and transportation technology have enabled transnational ethno-religious identities to intensify. Advanced weaponry has put China and India closer than ever before in terms of ballistic missile striking distances; PRC political repression and economic inequalities have exacerbated tensions in China's far west between ethnic minorities and the Han majority, encouraging those minorities to reach across the Himalaya and Pamir mountain ranges. Continued tensions between China and India coexist with growing economic interaction. Indeed, China's greater maritime activism has meant Chinese commercial vessels traversing the sealanes of the Indian Ocean on their journeys to and from Europe, Africa, and the Middle East. It is China's economy that has led to Beijing's far greater interest and involvement in both the continental and maritime reaches of South Asia.

Key Chinese Activities in the Region

Persistent disaffection among ethnic Tibetans and rising alienation among Uighurs has increased the unease of PRC leaders. Under Xi Jinping, China's relations with its neighbors have been reemphasized and the Belt and Road Initiative means that South Asia has become ever more important to the PRC, both as a key overland node and a critical maritime nexus.

Among the South Asian countries, Pakistan is China's closest partner (Figure 6.1). This relationship was capped in April 2015 when China and Pakistan signed agreements promising investments of up to $46 billion and the construction of a China Pakistan Economic Corridor of roads, rail lines, and pipelines.[1] The corridor is to run from Gwadar port in Pakistan, now envisioned as part of the Maritime Silk Road (the "Road" of Belt and Road) through Lahore and Islamabad to Xinjiang Uighur Autonomous Region in China. China's biggest rival, but also a partner, is India, the world's other giant. Although

Figure 6.1
China's Relations with Countries in South Asia, 2015

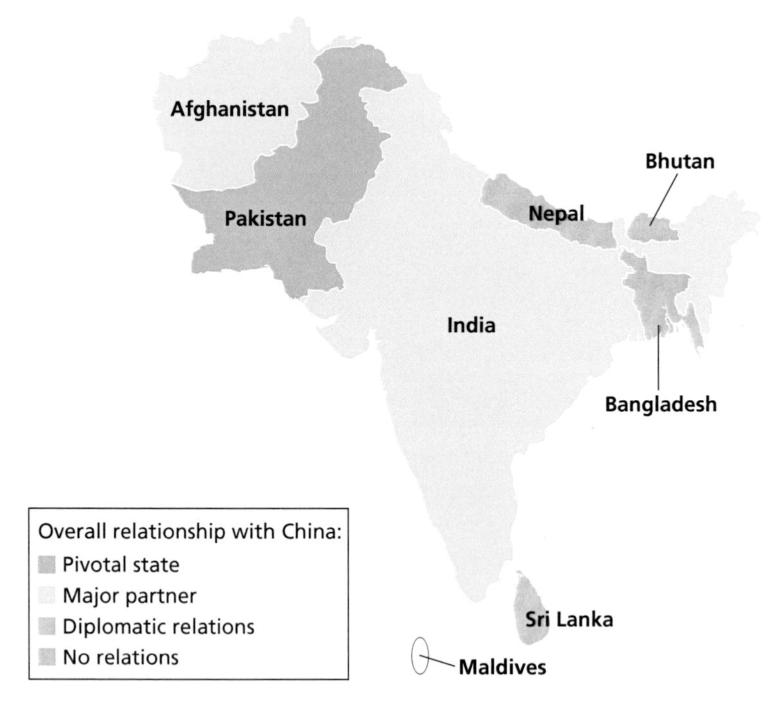

NOTE: Due to small scale of map, not all countries are displayed and labeled.
RAND *RR2273A-6.1*

1 "China's Xi Jinping Agrees $46bn Superhighway to Pakistan," *BBC News*, April 20, 2015.

they are rivals for influence in South Asia and Central Asia, China has also envisioned India as part of the Maritime Silk Road, and India recently joined the SCO as an observer; as of late 2015, it was expected to become a member. The greatest threat to China within the region stems from Afghanistan. Although the country is a partner, the unrest there, its production of heroin, and its proximity to Xinjiang raises the specter of terrorism that Chinese leadership fears. Finally, within the region, Bhutan alone does not recognize China.

Drivers of Chinese Engagement

Chinese Activities in the Region Prior to 2000

The history of the four decades prior to 2000 is largely one of tensions and rivalry with India. After an initial decade of warm ties between Beijing and New Delhi during the 1950s, relations soured following the flight into exile of the Dalai Lama (after violence in Tibet in 1959), the spiritual leader of Tibetan Buddhism, and the two countries fought a brief border war in 1962. China became a key patron of India's nemesis, Pakistan, and backed Islamabad in a series of Indo-Pakistan conflicts, notably in 1965 and 1971. Nevertheless, since the 1980s, China has attempted a rapprochement with India with some success. Prime Minister Rajiv Gandhi visited Beijing is 1988—the first visit by an Indian head of government in more than thirty years. PRC Premier Li Peng visited New Delhi three years later—becoming the most senior Chinese official to step foot in India since Premier Zhou Enlai did so in 1960. The road has been bumpy but China-India relations have become more cordial, and Beijing has shifted to more neutral positions on issues between New Delhi and Islamabad. Border clashes and periodic tensions between India and Pakistan—including the Kargil Crisis of 1999, a limited war following Pakistan's incursion into the Kargil-Dras sector of disputed Jammu and Kashmir[2]—witnessed corresponding upsurges in tensions between China and India. China has provided considerable

[2] Ashley J. Tellis, C. Christine Fair, and Jamison Jo Medby, *Limited Conflicts Under the Nuclear Umbrella: Indian and Pakistani Lessons from the Kargil Crisis*, MR-1450-USCA, Santa Monica, Calif.: RAND Corporation, 2001.

military assistance to Pakistan, including helping to develop Islamabad's nuclear program (see Chapter 9). These tensions have become more dangerous, with both Pakistan and India conducting nuclear tests in May 1998 and becoming full-fledged nuclear powers.

Current Chinese Policy Toward the Region

Chinese Priorities and Policies

Since the 1990s China has expanded its South Asia policy well beyond simply India and Pakistan, paying more attention to other states in the region, including Bangladesh and Sri Lanka. China's broader economic interests necessitate taking a more comprehensive approach rather than perceiving South Asia only in terms of the India-Pakistan dyad. Although China has continued to align itself with Pakistan since 2000, it has also sought to stabilize relations with India and adopted a more equidistant approach on Indo-Pakistan issues, such as the dispute over Kashmir. Beijing's rivalry with New Delhi contains elements of cooperation as well as competition.[3] Despite this, Pakistan continues to be "the linchpin of China's South Asia policy."[4] China continues to maintain its very close ties with Pakistan for three overarching reasons:

1. To ensure China's internal stability
2. To balance against India
3. To defend China's burgeoning economic interests, including safeguarding trade and transportation routes, and protecting PRC citizens.

1. Ensuring China's Internal Stability. Pakistan is considered key for maintaining stability inside the PRC, especially in China's far west autonomous regions of Xinjiang and Tibet. Since 2000, China has faced an increasingly restive Uighur ethnic minority, of Turkic stock, approximately ten million strong concentrated in Xinjiang.[5] Islamabad

---

[3] T.V. Paul, ed., *The China-India Rivalry in the Globalization Era*, Washington, D.C.: Georgetown University Press, forthcoming, 2018.

[4] Scobell, Ratner, and Beckley, 2014, p. 62.

[5] See Gardner Bovingdon, *The Uyghurs: Strangers in Their Own Land*, New York: Columbia University Press, 2010, and Scobell, Ratner, and Beckley, 2014, pp. 10–12.

is considered a key capital to help Beijing deal with the challenge both in terms of cracking down on radical Islamic groups supporting and training Uighurs in Pakistan as well as helping to cast China as friend of the Muslim world. While Beijing has used extremely repressive tactics against Uighurs in recent years, it has worked hard to portray itself as a regime that is tolerant and indeed supportive of Muslims within the borders of the PRC.

Pakistan is also important to China because it is considered critical to stabilizing neighboring Afghanistan—a country that has become of growing concern to China as a source of terrorism and heroin. Since the early 1990s, China has viewed Afghanistan as the regional center of Islamic radicalism, which Beijing fears, if unchecked, can spread throughout Central Asia and spill over into Xinjiang. According to one prominent Chinese analyst, "Afghanistan is still a crucial focus for China" because terrorists remain active in that country, "Afghanistan remains the spiritual pillar" for radicals, and Afghanistan's "production and transaction of narcotics," provides "significant funds" for terrorists throughout the region.[6] Although there is no easy access from Afghanistan directly to China (the Wakhan Corridor is remote, the terrain is inhospitable, and infrastructure is nonexistent),[7] Pakistan provides better access to Xinjiang, and China complains that Uighur extremists have received weapons, explosives, and training in Pakistan.[8]

Pakistan has also long been important vis-à-vis Tibet because it serves as a massive distraction for India. The threat to the west meant that New Delhi could not focus greater attention on complicating matters for Beijing in the Himalayas.

---

[6] On the significance of Afghanistan, see Pan Guang, "The Role of a Multilateral Anti-Terror Mechanism in Central Asia," in Charles Hawkins and Robert R. Love, eds., *The New Great Game: Chinese Views on Central Asia*, Fort Leavenworth, Kan.: Foreign Military Studies Office, 2006, p. 113.

[7] See Michael Swaine, "China and the 'AfPak' Issue," *China Leadership Monitor*, No. 31, February 23, 2010, pp. 6–7. The Chinese have built some infrastructure for troops stationed near the border. See Russell Hsiao and Glen E. Howard, "China Builds Closer Ties to Afghanistan Through Wakhan Corridor," *China Brief*, Vol. 10, No. 1, January 7, 2010.

[8] For example, Brian Spegele, "China Points Finger at Pakistan Again," *Wall Street Journal*, March 8, 2012, p. 8.

2. Balancing Against India. Pakistan's greatest geostrategic value to China has been to offset India.[9] For Beijing, Islamabad has proved to be an invaluable friend in South Asia. This is especially because relations between Beijing and New Delhi have been tumultuous and prickly. While Beijing-New Delhi ties have improved noticeably, major problem areas persist—significant mutual distrust continues and border disputes remain unresolved. Pakistan is seen as an extremely important counterweight to India. India is the only state on the Asian landmass that compares with China in terms of size, population, economic potential, and military power. Geopolitically, it may be China's only long-term rival in Asia, since Japan appears weakened by economic malaise and an aging population, and Russia confronts severe demographic distress in addition to chronic economic and political problems.[10] In recent years, India has been the only state in the Asia-Pacific to rival China's economic growth rates, and, according to a United Nations Department of Economic and Social Affairs report, the South Asian giant is poised to surpass the PRC as the world's most populous country by approximately 2030.[11] The result is considerable wariness by Beijing of New Delhi's intentions and capabilities.[12] Thus, China's main geopolitical interest in its relationship with Pakistan is, as Stephen Cohen puts it, to pursue a "classic balance of power strategy," using Pakistan to confront India with a potential two-front war.[13] Nevertheless, there is a fundamental ambivalence about India's challenge to China in Beijing: India is not considered China's equal—

---

[9] This section draws upon Scobell, Ratner, and Beckley, 2014, p. 65.

[10] For a systematic comparison of China and India, see George J. Gilboy and Eric Heginbotham, *Chinese and Indian Strategic Behavior: Growing Power and Alarm*, New York: Cambridge University Press, 2012.

[11] United Nations Department of Economic and Social Affairs, *Population Challenges and Development Goals*, New York, 2005, p. 5.

[12] For a good overview of China-India relations, see Murray Scot Tanner, Kerry Dumbaugh, and Ian Easton, *Distracted Antagonists, Wary Partners: China and India Assess Their Security Relations*, Alexandria, Va.: Center for Naval Analyses, September 2011.

[13] Stephen P. Cohen, *The Future of Pakistan*, Washington, D.C.: Brookings Institution Press, 2011, p. 60.

either as a partner or adversary. Despite this, Beijing desires cordial relations and a modicum of cooperation with New Delhi, including in such multilateral forums as the BRICS and the SCO (India has been an observer in the latter and was admitted to membership in the SCO—along with Pakistan—in 2017).

3. Safeguarding Transportation and Economic Interests and Protecting PRC Citizens. While China views Pakistan as a valuable counterweight to India, Beijing has no interest in increased tensions or military conflict between Islamabad and New Delhi. A heightened state of tensions between India and Pakistan or a war—even a limited one—along the lines of the Kargil crisis of 1999 is something China would strongly prefer to avoid. China's strong preference is for stability in South Asia because turmoil on China's periphery is alarming for Beijing and very bad for business. A top priority for PRC leaders is robust economic growth for China and continued material prosperity for China's people. This is predicated upon unimpeded and flourishing economic interactions between China, its neighbors, and the wider world.

From China's perspective Pakistan has a key role to play both in sustaining stability and peace on the subcontinent and in actively advancing China's economic relations with the region and the world. Beijing seeks a government in Islamabad that can maintain order inside Pakistan and also help stabilize Afghanistan. China also wants Islamabad to get along with New Delhi and refrain from provocations, including supporting terrorist activity in India or elsewhere. But beyond this, Beijing has ambitious plans for Pakistan to play a central role in China's economic plans for South Asia—as a maritime and continental transportation and trading hub.

Along with increased economic activity beyond China's borders, growing numbers of Chinese citizens are traveling for temporary or extended business and leisure abroad. The challenge for Beijing is how to protect all these burgeoning overseas interests. China looks to Islamabad to help protect China's interests in Pakistan and in neighboring Afghanistan. There are an estimated 13,000 PRC citizens in Pakistan, and their safety has been increasingly precarious, including the threat of being kidnapped or killed.[14] The one episode that crystalized the problem for China and prompted Beijing to demand action from Pakistan was the Red Mosque incident of 2007, when PRC citizens were seized by Islamic radicals in the heart of Islamabad.[15]

Political Engagement

In the 2013 to 2015 period, China made 18 visits to South Asia at the level of head of state or head of government. Moreover, South Asia and Central Asia together receive more high-level visits from Chinese leaders than any other regions in the world. The distribution of visits, however, has been uneven. The most frequent destination was India, which received six such visits, and the frequency has continued to increase. The Maldives, Nepal, Pakistan, and Sri Lanka received three visits each. Bangladesh has received one head of government, in 2005, but also had a visit from the vice president in 2010 and the foreign minister in 2014. Afghanistan is not a regular stop for senior PRC leaders, but this does not mean that Beijing has ignored Kabul. China reopened its embassy in February 2002 following the overthrow of the Taliban, and PRC Foreign Minister Tang Jiaxuan visited Kabul in June 2002. As of late 2015, the most senior Beijing official to visit Afghanistan was then CCP Politburo Standing Committee Member Zhou Yongkang, who made a four-hour stopover in Kabul in September 2012. Moreover, Afghanistan leaders are regular visitors to Beijing—former president Hamid Karzai visited China five times during his tenure, and his successor Ashraf Ghani's first visit abroad as head of state was to Beijing in October 2014. Furthermore, Chinese and Afghan leaders also meet each other at venues such as the annual SCO heads of state summit.[16]

---

[14] Isaac B. Kardon, *China and Pakistan: Emerging Strains in the Entente Cordial Project 2049*, Washington, D.C.: Project 2049, 2011, pp. 14–16.

[15] Andrew Small, *The China-Pakistan Axis: Asia's New Geopolitics*, New York: Oxford University Press, 2015, preface.

[16] Andrew Scobell, "China Ponders Post-2014 Afghanistan: Neither 'All In' nor Bystander," *Asian Survey*, Vol. 55, No. 2, March-April 2015, pp. 328–329.

Diplomatic Relations and Presence

China maintains ambassador-level relations with diplomatic mission in all countries in South Asia with the exception of Bhutan. This bilateral relationship is unusual because of Bhutan's special status since 1947 as a protectorate of India. New Delhi handled all aspects of the kingdom's foreign relations until the 1970s when Bhutan became a member state of the UN. While China and Bhutan still do not have formal diplomatic ties, the two countries have held routine dialogues on matters of common interest since the 1980s.[17]

Pivotal State and Major Partners

For China, the pivotal state in South Asia is Pakistan. Underscoring this is the fact that it is the only country in the region to have a free trade agreement with China.[18] Pakistan is also an "all weather" strategic cooperative partner—the only country anywhere in the world that is so described by Beijing. That being said, China has not neglected other countries in the region. It has, for example, various forms of comprehensive cooperative partnerships with Nepal, the Maldives, and Bangladesh and is negotiating free trade agreements with both Sri Lanka[19] and the Maldives.[20] More broadly, India is a negotiating partner in the Regional Comprehensive Economic Partnership trade deal, which includes China, the ten ASEAN countries, Japan, Korea, Australia, and New Zealand. In addition, since 2005 China has been an observer of the South Asian Association for Regional Cooperation (SAARC). China holds one of nine SAARC observer seats, the others being held by Australia, Iran, Japan, the European Union, Myanmar, Mauritius, South Korea, and the United States.

---

[17] Garver, 2000, pp. 175–186. Thus, Bhutan is a sovereign state, unlike Sikkim, which was absorbed by India.

[18] "China-Pakistan FTA," Ministry of Commerce of the People's Republic of China, undated.

[19] "China-Sri Lanka FTA," Ministry of Commerce of the People's Republic of China, undated.

[20] "China-Maldives FTA," Ministry of Commerce of the People's Republic of China, undated.

India is by far the most powerful state in the region, whether economically, politically, or militarily. However, relations with China have historically been tense since a 1962 border war, and today, there remain many outstanding issues, including competing claims to Aksai Chin and Arunachal Pradesh. Despite this, China maintains a strategic cooperative partnership with India, just as it does formally with Afghanistan and Sri Lanka. China and India investigated the possibility of establishing a regional trading arrangement and established a Joint Study Group to consider the issue. The group rendered its report in 2007, arguing that such an arrangement would be mutually advantageous, but there has since then been little follow-up.[21]

High-Level Exchanges

Of particular note were high profile visits by top Chinese leaders to India, Pakistan, the Maldives, and Sri Lanka, all since 2012. PRC Premier Li Keqiang visited India and Pakistan in May 2013. Li's visit to New Delhi was clouded by an incident on the disputed Sino-Indian border. Earlier in the year a small detachment of Chinese troops reportedly crossed into remote territory controlled by India, pitched tents, and remained encamped for weeks even after being discovered by Indian forces. The Chinese troops withdrew just prior to Li Keqiang's visit. Beijing's message appeared to be that it desires cooperation with New Delhi but China is in no mood to compromise or make concessions to India in the on-again off-again border talks. In September 2014 PRC President Xi Jinping paid a state visit to New Delhi in an effort to maintain cordial relations with a key rival on the subcontinent. Xi's visit occurred a week after an extended incursion by several hundred PLA troops into disputed territory in a remote western portion of the Sino-Indian Himalayan frontier.[22]

India was the third stop in a 2014 regional trip that also took Xi to the Maldives and Sri Lanka—the latter both strategic locations in

---

[21] "China-India Regional Trade Arrangement Joint Feasibility Study," Ministry of Commerce of the People's Republic of China, undated.

[22] Jason Burke and Tania Branigan, "India-China Border Standoff Highlights Tensions Before Xi's Visit," *The Guardian*, September 16, 2014.

the Indian Ocean. In the Maldives, the Chinese president signed agreements on infrastructure projects, including one to construct a bridge linking the capital with the country's international airport. By visiting Sri Lanka, Xi became the first PRC head of state in three decades to set foot in that country. There he discussed economic issues, including the negotiation of a free trade agreement. Most recently, in April 2015, Xi paid a state visit to Islamabad where he emphasized Beijing's continued commitment to Pakistan with the announcement of China's intent to invest $46 billion in infrastructure projects in the country.

Cultural Influence

China currently has established eight Confucius Institutes across six countries in South Asia. India and Pakistan have two each. Afghanistan, Bangladesh, Nepal, and Sri Lanka each have a single institute. The small states of Bhutan and Maldives do not possess any Confucius Institutes. Overall, China's cultural influence in South Asia is weak. This reality is highlighted by the fact that cultural influence has tended to flow in the other direction. Arguably, South Asia's most important export to China over the centuries was cultural—Buddhism traveled northward into China. In the twenty-first century, it is perhaps not surprising that Beijing seems most worried about the penetration into China from South Asia of religious influences—radical Islam via Afghanistan and Pakistan and Tibetan Buddhism via the Tibetan Government-in-Exile headquartered in Dharamsala, India.

In general, the estimates of Chinese citizens in South Asia suggest low numbers. These include fewer than 10,000 in Pakistan[23] and India,[24] each. We believe these figures to be low, however. Other estimates place the number in Bangladesh much higher.[25]

---

[23] Zahid Gishkori, "Economic Corridor: 12,000-Strong Force to Guard Chinese Workers," *The Express Tribune*, March 30, 2015.

[24] Megha Mandavia, "Why India Remains a Difficult Terrain for 7,000 Chinese Expatriates Living in the Country," *The Economic Times*, August 31, 2015.

[25] A source of which the accuracy we cannot fully assess reports that 168,000 Chinese reside in Bangladesh. See "1 Nian You 16 Wan Duo Zhongguo Renmin 'Yimin' Mengjiala? Hai Zheng You Ke Neng" ["160,000 Chinese 'Immigrating' to Bangladesh in a Year? It Actually Is a Possibility"], *Aboluowang*, October 16, 2016.

Economic Engagement

Despite its large population, South Asia as a whole does not play a large role in China's international economic engagement. However, this may change. During an April 2015 visit to Pakistan, PRC President Xi Jinping announced that China intended to invest $46 billion in the country to fund various infrastructure projects, including overland and maritime as part of a China-Pakistan Economic Corridor (CPEC).[26] If China's investment plans for Pakistan succeed, if RCEP negotiations succeed, and if China's Maritime Silk Road plans are carried out, then South Asia will have stronger links to China. But it will also have stronger links to the rest of the world, as will the rest of the world with it, enabling greater economic exchange beyond China.

Trade

India is by far China's largest trading partner in the region and is both its largest source of imports and its largest export destination. Indeed, China's two-way trade with India now dwarfs that with Pakistan. Between 2000 and 2013, Sino-Indian two-way trade jumped 22-fold to $65 billion. In contrast, Sino-Pakistani two-way trade has increased very slowly over the same period, to reach a modest $14 billion in 2013.

Unlike most other developing regions, China's imports from South Asia include a high proportion of manufactured goods (Figure 6.2). This is largely due to India, which exports mainly manufactured goods to China. Most other South Asian countries export raw materials. During the commodities boom of the mid-2000s, the share of commodities in imports rose dramatically, but the commodity mix has returned to what it had been at the beginning of the 2000s.

Along the lines of China's exports to other regions, China's exports to South Asia are almost completely manufactured items of various types, including machinery and transportation equipment (39 percent in 2013), manufactured goods (27 percent), chemicals (17 percent), and miscellaneous manufactured items (14 percent) for a

---

[26] Louis Ritzinger, "The China-Pakistan Economic Corridor: Regional Dynamics and China's Geopolitical Ambitions," *Commentary*, Seattle, Wash.: National Bureau of Asian Research, August 5, 2015.

Figure 6.2
Composition of Imports from South Asia

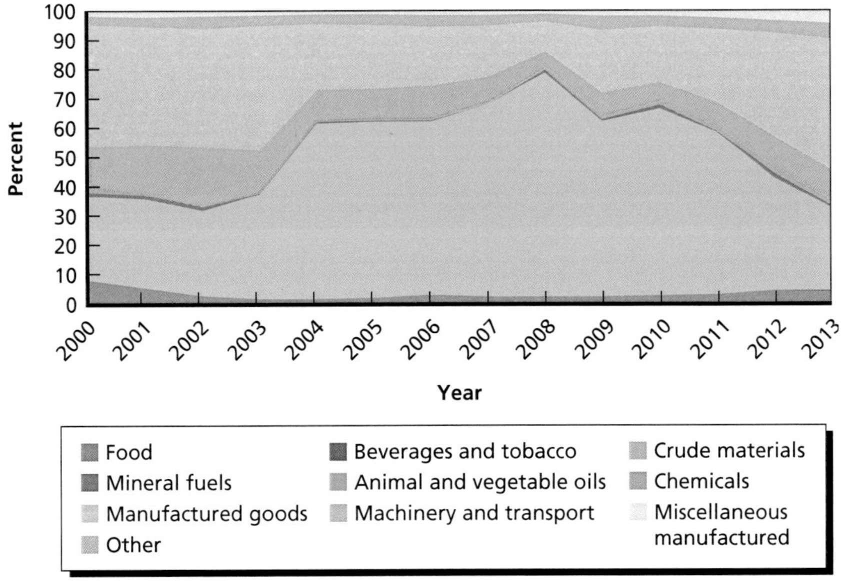

Percent: 0, 10, 20, 30, 40, 50, 60, 70, 80, 90, 100
Year: 2000, 2001, 2002, 2003, 2004, 2005, 2006, 2007, 2008, 2009, 2010, 2011, 2012, 2013

Food; Beverages and tobacco; Crude materials; Mineral fuels; Animal and vegetable oils; Chemicals; Manufactured goods; Machinery and transport; Miscellaneous manufactured; Other

SOURCE: UN Comtrade Database.
RAND *RR2273A-6.2*

total of 97 percent (Figure 6.3). This has been consistent through time, although the share of machinery and transportation equipment exports has risen dramatically.

South Asia has had a large trade deficit with China, which has only expanded over the 2000 to 2013 time period (Figure 6.4). China is in surplus with all South Asian countries, but the South Asia trade deficit is driven mainly by India, which in 2013 recorded a trade deficit of almost $30 billion.

Foreign Direct Investment and Lending

There has been a buildup of the stock of China's FDI in South Asia since 2003 (Figure 6.5). In 2003, China had only $45 million in FDI stock in South Asia. By 2012, this was more than $4 billion—an increase of almost 100-fold. In contrast to trade flows, much of this increase in investment has been to Pakistan, which in 2012 had more

Figure 6.3
Composition of Exports to South Asia

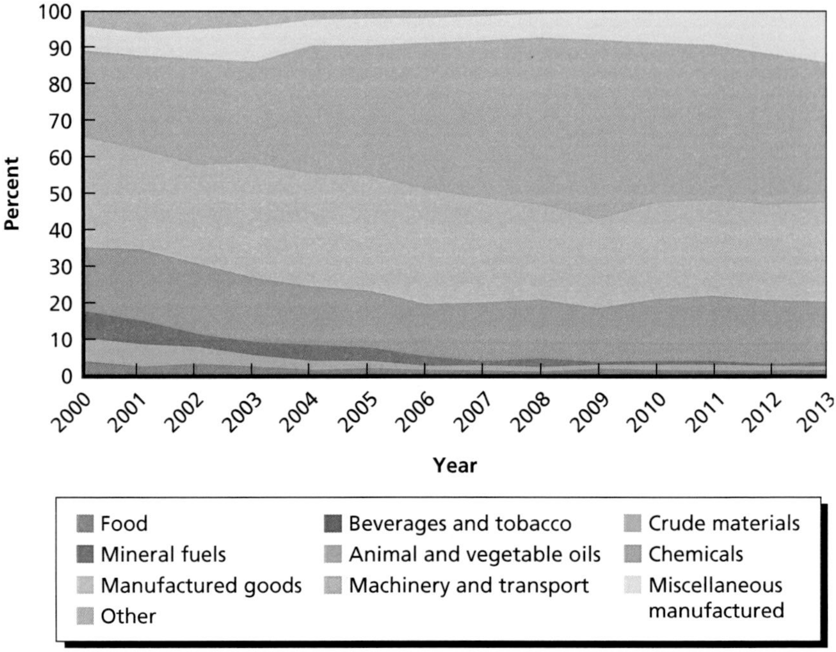

SOURCE: UN Comtrade Database.
RAND *RR2273A-6.3*

than $2 billion in Chinese FDI stock. Despite the much larger size of India's economy, there is very little investment by China in that country—hardly more than $1 billion in 2012. By comparison Chinese corporations have made substantial investments in Afghanistan. In 2007 a consortium of two Chinese companies successfully won a contract to develop the Aynak Copper Mine 35 miles from Kabul, reportedly agreeing to invest more than $4 billion. Four years later another Chinese corporation won the rights to look for oil in northwestern Afghanistan.[27] Certainly, not all of this has been invested. But by 2012, China had FDI stock of $483 million in Afghanistan.

---

[27] Erica Downs, "China Buys into Afghanistan," *SAIS Review*, Vol. 32, No. 2, Summer-Fall 2012, pp. 56–72.

Figure 6.4
Level of Exports to and Imports from South Asia

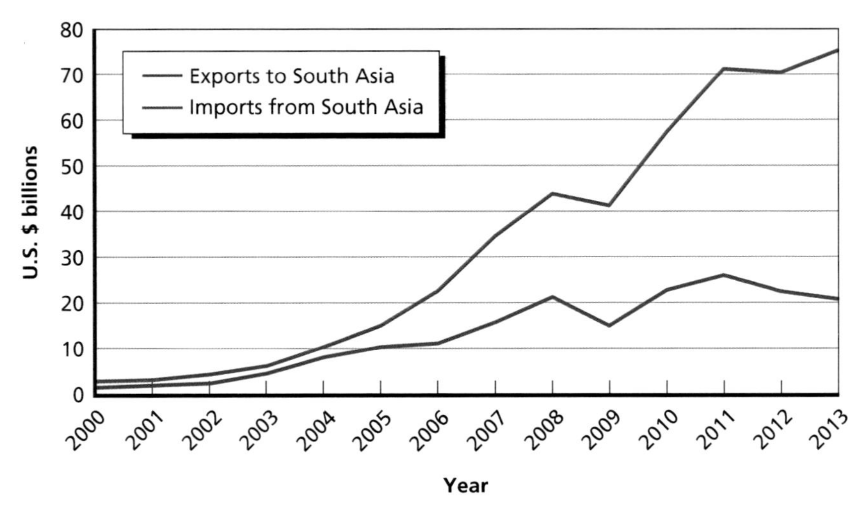

SOURCE: UNCTAD.
RAND *RR2273A-6.4*

Figure 6.5
China's FDI Stock in South Asia by Receiving Country

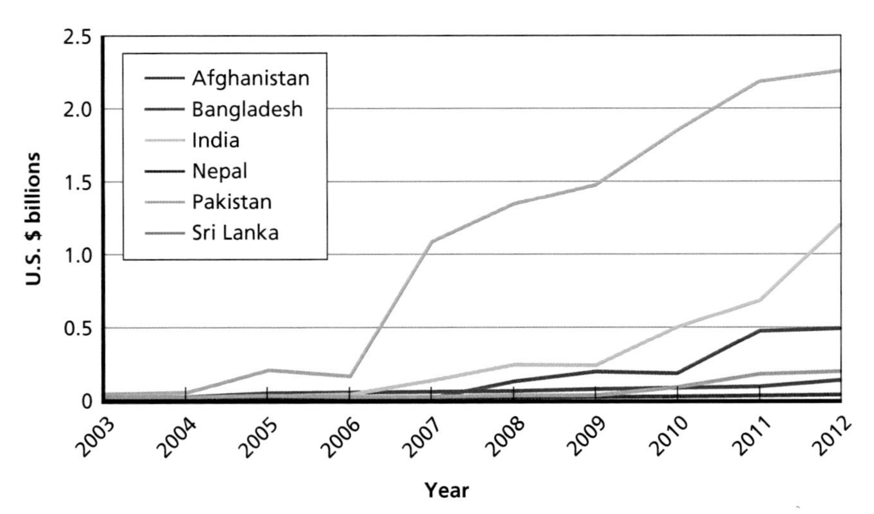

SOURCE: UNCTAD.
RAND *RR2273A-6.5*

Agreements and Other Issues

China has BITs with half the countries in South Asia. It negotiated BITs in the 1980s with Pakistan and Sri Lanka, and then Bangladesh in the mid-1990s. Emblematic of China's recent reaching out to India, the two countries negotiated their BIT in 2006; it entered into force in 2007. China has five tax treaties—covering either income only or income and capital. Pakistan was the first, in 1989, but India came soon after, in 1994. Others include Bangladesh, Nepal, and Sri Lanka.

China is exploring the possibility of a free trade agreement with India.[28] But even before that, China and India were both negotiating partners in the RCEP. Although there had been hope of completing negotiations before the end of 2015, negotiations have continued well beyond that date. No South Asian countries are partners with the United States in the TPP, signed in October 2015.

While China has focused on Belt and Road, of which it pictures India being part, India has countered this with Project Mausam, aimed at making India the dominant trade force in the Indian Ocean region. These competitive initiatives are manifestations of the rivalry between China and India. Such efforts do not automatically put Beijing and New Delhi at loggerheads; indeed, these projects can be justifications for greater cooperation. However, of the two, China's Belt and Road Initiative is far more ambitious and is already a work in progress.

China's vision is to link the port of Gwadar in Pakistan to Xinjiang with roads, railways, and an oil pipeline.[29] Pakistan has drawn up plans to build a railway between Havelian, a Pakistani city close to Islamabad, and Kashgar in Xinjiang. This railway would roughly parallel the Karakoram highway. In 2006, Pakistan awarded a $1.2 million contract to an international consortium to carry out a feasibility study for establishing this rail link, but so far no plans have been finalized to begin construction. In 2006, the Pakistani government presented

---

[28] "China FTA Network," Ministry of Commerce of the People's Republic of China, webpage, undated.

[29] These three paragraphs are drawn from Scobell, Ratner, and Beckley, 2014, pp. 73–75.

plans for a 3,300 km oil pipeline between Gwadar and Kashgar costing an estimated at $4.5 billion to $5 billion.[30] And then in April 2015, PRC President Xi Jinping announced the intention to fund $46 billion worth of CPEC projects.

Beijing is especially concerned about energy security, especially where petroleum is concerned. China has been a net importer of oil since 1993, and the overwhelming majority of this petroleum from overseas arrives in the PRC via Southeast Asia. The CPEC is an effort to diversify the routes. Nevertheless, China is likely to continue to rely heavily on the sea-lanes to supply its external energy needs. To improve security in the Indian Ocean China has adopted what one U.S. consulting firm dubbed a "String of Pearls" strategy working to establish a network of port facilities in countries around the Indian Ocean region.[31]

A key element in this strategy is developing Pakistan's port of Gwadar, a remote fishing village some 50 miles from the Iranian border and approximately 300 miles from the Strait of Hormuz. The port was reportedly leased by a Chinese company.[32] Gwadar was reported to be 11.5 meters deep, enough to accommodate submarines and aircraft carriers, and as of late 2015 could already function as a "listening post" to monitor U.S. naval activity in the Indian Ocean and Persian Gulf.[33] China also reportedly sent 450 engineers to provide technical expertise and committed $200 million to build a 725 km highway connecting

---

[30] For an overview of these developments, see Vijay Sakhuja, "The Karakoram Corridor: China's Transportation Networks in Pakistan," *China Brief*, Vol. 10, No. 20, October 8, 2010, pp. 5–7; Fazal-ur-Rahman, "Prospects of Pakistan Becoming a Trade and Energy Corridor for China," *Strategic Studies*, Vol. 28, No. 2, Summer 2007.

[31] Juli A. MacDonald, Amy Donahue, and Bethany Danyluk. *Energy Futures in Asia*, McLean, Virginia: Booz Allen Hamilton, 2004. The term was actually suggested by two Indian participants at a workshop. See also Christopher Pehrson, *String of Pearls: Meeting the Challenge of China's Growing Power Across the Asian Littoral*, Carlisle Barracks, Pa.: U.S. Army War College Strategic Studies Institute, 2006. These ports, including Gwadar, have everyday economic value and, in the event of a conflict, considerable military value.

[32] Summer Zhen, "Chinese Firm Takes Control of Gwadar Port Free-Trade Zone in Pakistan," *South China Morning Post*, November 11, 2015.

[33] On the current depth, see Li Xuanmin, "Gwadar Port Benefit to China Limited," *The Global Times*, November 23, 2016.

Gwadar with Pakistan's largest city, Karachi, which is itself connected to the northern Pakistan via railway.[34]

Military and Security Engagement

This section presents a brief overview of Chinese military engagement activities as an instrument of Chinese foreign and security policy in South Asia. It examines Chinese arms sales, military diplomacy, joint exercises, and port visits, as well as Chinese participation in UNPKOs and PLA MOOTW activities.

PRC Arms Sales

Since 2000, China has been a key supplier of major conventional weapons to South Asia, especially Pakistan and Bangladesh. Arms sales to these two countries alone comprised over half of China's total arms sales from 2000 to 2014, with Pakistan accounting for 42 percent and Bangladesh 11 percent, thus helping China to supplant Germany as the world's third-largest arms exporter. Chinese arms sales to South Asia appear to be increasing and have exceeded U.S. arms sales to the region (although U.S. arms sales also appear to be increasing). While arms transfers from China have made up roughly half of Pakistan's total arms imports since 2009, China has supplied approximately three-quarters of Bangladesh's arms imports since 2006 (in years where Bangladesh purchased arms), making China the primary supplier of arms to both countries in recent years. Probably the most notable Chinese sale to South Asia was the sale of JF-17 fighters to Pakistan followed by an agreement to build the jets in Pakistan as part of a Sino-Pakistani joint venture: the Pakistan Aeronautical Complex/Chengdu Aerospace Corporation.[35]

PLA Military Diplomacy

Between 2004 and 2014, CMC members made 11 visits to five countries in the region. Pakistan and India received three visits each (Table 6.1).

---

[34] Pehrson, 2006, p. 4, and Sudha Ramachandran, "China's Pearl in Pakistan's Waters," *Asia Times Online*, March 4, 2005.

[35] See, for example, Franz-Stefan Gady, "Déjà Vu: Pakistan and Nigeria to Sign JF-17 Fighter Jet Deal in November," *The Diplomat*, September 19, 2016.

Other destinations for such high-level visits were Nepal and Sri Lanka. There were no high-level military visits to Afghanistan, Bhutan (with which China has no official relations), or the Maldives.

One important example of Chinese military diplomacy in South Asia is Sri Lanka, a country in which many analysts view China as

Table 6.1
Chinese High-Level Military Visits to South Asia, 2003–2014

Year of Visit	Country Visited	CMC Member	Foreign Counterparts	Summits
2004	Pakistan	Cao Gangchuan, CMC Vice Chair/DM	PM Zafarullah Khan Jamali; DM Rao Sikander	
2004	India	Cao Gangchuan, CMC Vice Chair/DM	PM Atal Bihari Vajpayee; DM George Fernandes	
2005	India	Liang Guanglie, CGS	DM Pranab Mukherjee; NSA M. K. Narayanan	
2007	Bangladesh	Chen Bingde	Pres. Iajuddin Ahmed; Naval Chief Sarwar Jahan Nizam; Army and Air Force Chiefs	
2010	Pakistan	Liang Guanglie, DM	DM Chaudhry Ahmad Mukhtar	
2011	Nepal	Chen Bingde	Chief of Staff of Army Chhatra Man Singh Gurung; PM Jhalanath Khanal; Pres. Ram Baran Yadav	
2012	Sri Lanka	Liang Guanglie, DM	Pres. Mahinda Rajapaksa; DM Gotabaya Rajapaksa	First Chinese defense minister visit to Sri Lanka
2012	India	Liang Guanglie, DM	PM Manmohan Singh; DM A. K. Antony	
2014	Pakistan	Chang Wanquan, DM	Pres. Mamnoon Hussain; PM Nawaz Sharif; DM Khawaja Asif	
2014	Sri Lanka	Xu Qiliang, Vice Chair CMC	Pres. Mahinda Rajapaksa	
2014	Bangladesh	Xu Qiliang, Vice Chair CMC	Pres. Abdul Hamid; PM Sheikh Hasina	

attempting to make inroads despite India's traditional influence.[36] In August 2012 to September 2012, Chinese Defense Minister Liang Guanglie visited Sri Lanka on the way to India. This was the first ever visit to Sri Lanka by a Chinese defense minister.[37] Following Liang's groundbreaking visit, in May 2014, CMC Vice Chair Xu Qiliang visited Colombo, where he met with Sri Lanka President Mahinda Rajapaksa as well as the head of Sri Lanka's Ministry of Defense and several high-ranking officers from Sri Lanka's armed forces.[38] Highlighting the linkage between China's high-level military exchanges and its overall diplomacy in the region, Xu's visit preceded President Xi Jinping's September 2014 state visit to Colombo, during which Xi and Rajapaksa promised to strengthen the two countries' strategic cooperative partnership.[39] Sri Lanka followed up with a high-level defense delegation visit to Beijing later in September, during which Xu and Sri Lanka's defense secretary pledged to strengthen cooperation and enhance military-to-military ties.[40]

Combined Exercises

China has held a number of combined exercises in South Asia in recent years, including with Pakistan, India, and Sri Lanka (Table 6.2). Many of these exercises have focused on counterterrorism operations.

Chinese combined field exercises tend to be small scale, relatively few in number, and infrequent. They are purposefully selected and are

---

[36] China's approach may prove much more challenging following the recent leadership change in Colombo. See, for example, Ellen Barry, "New President in Sri Lanka Puts China's Plans in Check," *New York Times*, January 9, 2015.

[37] During Liang's visit, he met with Sir Lankan President Rajapaksa and Sri Lanka's defense secretary. In addition, the two sides announced plans for China to provide development assistance for an academic building complex for the Sri Lanka Military Academy. See "General Liang Guanglie Calls on Secretary [of] Defence," Ministry of Defense, Sri Lanka, August 31, 2012.

[38] Guo Renjie, "Sri Lanka President Meets with Xu Qiliang," *China Military Online*, May 19, 2015.

[39] Dharisha Bastians and Gardiner Harris, "Chinese Leader Visits Sri Lanka, Challenging India's Sway," *New York Times*, September 16, 2014.

[40] See "China, Sri Lanka Pledge Military Cooperation," *Xinhua News*, September 23, 2014.

Table 6.2
Selected Chinese Combined Exercises in South Asia, 2002–2014

Year	Name of Exercise	Partner(s)	Exercise Content
2003	Dolphin 0311	India	Naval search and rescue
2003	Dolphin 0310	Pakistan	Naval search and rescue
2004	Friendship 2004	Pakistan	Counterterrorism
2004	China-India Mountaineering Training	India	
2005	China-India Friendship	India	Naval search and rescue
2005	China-Pakistan Friendship	Pakistan	Naval search and rescue
2006	Friendship 2006	Pakistan	Counterterrorism
2007	Aman 2007	Pakistan; Others	Maritime counterterrorism
2007	Hand-in-Hand 2007	India	Counterterrorism
2007	2nd Western Pacific Naval Forum	India; Pakistan; Others	Maritime
2008	Hand-in-Hand 2008	India	Counterterrorism
2009	Aman 2009	Pakistan; Others	Maritime security
2010	Friendship 2010	Pakistan	Counterterrorism
2011	Shaheen I	Pakistan	Air Force training
2011	Aman 2011	Pakistan; Others	Maritime anti-piracy
2011	Friendship 2011	Pakistan	Counterterrorism
2012	Cormorant Strike 2012	Sri Lanka	Special operations
2013	[Unknown]	Pakistan	Counterterrorism
2013	Aman 2013	Pakistan; Others	Maritime counter-terrorism, anti-submarine warfare, anti-piracy, and search and rescue
2013	Shaheen II	Pakistan	Air Force training
2013	Hand-in-Hand 2013	India	Counterterrorism
2014	Peace Angel 2014	Pakistan	Medical drill
2014	Shaheen III	Pakistan	Air force training
2014	Hand-in-Hand 2014	India	Counterterrorism

SOURCE: Department of Defense China Military Power Report and Chinese Ministry of Defense website.

NOTE: China did not begin engaging in combined exercises with foreign militaries until 2002.

important indicators of China's interests and intentions. It is significant that from 2002 to 2014, two-thirds of all the exercises China conducted with South Asian states (16 of 24) were with one country: Pakistan. From Beijing's perspective, the security relationship with Islamabad is quasi-alliance in nature. But it is also noteworthy that during the same period China has held five field exercises with India, suggesting Beijing does not want its close ties with Islamabad to come at the expense of a confrontational relationship with New Delhi. China has not held any military exercises with Bangladesh.

PLAN Port Visits

From 2000 through 2014, China conducted 18 port visits to countries in this region. Of note, 17 of the 18 total port visits, including nine associated with Chinese anti-piracy task forces conducting escort missions in the Gulf of Aden and five port visits by the PLAN's hospital ship, took place from 2009 to 2014, representing a major increase in China's naval activity in the region in the years since it began conducting anti-piracy operations in the Gulf of Aden. The most notable and probably most controversial Chinese port calls in the region were a pair of PLAN submarine port calls in Colombo, Sri Lanka, in 2014. China made headlines throughout the region when a PLAN Type 039 Song-class conventional submarine and the PLAN's *Changxing Dao* submarine support ship visited Colombo, Sri Lanka, in September 2014 on the way to participate in counter-piracy operations in the Gulf of Aden. The same submarine visited Colombo again in October–November 2014 on the way back to China. The September 2014 port call was the first PLAN submarine foreign port visit, reportedly marking the second instance of a PLAN submarine operating in the Indian Ocean.[41] Sri Lanka called it a routine "good-will visit," but it exacer-

---

[41] The first PLAN submarine to operate in the Indian Ocean was a Type 093 SSN that operated in the Indian Ocean from December 2013–February 2014. China notified India and several other countries in advance of that deployment. See Felix K. Chan, "Chinese Submarines and Indian ASW in the Indian Ocean," *Geopolitcus*, November 24, 2014.

bated India's concerns about Chinese naval operations in the Indian Ocean.[42]

UN Peacekeeping Operations

There is no Chinese participation in UN peacekeeping operations in South Asia at this time. The only UNPKO in the region is the United Nations Military Observer Group in India and Pakistan (UNMOGIP)—in the disputed territory of Jammu and Kashmir—and China is not among the participant nations.

Military Operations Other than War

Chinese military operations other than war activities are also an important aspect of Chinese military engagement in South Asia. For example, the PLA played a prominent role when China provided disaster relief to Nepal following the devastating earthquake that killed thousands of people and caused massive damage in Kathmandu and other parts of the mountainous country in April 2015. Within days, China dispatched four PLAAF Il-76 transport aircraft[43] along with two teams of PLA relief personnel and specialized rescue equipment to aid in the search for survivors.[44] Some analysts in the region see Nepal as a strategically important country where China and India are increasingly competing for influence diplomatically and economically,[45] suggesting that, in addition to humanitarian concerns, China likely intended its support to signal its commitment to Nepal in the aftermath of the disaster.

---

[42] For more on the submarine visiting Sri Lanka, see "PLA Navy Submarine Visits Sri Lanka," *China Military Online*, September 24, 2014; "Sri Lanka Allows Chinese Submarine to Dock," *China Daily*, November 3, 2014; "China Says Its Submarine Docked in Sri Lanka 'for Replenishment,'" *The Hindu*, November 28, 2014.

[43] "Four Chinese Military Aircraft to Join Nepal Earthquake Relief," *China Military Online*, April 27, 2015.

[44] Chinese media highlighted the team's experience participating in other earthquake relief operations in recent years, including in the aftermath of major earthquakes in Sichuan and Yunnan Provinces. See "Chinese Army Rescuers Leave for Nepal After Quake," *Xinhua*, April 27, 2015.

[45] See, for example, Natalie Obiko Pearson, Sandrine Rastello, and David Tween, "Nepal Has Powerful Friends in High Places: India and China," *Bloomberg*, April 27, 2015.

Conclusion

In the twenty-first century, China's national priority is economic development and therefore Beijing has no interest in a state of heightened tensions or conflict in South Asia. Moreover, China foreign economic goals have become more ambitious under the leadership of Xi Jinping, and the region is an integral part of these plans. More notably, China's Belt and Road Initiative entails multiple overland routes through South Asia, and Southeast Asia lanes through the Indian Ocean. This vision builds on existing Chinese efforts to develop roads, railways, and pipelines across mountain ranges and through jungles and to build ports and facilities around the rim of the Indian Ocean.

Nevertheless, there are elements of continuity in China's policy toward South Asia with pre-2000 and Cold War eras. These include alarm over internal dangers to domestic stability combining with significant external challenges, which threatens to undermine CCP rule and split China apart. The persistent traditional security threat has been India, while a more recent nontraditional security threat has emerged—terrorism in the form of Islamic extremism. India, regarded as China's long-term geostrategic rival in South Asia, poses a more significant challenge if it aligns with the global hegemon, the United States. Moreover, India also poses a threat to Chinese territorial integrity and national unity through its territorial claims in the Himalayas and its tacit support for the Tibetan Government-in-Exile. Despite enduring Sino-Indian tensions, "because so many sources of dispute exist between China and India, both sides have come to recognize the need to prevent these tensions from leading to costly overt rivalry," the result is what one U.S. scholar dubs "quiet competition."[46]

China's continuity and change in policy toward South Asia come together in one partner: Pakistan. Islamabad continues to be seen as the key to countering New Delhi, especially as India grows stronger economically and more powerful militarily. And while India has sig-

---

[46] Mark W. Frazier, "Quiet Competition and the Future of Sino-Indian Relations," in Francine R. Frankel and Harry Harding, eds., *The India-China Relationship: What the United States Needs to Know*, New York: Columbia University Press, 2004, p. 295.

naled an interest in maintaining cordial relations with China, it has also indicated a desire to improve security and economic relations with other states, including the United States and its allies. Beijing perceives these developments as threatening. As the most powerful and sprawling state in South Asia, India not only dominants the subcontinent but also straddles the Indian Ocean. Chinese observers worry about India's dominant position astride China's most important oil routes and Chinese naval and maritime affairs publications closely track Indian naval developments.[47] And yet, China sees its rivalry with India as one that can and should be managed in the near to medium term.[48]

Implications for the United States

For Beijing, South Asia is only likely to become more important and China is only likely to become more active in the region. These trends raise the prospect of both cooperation and conflict. Rising tensions between China and India are certainly possible but so is greater cooperation to counter nontraditional security threats and protect the global commons. The Indian Ocean, for example could become a venue for greater cooperation or conflict.[49] At least some Chinese analysts argue that China should seek international cooperation to manage the security of the Southeast Asia lines of communication in the Indian Ocean because China is not strong enough to secure them itself.[50]

In a cooperative future trajectory for South Asia, Pakistan is likely to continue to be an important partner for China. However, in a more conflictual future for the region, Pakistan takes on even greater importance to China. Pakistan's political stability and national unity is crucial to China, not only to ensure that Islamabad remains a counterweight to

---

[47] Scobell, Ratner, and Beckley, 2014, p. 73.

[48] Frazier, 2004.

[49] For research highlighting the potential for increased maritime tensions, see Geoffrey Till, *Asia's Naval Expansion: An Arms Race in the Making?* London: International Institute for Strategic Studies, 2012. For research that provides a more balanced approach outlining both the prospects for cooperation and conflict, see John Garofano and Andrea J. Dew, eds., *Deep Currents and Rising Tides: The Indian Ocean and International Security*, Washington, D.C.: Georgetown University Press, 2013.

[50] Scobell, Ratner, and Beckley, 2014, p. 76.

India but also because, as an Islamic state and nuclear power its instability or disintegration would send shockwaves cascading far and wide. Moreover, severe upheaval or cataclysmic violence in Pakistan almost certainly will spill over into Afghanistan (and China). Beijing considers Afghanistan to be the terrorist epicenter of Central Asia and fears an overflow of Islamic extremism into neighboring states, including China.

While U.S. intervention in Afghanistan in late 2001 and subsequent persistent U.S. military presence in Afghanistan made China uneasy, Beijing is worried that an American drawdown will create a power vacuum and facilitate the return of the Taliban to power in Kabul. Therefore, there is the possibility of greater Chinese involvement in Afghanistan. This has already been seen in a modest manner diplomatically, but there is also potential for greater security involvement. China is unlikely to step up its involvement unilaterally; rather it would almost certainly require cooperation with Pakistan and might include coordination with other powers, including the United States.[51] Therefore, greater counterterrorism cooperation with China vis-a-vis Afghanistan and Pakistan is possible, although the potential is rather modest. The CPEC is likely to encounter difficulties and delays but Pakistan's seaports are certain to remain strategically and economically valuable for China.

The narrative in recent years about China establishing a "string of pearls" in the Indian Ocean is overhyped. Nevertheless, if conceived of as a network of ports of call for a range of PRC civilian and military vessels, from merchant ships to oil tankers to PLAN warships, then the "string" is more mundane but still significant. In particular, the new port facility at Gwadar is a useful "pearl" for Chinese commercial or military vessels. But even if China were to turn Gwadar into a naval base, it would likely not undermine American and Indian dominance of the Indian Ocean. India's navy has seven bases and three listening posts along the shores of the Indian Ocean, and the U.S. Navy maintains a large presence at Diego Garcia.[52]

---

[51] For more discussion and analysis, see Scobell, 2015.

[52] For more discussion, see Scobell, Ratner, and Beckley, 2014, p. 77.

CHAPTER SEVEN

China in the Middle East

The Middle East is the Developing World region of greatest growing importance to China outside of its Asia-Pacific neighborhood. The Middle East is geographically well beyond China's immediate neighborhood and made up a modest 6.3 percent of total Chinese goods trade with the world in 2013, although this was almost double the 2000 share. Nevertheless, the Middle East is important to China's Belt and Road Initiative, the flagship foreign policy initiative of PRC President Xi Jinping. Chinese involvement in the Middle East has expanded in recent decades and China is now an important presence in the region. In 2015 Beijing had significant interests in the Middle East and was grappling with how best to protect these. While keen to increase its influence, China is wary of escalating its involvement in the region and reluctant to enhance its commitments in the Middle East for fear of becoming ensnared in regional tensions and upheaval.[1] At the same time, it is aware of new opportunities, as suggested by a visit to Iran by PLA Deputy Chief of Staff Admiral Sun Jianguo in October 2015, during which Sun said China wants to deepen cooperation and "exchange views with Iran on bilateral military ties."[2]

---

[1] Andrew Scobell and Alireza Nader, *China in the Middle East: The Wary Dragon*, Santa Monica, Calif.: RAND Corporation, RR-1229-A, 2016.

[2] "China Said to Seek Deeper Military Ties with Iran," Radio Free Europe/Radio Liberty, October 15, 2015.

Key Chinese Activities in the Region

China is not seeking to challenge or confront the United States in the Middle East. Economics and trade have been the main focus of Beijing's engagement with the region, and the Middle East is an important source of energy (petroleum) for China. After Iraq opened its oilfields to outside operators starting in the late 2000s and held four bid rounds for 11 oil field and three gas field technical service contracts, China became a foreign partner in five oil fields.[3] China also exports machinery and consumer goods to the region and is investing in infrastructure and telecommunications.

Nevertheless, since the end of the Cold War, geopolitical considerations have played a greater role in Chinese engagement with the Middle East. China seeks to strengthen its relations with developing countries and increase its influence in a pivotal part of the world. Beijing cultivates the support of Middle Eastern capitals for policies China favors in key forums such as the UN Indeed, Beijing has worked hard to maintain good relations with all states in the region, and as of 2015, China was the only major power in the world to enjoy cordial relations with every country or governing authority in the Middle East, including Iran, Israel, Saudi Arabia, and the Palestinian Authority. Beijing views Iran and Saudi Arabia as its most important regional partners (Figure 7.1). Other major partners in the region include Egypt, Israel, and members of the Gulf Cooperation Council (GCC).

Drivers of Chinese Engagement

Chinese Activities in the Region Prior to 2000

In the Cold War era, Beijing felt largely closed out of the Middle East as Washington and Moscow fought for influence and power via regional proxy forces. Moreover, until the 1980s, the PRC's Chinese rival, the Republic of China on Taiwan, continued to be the one China diplo-

[3] U.S. Energy Information Administration, "Country Analysis Brief: Iraq," U.S. Department of Energy, January 30, 2015.

Figure 7.1
China's Relations with Countries in the Middle East, 2015

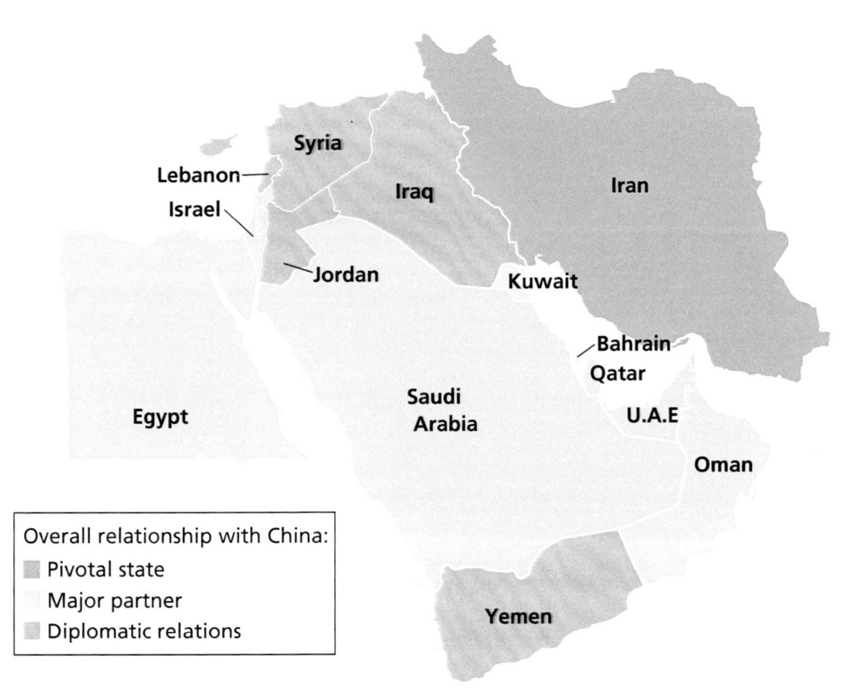

NOTE: Due to small scale of map, not all entities are displayed and labeled.
RAND *RR2273A-7.1*

matically recognized by many states in the region. Until the 1990s, the PRC was almost completely absent from the Middle East economically and militarily with the exception of serving as a supplier of bargain-priced or hard-to-get weaponry for states such as Iraq, Iran, and Saudi Arabia.[4]

In the months following the June 1989 Tiananmen Massacre, the Middle East leapt to prominence for China as Western capitals ostracized Beijing and imposed sanctions. China reached out to developing countries to counter the cold shoulder from developed states. Middle Eastern capitals were central targets of Beijing's counterstrategy in the

---

[4] See, for example, John Calabrese, "From Flyswatters to Silkworms: The Evolution of China's Role in West Asia," *Asian Survey*, Vol. 30, No. 9, September 1990, pp. 862–876.

early 1990s.[5] Moreover, this initiative coincided with growing demand for imported energy resources and commodities as China reinvigorated its economic reform and opening policy.

By 2000, all states in the Middle East had broken official ties with Taiwan and established full diplomatic relations with the PRC, which they recognized as the sole legitimate government of China. The PRC is now a key economic actor in countries throughout the region with modest but significant military relationships with many Middle Eastern states.

Current Chinese Policy Toward the Region

Chinese Priorities and Policies

By 2015, the region had become of greater importance to China than ever before. Beijing seems to perceive the Middle East as an extension of China's periphery as well as a zone of fragile stability. Moreover, China has become concerned about the stability of regimes in the region after being largely agnostic for many years.[6] Factors causing this include the advent of color revolutions in former communist states, the emergence of the Arab Spring in 2011, and continued turmoil in a range of Middle Eastern states. In addition, the rise of radical Islamic movements such as the Islamic State (also known as the Islamic State of Iraq and Syria [ISIS]) has forced China to rethink its preferences. All these dynamics not only threaten Chinese economic interests in the Middle East, including energy supplies, transportation routes, and PRC citizens in the region, but also are seen to pose a threat to CCP rule. Beijing is worried that these popular and extremist movements may inspire ethnic Han dissidents to push for greater democracy in China and Uighur activists to press for greater autonomy or religious freedom in Xinjiang.[7]

---

[5] See, for example, Yitzhak Shichor, "China and the Middle East Since Tiananmen," *The Annuals of the American Academy of Political and Social Science*, Vol. 519, January 1992, pp. 86–100.

[6] Jon B. Alterman and John W. Garver, *The Vital Triangle: China, the United States, and the Middle East*, Washington, D.C.: CSIS, 2008, p. 127.

[7] For elaboration on this point, see Scobell and Nader, 2016, pp. 10–12.

Beijing has three overarching interests in the Middle East:

1. Sustaining Chinese access to the energy resources, continuing the flow of trade, protecting Chinese investments, and ensuring the safety of PRC citizens in the region
2. Enhancing China's stature and influence in a region of geostrategic importance
3. Preserving China's domestic stability, defending China's sovereignty and territorial integrity, as well as securing the PRC's periphery in an ostensibly distant out-of-area region that Beijing has concluded is intimately intertwined with pressing security challenges back home.

1. Sustaining Energy Security, Protecting Investments, and Ensuring the Safety of People. The Middle East is an important source of imported energy for China. China is thirsty for petroleum; in 2014, China was the largest net oil importer in the world at 6.1 million barrels per day. In 2014, the region supplied 52 percent of China's gross imports, or 3.2 million barrels per day.[8] Moreover, in recent years China has invested billions in the region. Protecting these economic interests is of great concern for Beijing. Also at risk are PRC citizens living and working overseas, although reliable figures on the number of Chinese nationals in various countries and regions of the world are notoriously difficult to come by. Nevertheless, according to one Chinese analyst, in the second decade of the twenty-first century there are some five million Chinese citizens overseas around the globe, and of these he estimates approximately 550,000 are living and working in the countries of the Middle East.[9]

2. Enhancing Regional Influence and Global Status. Beijing has taken steps to raise its profile in the Middle East in search of greater

---

[8] U.S. Energy Information Administration, "China," U.S. Department of Energy, May 14, 2015.

[9] See Niu Xinchun, "China's Interests in and Influence over the Middle East," *Contemporary International Relations*, Vol. 24, No. 1, January/February 2014, pp. 42–43, and Mathieu Duchâtel, Oliver Bräuner, and Zhou Hang, *Protecting China's Overseas Interests: The Slow Shift Away from Non-Interference*, Policy Paper No. 41, Stockholm, Sweden: Stockholm International Peace Research Institute, 2014, pp. 41–42.

regional influence and projecting the image of a major power. These efforts include the creation of the position of PRC special envoy to the Middle East in 2002 and releasing a conspicuous but bland formal proposal for Israeli-Palestinian peace in 2013.[10] By publicly proclaiming an interest in addressing the Israeli-Palestinian problem, Beijing has made a grand albeit symbolic gesture that projects to a troubled region the image of an engaged outside power and morally upright pillar of the world community. According to one analyst, China's involvement in the Middle East peace process has been "merely diplomatic rhetoric," and "China's impact," has been assessed as having "hardly been felt."[11]

Although Beijing has issued several policy statements that outline its objectives in the region, the PRC has yet to issue a white paper on the Middle East as it has done for Africa and other areas of the world. The reason appears to be because of the extreme sensitivity of the region: China does not want to jeopardize its unique status as the one outside power to have cordial relations with every Middle Eastern state. Therefore, China tends to spout high-minded rhetoric and make very modest but high profile diplomatic gestures and small but well publicized tangible commitments of resources. Yet, on occasion, Beijing has been an energetic team player. One case in point is China's efforts to facilitate the now-completed nuclear deal between Iran and the P5+1, the five permanent members of the UN Security Council plus Germany. Indeed, according to some accounts, China's role was vital in making the deal.[12] China likely had a major interest in the deal because it would mean the lifting of economic sanctions that were hampering Chinese trade with and investment in Iran.[13]

3. Preserving Domestic Stability in China. Beijing is fearful that dynamics in the Middle East, notably the persistence of Islamic

---

[10] See Matt Schiavenza, "What Is China's Plan for the Middle East?" *The Atlantic*, May 10, 2013; President Xi actually invited both Mahmoud Abbas and Benjamin Netanyahu to China and they both came but did not meet each other while there.

[11] Modechai Chaziza, "China's Policy in the Middle East Peace Process After the Cold War," *China Report*, Vol. 49, No. 1, 2013, pp. 161, 199.

[12] Harold Pachios, "Let's Look at China's Role in the Iran Nuclear Deal," *The Hill*, August 21, 2015.

[13] Conversations with knowledgeable U.S. experts, 2015.

extremism, chronic political instability, and ethnic feuds, will penetrate into China. Although the region does not geographically border the PRC, ethnic, religious, and cultural linkages do extend from the Middle East through Central and South Asia to China. "As the strategic extension of China's western border region," according to a prominent PRC Middle East analyst, "the trends governing the situation in the Middle East and the region's pan-nationalisms and extremist religious ideological trends have a direct influence on China's security and stability."[14] In Beijing's eyes, these dynamics all come together in the case of the Uighurs, a mostly Muslim Turkic ethnic group. A formally recognized ethnic minority in China, the Uighurs officially have autonomy in the Xinjiang Uighur Autonomous Region in the westernmost portion of the PRC. The reality is quite different, and there is considerable disaffection among China's Uighur populace manifest in high profile episodes of violence across China and harsh PRC repression in the Xinjiang Uighur Autonomous Region in recent years.[15] Beijing is especially alarmed by cooperation and coordination between PRC Uighurs, the Uighur diaspora abroad, and Muslim groups in Central Asia, South Asia, and the Middle East. Uighur radicals have reportedly been trained in Pakistan, fought with the Taliban in Afghanistan, and joined the ranks of ISIS in Syria and Iraq. As a result, the PRC has become more vocal about the threat of terrorism and is energized to take action.[16]

Political Engagement

China's main political interest in the Middle East is to increase relations with regional countries to provide international support and

[14] Li Weijian, "Zhongdong Zai Zhongguo Zhanlue Zhong De Zhongyaoxing Ji Shuangbian Guanxi" ["The Middle East's Importance in China's Strategy and Bilateral Relations"], *Western Asia and Africa*, No. 6, 2004, pp. 18–19.

[15] See, for example, the excellent treatment in Bovingdon, 2010.

[16] See, for example, "Part I National Security Situation" in *China's Military Strategy*, 2015. See also Andrew Scobell, "Terrorism and Chinese Foreign Policy," in Yong Deng and Fei-ling Wang, eds., *China Rising: Power and Motivation in Chinese Foreign Policy*, Lanham, Md.: Rowman and Littlefield, 2004b, pp. 305–324.

legitimacy. China seeks closer relations with countries that have either significant regional or global roles.

In the twenty-first century, Beijing has been actively engaged in the Middle East with greater diplomatic activity in the region. This activity included one trip by then president Jiang Zemin in April 2002, when he visited Iran and three other developing states: Libya, Tunisia, and Nigeria. Jiang's successor, Hu Jintao, made three trips to the Middle East during his ten-year tenure, in 2004, 2006, and 2009. On his first trip, President Hu visited Egypt, and while there also met with the Arab League Chairman Amr Moussa and delegates from all of the organization's 22 member states; Hu also visited Algeria on the trip. The Arab League Secretariat and PRC Foreign Ministry issued a joint communiqué proclaiming the establishment of the China-Arab States Cooperation Forum (CASCF)—a mechanism intended to facilitate cooperation between Beijing and the Arab world.[17] In fact, China has leveraged CASCF as a mechanism for emphasizing China's rhetorical and symbolic solidarity with the Arab states on the Middle East peace process and also to inoculate itself against Arab criticism of Chinese policies in Xinjiang.[18]

During Hu Jintao's second trip to the region, in 2006, the PRC head of state visited Saudi Arabia and Morocco. During Hu's third trip to the Middle East he once again visited Saudi Arabia. In addition to meeting with King Abdullah and other Saudi officials, Hu also met with Secretary General Abdul Rahman Al-Attiyah of the Gulf Cooperation Council (GCC) to explore cooperation between the GCC and PRC.

Under President Xi Jinping's leadership, China's relations with the Middle East have remained generally good but politically shallow. In fact, top tier PRC leaders have largely ignored the region. President Xi

---

[17] Degang Sun and Yahia H. Zoubir, "China's Economic Diplomacy Towards the Arab Countries: Challenges Ahead?" *Journal of Contemporary China,* Vol. 24, No. 95, 2015, p. 912.

[18] See the fascinating analysis in Dawn Celeste Murphy, "Rising Revisionist? China's Relations with the Middle East and Sub-Saharan Africa in the Post–Cold War Era," dissertation, George Washington University, August 2012, pp. 172–178.

did not visit the Middle East until January 2016, after he had traveled to almost every other region of the world during the first three years of his tenure, including two visits to far-flung Latin America. As of late 2015, Premier Li Keqiang had yet to visit the Middle East.[19] The reason for the dearth of high-level attention appears to be that the current Beijing leadership considers the Middle East a complicated and opaque minefield to be navigated extremely carefully.[20]

Diplomatic Relations and Presence

Along with Southeast Asia, the Middle East is one of two developing regions in which China has diplomatic relations with all regional actors. China has one embassy in each of the 14 regional countries and five consulates across the region. Beijing also has an embassy-level mission to the Palestinian Authority. China may be the only major power from outside the region to be on good terms with every state in the Middle East, including Saudi Arabia, Iran, Israel, and even Syria.

Pivotal State and Major Partners

Within the Middle East, the pivotal state from the Chinese perspective is Iran. That being said, China has also attempted to maintain generally friendly relations throughout the region. It has, for example, strategic partnership agreements with both Qatar and the United Arab Emirates. It has further established a strategic cooperative relationship with Egypt. Also important is China's cooperative and strategic friendly relationships with Saudi Arabia and the Saudi-dominated GCC.[21] To date, China has successfully balanced robust ties with the two major Middle East rivals—Iran and Saudi Arabia.[22]

---

[19] Mu Chunshan, "Revealed: How the Yemen Crisis Wrecked Xi Jinping's Middle East Travel Plans," *The Diplomat*, April 22, 2015.

[20] Liu Zhongmin, "Zhongguo Bugai Zhuiqiu Zhong Dong Shiwu Lingdaozhe Jiaose" ["China Should Not Pursue a Leadership Role in Middle Eastern Affairs"], *Oriental Morning Post*, August 26, 2011.

[21] "China-GCC FTA," Ministry of Commerce of the People's Republic of China, undated.

[22] Scobell and Nader, 2016.

High-Level Exchanges

From 2003 to 2014, Chinese political leaders paid 40 visits to 15 countries or entities in the Middle East. Of these, four were visits by the president, and another five were visits by the premier. The key countries visited during this period were Egypt, Saudi Arabia, and the United Arab Emirates (UAE). Moreover, since 2003, there has been an increasing frequency of visits to Iran and the UAE and a simultaneous decreasing frequency of visits to Saudi Arabia. There were no visits to the region at the level of head of state since 2011 through the end of 2015.

Cultural Influence

Beijing has neglected—although not completely ignored—cultural and educational exchanges with countries of the Middle East and has focused almost single-mindedly on economic cooperation.[23] China has a modest number (11) Confucius Institutes across seven countries in the Middle East. The United Arab Emirates, Israel, Jordan, and Egypt each host two institutes. Bahrain, Lebanon, and Iran also each have a single institute. The remaining states in this region—Iraq, Kuwait, Oman, Qatar, Saudi Arabia, Syria, and Yemen—have no Confucius Institutes.

The Middle East has traditionally not had significant concentrations of ethnic Chinese but the region now reportedly contains more than half a million PRC citizens who live and work there. The largest concentration is in Dubai, where as many as 200,000 Chinese are working as traders. There are other concentrations, including reportedly more than 16,000 PRC citizens in Saudi Arabia.[24]

Economic Engagement

The Middle East is most important to China as a source of energy. Because oil is one world market, it is possible to make too much of bilateral trade relationships—suppliers can be substituted. But long-term relations develop, and China has been concerned about the security of its energy supplies. Beyond energy, China has included

[23] Sun and Zoubir, 2015, p. 920 (on neglect of culture), p. 913 (on cultural and educational exchanges).

[24] Sun and Zoubir, 2015, p. 919.

the region in its Belt and Road Initiative. Linking China to Europe through the Persian Gulf and West Asia is noted in the main Belt and Road document.[25] And emblematic of China's good relations with all parties in the Middle East, the Maritime Silk Road includes Israel, in which China is building a new port in Ashdod on the Mediterranean with the idea of rail link from Eilat on the Red Sea.[26]

Trade

Trade between China and the Middle East is dominated by imports of mineral fuels, which make up more than 80 percent of the total (Figure 7.2). Additionally, roughly 13 percent of total imports are

Figure 7.2
Composition of Imports from Middle East

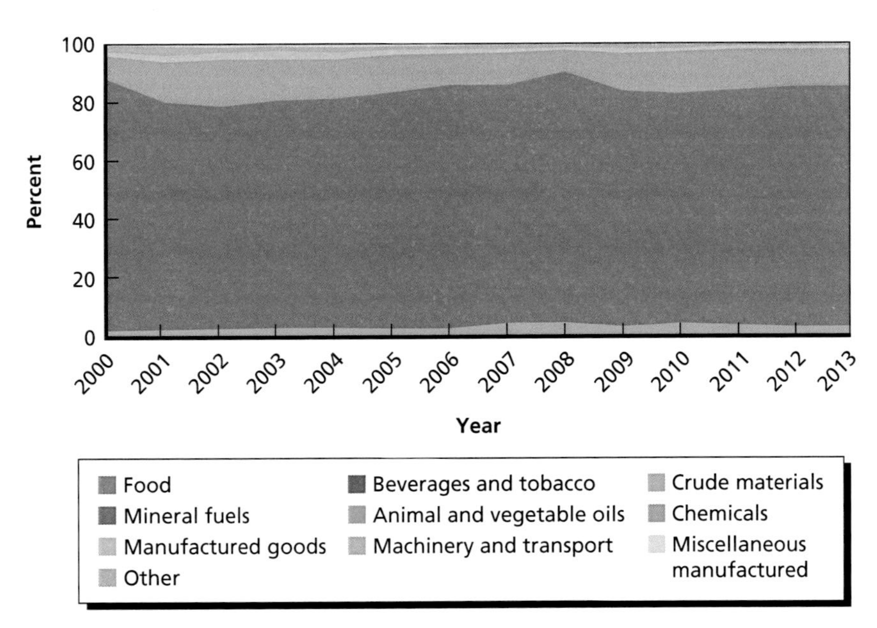

SOURCE: UN Comtrade Database.
RAND *RR2273A-7.2*

---

[25] *Vision and Actions on Jointly Building Silk Road Economic Belt and 21st-Century Maritime Silk Road*, 2015.

[26] Aryeh Tepper, "China's Deepening Interest in Israel," *The Tower Magazine*, No. 30, September 2015.

chemicals driven mainly by petrochemical products such as plastics. Saudi Arabia provides roughly a third of all fuel from the region and 16 percent of China's worldwide fuel imports. Another 50 percent of fuel imports from the region is equally divided between Iran, Iraq, and Oman.

Exports to the Middle East are dominated by manufactured items and machinery, which totaled over 90 percent over the entire 2000 to 2013 time period (Figure 7.3). The largest destinations for exports in the Middle East are Iran, Saudi Arabia, and the United Arab Emirates, although exports to the UAE may be destined for other countries due to UAE's role as a global entrepôt.

There is a significant trade imbalance between the Middle East and China in favor of the Middle East (Figure 7.4). Of the petroleum

Figure 7.3
Composition of Exports to Middle East

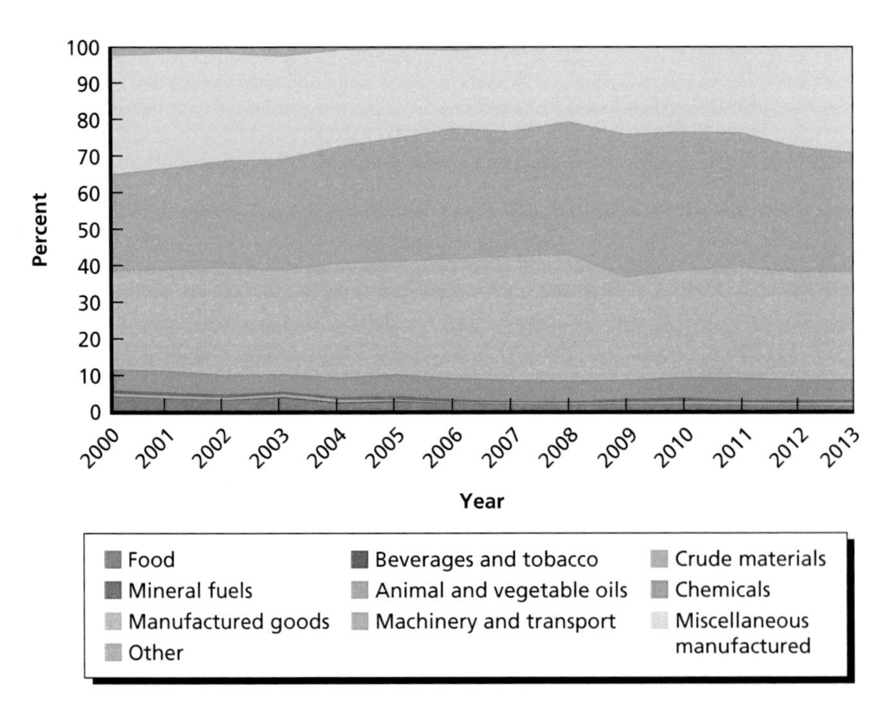

SOURCE: UN Comtrade Database.

RAND *RR2273A-7.3*

Figure 7.4
Level of Exports to and Imports from Middle East

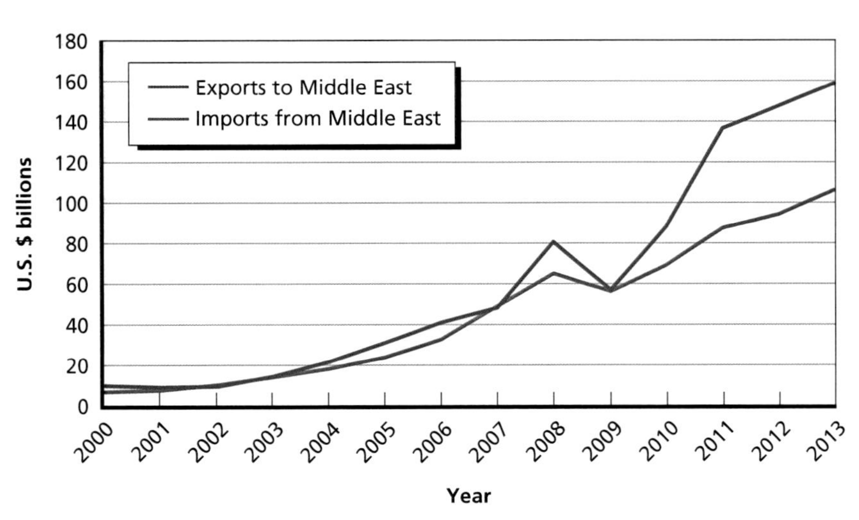

SOURCE: UNCTAD.
RAND *RR2273A-7.4*

exporting countries, only the United Arab Emirates had a trade deficit with China in 2013. As noted, this may be because many of China's exports there may have been destined to be re-exported.

Foreign Direct Investment and Lending

There have been large investments into the Middle East by China since 2008. The most dramatic increase has been in Iran since 2009, with FDI stock reaching more than $2 billion in 2012 (Figure 7.5). There have also been growing Chinese investments in the UAE ($1.3 billion), Saudi Arabia ($1.2 billion), and Iraq (which stood at $437 billion in 2003, declined to $21 billion in 2008, but had risen to $754 billion by 2012). Not only have the Chinese been large investors in Saudi Arabia but also there has been considerable investment by the Saudis in China. In 2012, Saudi Basic Industries Corporation (SABIC) announced plans to build an $11 billion project for petrochemical plants in Tianjin and Chongqing.[27] By 2015, the Sinopec

[27] http://www.wantchinatimes.com/news-subclass-cnt.aspx?id=20120411000118&cid=1103

Figure 7.5
China's FDI Stock in the Middle East by Receiving Country

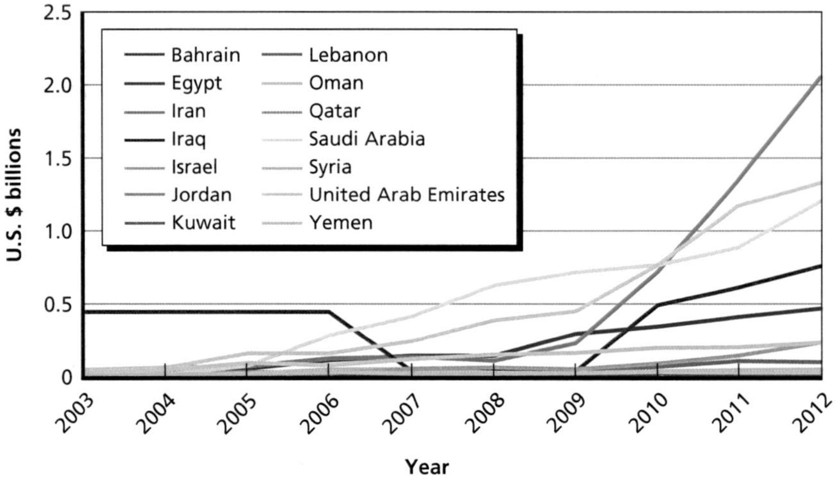

SOURCE: UNCTAD.
RAND *RR2273A-7.5*

SABIC Tianjin Petrochemical Company was producing 260,000 tons annually of polycarbonate.[28]

Agreements and Other Issues

China has bilateral investment treaties in force with every country in the region except Iraq and Jordan, and a treaty with Jordan has been signed but is not in force. The treaty with Kuwait was signed in 1985, and all others, except the treaties with Jordan and Iran, were signed in the 1990s. Likewise, China has tax treaties with all but Iraq, Jordan, Lebanon, and Yemen. These were negotiated somewhat later than the BITs.

Just as the Middle East is a component of China's Belt and Road, Middle Eastern countries have signed up to participate in the Asian Infrastructure Investment Bank. Of the 50 signing founding members, eight are from the Middle East: Egypt, Iran, Israel, Jordan, Oman, Qatar, Saudi Arabia, and UAE. A ninth, Kuwait, enlisted as a prospec-

---

[28] Dania Saadi, "Sabic Retains Expansion Plans Despite Oil Drop," *The National*, January 12, 2015.

tive founding member but did not sign the articles of incorporation in June 2015, deferring its membership.

Beyond regional participation, China has zeroed in on Israel for innovation cooperation. One of China's main economic challenges is shifting from manufacturing and assembly to innovation. Accordingly, it has deepened its relations with Israeli innovators and venture capitalists. Israel's leading high-tech university, the Technion, announced in 2013 that it would open a campus at Shantou University in Guangdong.[29] And as of June 2015, it was expected that China would invest $500 million in venture capital funds in Israel during the calendar year.[30]

Military and Security Engagement

This section presents a brief overview of Chinese military engagement activities as an instrument of Chinese foreign and security policy in the Middle East. It surveys Chinese arms sales, military diplomacy, joint exercises, and port visits as well as Chinese participation in UNPKOs and PLA MOOTW activities.

PRC Arms Sales

Total Chinese arms sales to countries in the Middle East over the 15 years from 2000 have been far lower than total U.S. arms sales to countries in the region during the same period. Moreover, unlike in some other parts of the Developing World, PRC arms sales to countries in the Middle East have declined in recent years, according to the SIPRI Arms Transfers Database. Nevertheless, Chinese arms sales still offer Beijing some opportunities to bolster relations with key partners in the Middle East. For example, in April 2014, China agreed to sell Wing Loong (Pterodactyl) medium-altitude long-endurance UCAVs to Saudi Arabia.[31] The Wing Loong is similar in appearance to the

---

[29] Tepper, 2015.

[30] Idan Rabi, "China VC to Invest $500m in Israel in 2015," *Globes*, June 3, 2015.

[31] On the sale of armed UAVs to Saudi Arabia, see Zachary Keck, "China to Sell Saudi Arabia Drones," *The Diplomat*, May 8, 2014.

U.S. Predator UCAV and is capable of carrying two air-to-ground missiles. China's UCAV sale to Saudi Arabia is suggestive of China's potential to become a major global supplier of UCAVs and appears intended to further strengthen China's relationship with Saudi Arabia.

China has also supplied hundreds of millions of dollars of weapons to Iran since 2000. In fact, Beijing is second only to Moscow in terms of the value of armaments sold to Tehran during the 2000s. China has provided Iran with hundreds of anti-ship and antiaircraft cruise missiles.[32] Beijing has a long history of cooperation with Tehran's missile and nuclear programs although Chinese support for the latter appears to have ended.[33] In addition, China has on occasion sought to purchase select systems from countries of the region. At the turn of the century, for example, Beijing attempted to purchase the airborne early warning radar system Phalcon from Israel, but Tel Aviv relented under intense U.S. opposition to the proposed sale.[34]

PLA Military Diplomacy

Chinese military diplomacy is another important part of PLA engagement in the Middle East, as reflected by eight high-level trips to the region between 2004 and 2011. This puts the Middle East on par with Africa in terms of the number of visits, but well below South and Central Asia and Southeast Asia, which are by far the most frequent destinations during the ten-year period of 2003–2014. The following are the high-level visits to the Middle East between 2004 and 2011:

- In July 2004, CMC Vice Chair (VC) Guo Boxiong visited Egypt.
- In April 2005, CMC VC and Defense Minister (DM) Cao Gangchuan visited Egypt.

---

[32] See, for example, John Garver, "China-Iran Relations: Cautious Friendship with America's Nemesis," *China Report*, Vol. 49, No. 1, 2013, p. 84.

[33] Evan S. Medeiros, *Reluctant Restraint: The Evolution of China's Nonproliferation Policies and Practices, 1980–2004*, Stanford, Calif.: Stanford University Press, 2007. See also Scobell and Nader, 2016, pp. 55–57.

[34] See, for example, Sameer Suryakant Patil, "Understanding the Phalcon Controversy," *Israel Journal of Foreign Affairs*, Vol. 2, No. 2, 2008, pp. 91–98.

- In November 2007, CMC VC and DM Cao Gangchuan visited Kuwait.
- In January 2008, CMC VC and DM Cao Gangchuan visited Saudi Arabia.
- In November 2008, DM Liang Guanglie visited UAE, Oman, Bahrain, and Qatar.
- In November 2010, CMC Vice Chair Xu Caihou traveled to UAE, Syria, and Jordan.
- In May 2011, PLAN Commander Wu Shengli visited Israel.
- In August 2011, CGS Chen Bingde visited Israel.

However, since the flowering of the Arab Spring in 2011 and its aftermath—the fall of Gadhafi in Libya, the continuing civil war in Syria, and the rise of ISIS—PRC high-level military visits have been curtailed just like high-level civilian diplomatic travel.

Combined Exercises

As of late 2015, China had conducted just one combined exercise in the Middle East. In September 2014, the PLA Navy visited Iran for the first time, bringing two warships associated with the PLAN's anti-piracy task force in the Gulf of Aden—the guided missile destroyer *Changchun* and the frigate *Changzhou*—to the Iranian port of Bandar Abbas to conduct four days of basic search and rescue exercises with the Iranian navy.[35] Roughly 650 Chinese sailors reportedly participated in this unprecedented exercise.[36]

PLAN Port Visits

PLAN port visits, many of them associated with anti-piracy patrols, are also becoming a regular feature of Chinese military engagement in the Middle East. Indeed, the Middle East was the region with the

[35] Sam LaGrone, "Chinese Ships in Iran for Joint Exercises," *USNI News*, September 22, 2014; Ankit Panda, "China and Iran's Historic Naval Exercise," *The Diplomat*, September 23, 2014; "Zhongguo Haijun Jianting Biandui Shouci FangwenYilang" ["Chinese Navy Ship Formation Visits Iran for the First Time"], PRC government web portal, September 20, 2014.

[36] Thomas Erdbrink and Chris Buckley, "China and Iran to Conduct Joint Naval Exercises in the Persian Gulf," *New York Times*, September 21, 2014.

largest number of Chinese port visits from 2000 to 2014, with 45 ports visits. Notably, 44 of the 45 took place from 2009 to 2014, and all of these were associated with the participation of PLAN task forces in anti-piracy operations in the Gulf of Aden, which began in December 2008. Countries the PLAN has visited include Bahrain, Egypt, Israel, Oman, Kuwait, Qatar, Saudi Arabia, Yemen, and UAE. The most frequented ports in the region are Salalah, Oman (21); Aden, Yemen (eight); and Jeddah, Saudi Arabia (seven). Salalah is the PLAN's single most frequented port in the Developing World. The main purpose of many of these visits is for replenishment and overhaul activities, but others are essentially goodwill visits that take place on the way to the region or on the way back to China, and in many instances the port visits conducted by PLAN anti-piracy task forces support China's broader diplomatic agenda.[37] For example, China's ambassador to UAE portrayed a March 2010 port call by the PLAN frigate *Ma'anshan* and the supply ship *Qiandaohu* to Port Zayed, Abu Dhabi, as reflecting the strength of China's ties to the country.[38] In addition, the PLAN made its first port visit to Iran in September 2014; the guided missile destroyer *Changchun* docked in Bandar Abbas in anticipation of the first combined naval exercises between China and Iran.

UN Peacekeeping Operations

China's initial foray into UNPKOs came in 1990, when it sent a small number of observers to take part in the UN Truce Supervision Organization (UNTSO) mission in the Middle East. As of March 31, 2015, China was involved in two UNPKOs in the Middle East. Specifically, China has four experts on the mission taking part in UNTSO and 216 troops participating in the United Nations Interim Force in Lebanon (UNIFIL).[39]

---

[37] For a comprehensive review and assessment of this subject, see Erickson and Strange, 2015.

[38] China's ambassador to UAE, Gao Yusheng, said the visit was "because of the strength of political ties between our two countries, and the development that has been witnessed by the Emirates in recent years." See Mahmoud Haboush, "Middle Kingdom Visits Middle East as Chinese Navy Docks at Port Zayed," *The National*, March 25, 2010.

[39] United Nations, *UN Mission's Summary Detailed by Country*, March 31, 2015.

Military Operations Other than War

Chinese military operations other than war activities are another important part of Chinese military engagement in the Middle East.[40] Perhaps the most notable Chinese MOOTW activity in the Middle East in recent years was the PLA Navy's participation in the evacuation of Chinese and foreign citizens from Yemen. The evacuation began in March 2015 with China's withdrawal of about 570 PRC citizens from Yemen, along with eight foreigners from Romania, India, and Egypt.[41] Although this was a much smaller number of citizens than the Chinese evacuation from Libya in 2011, Chinese Ambassador to Yemen Tian Qi called the evacuation "a significant practice of major power diplomacy with Chinese characteristics." Important, the PLAN played a central role in the Yemen evacuation. China used two PLA Navy frigates and a supply ship from the 19th escort fleet participating in Gulf of Aden anti-piracy patrols to conduct the evacuation operations. The Ministry of Foreign Affairs still takes the lead in overseas evacuations, but the PLAN involvement in Yemen evacuation shows that the PLA's role is growing.[42] The PLA probably embraces this role because it demonstrates its importance to protecting China's increasingly global interests. It also displays the growth of Chinese power and influence in a relatively nonthreatening way and provides further justification for improvements in military capability. As editor Yu Jincui wrote in a *Global Times* op-ed, "The capability of a country to protect its citizens abroad is an embodiment of its national strength and influence... China in the future should make continuous efforts to reinforce its

---

[40] The PLAN's involvement in anti-piracy operations in the Gulf of Aden (off the coast of Somalia) is covered in a later section about Chinese MOOTW in Africa.

[41] Jane Perlez and Yufan Huang, "Yemen Evacuation Shows Chinese Navy's Growing Role," *New York Times*, March 31, 2015; James T. Areddy, "China Evacuates Citizens from Yemen," *Wall Street Journal*, March 30, 2015; Zhang Yunbi, "Over 500 Chinese Nationals Evacuated from Yemen," *China Daily*, March 30, 2015; "Evacuation of Chinese Nationals from Yemen Completed," *CGTN America*, April 22, 2015; "Zhongguo Haijun Jianting Biandui Fu Yemen Cheli Zhongguo Gongmin" ["Chinese Naval Detachment Sails to Yemen to Evacuate Chinese Nationals"], Ministry of National Defense of the People's Republic of China, March 30, 2015.

[42] This is a role the PLA evidently welcomes. According to China's Minister of National Defense, "Military officers must be the guardians of the people's security, and military ships must be like Noah's Ark for our compatriots."

naval strength to meet the soaring demands of protecting the expansion of its overseas interests."[43]

Following China's evacuation of its own citizens from Yemen in late March, Beijing employed the PLAN to conduct an unprecedented evacuation of foreigners from Yemen on April 2, 2015. The PLAN Type 054 frigate *Linyi* evacuated about 225 foreign nationals from Aden to Djibouti. Chinese official statements indicate that the evacuees came from ten countries, including Pakistan (176 citizens), Ethiopia (29), Singapore (five), Italy (three), Germany (three), Poland (four), Ireland (one), Britain (two), Canada (one), and Yemen (one). Chinese officials stated this was the first time the PLA Navy had evacuated non-Chinese in a humanitarian mission, and that its involvement in the operation reflected principles of "internationalism and humanitarianism." According to Chinese commentators, by helping evacuate foreign nationals, China boosted its image regionally and globally and showcased the PLA as a force that can help other countries.[44]

Conclusion

During the Cold War, China viewed the Middle East primarily as a key region of contestation between the superpowers and competition with Taiwan, and China was simply seeking to become relevant in the region. In the twenty-first century, China is now a key player with significant interests in the Middle East. As of 2015, Beijing's top regional priorities were fostering peace and stability.[45] Indeed, recent public opinion surveys indicate majorities or pluralities in five states believe

---

[43] Yu Jincui, "Overseas Evacuation Attests to Nation's Responsibility," *Global Times*, March 31, 2015; Zhang Yunbi, 2015.

[44] Moreover, as Shen Dingli of Fudan University observed, China would have risked looking bad if it didn't help, especially given the availability of PLAN vessels in the Gulf of Aden, where they were conducting anti-piracy operations. See Ankit Panda, "China Evacuates Foreign Nationals from Yemen," *The Diplomat*, April 6, 2015, and Megha Rajagopalan and Ben Blanchard, "China Evacuates Foreign Nationals from Yemen in Unprecedented Move," *Reuters*, April 3, 2015.

[45] See, for example, Scobell and Nader, 2016.

that China has already surpassed—or will soon surpass—the United States as the dominant power in the region and world (Table 7.1).

In the Middle East, the PRC has skillfully managed to remain a friend to all and enemy of no one. China is seen in generally positive terms, especially with regard to Chinese economic impact on countries in the region. A majority of those surveyed in Egypt, Israel, and Jordan, for example, view China's involvement in the Middle East as economically beneficial to their country.

Many of the partnerships are broad and comprehensive but superficial in terms of level of commitment. However, at least four of these partnerships have proved quite robust, comprehensive, and enduring, and most have a military or security component; these include Egypt (since the 1950s), Iran (since the 1970s), Israel (since the 1980s), and,

Table 7.1
Global Attitudes Toward China

	General View of China		Is China's Economic Growth Good or Bad for Your Country?		Will or Has China Replaced the United States as Leading Superpower?	
	Favorable (%)	Unfavorable (%)	Good (%)	Bad (%)	Will or Has Replaced (%)	Will Never (%)
Tunisia	64	21	66	18	54	30
Palestinian Territories	61	29	53	22	53	35
Lebanon	53	44	64	27	49	45
Israel	49	50	62	21	57	36
Egypt	46	53	53	42	42	47
Jordan	35	63	58	37	52	42
Middle East median	**51**	**47**	**60**	**24.5**	**52.5**	**39**
Global median	**49**	**32**	**53**	**27**	**49**	**34**

SOURCE: Pew Research Center, Global Indicators Database, July 2014.

more recently, Saudi Arabia (since the 1980s). All of these have involved cooperation in the security realm, often conducted in secret, involving arms sales, and, at least at one point in time, the potential sharing of sensitive technology.[46]

Implications for the United States

For at least two decades, an emerging concern in Beijing has been how to maintain some semblance of stability in the Middle East. Beijing's thinking has transformed from not caring about conflict or turmoil in the region to a clear preference for peace and order. In an earlier time, upheaval in the Middle East was not seen as negative because it served to sap the strength of the United States and Soviet Union and divert the attention of Washington and Moscow away from Beijing and Asia. During the Cold War, leaders such as Mao Zedong and Deng Xiaoping viewed the Middle East as a distant zone of contestation for influence with the two superpowers and rivalry with Taiwan. But by the 2000s, China had a strong preference for a tranquil region, and Chinese analysts expressed a clear desire for the United States to "uphold stability in the Middle East."[47]

China and the United States appear to hold overlapping but not identical views on the region. Beijing does not seek to subvert or replace the U.S. role as the key external security guarantor for the region. China opposes the overthrow of Middle Eastern regimes and refuses to sanction external intervention to stabilize turmoil in countries such as Syria. Beijing feels burned by the UN Security Council vote in support of the imposition of a no-fly zone over Libya in 2011 because this led to the overthrow of Gadhafi. While China tends to line up with Russia in terms of positions on Middle East issues, there are real differences. Beijing, for example, is far more reluctant than Moscow to intervene militarily to protect its interests. Russia's military base in Syria and the insertion of additional forces into that country in late 2015 to bolster Assad contrast starkly with China's more hands-off military stance.

---

[46] On cooperation between China and Iran and China and Saudi Arabia, see Scobell and Nader, 2016, Chapters 3 and 4, respectively.

[47] Alterman and Garver, 2008, p. 18.

Arguably China does have a larger military footprint in the Middle East than Russia, but this presence is limited to UNPKO missions, ships in the Gulf of Aden anti-piracy flotilla and associated port visits and replenishment efforts, and Chinese arms sales in the region. While Beijing insists that it does not have military bases overseas, it does have facilities with Chinese military personnel or contractors active in the Middle East. The most notable location of a PRC military facility is in the small Red Sea state of Djibouti, which China refers to as a facility to provide logistical support but that others have subsequently described as China's first overseas military base (see Chapter 8).

China has also shown that, in modest but significant ways, it can work with the United States and like-minded countries in the Middle East on issues from counter-piracy to counter-proliferation (that is, the Iran nuclear deal). The United States should consider establishing a military-to-military dialogue with China to discuss Middle East security issues to build on these modest successes.

CHAPTER EIGHT

China in Africa

China is a long-established diplomatic partner to Africa, and Chinese interests on the continent extend beyond acquiring natural resources to encompass trade, security, diplomacy, and soft power. Located beyond China's immediate neighborhood, African governments do not have any territorial disputes with China and largely welcome Chinese engagement. While the PRC's relations with Africa were dominated by ideological imperatives in the early days, Beijing has focused on advancing its economic interests and winning political legitimacy in recent years. As of late 2015, Beijing had diplomatic relations with 51 of the 54 African nations and was the continent's top trade partner. Since 2000, Chinese imports from the region have grown 20-fold. Indicative of the region's importance to China, Africa also receives roughly half of China's total foreign aid.

Key Chinese Activities in the Region

China has significant political and economic engagement with the region and views its activities there as important to supporting continued Chinese economic growth and international development. Politically, close relations with African countries provide China with a strong dose of international legitimacy and support for a range of international and political issues. China has ongoing high-level political and economic engagement with African countries both bilaterally and multilaterally through the Forum on China-Africa Cooperation (FOCAC). While South Africa is China's most important regional partner, Beijing views half a dozen other nations as also playing crucial political or economic roles (Figure 8.1). Economically, Beijing has focused on gaining access to natural resources, creating markets for Chinese-manufactured goods, and developing manufacturing facilities that can take advantage of the continent's low labor costs. China's Belt and Road Initiative also envisions linking at least the east coast of Africa to its 21st Century Maritime Silk Road, although Africa is likely to play a lesser role than regions such as Central Asia or Southeast Asia. Militarily, China

Figure 8.1
China's Relations with Countries in Africa, 2015

NOTE: Due to small scale of map, not all countries are displayed and labeled.
RAND *RR2273A-8.1*

is developing ties to African armed forces, participating in several UN peacekeeping missions in the region, pledging $100 million to the African Union (AU) to create an immediate response unit,[1] and taking proactive measures to ensure the safety and security of Chinese citizens and investments abroad. Overall, Chinese activities in the region are still predominantly economic, and there is little indication that the United States and China are headed for conflict or competition in Africa.

Drivers of Chinese Engagement with the Region

Chinese Activities in the Region Prior to 2000

In its early days, the PRC's relations with Africa were dominated by ideological imperatives of Third World solidarity, anti-colonialism, and support for African independence movements. In accordance with the principles of 1955 Bandung Conference, China based its relations with newly independent African states on the principles of equality, mutual interest, and noninterference.[2] China's ideological engagement shifted to a greater political pragmatism as Beijing sought allies in the international arena, which paid off most dramatically when support from 26 African states helped ensure passage of UN General Assembly Resolution 2758, which expelled Taiwan from the organization and declared that the People's Republic was the sole legitimate representative of China at the UN.[3] As China began to pursue market economics in 1978, it reached out economically to Africa.[4] Chinese companies initially had trouble competing with more experienced Western firms, but—aided by Chinese subsidies, loans to African governments, and high-profile

---

[1] Jane Perlez, "China Surprises U.N. with $100 Million and Thousands of Troops for Peacekeeping," *New York Times*, September 28, 2015.

[2] See Final Communiqué of the Asian-African conference of Bandung (April 24, 1955).

[3] United Nations General Assembly, Resolution 2758 (XXVI), October 25, 1971. Also see Marius Fransman, "Keynote Address to the Ambassadorial Forum on China–South Africa Diplomatic Relations at 15 Years," Pretoria, South Africa, September 19, 2013.

[4] See Larry Hanauer and Lyle J. Morris, *Chinese Engagement in Africa*, Santa Monica, Calif.: RAND Corporation, RR-521-OSD, 2014. Also See Li Anshan, "China and Africa: Policy and Challenges," *China Security*, Vol. 3, No. 3, Summer 2007, pp. 70–73.

public works gifts that won local leaders' favor—they eventually made inroads in the resource- and labor-intensive petroleum, mining, and construction sectors.

By the late twentieth century, China's economic and commercial activities came to be widely viewed as one-sided, neo-colonial, mercantilist ventures that exploited the region's resources while undermining local industries, burdening African governments with heavy debts and providing few long-term economic benefits for Africans. Beijing in 2000 created the Forum on China-Africa Cooperation as a regional venue for coordinating and repositioning China's engagement with the region as a "win-win" relationship.

Current Chinese Strategy and Policy Toward the Region

Chinese Priorities and Policies

China has four overarching interests in Africa:[5]

1. Access to natural resources, particularly oil and gas
2. Export markets for Chinese manufactured goods
3. International political legitimacy as a global power, including recognition of Beijing as the sole representative of China (the "One China" policy) and acknowledgement of the principle of noninterference in sovereign countries' internal affairs[6]
4. Sufficient political stability and security for China to safeguard its citizens and pursue its economic and commercial interests.

The four interests are intertwined in the various policy documents that China has issued to define its policy objectives in Africa. Its January 2006 Africa Policy White Paper states that the general principles and objectives of China's African policy include support for African countries' sovereignty, mutually beneficial economic cooperation, mutual support in international forums, sustainable develop-

[5] See Hanauer and Morris, 2014.

[6] China is a beneficiary as well as a practitioner of the principle of noninterference; Beijing ardently opposes criticism of its policies toward the restive regions of Tibet and Xinjiang as unmerited interference in its domestic affairs.

ment, and African support for the "One China" principle.[7] In 2011, China issued a White Paper on its global foreign aid—46 percent of which went to Africa—in which it emphasized sustainability and the absence of political preconditions, vowing "never [to] use foreign aid as a means to interfere in recipient countries' internal affairs or seek political privileges for itself."[8] In a revised 2014 Foreign Aid White Paper, China asserted it had prioritized agriculture, education, health care, and emergency humanitarian aid[9] and that more than half of its foreign aid was provided to African nations between 2010 and 2012.[10]

In 2013, China's Ministry of Defense issued a White Paper in which it committed military resources to participate in UNPKOs, including those in Liberia, Congo, South Sudan, and Darfur; deliver humanitarian assistance, including medical care and demining assistance in Africa; and safeguard the security of international sea lines of communication, including in the Gulf of Aden.[11] Also in 2013, China published an updated version of its 2010 White Paper on China-Africa economics and trade, in which it noted China's aspirations to promote sustainable growth in trade, increase Chinese investment, strengthen agricultural cooperation, support construction of African infrastructure, build local capacity, and build multilateral cooperation.[12] More recently, China has made efforts to incorporate Africa into its Belt and Road Initiative. Nairobi, for example, is one of the designated stops along the Maritime Silk Road.[13] Prominent

---

7 "China's African Policy," *Xinhua News*, January 12, 2006.

8 *China's Foreign Aid (2011)*, Information Office of the State Council of the People's Republic of China, April 2011.

9 "White Paper Details China's Foreign Aid Priorities," *Xinhua News*, July 10, 2014.

10 "China Issues White Paper on Foreign Aid," *Xinhua News*, July 10, 2014.

11 *The Diversified Employment of China's Armed Forces*, 2013, Section V.

12 *China-Africa Economic and Trade Cooperation*, Information Office of the State Council of the People's Republic of China, August 2013.

13 "China Pushes 'One Belt, One Road,'" *CCTV*, March 8, 2015.

voices have further called for increased involvement from the rest of the African continent.[14]

In general, close relations with the majority of Africa's 54 countries provide China with a strong dose of international legitimacy. Having experienced its own rapid economic growth and development, China offers itself as a model that African leaders can emulate as they attempt to lead their own nations to prosperity. Beijing is also eager to have African allies at the UN, where African votes have helped defeat anti-Chinese resolutions at UN human rights bodies.[15] Beijing also works diligently to advance its One China policy by isolating African countries that recognize Taiwan and rewarding countries that switch their allegiance to Beijing with aid and investment, leaving only three countries on the continent that recognize Taiwan.[16]

China has historically preferred to engage on a government-to-government level, including when it comes to economic activities undertaken by state-owned enterprises (SOEs) and state-backed finance institutions. China tends to establish relationships and win favor with local political elites through promises of aid, trade, and investment with no strings attached, then use their influence to win contracts in nontransparent negotiations behind closed doors.[17] Political elites can take Chinese loans and produce concrete deliverables, such as factories or infrastructure, without having to make politically tough decisions (like economic reforms or eliminating subsidies) that might be

---

[14] These have included Justin Yifu Lin, former chief economist of the World Bank, and He Wenping, director of African studies at the Chinese Academy of Social Sciences (CASS). See He Wenping, "'One Belt, One Road' Can Find Place for Africa," *Global Times*, January 29, 2015.

[15] Joshua Eisenman, "China's Post–Cold War Strategy in Africa: Examining Beijing's Methods and Objectives," in Joshua Eisenman, Eric Heginbotham, and Derek Mitchell, eds., *China and the Developing World*, New York: M.E. Sharpe, 2008, pp. 35–36. Also see Richard T. Nenge, Takavafira M. Zhou, Tompson Makahamadze, "Analysing the Extent to Which China Uses the Non-Interference Policy to Promote Peace and Security in Africa," in China-Africa Think Tanks Forum, "The 2nd Meeting of the China-Africa Think Tanks Forum," conference report, Bisoftu, Ethiopia, October 12–13, 2012, p. 111.

[16] Pete Guest, "And Then There Were Three: China's Spending Power Entices Taiwanese Ally," *Forbes*, November 26, 2013.

[17] Richard Aidoo and Steve Hess, "Non-Interference 2.0: China's Evolving Foreign Policy Towards a Changing Africa," *Journal of Current Chinese Affairs*, Vol. 44, No. 1, 2015, pp. 118–119, 126.

demanded by Western donor governments or international financial institutions. Economic benefits from Chinese investment also tend to accrue principally to elites. Chinese investment in large-scale extractive ventures tends to produce profits for local businesspeople and revenues (often illicit) for government officials, whereas they tend to create few jobs for ordinary citizens. As a result of these dynamics, African elites have generally welcomed Chinese trade and investment,[18] while ordinary Africans perceive Chinese investment as benefitting the rich and powerful—in part through corrupt activities[19]—but not themselves.[20] More broadly, according to an assessment by the Ethics Institute of South Africa, "China's interests are seemingly vested in African leaders rather than African citizens."[21]

Private Chinese nationals, however, are increasingly pursuing economic opportunities in Africa independent of government-directed initiatives.[22] In many cases, nonofficial Chinese seem to undermine Beijing's official efforts to win friends and influence people. In March 2015, for example, the decision by a Chinese restaurant owner in Nairobi to refuse service to black people after dark generated considerable anti-Chinese hostility that undermined Beijing's official efforts to improve China's image in Kenya through media outreach, investment, and job creation.[23] Indeed, U.S. academics Fei-Ling Wang and Esi A. Elliot note that "the lack of good coordination between the cautious and friendly Beijing and the increasingly numerous cowboy-like Chinese fortune

---

[18] Fei-Ling Wang and Esi A. Elliot, "China in Africa: Presence, Perceptions and Prospects," *Journal of Contemporary China*, Vol. 23, No. 90, 2014, p. 1029.

[19] Ethics Institute of South Africa, "Africans' Perceptions of Chinese Business in Africa: A Survey," Pretoria, 2014, pp. 24–25.

[20] Richard Aidoo and Steve Hess, 2015, pp. 117, 125.

[21] Commenting on the incident, Kenya's *Mail & Guardian* newspaper wrote, "Official China does a good job of not offending African sensibilities, but its businessmen and women don't have the same diplomatic skills." See Ethics Institute of South Africa, 2014, p. 12.

[22] Gilles Mohan and May Tan-Mullins, "Chinese Migrants in Africa as New Agents of Development? An Analytical Framework," *European Journal of Development Research*, Vol. 21, No. 4, 2009, p. 589.

[23] "Beijing's Africa Problem: 'No Blacks' Chinese Restaurant Shut Down in Kenya," *Mail & Guardian*, March 25, 2015.

seekers in the wild west of Africa is . . . a major problem" for state-run Chinese development and investment organizations.[24] Although Beijing has little ability to control private Chinese citizens, the behavior and conduct of thousands of Chinese businessmen in Africa will be as important as government diplomacy and concessions in shaping China's engagement in the region.[25]

Political Engagement

China has increased political engagement with all African countries that recognize Beijing. Its commitment to avoid interfering in, or even passing judgment on, sovereign nations' behavior and policies allows it to pursue its political and economic interests across the continent with democrats and despots alike. Beijing's willingness to pursue political ties and economic opportunities with pariah governments—whether arms sales to Zimbabwe or oil exploration in Sudan—have, without question, provided some African regimes with the resources they need to perpetuate their undemocratic, and often abusive, rule. Such engagement has proven at times to be a source of contention with the United States and Europe, which argue that governments that show little respect for human rights, democratization, and the rule of law should not be rewarded with political support or extensive aid and investment.[26]

To elevate its engagement with Africa and make its largesse highly visible, the Ministry of Foreign Affairs established the Forum

---

[24] Wang and Elliot, 2014, p. 1021.

[25] Chris Alden, *China in Africa*, London: Zed Books, 2007, p. 128. Note that Western companies have not necessarily had easy relations with Africans; most often, problems have been in the context of major resource extraction companies operating under government auspices. Protests and direct action against oil companies in the Niger Delta provide one example (John Ghazvinian, *Untapped: The Scramble for Africa's Oil*, Orlando, Fla.: Harcourt, Inc., 2007).

[26] Critics would note that despite their rhetoric, the United States and Europe have established close political and economic relations with many undemocratic countries in Africa, providing military assistance to governments (such as Somalia, Chad, Mali, Mauritania, Ethiopia, and Djibouti) that are assessed to be highly corrupt and to deny their populations even basic political and civil rights. See, for example, Transparency International, *Corruption Perceptions Index 2014*, 2014; see also *Freedom House, Map of Freedom 2014*, 2014.

on China-Africa Cooperation (FOCAC), a pan-African umbrella for China's bilateral relations with 50 individual countries. FOCAC organizes highly staged triennial summit meetings—held in 2000, 2003, 2006, 2009, 2012, and 2015—at which China announces new three-year regional engagement strategies, launches new regional initiatives, and unveils large bilateral trade, investment, and aid deals. Moreover, each African head of state is able to meet with the Chinese president on the margins of the summits, which enables Beijing to highlight its close relations and commitment to each African nation.

FOCAC has covered a wide range of issues and provided Chinese deliverables in multiple areas.[27] The FOCAC 2013–2015 Action Plan,[28] which resulted from the 2012 summit, identified five key areas of concentration in Sino-African relations:

5. *Political Affairs and Regional Peace and Security*, including high-level visits; exchanges of legislative, judicial, and local government officials; conflict resolution; and security cooperation
6. *Cooperation in International Affairs*, including climate change, food security, human rights, global trade, and participation in international financial institutions
7. *Economic Cooperation*, including in the areas of agriculture, private investment, infrastructure, trade, banking, energy, communications, and transportation
8. *Cooperation in the Field of Development*, including human resources development, technology transfer, poverty reduction, public health
9. *Cultural and People-to-People Exchanges and Cooperation*, including exchanges in education, academia, media, think tanks, journalism, youth, women, and sports.

Although the FOCAC Action Plan expressed commitment to the promotion of "mutual" cooperation, investment, learning, trust,

---

[27] Huang Meibo and Qi Xie, "Forum on China-Africa Cooperation: Development and Prospects," *African-East Asian Affairs/The China Monitor*, Vol. 74, 2012, p. 10.

[28] "The Fifth Ministerial Conference of the Forum on China-Africa Cooperation Beijing Action Plan (2013–2015)," July 23, 2012.

understanding, and benefit, the "Chinese extravaganza of largesse and ostensible generosity"[29] that takes place at FOCAC summits also highlights the asymmetric nature of the Chinese-African relationship. China exerts significant control on the process and sets the agenda, declarations, and outcomes.[30] Although private companies are increasingly prominent components of China's overall engagement with the continent, FOCAC is a critical tool for the Chinese government to manage its relations with the region.[31]

Along with FOCAC, China has augmented its collaboration with the African Union as a way to give its engagement greater regional impact and legitimacy. In 2006, China declared it would work closely with the AU on peace and security issues, committing in the 2006 FOCAC Action Plan to "support the AU's leading role in resolving African issues, and take an active part in UN peace-keeping operations in Africa."[32] In 2007, Beijing established a security consultative mechanism, the China-AU Strategic Dialogue, which addressed security challenges in Sudan, Zimbabwe, eastern Congo, and Somalia.[33] China has since provided training, materiel, and funds for AU military operations and mediation efforts in Somalia, Mali, and other countries.[34]

---

[29] Ian Taylor, "From Santa Claus to Serious Business: Where Should FOCAC Go Next?" *African-East Asian Affairs/The China Monitor*, Vol. 74, 2012, p. 32.

[30] Ian Taylor, 2012, p. 31.

[31] Ian Taylor, *The Forum on China-Africa Cooperation (FOCAC)*, Abingdon: Routledge, 2011, p. 103.

[32] Forum on China-Africa Cooperation, "Forum on China-Africa Cooperation Beijing Action Plan (2007–2009)," November 16, 2006, para 2.5.2.

[33] See Georg Lammich, "China's Impact on Capacity Building in the African Union," paper presented at a workshop regarding South-South Development Cooperation Chances and Challenges for the International Aid Architecture, Heidelberg University, September 26–27, 2014, p. 12.

[34] Yun Sun, "Xi Jinping's Africa Policy: The First Year," Brookings Institution *Africa in Focus* blog, April 14, 2014; also, Georg Lammich, 2014, pp. 12–13; see also Jia Qinglin, Chairman of the National Committee of the Chinese People's Political Consultative Conference, "Towards a Better Future with Stronger China-Africa Solidarity and Cooperation," speech to the 18th Ordinary Session of the Assembly of the African Union, Addis Ababa, January 29, 2012.

By 2009, China argued that it "support[s] the AU playing a bigger role in regional and international affairs" beyond just peace and security.[35] In March 2015, China accredited its first full-time ambassador to the AU, making it only the second country other than the United States to do so. The newly accredited Chinese ambassador stated, "For many years, China has mainly relied on bilateral cooperation. . . . China is ready to do more with Africa."[36]

In recent years, Chinese engagement with Africa has triggered growing grassroots hostility and locals widely perceive Chinese activities—particularly its economic investments—as benefitting China more than its Africa partners. Beijing responded by emphasizing the mutually beneficial nature of its engagement, bolstered by a proactive public diplomacy campaign consisting of job training, educational and cultural exchanges, funding for humanitarian relief and health care, and a comprehensive media outreach effort.[37] After being criticized for failing to provide assistance in the early days of the Ebola outbreak in West Africa,[38] for example, China contributed $123 million, donated medical equipment and vehicles, announced plans to train 10,000 local health care workers, and deployed 1,000 medical and disease control personnel.[39] The overall intention of these broad-based programs is to build positive perceptions of China and counter what it saw as unfairly negative representations of China in Western-dominated media.[40]

---

[35] Forum on China-Africa Cooperation, "Forum on China-Africa Cooperation Sharm El Sheikh Action Plan (2010–2012)," November 12, 2009, para 2.5.2.

[36] AFP, "China Boosts Africa Diplomacy," March 13, 2015.

[37] Interestingly, China's people-to-people exchanges—academic scholarships, cultural exchanges, language training, job training, etc.—almost all involve Africans going to China or Chinese trainers/teachers working in Africa. Thus, although China speaks of "exchanges," the transfer of knowledge and experience is mostly one-way. See Kenneth King, *China's Aid and Soft Power in Africa: The Case of Education and Training* (Suffolk, UK: James Currey, 2013), pp. 66, 99, 101.

[38] Chris Leins, "China's Evolving Ebola Response: Recognizing the Cost of Inaction," Atlantic Council *New Atlanticist* blog, November 10, 2014.

[39] United Nations Development Programme, "The Ebola Virus Outbreak and China's Response," Issue Brief No. 6, December 2014.

[40] Wang and Elliot, 2014, p. 1030.

Diplomatic Relations and Presence

China, as of late 2015, had diplomatic relations with 51 of the 54 countries in Africa. The three exceptions were Burkina Faso, Sao Tome and Principe, and Swaziland, which had diplomatic relations with Taiwan instead. China operates embassies in 49 of the remaining African countries. It also has seven consulates in five of these countries, with three in South Africa alone.

China has signed a range of political partnership agreements with several African states. The most important of these are with Algeria and South Africa, both of which China has designated as comprehensive strategic partners. Following them are Equatorial Guinea, Ethiopia, the Republic of the Congo, Tanzania, and Kenya, which are comprehensive cooperative partners. Finally, China has strategic partnerships with the African Union as an organization, Angola, and Nigeria. These political agreements help identify some, but not all, of China's most important partners in the region.

Pivotal State and Major Partners

In terms of individual countries, China's most significant relationships are with South Africa, its pivotal partner on the continent, and Tanzania. South Africa is one of the five BRICS countries and is a cofounder of the New Development Bank. The country's attractiveness as a partner stems in part from its economy, the second largest in sub-Saharan Africa. Moreover, because of its strong financial sector, rule of law, and infrastructure, it is a destination of choice for Chinese businesses and serves as a gateway to the rest of the continent. Beyond economics, South Africa is a regional leader and active in a number of regional organizations, including the African Union and the Southern African Development Community, making it widely considered a "continental leader."[41] Tanzania, on the other hand, has become an increasingly important Chinese partner in military affairs. Both Tanzania and South Africa received the most visits from members of the

---

[41] The quotes in this paragraph can be found in Sven Grimm, Yejoo Kim, and Ross Anthony, with Robert Attwell and Xin Xiao, *South African Relations with China and Taiwan: Economic Realism and the "One-China" Doctrine*, Stellenbosch, South Africa: Stellenbosch University Centre for Chinese Studies, February 2014, pp. 15–16, 16, respectively.

Central Military Commission in recent years. Two of China's three joint military exercises in Africa were held with Tanzania.

Other important relationships in the region include those with Algeria, Angola, Equatorial Guinea, Ethiopia, Kenya, Nigeria, and the Republic of the Congo. Both Angola and Algeria, for example, are major oil-producing states, and because of this, China has sought to build ties with them both. Angola's trade with China matches the total of trade with its next ten biggest partners combined and is overwhelmingly based on oil. That said, during his state visit in June 2015, Angola President Jose Eduardo Dos Santos sought to expand the relationship to include new areas such as trade, transport, electricity, and finance.[42] A series of equally high-level meetings have taken place between Chinese and Algerian leaders this year. In February 2015, Yang Jiechi, state councilor responsible for foreign affairs, traveled to Algeria and met with both President Abdelaziz Bouteflika and Prime Minister Abdelmalek Sellal.[43] Later in the year, Abdelkader Bensalah, president of the upper house of the Algerian Parliament, and Prime Minister Sellal made separate trips to China to push for deeper economic ties.[44]

Other countries are appealing because of their economic strength. Ethiopia, specifically, is one of the five fastest growing economies in the world, according to the IMF.[45] It is, moreover, a regional power in East Africa and has been involved in fighting Al-Shabaab in neighboring Somalia.[46] Consequently, China has sought closer ties with Ethiopia, such as by signing 16 deals during Premier Li Keqiang's visit in May 2014.[47]

---

[42] "Angola President Seeks More Non-Oil Deals in His Visit to China," *Bloomberg*, June 12, 2015.

[43] "China, Algeria to Jointly Push for Progress in Partnership," *China Daily*, February 8, 2015.

[44] "Xi Jinping Meets with Prime Minister Abdelmalek Sellal of Algeria," Ministry of Foreign Affairs of the People's Republic of China, April 29, 2015; "Li Keqiang Meets with President of the Council of the Nation Abdelkader Bensalah of Algeria," Ministry of Foreign Affairs of the People's Republic of China, September 4, 2015.

[45] "Ethiopia Economic Outlook," African Development Bank Group, 2015.

[46] "Obama Praises Ethiopia over Fight Against al-Shabab," *BBC News*, July 27, 2015.

[47] Aaron Maasho, "China Signs Deals with Ethiopia as Premier Starts Africa Tour," *Reuters*, May 4, 2014.

Countries, however, also have shortcomings that reduce their appeal as partners to China, even in spite of possessing major strengths. Nigeria, for example, is a member of OPEC and a major oil-producing state. Recent recalculations of its GDP also revealed that it accounts for roughly 26 percent of the entire continent's GDP, making it in overall terms the largest economy in Africa. However, it also suffers from poor infrastructure, corruption—especially troublesome within the state-owned Nigerian National Petroleum Corporation—and internal instability because of the ongoing Boko Haram insurgency.

Finally, Djibouti is an important major partner with growing military links to China. In 2014, for instance, the two countries signed a security and defense strategic partnership agreement giving port access to PLAN ships. As of 2015, the two countries agreed to establish what China refers to as a facility to provide logistical support but that others have subsequently described as China's first overseas military base.

High-Level Exchanges

China continues to regularly engage in high-level exchanges and visits to the region. From 2003 to 2014, Chinese leaders made 91 high-level visits to 53 countries in Africa. Of these, 32 were at the level of head of state or government, with 20 having taken place from 2003 to 2008 and 12 having taken place from 2009 to 2014. Moreover, there has been an increasing frequency of visits to Ethiopia, Morocco, South Africa, Sudan, and Tanzania in particular.[48]

Cultural Influence

China has engaged in significant public diplomacy in Africa to counter negative public perceptions of China and increase the region's affinity toward China. One of the principal (and most costly) elements of

---

[48] In contrast to China's emphasis on high-level diplomacy, few senior U.S. officials have visited the continent. U.S. presidents have visited only 14 sub-Saharan African countries—plus four North African countries (Morocco, Tunisia, Algeria, and Egypt)—since Franklin D. Roosevelt made the first presidential trip to the region in 1943. See Andrew Katz, "All the Presidents' Trips to Africa, Mapped," *Washington Post*, July 27, 2015.

China's public diplomacy strategy has been to expand outreach by its state media.[49]

Beijing launched its media expansion in January 2009 with a $6.6 billion investment.[50] Starting in 2009, Xinhua opened additional news bureaus throughout the continent, and by 2012 the English-language *China Daily* launched an African edition and state-run China Central Television, which changed at the end of 2016 to China Global Television Network, opened a broadcast studio—its first outside China—in Kenya.[51] Aside from producing news with a Chinese angle, China has also promoted Chinese pop culture for broadcast in Africa. It has dubbed Chinese TV soap operas into Swahili, for example, to promote a more positive image of Chinese culture and family life.[52]

Under the auspices of FOCAC, China has also increased the number of scholarships and job training programs that bring Africans to China.[53] For example, from 2010 to 2011, the number of Chinese government scholarships increased from 5,710 to 6,316.[54] Meanwhile, at the July 2012 FOCAC ministerial meeting, Hu Jintao promised that the Chinese government would increase the number of scholarships to 18,000 in the next three years.[55] Similarly, China increased the number of vocational training programs for Africans. At the end of 2012, for example, "China had trained more than 53,700 Africans

---

[49] Liu Guangyuan, "Deepen China-Africa Media Cooperation and Enrich the China-Africa Community of Shared Destinies," speech at the seminar on China-Africa Media Cooperation on 18 November 2013, Chinese Embassy in Kenya, November 19, 2013.

[50] "Beijing in 45b Yuan Global Media Drive," *South China Morning Post*, January 13, 2009.

[51] See Hanauer and Morris, 2014, pp. 74–75.

[52] "Chinese Soft Power in Africa," *Economist Intelligence Unit*, August 21, 2014.

[53] King, 2013, p. 69.

[54] Forum on China-Africa Cooperation, "Forum on China-Africa Cooperation (FOCAC)," July 18, 2012.

[55] More than 35,000 Africans were studying in China in 2013, most of whom received Chinese government-funded scholarships, according to the *Economist Intelligence Unit*. China has provided academic scholarships to all 50 African countries with which it has diplomatic relations, though it is not clear if there is a pattern to the way in which China distributes these grants. See Forum on China-Africa Cooperation, "FOCAC ABC," April 9, 2013, and "Chinese Soft Power in Africa," *Economist Intelligence Unit*, August 21, 2014.

in China and sent more than 350,000 technical personnel to Africa."[56] A study of short-term training courses provided by China's Ministry of Commerce to government officials from developing countries concluded that an estimated 86,000 African officials will have attended such classes between 2000 and 2015.[57]

China has also greatly expanded the number of "people-to-people" exchanges involving academics, students, government officials, think tank analysts, journalists, and others. The 2009 FOCAC meeting established an exchange of scholars, the China-Africa Joint Research and Exchange Programme, which first met in March 2010.[58] The China-Africa Think Tank Forum, for example, first met in October 2011 "to generate policy recommendations for the sustainable development of Sino-African relations,"[59] particularly in the areas of peace and security, finance and investment, and people-to-people and cultural exchanges.[60]

Confucius Institutes also support China's public diplomacy toward the region. China currently possesses 34 Confucius Institutes throughout 26 countries in Africa. The most are located in South Africa, which has four. Kenya is next with three institutes, followed by Nigeria, Morocco and Tanzania, which possess two each.

As with other regions, there are no definite estimates of the number of Chinese citizens in Africa. However, the number in sub-Saharan Africa is thought to have peaked at about one million in 2013.[61]

---

[56] Hou Liqiang, "Drive to Improve Vocational Education," *China Daily*, January 16, 2015.

[57] Although a high percentage of participants have difficulty applying the training because of a lack of resources in their home countries, these training courses for African officials "have become one of China's most successful public diplomacy efforts." See Henry Tugendhat, "Chinese Training Courses for African Officials: A 'Win-Win' Engagement?" SAIS China-African Research Initiative Policy Brief No 3, December 2014.

[58] "China and Africa Joint Research and Exchange Program Formally Launched," FOCAC website, March 31, 2010; see also "Chinese Premier Wen Jiabao Announces Eight New Measures to Enhance Cooperation with Africa," *Xinhua News*, November 9, 2009.

[59] China-Africa Think Tanks Forum, "The 2nd Meeting of the China-Africa Think Tanks Forum," conference report, Bisoftu, Ethiopia, October 12–13, 2012, p. 5.

[60] Forum on China-Africa Cooperation, "Declaration of the 1st Meeting of the China-Africa Think Tank Forum," November 23, 2011.

[61] Tom Hancock, "Chinese Return from Africa as Migrant Population Peaks," *Financial Times*, August 28, 2017.

Some Chinese public diplomacy activities seem aimed at convincing non-African countries that China can be a responsible actor in the region. China has taken some modest steps to crack down on ivory smuggling, for example—an issue that tends to resonate more with Western publics and policymakers than with Africans. Seeking to demonstrate that it is working to reduce demand for ivory, in 2013, users of Chinese mobile phones began receiving SMS messages on landing in Kenya warning them not to buy ivory, rhino horn, or other wildlife products.[62] In January 2014, China crushed six tons of confiscated ivory in Dongguan,[63] and in April 2014, China passed a law prohibiting the purchase or consumption of more than 400 imperiled or endangered species.[64]

Economic Engagement

China's economic engagement has focused on gaining access to natural resources, creating markets for Chinese-manufactured goods, and developing manufacturing facilities that can take advantage of the continent's low labor costs. China's principal interest in Africa is to ensure access to the raw materials it needs to fuel its own economy—principally oil, gas, metals, and minerals. It has, thus, invested heavily in countries that are richly endowed with such resources, and its trade with the continent is overwhelmingly concentrated in raw materials. From 2003 to 2010, more than half of China's investment in Africa was concentrated in the oil sector, almost all of it coming from well-resourced SOEs. China's imports from Africa consist overwhelmingly of natural resources; in 2011, 64 percent of its imports from the continent consisted of petroleum, 16 percent consisted of iron and other metals, and 6 percent consisted of copper.[65]

[62] "Say No to Ivory and Rhino Horn Chinese Cell Phone Users Told," WildAid, September 30, 2013.

[63] Brian Clark Howard, "China Crushes Six Tons of Confiscated Elephant Ivory," *National Geographic*, January 7, 2014.

[64] Zoe Lin, "Off the Menu: China Moves to Protect Endangered Species," CNN.com, May 5, 2014.

[65] Lauren Gamache, Alexander Hammer, and Lin Jones, "China's Trade and Investment Relationship with Africa," USITC Executive Briefings on Trade, April 2013.

China also looks to Africa as a growing market for Chinese-made products. Although Africa is the destination for only 3.7 percent of China's exports ($81.7 billion in 2013), this figure has risen more than 19-fold since 2000, more than China's worldwide exports but less than growth in exports to Central and South Asia, and on par with exports to Latin America. Some Chinese products—machinery and transportation equipment, for example, which comprised 38 percent of Chinese exports to Africa in 2011—are components of other Chinese economic activities in the region.[66]

Finally, as the cost of labor in China increases, Chinese companies have increasingly opened manufacturing facilities in Africa (as well as other countries), where manufacturing costs may be less.[67] Chinese firms now manufacture everything from electronics to vehicles to shoes in African countries, in some cases from Special Economic Zones that host nations have established to attract such Chinese investment.[68] Some of this investment has taken place to take advantage of trade preferences offered by Europe and the United States, such as the U.S. African Growth and Opportunity Act.

Over time, however, many Africans have come to resent China's economic engagement for failing to create large numbers of skilled jobs, failing to train African workers or transfer manufacturing technologies, creating abusive and polluting work environments, and undercutting domestic industries. Separately, Chinese emigrants to Africa increasingly consist of private entrepreneurs and businessmen who are not subject to Beijing's control (and who sometimes seek their economic opportunity through illegal or illicit activities). These Chinese expatriates have often clashed with locals in ways that undermine Chi-

---

[66] Source for data: IMF Direction of Trade Statistics and UN Comtrade. See Hanauer and Morris, 2014, p. 31.

[67] Xiaoqing Pi, "China Wages Seen Jumping in 2014 Amid Shift to Services," *Bloomberg*, January 6, 2014; China's 12th Five-Year Plan (2011–2015) calls for a 13 percent annual increase in the minimum wage and requires employers make social welfare contributions (housing, health insurance, pensions, etc.) that will increase labor costs by more than 35 percent. See Ernst and Young, "China's Productivity Imperative," 2012, p. 14.

[68] See, for example, Peter Wonacott, "China Inc. Moves Factory Floor to Africa," *Wall Street Journal*, May 14, 2014; see also "The Awakening Giant," *The Economist*, February 8, 2014.

na's overall message of win-win bilateral economic and cultural cooperation. The secondary effects of China's trade and investment have, thus, contributed to an anti-Chinese backlash that has driven China to modify its approach to the continent.

Trade

China's total goods trade with Africa grew 20-fold over the period 2000 to 2013, more than growth with any other region other than Central Asia and Latin America. Imports have grown from $5 billion in 2000 to $111 billion in 2013. Roughly 80 percent of imports from Africa are fuel and raw materials (Figure 8.2). This has remained relatively constant, except for fluctuations driven by commodity prices. The only other commodity group of any size is manufactured goods.

Figure 8.2
Composition of Imports from Africa

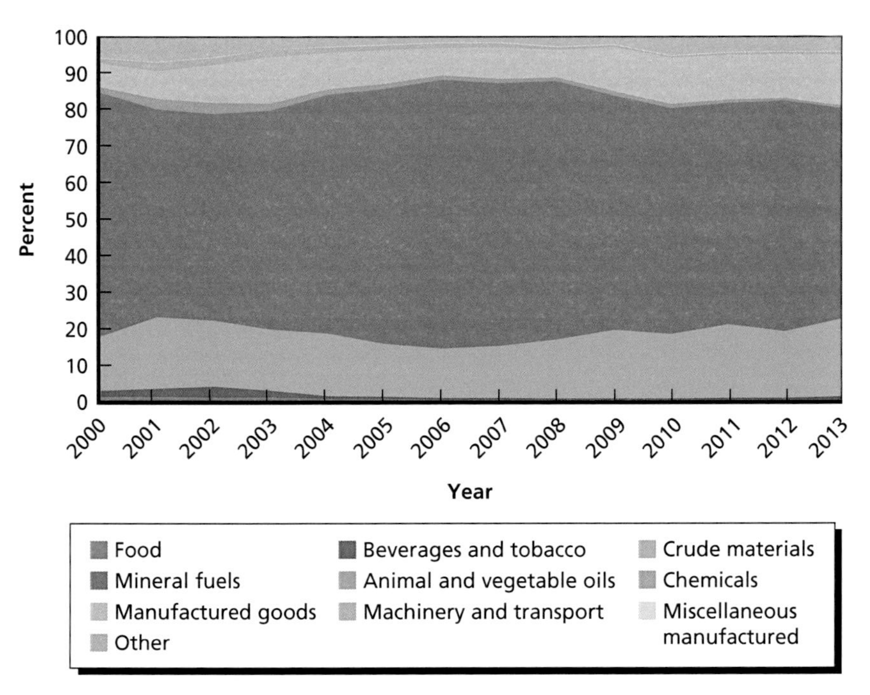

SOURCE: UN Comtrade Database.
RAND *RR2273A-8.2*

Exports have grown from $4 billion in 2000 to $82 billion in 2013. They are characterized by different categories of manufactured items, including chemicals, manufactured goods, machinery and transport equipment (the largest group), and miscellaneous manufactures (Figure 8.3). Exports of food were almost 10 percent of the total at the beginning of the period, but have declined to about 3 percent.

China runs a trade deficit with Africa (Figure 8.4). Much of that deficit is driven by South Africa and Angola. South African exports represent at least 20 percent of total African exports across all categories. Since the breakup of Sudan, when trade with Sudan collapsed, Angola has filled the supply in fuel exports, further increasing its trade surplus with China. China is in surplus with Nigeria, driven primarily by Nigerian imports of machinery and chemicals.

Figure 8.3
Composition of Exports to Africa

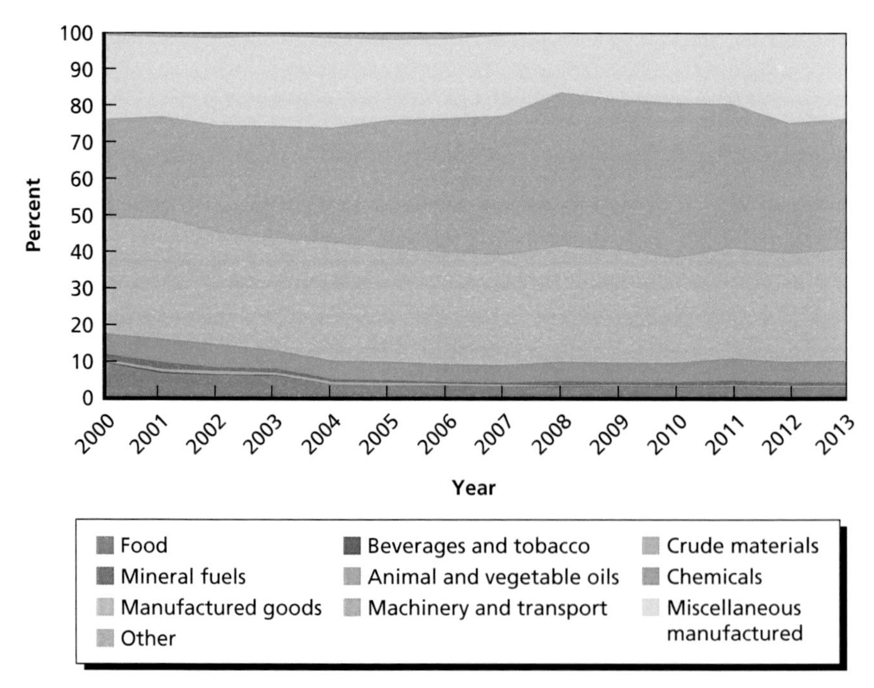

SOURCE: UN Comtrade Database.

RAND *RR2273A-8.3*

Figure 8.4
Level of Exports to and Imports from Africa

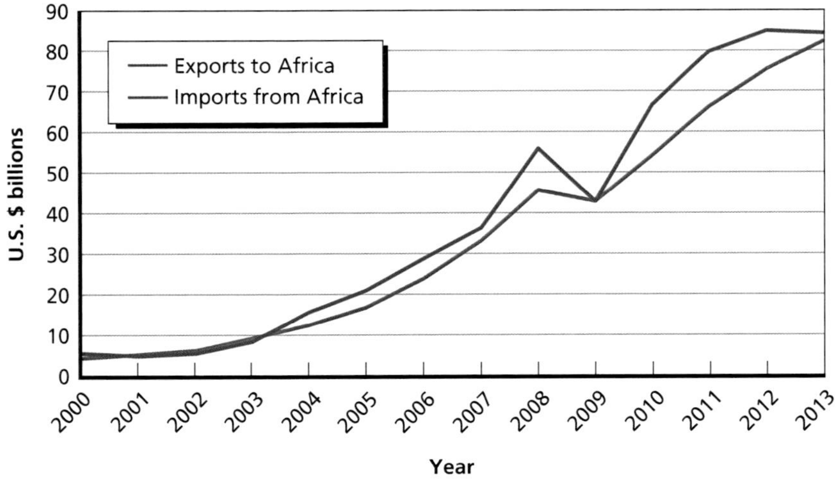

SOURCE: UN Comtrade Database.
RAND RR2273A-8.4

Foreign Direct Investment, Lending, and Aid

As with its trade, China's stock of FDI in Africa has risen dramatically, from $477 million in 2003 to $21.3 billion in 2012. Of this, the top recipients include South Africa, at almost $5 billion in 2012, and then Zambia, Nigeria, Algeria, Angola, and Sudan, all between $1 billion and $2 billion (Figure 8.5). Together, these countries have attracted almost 60 percent of all Chinese FDI in Africa.

China does not emphasize "poverty mitigation" in its aid; instead, it claims to emphasize mutual cooperation among fellow developing countries (as opposed to a hierarchical donor-recipient relationship).[69] In 1964, Premier Zhou Enlai outlined eight principles of China's aid to foreign countries, the first of which is: "The Chinese Government always bases itself on the principle of equality and mutual benefit in providing aid to other countries. It never regards such aid as a kind of

[69] King, 2013, pp. 5–6, 8.

Figure 8.5
China's FDI Stock in Africa by Top Receiving Countries

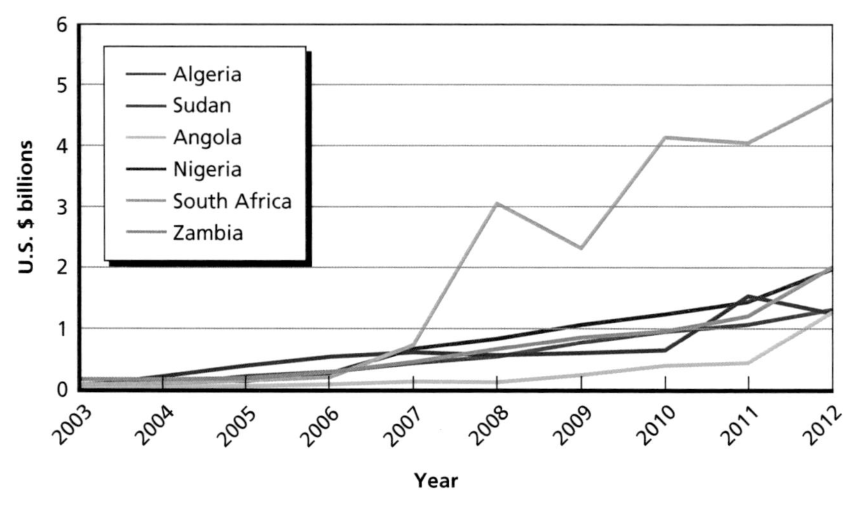

SOURCE: UNCTAD.
NOTE: Figure shows only those countries with greater than $1 billion in Chinese outward FDI stock in 2012.
RAND *RR2273A-8.5*

unilateral alms but as something mutual."[70] Decades later, China's 2011 White Paper on foreign aid noted that "Mutual benefit and common good or common development have been the explicit rationale for China's cooperation with Africa over 60 years."[71] Aside from that claimed difference, much Chinese aid come in forms that would not necessarily be considered aid by Western governments. Forms include concessional loans, resource-backed loans, and tied aid, along with more traditional forms of aid.

China's second foreign aid White Paper, produced in 2014, reported that in the three years of 2010 through 2012 since the last report, China had provided Africa $14.4 billion in official development assistance, almost 52 percent of all aid from China and a 6.1 percent

[70] "Premier Zhou Enlai's Three Tours of Asian and African Countries," Ministry of Foreign Affairs of the People's Republic of China, undated.

[71] King, 2013, p. 64.

increase from the previous period. The annual average of $4.8 billion per year was divided into $2.68 billion in concessional loans, $1.74 billion in grants, and $0.39 billion in interest-free loans.[72] The paper noted additional aid in the form of $430 million annually provided through the UN and multilateral and regional development banks, and $76.3 million annual of debt relief of interest-free loans.

At the 2015 FOCAC meeting, President Xi pledged $60 billion to support development in Africa. Of this, $5 billion was to be in interest-free loans and $35 billion was to be in preferential financing, export credits, and other forms of concessional loans. It is not clear what form the other $20 billion was to take.[73] Even with preferential rates, this $40 billion will need to be paid back by the governments or firms that borrow it.

Much of China's domestic growth has been driven by the construction, engineering, and machinery sectors that are well suited to compete for similar infrastructure projects in Africa. Often, these projects are funded with concessional loans from China's policy banks. In 2012, China received roughly $40 billion in construction contracts from Africa. Africa is the second largest foreign market for Chinese construction projects and represents roughly a third of all construction projects abroad.[74] Examples include a $9 billion rail and road network contract with the Democratic Republic of Congo (more than that country's national budget);[75] a $12 billion contract to build an 850-mile long rail line in Nigeria;[76] and a $700 million airport for Khartoum, to be repaid over 15 years.[77]

---

[72] 2012 USAID assistance to Africa was $8.1 billion, a figure that does not include other forms the United States grants.

[73] Rene Vollgraaff, Amogelang Mbatha, and Mike Cohen, "Xi Unveils $60 Billion Funding Pledge at South Africa Summit," *BloombergBusiness*, December 4, 2015.

[74] *China-Africa Economic and Trade Cooperation*, 2013.

[75] Nirit Ben-Ari, "On Bumpy Roads and Rails," Africa Renewal, April 2014.

[76] Konye Obaji Ori, "China Signs Deal with AU to Connect Africa's Big Cities," *The Africa Report*, January 28, 2015.

[77] Mikolaj Radlicki, "From Sudan to Senegal, Africa's Head-Turning New Airports . . . with a Helping Hand from Chinese Friends," *Mail & Guardian Africa*, March 6, 2015.

China has also provided traditional development aid in such areas as health care and the environment. For example, China sent more than 1,000 health care workers to West Africa during the Ebola crisis, built Ebola treatment centers, and provided assistance.[78] And during his May 2014 visit to Africa, Premier Li Keqiang pledged $10 million to promote conservation, including funds to help Kenya combat poaching.[79]

Agreements and Other Issues

Africa lags in bilateral investment treaties with China, given the number of countries in the continent. Seventeen have BITs in force, although an additional 15 have signed BITs that have not yet entered into force. Except for the BIT with Ghana, which entered into force in 1990, all the effective BITs entered into force in 1997 or later, and 11 of them entered into force in 2000 or later. China has few tax treaties with Africa, with only eight income or income and capital tax treaties.

Africa is becoming increasingly linked to China's Belt and Road Initiative.[80] While the Silk Road Economic Belt runs from China through Asia and the Middle East to Europe, the 21st Century Maritime Silk Road does touch the east coast of Africa. The Silk Road may include an East African railway in Kenya from Nairobi to Mombasa, a port on the Indian Ocean.[81] Early diagrams of the maritime route also suggest a transit through Bab el-Mandeb Strait, a key maritime chokepoint that borders Djibouti and Eritrea on the African continent. China has conducted multiple port calls to Djibouti and views establishing a naval supply facility or base there as a logical extension of increasing Chinese maritime interests.

---

[78] "China to Cooperate with Africa on Industrialization, Sanitation, Security: FM," *China Daily*, March 8, 2015.

[79] Fredrick Nzwilim, "China Pledges $10 Million in Support of Wildlife Conservation in Africa," *National Geographic Voices* blog, May 13, 2014.

[80] Yun Sun, "Inserting Africa into China's One Belt, One Road Strategy: A New Opportunity for Jobs and Infrastructure?" Brookings Institution, March 2, 2015.

[81] Wang Shengwei, "HK Must Embrace the 'One Belt, One Road' Initiative," *China Daily*, August 12, 2015.

No African countries signed up as founding members of the Asian Infrastructure Investment Bank. However, South Africa is a full participant in another China-inspired development bank, the New Development Bank, also known as the BRICS bank, with Brazil, India, and Russia. The five BRICS countries completed the establishment of the New Development Bank in July 2015.[82]

Not all Chinese commercial activities are carried out by SOEs or major companies with favored state access. Although reliable statistics are unavailable, private Chinese companies—primarily construction firms and small- to medium-sized enterprises—comprise an increasing share of Chinese commercial activity in Africa.[83] Many such firms, lacking the resources to engage in costly natural resource extraction, have pursued opportunities in construction and manufacturing.[84] Individual Chinese nationals are also increasingly migrating to Africa on their own in search of economic opportunity.[85] Many of these migrants have set up small shops that compete with local entrepreneurs. Many of these shops remain segregated from local communities, and tensions with locals have erupted into violence or otherwise created negative impressions of Chinese.[86]

Indeed, while some public opinion polls have shown that Africans believe China is contributing to their nations' development,[87] other polls have shown that Chinese investment is viewed negatively or has little or no influence on public opinion of China, in part because it

---

[82] "BRICS Countries Launch New Development Bank," *BBC News*, July 21, 2015.

[83] See Gu Jing, "China's Private Enterprises in Africa and the Implications for African Development," *European Journal of Development Research*, Vol. 21, No. 4, 2015, p. 574.

[84] See Mohan and Tan-Mullins, 2009. Also see Jian-Ye Wang, "What Drives China's Growing Role in Africa?" IMF Working Paper WP/07/211, October 2007; also see Gu Jing, 2015, p. 573.

[85] For an excellent description of individual Chinese migrants' search for economic opportunities in Africa, see Howard French, *China's Second Continent: How a Million Migrants are Building a New Empire in Africa*, New York: Knopf, 2014.

[86] Mohan and Tan-Mullins, 2009, pp. 597–598.

[87] Pew Global Attitudes Project, "America's Global Image Remains More Positive than China's," Washington, D.C.: Pew Research Center, July 18, 2013.

is too unrelated to ordinary citizens' daily lives.[88] To the extent that Africans are aware of Chinese investment, they generally see these projects as having failed to meet promises of new jobs and greater prosperity.[89] African publics are often aware of highly visible Chinese-backed infrastructure and construction projects. Many such projects have been widely criticized, however, for poor quality work that deteriorates quickly and for employing large numbers of Chinese laborers rather than locals. As a result, they often damage rather than improve China's image.[90] While Chinese trade has a greater influence on public opinion, higher trade with China has tended to result in more negative views of the country, as many Africans view Chinese products as poor quality and believe they unfairly compete with locally made products.[91]

There appears to be widespread grassroots opposition in Africa to China's activities.[92] China has been widely criticized across the continent—by civil society groups, journalists, and some government officials—for a wide range of practices. Among them are abusive

---

[88] Capturing the dichotomy, a 2014 opinion poll conducted by the Ethics Institute of South Africa found the following: "Considering the question whether China has a positive impact on the development of their respective countries, 38% agree and 11% strongly agree. But when asked if Africans have personally benefited from Chinese business, most disagree (24%) or strongly disagree (29%)." See Ethics Institute of South Africa, 2014, pp. 16–17.

[89] See Aleksandra Gadzala and Marek Hanusch, "African Perspectives on China-Africa: Gauging Popular Perceptions and Their Economic and Political Determinants," *Afrobarometer Working Paper*, No. 117, January 2010, p. 7. Also see Hanauer and Morris, 2014, p. 61.

[90] Claims of rapidly collapsing Chinese-built infrastructure may very well be exaggerated. (See Deborah Brautigam, "The Chinese in Africa: *The Economist* Gets Some Things Right, Some Wrong," blog post, *China in Africa: The Real Story*, May 20, 2011.) Moreover, African governments may be partly to blame for poor quality construction work, either because they set low standards, rushed completing for political purposes, or siphoned off resources meant for public works. (David H. Shinn, correspondence with authors, September 2, 2013.) Nevertheless, the perception that Chinese work is substandard is widely held and has undermined China's efforts to portray its investments as beneficial for African nations rather than moneymaking opportunities for Chinese companies.

[91] Brautigam, 2011. See also *Afrobarometer*, which found in a 2010 public opinion poll that "African support of the Chinese declines as the percentage of Chinese imports increases," Gadzala and Hanusch, 2010, p. 15.

[92] Wang and Elliot, 2014, p. 1030.

labor practices;[93] low wages;[94] pollution and violation of environmental laws;[95] corruption;[96] and importation of Chinese laborers, which minimizes the number of local jobs created.[97] Even the tendency of Chinese SOE workers to live apart from local communities in separate compounds has inspired views that Chinese are aloof[98] and generated rumors that Chinese laborers are actually prisoners.[99] In some cases, anti-Chinese sentiment has led to violence at factories, mines, and Chinese residential compounds.[100] A 2014 South African survey

---

[93] See, for example, Human Right Watch's comprehensive report on low wages, long hours, hazardous conditions, retaliation against whistleblowers, and other health, safety, and labor practices in Chinese copper mines in Zambia. "'You'll Be Fired If You Refuse': Labor Abuses in Zambia's Chinese State-Owned Copper Mines," *Human Rights Watch*, 2011.

[94] Alexis Okeowo, "China, Zambia, and a Clash in a Coal Mine," *The New Yorker*, October 9, 2013.

[95] Despite the fact that China purchases 7 percent of Chad's oil and has invested heavily in the country's vital oil sector, the Chadian Environment Ministry fined the local subsidiary of the China National Petroleum Corporation $1.2B in March 2014 for "repeated violations" of environmental rules. See "Chad Imposes US$1.2bn Fine on Chinese Oil Firm," *Economist Intelligence Unit*, April 7, 2014.

[96] In March 2015, a report by Kenya's anti-corruption watchdog implicated a cabinet minister and a senator in a scheme to award a $500M pipeline contract to Sinopec in exchange for a $15M payoff. See Edith Honan, "Kenya Corruption Watchdog Makes Allegations Against 175 Officials," *Reuters*, April 1, 2015.

[97] The previous president of Zambia, Michael Sata, ran for election on an anti-Chinese platform, deriding China for stealing, rather than creating, local jobs and promising to kick out Chinese "infesters" if elected. In March 2015, in large part because of resentment of Chinese workers, Tanzania's parliament passed a law (the Non-Citizens Employment Regulation Bill) that requires businesses to assert that no local could do a job before it can hire a foreigner and also requires firms to develop plans for locals to eventually take over the jobs. See "Tanzania's MPs Approve Anti-Foreigner Law," *BBC News*, March 19, 2015; see also Masato Masato, "Tanzania: Labour Ministry to Regulate Foreigner's Employment," *Daily News*, March 19, 2015.

[98] Terence McNamee, "Africa in Their Words: A Study of Chinese Traders in South Africa, Lesotho, Botswana, Zambia and Angola," Brenthurst Foundation, discussion paper 2012/03, April 2012.

[99] Deborah Brautigam, "Is China Sending Prisoners to Work Overseas?" blog post, *China in Africa: The Real Story*, August 13, 2010.

[100] Alexis Okeowo, "China, Zambia, and a Clash in a Coal Mine"; see also Yaroslav Trofimov, "In Africa, China's Expansion Begins to Stir Resentment," *Wall Street Journal*, February 2, 2007.

found that large majorities of Africans believe Chinese companies are not socially responsible and that they do not engage with local communities.[101]

Military and Security Engagement

China has been increasing its military and security engagement with the region. In recent years, there have been more PRC arms sales to the region, more senior military leadership visits to the region, and more PLAN port visits. China also participated in three joint exercises with African forces and has engaged in significant peacekeeping operations as well as military operations other than war in the region.

Most important, China has become more invested in helping provide regional security. While China had long maintained a hands-off approach to security matters in Africa,[102] regional instability has threatened Chinese investments and citizens in Africa.[103] Beijing has responded by building up host nation capacity, making greater use of private Chinese security firms, and even using government assets and resources to evacuate Chinese citizens from conflict zones. This has culminated in the announcement of China's first overseas military out-

---

[101] Ethics Institute of South Africa, 2014, p. 22.

[102] China views that the Western concept of promoting security as a means to advance economic development is merely a way to interfere in the sovereign affairs of African nations. Instead, China argued that African countries should first strive to advance their economies as a way of promoting security and stability. See Wang Xuejun, "Developmental Peace: Understanding China's Policy Towards Africa in Peace and Security," Institute for Africa Studies, Zhejiang Normal University, September 12, 2014.

[103] A problem Beijing faces is that Chinese companies often do not evaluate potential instability and political risk when deciding whether to invest abroad. When they do, according to a World Bank study, they see Africa as a highly risky investment environment. In a 2005 survey of 150 Chinese firms investing abroad, 94 percent of the firms surveyed viewed Africa as the riskiest and least attractive region in which to do business. Operations to extract natural resources in Africa are typically in remote areas, where state power projection is often limited and security risks are often escalated. See Peter Ford, "Why Chinese Workers Are Getting Kidnapped Abroad," *Christian Science Monitor*, February 1, 2012; Harry G. Broadman, *Africa's Silk Road: China and India's New Economic Frontier*, Washington, D.C.: The World Bank, 2007, p. 99.

post, in Djibouti, which China refers to as "a facility to provide logistical support to Chinese fleets performing escort duties in the Gulf of Aden and the waters off the Somali coast"[104] but that others have subsequently described as China's first overseas military base.[105]

The following sections first discuss Chinese efforts to strengthen regional security and then detail PRC arms sales, military diplomacy, military exercises and training, PLAN port visits, peacekeeping activities, and military operations other than war.

PRC Efforts to Strengthen Regional Security

As Chinese companies ventured further into ungoverned and unstable areas of the continent, Chinese investments and citizens became increasingly threatened by political violence, terrorism, and social unrest that host nations proved unable (and sometimes unwilling) to control. Beijing realized it would have to take a more active involvement in local political and military disputes. In a marked change from its noninterference principle, Beijing became actively involved in diplomatic efforts to resolve conflict between Sudan and South Sudan—the source of roughly 5 percent of China's oil imports and the location of significant amounts of Chinese-built oil infrastructure.[106] In addition, Beijing contributed peacekeepers—including, for the first time, infantry troops—to UN peacekeeping operations in Darfur, South

---

[104] Hong Lei, "Foreign Ministry Spokesperson Hong Lei's Regular Press Conference on January 21, 2016," Ministry of Foreign Affairs of the People's Republic of China, January 21, 2016.

[105] Jane Perlez and Chris Buckley, "China Retools its Military with a First Overseas Outpost in Djibouti," *New York Times*, November 26, 2015; Ben Blanchard, "China Sends Troops to Open First Overseas Military Base in Djibouti," *Reuters*, July 11, 2017.

[106] These security risks can cause critical disruptions to Chinese economic and business interests. The China National Petroleum Corporation (CNPC) has invested more than $7 billion in South Sudan's oil infrastructure, which has been threatened by instability there. Fighting in December 2013 caused Chinese oil production in South Sudan—which represented 1 percent of China's total oil imports in the first ten months of the year—to plummet by 20 percent. See Haggai Matsiko, "Is It time for a China-Africa Command?" *The Independent* (Uganda), November 16, 2014; Yuwen Wu, "China's Oil Fears over South Sudan Fighting," *BBC News*, January 8, 2014.

Sudan, Mali, Cote d'Ivoire, Liberia, Democratic Republic of Congo, and Western Sahara.[107]

China has ramped up its engagement in security matters only in the past few years. The first FOCAC conference pledged support for nuclear weapon-free zones and greater attention to small arms smuggling.[108] The second FOCAC action plan called for coordination on a range of nontraditional security issues, including terrorism, drug trafficking, transnational crime, and other challenges.[109] The FOCAC action plan for 2012–2015 promised Chinese support to African Union conflict resolution initiatives, UN peacekeeping operations, counterpiracy patrols, and political mediation by China's Special Representative for African Affairs.[110] In March 2013, Foreign Minister Wang Yi said security would be one of the three focus areas of China's cooperation with Africa.[111]

Chinese firms often rely on host nation police and security forces to protect their facilities, but these forces are often poorly equipped and trained.[112] Moreover, it is politically risky for an African government to provide better (or even just more visible) security for Chinese firms while locals complain about inadequate or abusive security forces.[113] China is developing new ways of protecting its economic assets and citizens in Africa.

Chinese companies are also increasingly taking their own measures to provide security for their workers in Africa. Private Chinese

---

107 See United Nations, "Current Peacekeeping Operations," webpage, undated.

108 The First Ministerial Conference of the Forum on China-Africa Cooperation, "Beijing Declaration of the Forum on China-Africa Cooperation," October 12, 2000.

109 The Second Ministerial Conference of the Forum on China-Africa Cooperation, "Addis Ababa Action Plan," September 25, 2009.

110 The Fifth Ministerial Conference of the Forum on China-Africa Cooperation, "Beijing Action Plan (2013–2015)," July 23, 2012, section 2.6.

111 "China to Cooperate with Africa on Industrialization, Sanitation, Security," 2015.

112 Ford, 2012.

113 Shaio H. Zerba, "China's Libya Evacuation Operation: A New Diplomatic Imperative—Overseas Citizen Protection," *Journal of Contemporary China*, Vol. 23, No. 90, 2014, p. 1110.

security companies—only legalized in China in 2010[114]—are beginning to enter the African market to provide security to Chinese firms. The director of one such security firm, Beijing Huayuan Weishi Security Service Co., traveled to Tanzania with Vice President Li Yuanchao in December 2014 to assess business potential in Tanzania, where it plans to have 800 guards, with sales of about $90 million within three years.[115] While private security contractors may mitigate security shortcomings for Chinese firms, it is also possible that poorly trained guards operating in Africa with minimal oversight could exacerbate local tensions with Chinese expatriates.

PRC Arms Sales

Chinese arms sales are an important component of Chinese military engagement in Africa. According to the SIPRI Arms Transfers Database, from 2010 through 2014, China sold arms to at least 18 countries in Africa, including Algeria, Cameroon, Chad, Congo, Ethiopia, Gabon, Ghana, Kenya, Namibia, Nigeria, Sudan, Tanzania, and Zambia.[116] SIPRI reports indicate that Chinese arms sales in Africa have increased in recent years, and China has sold more arms in Africa than has the United States in most years since 2000.

One notable deal was China's recent agreement to sell three Chinese-made surface ships to Algeria. China launched the first of three frigates built for Algeria by China State Shipbuilding Corporation in August 2014, and it is scheduled for delivery in May 2015. In addition, China is reportedly negotiating a contract for the sale of three more of the ships to Algeria.[117] Nigeria has also purchased significant amounts of Chinese military materiel for both coastal patrols and oper-

---

[114] Karthie Lee, "Chinese Private Security Firms Go Overseas: 'Crossing the River by Feeling the Stones,'" Frontier Services Group Analysis, September 8, 2014.

[115] Yang Yao, "Chinese Security Company Makes Foray into Africa," *China Daily Africa*, October 31, 2014.

[116] Pieter D. Wezeman and Siemon T. Wezeman, "Trends in International Arms Transfers, 2014," SIPRI Fact Sheet, March 2015.

[117] Kerry Herschelmann, "First Algerian C28A Corvette Launched in China," *IHS Jane's Defence Weekly*, August 20, 2014.

ations to counter Boko Haram, including two P-18N offshore patrol vessels, armored personnel carriers, antitank missiles, and, reportedly, armed CH-3 unmanned aerial vehicles (UAVs).[118] China has provided some military materiel as grants to selected African countries as well, sometimes as deliverables associated with high-level visits. While on a visit to Windhoek in March 2015, for example, Chinese Minister of Defense Chang Wanquan announced Beijing would provide $58 million worth of equipment to Namibia.[119] Similarly, between 2004 and 2014, China provided Liberia with $10 million in military equipment and training.[120]

Some African countries have acquired Chinese arms to support peacekeeping capabilities; Zambia, for example, used Chinese-made armored personnel carriers in Sudan,[121] and Ghana's $160 million arms agreement with China included peacekeeping-related training.[122] In other cases, however, Chinese arms have clearly fueled internal and regional conflicts. Chinese arms were used by both sides of conflicts in the Democratic Republic of Congo, Sierra Leone, and Sudan as well as in the border wars between Ethiopia and Eritrea.[123]

PLA Military Diplomacy

Chinese military diplomacy is another important aspect of Chinese military engagement in Africa. Africa is the region with the third highest number of visits by CMC members since 2003, with nine, though

---

[118] See, for example, Jeffrey Lin and P. W. Singer, "Did an Armed Chinese-Made Drone Just Crash in Nigeria?" *Popular Science*, January 28, 2015; see also "Nigeria Acquiring New and Second-Hand Military Hardware," *Cameroon Concord*, March 30, 2015.

[119] "China Donates Military Equipment to Namibia," *Star Africa*, March 31, 2015.

[120] Terrence Sesay, "China Donates $4m Worth of Equipment to Liberian Military," *Africa Review*, February 27, 2014.

[121] Bates Gill and Chin-Hao Huang, *China's Expanding Role in Peacekeeping: Prospects and Policy Implications*, SIPRI, Policy Paper 25, November 2009.

[122] Bernice Bessey, "Ghana: Gov't to Re-Equip Armed Forces," *Ghanaian Chronicle*, September 10, 2008.

[123] Kuruvilla Mathews, "China and UN Peacekeeping Operations in Africa," in China-Africa Think Tanks Forum (CATTF), "The 2nd Meeting of the China-Africa Think Tanks Forum," conference report, Bisoftu, Ethiopia, October 12–13, 2012, pp. 95–96.

it is well behind Southeast Asia and South and Central Asia, the two most frequent destinations, with 27 and 20 such trips, respectively. Senior Chinese military officers visited a number of countries in Africa during the period reviewed as part of this study, with Tanzania and South Africa appearing to be countries of particular interest to China. The frequency of such visits also appears to be increasing.

Combined Exercises and Training

PLA troops have participated in just three joint exercises with African armed forces. China's first joint exercise in Africa, "Peace Angel-2009," was a humanitarian medical rescue mission with Gabon.[124] China also held a 2011 counter-piracy training with Tanzania. In 2014, this was expanded in "Transcend-2014," a month-long exercise conducted at Kigamboni Naval Base involving the PLAN South Sea Fleet and the Tanzanian Marine Corps.[125] Transcend-2014 focused on marine tactics, anti-piracy, and counterterrorism; the specific scenario required the marines to rescue civilians held hostage on a small island after a terrorist hijacking.[126] China has also provided training to African militaries, although often the training is related to weapons and materiel that China has provided.[127]

PLAN Port Visits

From 2000 to 2014, the PLA Navy conducted 35 total port visits to Africa. Since 2009 alone, the PLAN has made 33 port visits to the region, 28 of which have been associated with PLAN anti-piracy task forces. The PLAN's *Peace Ark* hospital ship made four port visits in

---

[124] "'Peace Angel 2009' Kicks Off," *Xinhua News*, June 21, 2009.

[125] Forum on China-Africa Cooperation, "The First Joint Training Exercise Between the Two Armed Forces of Tanzania and China to Be Conducted," October 23, 2014; Forum on China-Africa Cooperation, "Ambassador Lu Observed Transcend 2014 Joint Training Exercise of Marine Corps Between China and Tanzania," November 15, 2014.

[126] Forum on China-Africa Cooperation, November 15, 2014.

[127] As part of U.S. security cooperation efforts, the U.S. military often provides English language study centers to partner militaries so their personnel can acquire the language skills necessary to attend training courses in the United States.

Africa in 2010, stopping in Djibouti,[128] Kenya,[129] Tanzania,[130] and the Seychelles.[131] Over 400 Chinese soldiers, officers, and medical workers aboard the ship provided free medical services to local residents. The port most frequented by these task forces is Djibouti, a key port of supply in the region that has been visited 19 times between 2009 and 2014, making it the PLAN's second most frequented port overall (after Salalah, Oman).[132]

China's increasingly frequent calls on African ports raised the question of whether Beijing would seek to institutionalize its port access, either by establishing a permanent naval base of its own or by formalizing logistics agreements to service naval vessels. If the PLAN is to engage in non-PKO operations abroad, it would benefit from securing reliable access to fuel, supplies, and other forms of logistical support.[133] A Chinese naval presence would also help project Chinese military power and protect Chinese commercial shipping transiting the Indian Ocean, the Red Sea, and the Suez Canal.[134]

Related to this, the Seychelles reportedly invited China in December 2011 to set up a military base, and China considered setting up some type of facility, although characterizing it as a potential supply stop rather than a military base.[135] Chinese defense officials asserted at the time that PLAN ships had previously taken on supplies in Djibouti,

---

128 "China's Hospital Ship Peace Ark Leaves Djibouti," *Xinhua News*, September 29, 2010.

129 "Navy Hospital Ship 'Peace Ark' Arrives in Kenya," *China Daily*, October 14, 2010.

130 "China's Peace Ark Arrives in Tanzania," *China Daily*, October 20, 2010.

131 "China's 'Peace Ark' Mission Proves Success in Seychelles," *Xinhua News*, October 30, 2010.

132 Note that an alternate and potentially more complete count of port calls appears in Erickson and Strange, 2015.

133 Zerba, 2014, p. 1107.

134 Simon Allison, "Djibouti Welcomes China to the Playground of the Superpowers," *Daily Maverick*, May 14, 2015.

135 Zerba, 2014, p. 1107. See also Chris Buckley with additional reporting by Michael Martina, "Update 2—China Considers Seychelles Port Offer, Denies Base Plan," *Reuters*, December 13, 2011.

Yemen, and Oman.[136] In February 2014, Djibouti signed a security and defense strategic partnership agreement with China that granted port access to PLAN ships in exchange for Chinese assistance to Djibouti's navy and air force.[137] Fifteen months later, in May 2015, Djiboutian President Ismail Omar Guelleh announced that his country was negotiating with Beijing regarding the establishment of a Chinese military base.[138] That November, the establishment of a Chinese facility was announced. Although China referred to it as a logistical support facility, others have subsequently referred to it as a military base.[139]

China formally opened the base on August 1, 2017, with Deputy Chinese Naval Commander Tian Zhong and Djibouti's Defense Minister Ali Hassan Bahdon attending.[140] Analysis of satellite imagery showed the base to be fortified with three layers of security and to have about 250,000 square feet of underground space, allowing not only for storage but also for unobserved activity.[141] Subsequently, Chinese troops at the base have conducted at least one live-fire exercise with the stated purpose of testing their capacity to handle a variety of tasks and weapons in extreme heat and humidity.[142]

Although the strategic advantages of a naval facility in Djibouti are clear, some observers assert that Beijing's effort to establish a military facility in Djibouti is a direct challenge to the United States, which has leased Djibouti's 500-acre Camp Lemonnier as a base for

---

[136] Li Xiaokun and Li Lianxing, "Navy Looks at Offer from Seychelles," *China Daily*, December 13, 2011.

[137] "Djibouti and China Sign a Security and Defense Agreement," *AllAfrica.com*, February 27, 2014; see also, John Lee, "China Comes to Djibouti," *Foreign Affairs*, April 23, 2015.

[138] AFP, "Djibouti President: China Negotiating Horn of Africa Military Base," *Defense News*, May 10, 2015.

[139] Perlez and Buckley, 2015.

[140] "China Formally Opens First Overseas Military Base in Djibouti," *Reuters*, August 1, 2017.

[141] Joshua Berlinger, "Satellite Photos Reveal Underground Construction at Chinese Military Base," CNN, August 1, 2017.

[142] Minnie Chan, "Live-Fire Show of Force by Troops from China's First Overseas Military Base," *South China Morning Post*, September 25, 2017.

its regional counterterrorism operations since 2002[143] and signed a new 20-year lease for the base in 2014.[144]

UN Peacekeeping Operations

Chinese participation in UN Peacekeeping Operations is a central aspect of Chinese military engagement and conflict resolution in Africa. Chinese officials have promised to work to resolve conflicts in Africa, support African organizations, and participate in UN peacekeeping operations in the region.[145] As of March 31, 2015, China was involved in seven UNPKOs in Africa.[146]

China's participation in such operations in Africa has featured several notable firsts. This includes the first time a PLA officer led a UNPKO and the first time China sent guard forces to participate in a UNPKO, even though their role appears limited to providing security for the other Chinese personnel. China also achieved another milestone by deploying a larger number of security forces to Mali to participate in the United Nations Multidimensional Integrated Stabilization Mission in Mali (MINUSMA). Their responsibilities went beyond protecting other Chinese troops to include guarding MINUSMA headquarters and the living areas of the UNPKO personnel. China has also sent an entire infantry battalion to participate in the UN peacekeeping mission in South Sudan.[147] China's peacekeeping activities in Africa in recent years thus represent a key step beyond China's traditional practice of providing only noncombat forces to participate in UNPKOs.

---

[143] Craig Whitlock, "Remote U.S. Base at Core of Secret Operations," *Washington Post*, October 25, 2012; Frank Gardner, "US Military Steps Up Operations in the Horn of Africa," *BBC News*, February 7, 2014.

[144] Eric Schmitt, "U.S. Signs New Lease to Keep Strategic Military Installation in the Horn of Africa," *New York Times*, May 5, 2014.

[145] Wang Wei, "China and Africa Envision New Security Cooperation," *China.org.cn*, July 9, 2010.

[146] UN Missions Summary, detailed by country, March 31, 2015.

[147] "Xinhua Insight: Chinese Peacekeeping Troops Show Responsibility, Professionalism," *Chinese Military Online*, April 19, 2015.

China's participation in African stability operations benefits it in a number of important ways. These operations win China regional trust and international stature,[148] and China uses them to advance its own strategic interests. For example, when China's support of the Sudanese regime led international human rights groups to label Beijing's Olympic Games as the "Darfur Olympics" and the "Genocide Olympics," China pressured Sudan to accept the deployment of a UN peacekeeping operation.[149] This allowed Beijing to mitigate criticism of its Olympic Games and distance itself from the violence against civilians in Darfur. PKOs can also contribute directly to Chinese economic interests by maintaining stability in regions where Chinese companies operate.[150]

Military Operations Other than War

PLA participation in military operations other than war activities represents still another element of Chinese military engagement with countries in Africa. Prominent examples have included Chinese PLAN participation in anti-piracy patrols in the Gulf of Aden, PLA participation in Ebola treatment operations, and PLAN and PLAAF involvement in noncombatant evacuation operations.

China's navy has been participating in anti-piracy patrols in the Gulf of Aden since December 2008. Their participation in 22 successive task forces, and counting, has not only helped deal with piracy but also allowed China to boost its image internationally and given the PLAN an opportunity to improve its ability to operate far from China's shores. In addition, participation in anti-piracy patrols has positioned the PLAN to be able to participate in other missions, most notably China's evacuations from Libya in 2011 and Yemen in 2015.

In October 2014, China announced that it would dispatch hundreds of military medical personnel to West Africa to treat patients and help in the fight against Ebola. PLA involvement in relief operations in West Africa was unprecedented in that it marked the first time China had sent military medical units overseas to set up a hospital and

[148] Gill and Huang, 2009, p. 13.

[149] Gill and Huang, 2009.

[150] Gill and Huang, 2009.

participate in a humanitarian assistance mission.[151] PLA personnel sent to Liberia and Sierra Leone not only treated hundreds of patients but also provided training to numerous local health care workers.[152]

The protection of Chinese nationals abroad has taken on greater importance. There are at least hundreds of thousands of PRC citizens—perhaps as many as one million—living and working in Africa.[153] In March 2011, China managed a noncombatant evacuation operation from Libya, which Chinese officials describe as the "largest and most complicated overseas evacuation ever conducted by the Chinese government." At a cost of $152 million,[154] China evacuated more than 36,000 Chinese citizens and 2,100 foreign nationals from Libya in roughly ten days.[155] To coordinate the evacuation, the PRC established a special task force led by a vice premier.[156] The operation was particularly notable for its limited, but unprecedented, PLAN and PLAAF participation.[157]

Conclusion

China and the United States have similar interests in Africa. Both the United States and China seek security and stability in the region and

---

[151] Megha Rajagopalan, "China to Send Elite Army Unit to Help Fight Ebola in Liberia," *Reuters*, October 21, 2014.

[152] See, for example, "PLA Sends Two More Medical Teams to Fight Against Ebola in West Africa," *China Military Online*, January 14, 2015; and Tang Yingzi and Wang Xiaodong, "China Army Medics Join Ebola Battle," *China Daily*, November 15, 2014.

[153] French, 2014, p. 5.

[154] Zerba, 2014, p. 1112.

[155] Zerba, 2014.

[156] Mathieu Duchâtel and Bates Gill, "Overseas Citizen Protection: A Growing Challenge for China," SIPRI, February 12, 2012.

[157] China relied on 74 chartered aircraft, more than a dozen ships, and 100 buses to evacuate its citizens. However, in a first for China, the PLAAF sent four IL-76 large transport aircraft to Libya to participate in evacuation, and the PLAN Jiangkai II-class frigate *Xuzhou*, which had been conducting anti-piracy operations off Somalia, provided "support and protection." See Zerba, 2014, p. 1101, and Duchâtel and Gill, 2012.

the maintenance of political influence, although Washington and Beijing take different approaches to some of these interests. The United States has worked to promote good governance, provided aid that is focused on human development, and pursues investment led by private sector entities, whereas China has stressed political independence from outside interference while providing state-backed investment and tied aid focused on infrastructure and natural resource extraction. To some degree, Washington and Beijing are working at cross-purposes. In providing aid without preconditions, for example, Beijing encourages inefficiencies that Washington tries to mitigate through its governance initiatives; similarly, by insisting that African countries conduct feasibility studies and environmental impact assessments before building new infrastructure, Washington is hindering China's ability to do business.

Commercially, both seek access to natural resources and seek the creation of export markets for manufactured goods. Both hope to improve African economic development through aid, investment, and trade, but Beijing and Washington take different approaches. Chinese and American companies generally operate in different spheres; Chinese firms tend to pursue opportunities in capital-intensive industries using low-skilled labor, such as construction, mining, and manufacturing, while U.S. firms are involved in service industries and high-tech sectors such as banking and information technology.[158]

Critics of China's emphasis on political noninterference in its investment activities "characterize Chinese involvement on the continent as narrowly mercantilist at best and devoid of moral content at worst."[159] China has typically argued that economic development is the basis for peace,[160] but with its own investments increasingly threatened

---

158 Government Accountability Office, 2013, pp. 54, 67.

159 Chris Alden and Daniel Large, "On Becoming a Norms Maker: Chinese Foreign Policy, Norms Evolution and the Challenges of Security in Africa," *China Quarterly*, March 2015, p. 130.

160 Chinese Mission to UN Offices in Geneva, "Statement by Ambassador Wang Yinfan, Permanent Representative of China to the United Nations, at the 56th Session of the General Assembly on the Issue of 'the Causes of Conflict and the Promotion of Durable Peace and Sustainable Development in Africa,'" December 3, 2001.

by instability and anti-Chinese violence, China is increasingly seeking a way to promote peace and stability to promote economic development. Chinese involvement in African peace, security, and post-conflict reconstruction has been increasingly prominent focus areas at FOCAC meetings since 2006.[161] China is also adjusting its approach to foreign policy to move beyond strict noninterference to play a more substantive role in African security.[162] Some experts believe that China may well take similar approaches in other regions of the world. "Africa has become a terrain for demonstrating China's foreign policy activism and its willingness to strike a foreign policy formula integrating its economic interests, regional concerns and provisions for international public goods" that it may apply elsewhere.[163]

A decision by China to pursue a more activist foreign policy in Africa (and perhaps in other parts of the world) could have mixed results for the United States. On one hand, China's willingness to help resolve conflicts, contribute to peacekeeping missions, and encourage partner nations to moderate their own destructive policies could improve political and security conditions in countries where U.S. influence may be minimal. Beijing's successful efforts to convince Sudan to accept a UN peacekeeping mission in Darfur is one notable example of China's constructive activism. Moreover, China's rapidly growing investment in African infrastructure could yield economic benefits for African nations—provided they are managed well and are economically efficient, rather than just placing recipient countries in a debt hole—while also facilitating business opportunities for U.S. and other foreign companies. On the other hand, if China seeks a greater military presence on the continent, uses the access created by its economic engagement to push for the United States' exclusion from the region, or otherwise seeks to treat the region as a zero-sum battle for influence, China's growing influence in the region could be to the United States' detriment.

---

[161] Alden and Large, 2015, p. 131.

[162] Alden and Large, 2015, p. 123.

[163] Alden and Large, 2015, p. 128.

It is not clear, at least at this point, if Chinese involvement in the region has translated into greater regional (or country-specific) support for broader Chinese policy initiatives. With the exception of a small number of African states, such as Zimbabwe, the pariah status of which means it has few other friends in the international community, it is not clear whether Chinese trade, investment, or aid have enhanced Beijing's influence over regional politics or translated into a greater willingness to vote with China at the UN. To date, Beijing has seemed more interested in using its political clout and vast economic resources to secure additional business opportunities, particularly in the extractive industries and the relatively low-tech construction sector, both of which are dominated by SOEs.

Although Chinese economic pursuits may undermine U.S. efforts to promote good governance on the continent, for the most part the United States and China do not seem headed for conflict or competition in Africa. Indeed, in the political sphere, African countries appear eager to maintain close relations with both the United States and China. African governments participated at the highest levels (typically head of state) in the 2014 White House Africa summit without apparent concern, for example, that their doing so would jeopardize their relationship with China or their participation in the 2015 FOCAC summit. In the realm of foreign assistance, the United States focuses its assistance efforts on human development to a much greater degree than China, and in the commercial sphere, U.S. and Chinese firms generally do not compete in Africa (with the exception of the hydrocarbons sector). The Chinese government provides much more state backing to private investment in Africa than do U.S. equivalent entities like the Export-Import Bank, the Trade and Development Agency (TDA), and the Overseas Private Investment Corporation (OPIC). Finally, U.S. companies are often less willing to invest in countries with high political risk, poor infrastructure, and small domestic or regional markets.[164]

China has a different approach to security matters in Africa than the United States does, however. While both seek to protect their

[164] Hanauer and Morris, 2014, pp. 99–101.

nationals from violence, the United States is interested in mitigating and containing threats so they do not reach the U.S. homeland, while China is principally interested in eliminating threats to its economic activities in the region. The United States, thus, takes a more proactive approach to security matters, deploying U.S. military assets to engage in training and operations and providing extensive bilateral security cooperation designed to address shared threats, such as terrorism and violent extremism. In contrast, China focuses its military engagement on internationally endorsed multinational peacekeeping missions, arms sales tailored to African countries' own threat perceptions, and limited military deployments aimed at protecting Chinese commercial operations in the region.

Implications for the United States

While Washington's and Beijing's divergent strategies for pursuing their respective interests in Africa means that the two world powers are not likely to come into conflict, it also means that few opportunities for mutually beneficial collaboration exist.[165] The United States and China consult periodically on African affairs through the U.S.-China Sub-Dialogue on Africa, which meets at the assistant secretary level. Although launched in 2005 to discuss regional issues and promote U.S.-Chinese cooperation in the region, the initiative has produced no collaborative programs.

Health care and economic development are often sufficiently politically innocuous to permit collaboration.[166] Nevertheless, even when their interests have coincided, strategic mistrust between Washington and Beijing has led them to pursue parallel initiatives.[167] Even though both countries provided assistance to manage the spread of the Ebola virus in West Africa in 2014, for example, U.S. and Chinese

[165] Yun Sun, "The Limits of U.S.-China Cooperation in Africa," Brookings Institution, April 6, 2015.

[166] See Travis M. Miller, "Is There Room for U.S.-China Cooperation on the Ebola Crisis? (Parts 1 through 3)," The Carter Center, *U.S. China Perception Monitor* blog, October 15, 2014.

[167] Yun Sun, 2015.

responders engaged in only minimal deconfliction.[168] In a similar vein, humanitarian assistance and disaster relief may provide opportunities for U.S.-Chinese collaboration. However, the U.S. and Chinese armed forces play significant roles in official disaster response efforts, and it may be difficult to manage coordination between military forces that are accustomed to viewing each other as likely adversaries.

As Chinese citizens increasingly go overseas to pursue economic opportunities, they are likely to require assistance when conflicts erupt or disasters strike. The U.S. government has extensive experience conducting noncombatant evacuation operations. Cooperation on such operations could be promoted as a joint humanitarian effort, since the beneficiaries would be civilians caught in conflict or disaster zones, but distrust between the U.S. and Chinese militaries could make such collaboration difficult without a very senior-level commitment to work together.

---

[168] U.S. government official, "China and the US in Africa—Can Security Policy Promote Practical Cooperation?" Roundtable discussion, Johns Hopkins University School of Advanced International Studies, Washington, D.C., March 25, 2015.

CHAPTER NINE

China in Latin America and the Caribbean

Latin America and the Caribbean (hereafter Latin America) is the least important developing region for China. The region is geographically distant and made up only 6 percent of total Chinese goods trade with the world in 2013. Countries in the region neither have any territorial disputes with China nor view the country as a security threat. Many of them do view China as a good market and a source of capital for infrastructure and other projects, but some are also concerned about Chinese investment and competition.

The region is currently not part of China's Belt and Road Initiative. There are voices in China arguing that Latin America should be included in China's 21st Century Maritime Silk Road.[1] There is also speculation that China is deepening relations and engaging in significant infrastructure investments to facilitate the region's potential inclusion despite not characterizing its actions as such.[2] Beijing, however, is

---

[1] There are some in China urging the country to expand its maritime silk road to Latin America. See Tang Jun, "Ying Jiang '21 Shiji Haishang Sichou Zhi Lu' Yanshen Zhi Lamei Diqu" ["The '21st Century Maritime Silk Road' Should Be Extended to the Latin American Region"], *The Contemporary World*, February 6, 2015.

[2] Nathan Beauchamp-Mustafaga, "The New Silk Road and Latin America: Will They Ever Meet?" *Jamestown China Brief*, Vol. 15, No. 5, March 6, 2015; "Zhongguo Lamei Luntan Rang Meiguo Zhuakuang" ["China-Latin America Forum Drives America Mad"], *Creaders.net*, January 10, 2015.

cautious of U.S. sensitivities of being too active politically and militarily in the Americas.

Overall, China is increasing its involvement in the region and will likely become a more important player in the years to come. Relations will also likely become more complex as Chinese influence extends beyond the economic sphere. However, some of this will depend on China's growth path, its future demand for commodities, other demands on its capital, and the success or failure of its Latin American partners. There is interest and potential for deepening the relationship, but there are also concerns that Latin America is less receptive to Chinese activities than Africa and economic frictions could strain China's relations with the region.

Key Chinese Activities in the Region

China is not actively seeking to balance the United States in Latin America. Economics and trade have been the main focus of Beijing's engagement with the region. China is exporting manufactured goods to the region and investing in infrastructure, agriculture, telecommunications, and tourism. The region is also a source of energy (petroleum), raw materials (iron, copper, and nonferrous ores), and food (soy) for China.

In recent years, geopolitical considerations have played a greater role in Chinese engagement. China sees Latin America as an important region for China to strengthen its relations with developing countries and to work toward a more multipolar international system. This includes obtaining regional support in the UN for policies China favors as well as involving countries in Chinese multilateral initiatives. China is most intertwined with Venezuela. But Brazil serves as more of a partner in multilateral initiatives; it is the only Latin American founding member of the China-led AIIB, and it is a core member of the New Development Bank, or BRICS bank. Beijing also seeks to strengthen ties with countries in the region to decrease Taiwanese influence. Beijing views three countries in particular—Venezuela, Brazil, and Argentina—as its most important regional partners (Figure 9.1).

Figure 9.1
China's Relations with Countries in Latin America and the Caribbean, 2015

NOTE: Due to small scale of map, not all countries are displayed and labeled.
RAND *RR2273A-9.1*

Drivers of Chinese Engagement

Chinese Activities in the Region Prior to 2000

Early Chinese involvement in the region can be divided into the Cold War period and post–Cold War decade. During the Cold War, Beijing focused on transforming the international system by supporting nonalignment of third world countries as well as local Maoist movements that sought to overturn the established socioeconomic system. With the exception of communist Cuba, countries in the region did not establish diplomatic relations with Beijing until the 1970s as most had pro-Washington and anti-Communist governments run by conservative military leaders. After Sino-U.S. rapprochement in the early 1970s, the Nixon administration discreetly encouraged Latin American countries, such as Brazil, Chile, and Mexico, to open embassies in Beijing. As Beijing embarked on economic reforms and opened up to international trade in the late 1970s, it also shelved its attempts to foment socialist revolution in favor of developing bilateral relations and links to the Developing World. By the 1990s, China switched its emphasis in Latin America from political mobilization to economic engagement.[3]

Current Chinese Policy Toward the Region

Chinese Priorities and Policies

China has three overarching interests in Latin America:

- Solidarity and cooperation with developing countries to facilitate China's vision of a multipolar world, including Chinese support of a greater Latin American role in international affairs and Latin American support of Chinese international initiatives
- Economic trade and investment to support China's economic growth

---

[3] Adrian H. Hearn and Jose Luis Leon-Manriquez, "China and Latin America: A New Era of an Old Exchange," in Adrian H. Hearn and Jose Luis Leon-Manriquez, eds., *China Engages Latin America: Tracing the Trajectory*, Boulder, Colo.: Lynne Rienner Publishers, 2001, pp. 8–10.

- International political legitimacy, including recognition of Beijing as the sole representative of China (One China principle), acknowledgement of the principle of noninterference in sovereign countries' internal affairs, and support of Chinese sovereignty and territorial integrity.

Beijing has issued several policy documents that define its objectives in Latin America. China's 2008 White Paper on Latin America was its third such regional policy paper after its papers on the European Union and Africa.[4] The paper indicates that "the move towards multi-polarity is irreversible" and that Latin America as a region "is growing in strength and its international influence is rising." Beijing views relations with the region from a "strategic plane" and aims for "a comprehensive and cooperative partnership featuring equality, mutual benefit and common development." The paper listed four goals of Chinese policy toward the region: "promote mutual respect and mutual trust and expand common ground"; deepen cooperation, particularly economic cooperation; increase political and cultural exchanges; and uphold the One China principle.

In 2011 and 2014, China issued two different White Papers on its foreign aid.[5] Aid to Latin America constituted 12.7 percent of all Chinese foreign aid up to and including 2009 but only 8.4 percent of Chinese foreign aid from 2010 to 2012. The major recipients of Chinese aid were Asian and African countries[6] as well as the poorest LDCs.[7] Latin America was not a priority region, and only Haiti qualified as an LDC.

In recent years, Chinese engagement with the region has transitioned from bilateral to region-wide platforms. China has been a permanent observer in the Latin American Integration Association since

[4] "Full Text: China's Policy Paper on Latin America and the Caribbean," *Xinhua News*, November 6, 2008.

[5] *China's Foreign Aid (2011)*, 2011; *China's Foreign Aid (2014)*, Information Office of the State Council of the People's Republic of China, July 2014.

[6] Both regions received over 80 percent of global Chinese foreign aid.

[7] Chinese aid to LDC increased from 40 percent in 2009 to 52 percent in 2010–2012.

1994 and the Organization of American States since 2004. It became a formal member in the Inter-American Development Bank in 2009. In 2014, the China-Community of Latin American and Caribbean States (CELAC) forum was established. This multilateral forum provides a vehicle for China to conduct talks with all Latin American countries at the ministerial level and resembles Chinese regional arrangements in Africa (FOCAC) and Central Asia (SCO) as well as China's engagements with ASEAN in Southeast Asia.

Chinese policy in Latin America is shaped by a number of government, quasi-government, and nongovernment actors. There is limited but growing Chinese expertise on Latin America within and outside the government (see Appendix A). Similarly, on the Latin American side, regional countries are still grappling with how best to engage more systematically and institutionally with China. According to a 2015 Yellow Paper published by the Institute for Latin American Studies at the Chinese Academy of Social Science, Latin American countries are beginning to reassess and formulate strategies to engage with China. Brazil formulated a "China Agenda—Positive Action for Sino-Brazilian Economic and Trade Relations" in 2008 to increase exports to China and diversify economic partnerships. Similarly, Chile established a policy plan for China in 2009 and a China affairs group within its Foreign Investment Committee in 2010.[8] In 2013, Mexico agreed to establish a special trade office to facilitate bilateral cooperation with China.[9]

The following three sections explore China's political, economic, and military engagement with the region.

Political Engagement

China's main political interest in the region is to increase relations to provide international support and legitimacy. China seeks closer relations with countries that have either a significant regional or global role.

---

[8] "Zhongguo Shi Lamei Waijiao 'Taipingyang Zhanlue' De Youxian Mubiao" ["China Is the Primary Target of Latin America Foreign Policy's 'Pacific Strategy'"], *People's Daily*, May 15, 2015.

[9] Zhu Zhe, "China, Mexico Boost Relations," *China Daily*, June 5, 2013.

Often, China's actions have a strong economic component alongside their political and diplomatic components.

In Latin America, China has maintained and formed close relations with left-leaning and socialist countries such as Cuba, Venezuela, Argentina (when it was left-leaning), and Ecuador. While China has actively reached out to the entire region, left-leaning countries have particularly embraced and welcomed stronger relations with China. Cut off from or with limited access to U.S. and Western financing, these countries have also looked to China for economic support. Beijing is also advancing its One China policy by providing more financial rewards to countries that recognize Beijing. Of the 22 countries that still recognize Taiwan, 12 were located in Latin America as of late 2015. Although Beijing and Taipei agreed to a truce in 2008 to their competition to win diplomatic recognition, China still seeks to strengthen its position vis-à-vis Taiwan.

Under President Xi's leadership, China's relations with the region have deepened significantly. Since coming to power in 2013 and through the end of 2015, Xi has visited the region twice and Premier Li Keqiang traveled again to Latin America in 2015. Xi's June 2013 visit took him to Trinidad and Tobago, Costa Rica, and Mexico. In Trinidad and Tobago, the first Caribbean country to establish diplomatic ties with China, in 1974, he emphasized the need to enhance high-level exchanges and visits and to expand cooperation in infrastructure, energy, and mining. Xi also met with leaders from other Caribbean countries with diplomatic ties to China and promised $3 billion in loans for projects.[10] He then visited Costa Rica, the only Central American country that has diplomatic ties with China and the country that would serve as the CELAC chair in 2014. China and Costa Rica agreed to work together to establish a China-Latin America cooperation forum[11] and China agreed to provide the Central American country a $900 million credit for modernization of an oil refinery and $400 million in financing for a strategic highway.[12]

---

10 "China, Trinidad and Tobago Pledge to Bolster Ties," *Xinhua News*, June 2, 2013.

11 "China, Costa Rica Agree to Enhance Ties," *China Daily*, June 6, 2013.

12 "Costa Rica, China Sign Cooperation Agreements Worth Nearly $2 Billion," *Tico Times*, June 1, 2013.

In Mexico, Xi sought to smooth previous friction between the two countries and enhance economic cooperation.[13]

Thirteen months later, in July 2014, Xi traveled to Latin America again to attend a BRICS summit and the first meeting of the China-CELAC grouping in Brazil and to also visit Argentina, Venezuela, and Cuba. In Brazil, the BRICS countries agreed to establish the New Development Bank and a Contingency Reserve Agreement that will add to—and, some argue, rival—existing financial entities like the World Bank, the Asian Development Bank, and the International Monetary Fund.

During the trip, China also signed a number of agreements, totaling around $70 billion, in the areas of energy, mining, electricity, agriculture, science and technology, infrastructure, and finance. Xi also pushed for a "1+3+6" cooperation framework for future partnership, which included:

- One plan: Chinese-Latin American and Caribbean Cooperation Plan (2015–2019)
- Three engines of cooperation: trade, investment, and financial cooperation
- Six fields of emphasis: energy and resources, infrastructure, agriculture, manufacturing, scientific and technological innovation, and information technologies.

In early 2015, China and Latin American countries signed the China-Latin American and Caribbean Countries Cooperation Plan (2015–2019). China and Latin American states agreed to mutual respect of sovereignty and territorial integrity, greater economic cooperation, and more constructive and closer consultation on international affairs via institutionalized, high-level contacts. The plan recognized that China and Latin America were developing countries and emerging economies that were important international actors that could help promote "multilateralism and a multipolar world, and greater democracy in international relations." The sides agreed to enhance collabora-

---

[13] Zhu Zhe, 2013.

tion on major global issues and "strengthen the voice of developing countries in decision-making bodies of multilateral institutions."[14]

The Cooperation Plan itself included a number of goals for the coming decade and specified particular targets for its engagement:[15]

- Politically, expand exchanges and dialogue and China will invite 1,000 political leaders of CELAC countries to visit China from 2015–2019
- Economically, increase annual trade to $500 billion between China and Latin America and bilateral financial cooperation to $250 billion by 2025, with a particular emphasis on high technology and value-added goods
- Culturally, China will provide CELAC countries with 6,000 governmental scholarships, 6,000 training opportunities, and 400 opportunities for on-the-job master degree programs in China between 2015 and 2019.

In May 2015, Premier Li Keqiang visited four countries (Brazil, Colombia, Chile, and Peru) in Latin America to strengthen and upgrade China's relations with the region. At a speech at the UN Economic Commission for Latin America and the Caribbean, he characterized Latin America as "a rising high point in global politics and economy."[16] He also pushed for more industrial cooperation, including the transfer of Chinese industrial production capacity and equipment to the region.[17] Li's visit to Brazil was the highlight of the trip: China and

[14] "Beijing Declaration of the First Ministerial Meeting of the CELAC-China Forum," China-CELAC Forum, January 23, 2015.

[15] "China-Latin American and Caribbean Countries Cooperation Plan (2015–2019)," China-CELAC Forum, January 23, 2015.

[16] "Premier Li: Latin America Is the New Global High Point," Information Office of the State Council of the People's Republic of China, May 26, 2015; certainly, from the vantage point of late 2017, this laudatory statement seems either premature or overtaken by other events.

[17] "Premier Li Keqiang: Upgrade Practical Cooperation Between China and Latin America and the Caribbean Under the '3×3 Model,'" Ministry of Foreign Affairs of the People's Republic of China, May 22, 2015.

Brazil signed a Joint Action Plan for 2015–2021[18] and China agreed to nearly $53 billion worth of deals with Brazil in infrastructure, energy, mining, technology, and aviation.[19] The Joint Action Plan extended the previous high levels of strategic partnership between the two countries from 2014 to 2021. It laid out the two countries' plan to enhance bilateral cooperation across a dozen different fields, and Beijing and Brasilia also agreed to coordinate their positions in multilateral and international political and economic forums.

Diplomatic Relations and Presence

As of late 2015, 12 countries in Latin America continued to recognize Taipei instead of Beijing. With the exception of Paraguay in South America, most of these countries were in Central America and the Caribbean.[20] China has embassies in all the remaining 21 countries and consulates in six countries.

China has bilateral strategic partnership agreements with Brazil (1993/2004), Venezuela (2001), Mexico (2003), Argentine (2004), Peru (2008), and Chile (2012). China further elevated its relations with Brazil (2012), Mexico (2013), Argentina (2014), and Venezuela (2014) to a comprehensive strategic partnership.

Pivotal State and Major Partners

Venezuela, Brazil, and Argentina are priority countries for Chinese political, economic, and military engagement. Among these three, Brazil stands out in many ways. Brazil is the only country that President Xi and Premier Li visited on each trip, the only Latin American country that participated in AIIB, and a founder of the BRICS bank. Accord-

---

[18] For text of the Joint Action Plan, see "Joint Action Plan Between the Government of the Federative Republic of Brazil and the Government of the People's Republic of China, 2015–2021," *DefesaNet*, March 20, 2015.

[19] "BBC Brazil: Deals Show Waning US Influence," *China Daily*, May 21, 2015.

[20] These 12 are: Belize, El Salvador, Haiti, Nicaragua, Paraguay, St. Lucia, the Dominican Republic, the Republic of Guatemala, the Republic of Honduras, the Republic of Panama, Saint Christopher (Saint Kitts) and Nevis, and Saint Vincent and the Grenadines. See "Diplomatic Allies," Ministry of Foreign Affairs of the Republic of China (Taiwan), webpage, undated.

ing to President Xi, the country is also "China's first strategic partner among developing countries, and the first Latin American nation to forge a comprehensive strategic partnership with China."[21] However, China is deeply intertwined with Venezuela on all three dimensions we analyze—political, economic, and military—creating a partnership that may be as much burden as benefit (see Chapter 10).

High-Level Exchanges

China has been increasing its high-level exchanges and visits to the region. From 2003 to 2014, Chinese political leaders paid 45 visits to different countries in Latin America; 33 of the visits occurred from 2009 to 2014.[22] Chinese leaders were in Latin America for regional tours, to attend BRICs, APEC, or G20 summits, or for regional meetings. They did not visit every Latin American country but, instead, paid multiple visits to approximately half of the countries. Brazil and Mexico were the most visited countries, followed by Cuba, Argentina, and Venezuela. Chinese presidents during this period (Hu Jintao and Xi Jinping) visited only nine countries in Latin America.[23]

Cultural Influence

China does not have a significant cultural influence in the region and recognizes that it will not be easy for China to increase such ties. Chinese scholars identify Latin American countries as culturally and politically Western. They also view the United States as having substantial political, cultural, and economic influence in the region. Even among Asian countries, China may not be the favorite, since Japan has significant investment in the region and has had longer and more mature commercial and diplomatic ties with Latin American countries than

---

[21] "Chinese President Expects Stronger Ties with Brazil, L. America," *Xinhua News*, July 17, 2014.

[22] Chinese political leaders include the president, premier, vice president, minister of foreign affairs, and state councilor in charge of foreign affairs.

[23] These countries are: Argentina, Brazil, Chile, Costa Rica, Cuba, Mexico, Peru, Trinidad and Tobago, and Venezuela.

China.[24] Some Chinese strategists are concerned that Beijing is placing too much emphasis on Latin America and viewing the region too much like Africa; Latin America is less culturally and politically receptive to Chinese engagement than Africa.[25]

China currently has 32 Confucius Institutes in 14 Latin American countries, with Brazil having eight institutes, Mexico five, Peru four, Colombia three, Chile two, and Argentina two institutes. It also established a cultural center in Mexico City.[26] In 2012, China offered 5,000 scholarships spread over a period of five years for Latin American students studying in China.[27] The China-Latin American and Caribbean Countries Cooperation Plan (2015–2019) will further expand future cultural exchanges.

As in other regions, the number of Chinese citizens in Latin America is uncertain. One source suggested the number was 100,000 in 2010, up from 50,000 in 1990.[28]

Economic Engagement

China is increasing its economic engagement with the region. Chinese trade with and investment in Latin America has increased nearly

---

[24] 2014 polling by *BBC News* in Brazil, Argentina, Mexico, and Peru, for example, shows that only Argentina had a marginally more favorable view of China compared to Japan. Forty-three percent of Argentinians saw Japan as having a favorable influence and 45 percent saw China as having a favorable influence. In the other three countries, Japan was viewed more favorably than China. See "BBC World Service Poll," *BBC*, June 3, 2014; see also "Japan and China Compete for Latin American Clout," *Asia Sentinel*, August 11, 2014.

[25] "Zhongguo Buying Gaogu Lamei De Zhanlue Yiyi" ["China Should Not Overestimate Latin America's Strategic Value"], *Financial Times* (China), January 21, 2015; "Zhongguo Haiyao Fuhuo Nanmei De Xin" ["China Still Needs to Capture South America's Heart"], *Think.China.cn*, August 20, 2014.

[26] Zhu Zhe, 2013.

[27] Shen Zhiliang, "Zhongla Guanxi: Guanfang Waijiao Yu Gonggong Waijia Bing Zhong" ["China-Latin America Relations: The Equal Importance of Official Diplomacy and Public Diplomacy"], *PR World*, Vol. 2, 2014, p. 53.

[28] Jacqueline Mazza, *Chinese Migration to Latin America and the Caribbean*, Washington, D.C.: The Inter-American Dialogue, October 2016, p. 9.

20-fold since the early 2000s. Latin America has been a source of food and raw materials for continued Chinese manufacturing expansion as well as a destination for China to export manufactured goods and machinery. China seeks to strengthen trade with major regional economies and has been willing to provide significant financial support in exchange for resources.[29] China has been importing soy from Brazil and Argentina, and experts at the Inter-American Development Bank predict that China's food consumption will triple by 2030, whereas Latin America will have a food surplus.[30] Currently, Latin America plays a small role in Chinese energy consumption; it supplies less than 10 percent of China's oil and an even smaller share of its coal and natural gas.[31] Petroleum from Venezuela, Brazil, and Ecuador is China's main energy import from the region. China also imports iron ore from Brazil and its FTAs with Chile and Peru have incentivized Chinese mining in both countries, particularly for copper and nonferrous ore.[32]

Despite this growth in Sino-Latin American economic activities, there were few Chinese companies with a physical presence in Latin America prior to 2009. In recent years, Chinese companies have been sending more personnel to the region and setting up and expanding their operations on the ground.[33] China has also signed free trade and currency swap agreements with a handful of countries. Since 2015, China has been trying to rebalance its trade and investment in the region away from importing commodities from the region and is

---

[29] China has provided billions in loans to oil-rich Venezuela and Ecuador. See "China Steps in to Support Venezuela, Ecuador as Oil Prices Tumble," *Fortune*, January 8, 2015; "Venezuela to Get $5 Billion in Funding from China in Next Few Months: PDVSA Official," *Reuters*, June 16, 2015.

[30] "Latin America Set to Play Bigger Role for Chinese Firms," *China Daily*, September 12, 2014.

[31] Iacob Koch-Weser, "Chinese Energy Engagement with Latin America: A Review of Recent Findings," Inter-American Dialogue, January 12, 2015.

[32] For more on Chinese mining in Latin America, see Iacob Koch-Weser, "Chinese Mining Activity in Latin America: A Review of Recent Findings," Inter-American Dialogue, September 24, 2014.

[33] R. Evan Ellis, *China on the Ground in Latin America: Challenges for the Chinese and Impacts on the Region*, New York: Palgrave Macmillan, 2014.

encouraging Chinese companies to shift some of their industrial production capacity to Latin America. Chinese companies, however, still are learning to operate in Latin America and face a number of barriers to expanding their activities in the region.

Trade

China is currently Latin America's second largest trade partner. Chinese trade with Latin America as a whole from 2000 to 2013 has increased 20-fold. In contrast China has low levels of trade with the Caribbean states compared to all other regions of the Developing World and aggregate trade is on the order of $6 billion as of 2013. Although the data suggest that there are large Chinese investments in the Caribbean, most of these investments are either passed through to another foreign location or round-tripped back to China for tax reasons. These are simply holding companies for investments in other places and not investments in the Caribbean. Most of our subsequent economic analyses, thus, focus on Central and South America.

The composition of imports from Latin America has remained relatively constant with the exception of petroleum imports from Venezuela (Figure 9.2). In 2000, roughly 60 percent of all imports were food and crude materials, with the remaining mostly in manufactured goods and machinery. By 2013, food imports had fallen to just 4 percent and fuel imports had risen from just 2 percent in 2000 to 17 percent in 2013. Mineral products (crude materials) remained the largest single commodity group. Additionally, manufactured goods and machinery fell from 30 percent in 2000 to just 19 percent in 2013. Although this may seem like a dramatic change in composition, it is driven mainly by an increase in fuel imports from Venezuela of just more than $4 million in 2000 to more than $12 billion in 2013. China's largest import sources from Latin America are Brazil, Chile, Venezuela, and Mexico.

Exports to Latin America are concentrated in the three types of manufactured items—manufactured goods, machinery and transport, and miscellaneous manufactures. Together with chemical products, they made up roughly 94 percent of all exports over the entire time from 2000 to 2013 (Figure 9.3). There has been a relative increase in

Figure 9.2
Composition of Imports from Latin America

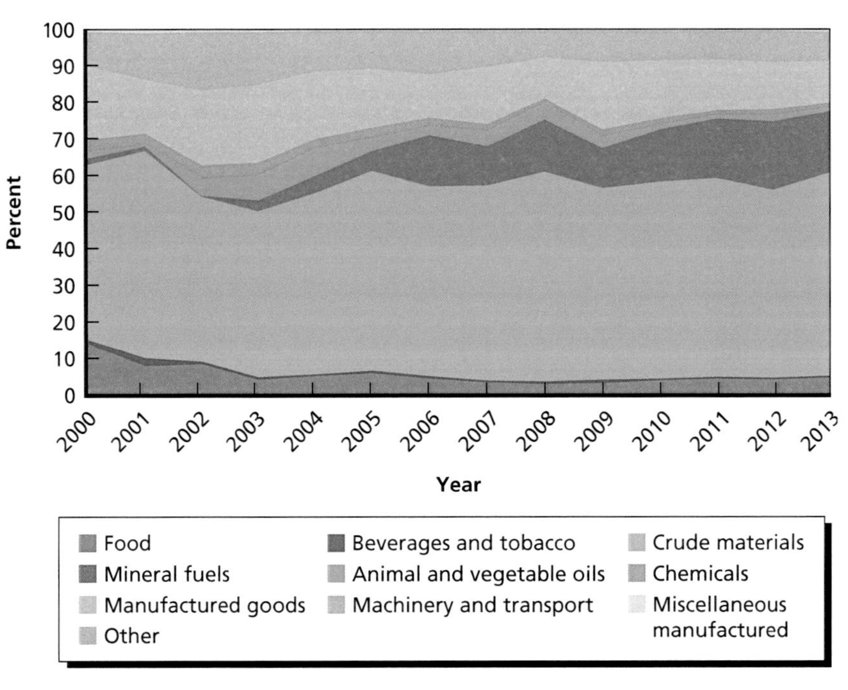

SOURCE: UN Comtrade Database.
RAND *RR2273A-9.2*

the proportion of machinery from 31 percent in 2000 to over 45 percent in 2013. This has come with a drop in proportion of manufactured goods from 60 percent to 42 percent. China's largest destinations for exports are Brazil, Mexico, Chile, and Panama.

Chinese imports from and exports to Latin America have been relatively balanced, mainly due to the large trade surpluses in Brazil and Venezuela and significant trade deficits for Mexico and Panama (Figure 9.4).

Foreign Direct Investment and Lending

There has been considerable growth in Chinese investment and loans to Latin America, especially in Venezuela and Brazil and, increasingly,

Figure 9.3
Composition of Exports to Latin America

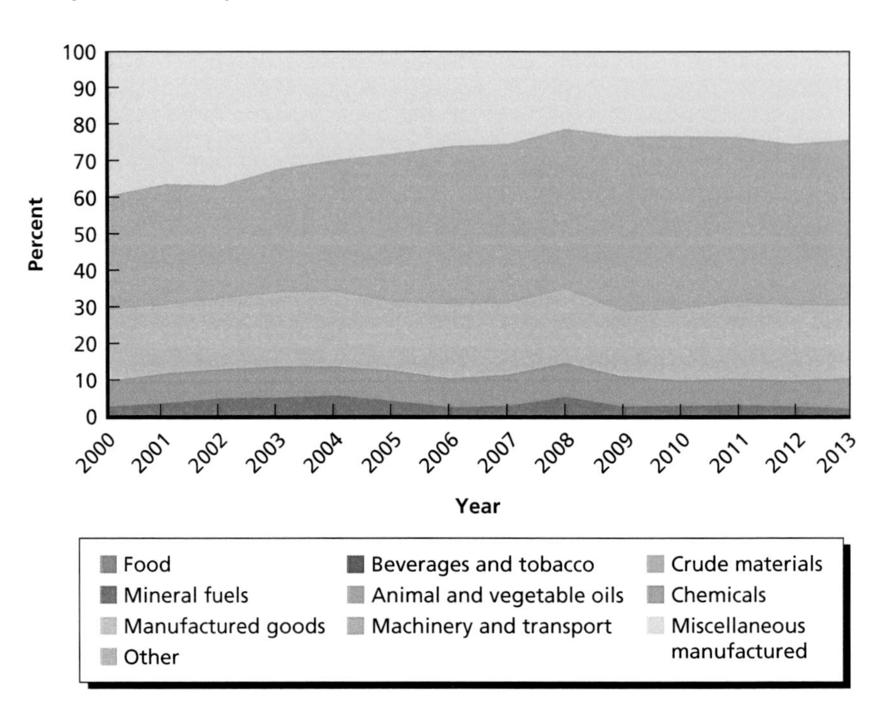

SOURCE: UN Comtrade Database.
RAND *RR2273A-9.3*

Argentina through 2015. As of the end of 2013, Chinese outward foreign direct investment stock totaled $86 billion, nearly 19 times its FDI in Latin America in 2003 (Figure 9.5). China is investing in energy, mining, agriculture, manufacturing, and basic infrastructure.

Since 2010, there has been a significant increase in Chinese lending activity to Latin America. In 2010 alone, Chinese lending to the region exceeded loans provided to the region from the World Bank, Inter-American Development Bank, and U.S. Export-Import Bank combined.[34] According to the Inter-American Dialogue, over a third of Chinese loans to the region since 2005 were for infrastructure.

---

[34] Kevin P. Gallagher and Margaret Myers, "China-Latin America Finance Database," Washington, D.C.: Inter-American Dialogue, 2014.

Figure 9.4
Level of Exports to and Imports from Latin America

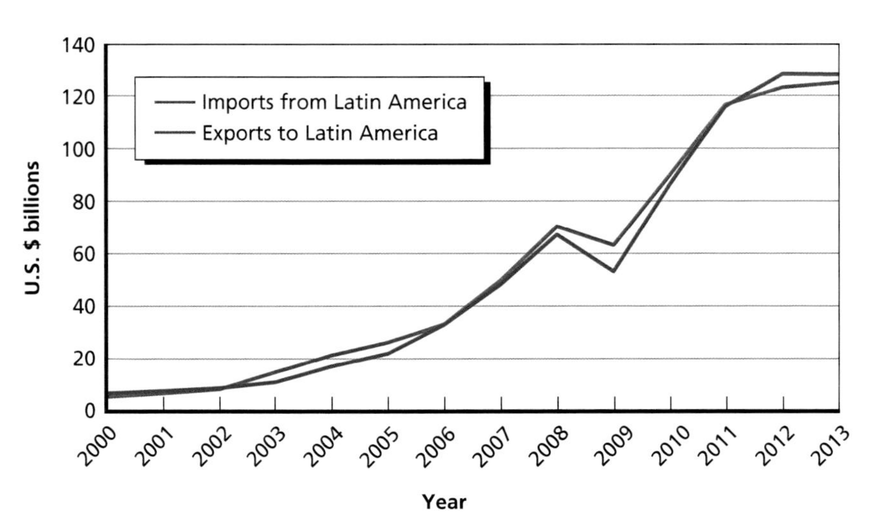

SOURCE: UN Comtrade Database.
RAND *RR2273A-9.4*

Chinese FDI and lending appear to follow similar patterns and are concentrated in several countries. China has invested the most in Venezuela. In 2013, its FDI stock in Venezuela reached $2.4 billion. It also loaned the country approximately $56 billion from 2005 through 2014, mainly in exchange for future oil shipments and more than double the amount it provided to Brazil ($22 billion) during the same time.[35] Investments in Brazil originally centered on minerals, oil and gas, and food, but have subsequently evolved into infrastructure, energy, and telecommunications.[36]

China's recent economic slowdown and lower demand for raw materials, however, have negatively affected Latin America, and Chinese strategists recognize that its "overdependence on commodity trade

[35] Inter-American Dialogue, China-Latin America Financial Database, 2015.

[36] China-Brazil Business Council, "Chinese Investments in Brazil from 2007–2012: A Review of Recent Trends," June 2013.

Figure 9.5
Chinese FDI Stock in Latin America and the Caribbean by Receiving Country, 2013

SOURCE: Chinese Ministry of Commerce, 2013 Statistical Bulletin of China's Outward Foreign Direct Investment.
NOTE: PRC FDI stock in Venezuela was $2.4 billion in 2013.
RAND *RR2273A-9.5*

[with the region] could not continue and needed to be transformed."[37] Beijing is adjusting its investment to focus more on infrastructure and local production of value-added products. In 2014, China offered CELAC a $20 billion fund from the China Development Bank to promote regional infrastructure, $10 billion in preferential loans from Exim Bank of China, and $5 billion in China-CELAC cooperation funds.[38] In May 2015, Chinese Premier Li Keqiang pushed for upgrading Chinese economic engagement with the region through the transfer of Chinese industrial production capacity and equipment to the region, particularly in the fields of logistics, power, and information.[39] He urged Chinese-invested companies to open local plants and promised to set up a $30 billion special fund to promote industrial cooperation between China and Latin America.[40] This fund was also to support infrastructure projects, including the ambitious project to connect the Atlantic Ocean to the Pacific Ocean by railroad through Brazil and Peru.[41]

Agreements and Other Issues

At present, China has fewer agreements with Latin America than with most other regions. It has three FTAs in the region, with Chile, Costa Rica, and Peru.[42] It is exploring a fourth with Colombia, but as of October 2015, negotiations had not been launched. It has nine BITs in Latin America, six of which entered into force in the mid-1990s and three of which entered into force in the 2000s and 2010s. It also has four BITs in force in the Caribbean, three of which entered into force in the 2000s. It has much less coverage with tax treaties, either for

---

[37] Quote from former Chinese vice foreign affairs minister Li Jinzhang. See "Li Keqiang Arrives in Latin America with Promise of US$50 Billion in Infrastructure Investments," *South China Morning Post*, May 19, 2015.

[38] Yu Lintao, "Vibrant Integration," *Beijing Review*, January 22, 2015.

[39] "Premier Li Keqiang," May 22, 2015.

[40] "Premier Li Keqiang," May 22, 2015.

[41] "Li Calls for Manufacturing Shift in Peru," *China Daily*, May 24, 2015.

[42] Asia Regional Integration Center, "Free Trade Agreements," webpage, Asian Development Bank, undated.

income only or for income and capital: only four in Latin America and four in the Caribbean. It also has the most contentious trade relations, as measured by cases filed with the WTO. Of the 39 cases filed against China in the WTO's dispute settlement system, Latin America has brought five: four by Mexico and one by Guatemala. This makes Latin America the only developing region with WTO cases against China.[43]

China has also signed financial and high technology agreements with Latin American countries, including bilateral currency exchange agreements with Brazil and Argentina and joint satellite development with Brazil, Venezuela, and Bolivia.[44] Since 2009, China has signed bilateral currency swap agreements to support trade and investment and to promote internationalization of the RMB. In the case of Argentina, the currency swap has also been used to facilitate loans. As of mid-2015, China has signed four multiyear currency agreements: Argentina (2009), Brazil (2013), Suriname (2015), and Chile (2015). The agreements range from highs of RMB 190 billion ($30 billion) with Brazil[45] and RMB 70 billion ($10.24 billion) with Argentina[46] to a low of RMB 1 billion ($160 million) in its agreement with Suriname.[47] They allow the respective countries access to Chinese credit, and companies can also trade in local currencies instead of U.S. dollars. Of these four countries, only Argentina has activated the swap line to withdraw $2.7 billion in 2014, and the RMB is still far from becoming the preferred currency in Latin America.[48] In 2015, China and Chile also agreed to establish an RMB clearing bank in Chile, the first of its kind in South America, that would help China establish an offshore RMB clearing network in the region.[49]

---

[43] World Trade Organization, "Chronological List of Dispute Cases," website, Geneva, undated.

[44] Shen Zhiliang, 2014, p. 53.

[45] "China and Brazil Sign $30bn Currency Swap Agreement," *BBC News*, March 27, 2013.

[46] "China and Argentina in Currency Swap," *Financial Times*, March 21, 2009.

[47] "China, Suriname Sign Currency Swap Deal," *Global Times*, March 18, 2015.

[48] Benn Steil and Dinah Walker, "Are China's RMB Swap Lines an Empty Vessel?" Council on Foreign Relations, May 21, 2015.

[49] China Construction Bank, "CCB Designated as the First RMB Clearing Bank in South America," May 26, 2015.

Economic Barriers and Hurdles

Chinese economic activities in the region have met with varying degrees of acceptance and criticism. Countries that are more politically or financially isolated or that in some manner stand in opposition to the United States, such as Argentina (until late 2015), Bolivia, Ecuador, and Venezuela, have welcomed Chinese investment. In other Latin American countries, stronger civil society and institutions are holding Chinese companies and investors to higher standards of corporate social responsibility than China has faced in Africa. A number of poor Chinese business practices, including neglect of local labor laws, lack of environmental safeguards, lack of transparency, and questionable managerial practices, have frustrated governments and populations.[50]

In practice, this means that China often faces a host of legal and commercial hurdles as it increases economic investments in the region. Brazil passed a 2010 law that restricted land purchases by foreigners partially out of concerns that China was trying to buy too much land in Brazil so as to have access to the natural resources there.[51] Costa Rica signed a free trade agreement with China in 2010 and is one of three Latin American countries to do so, but five years later and as of early 2015, the Costa Rican Legislative Assembly has yet to pass a bilateral investment protection bill. Additionally, each product for export to China has to undergo a specific quality and safety certification that takes approximately one year. This long process had led to only six Costa Rican products being approved for export since 2010. On the investment side, the $1.5 billion oil refinery that China agreed to finance in mid-2013 was delayed and then renegotiated in early 2015 after Costa Rican authorities found a contractual violation on the Chinese side.[52]

---

[50] Jon Brandt et al., "Chinese Engagement in Latin America and the Caribbean: Implications for US Foreign Policy," American University, School of International Service, December 2012, p. 19.

[51] "China Overtakes US as Brazil's Top Trade Partner," *JOC*, March 24, 2014.

[52] Costa Rican authorities delayed the deal when they found that a CNPC subsidiary conducted the project's feasibility study. This was a conflict of interest since CNPC was the Chinese company involved in the construction. See "Biofuels Could Be Produced at Chinese Refinery in Limon, Says Costa Rica Oil Chief," *Tico Times*, January 10, 2015.

One other barrier is actually on the Chinese side. Although financing for overseas projects had been relatively easy elsewhere, especially from China's policy banks, it has become more difficult for companies to invest, and this has affected their ability to invest in Latin America.[53] First, it has been harder to get loans for production projects as opposed to construction. Second, banks have recognized that they have a hard time assessing risk, so they have become more cautious about lending. Issues of collateral and the differential cost of RMB-based loans versus dollar loans, which are cheaper, have also affected financing. None of these barriers are insurmountable. They just mean that announcements of intention to invest may bear little relationship to actual investments, and those actual investments may not pay off in the end.

Military and Security Engagement

China has limited security interests in the region and has modest military engagement with Latin America. Given the geographic distance between China and the region, Beijing does not have any territorial or other disputes with countries in the region. China recognizes the proximity of Latin America to the United States and is sensitive to U.S. perceptions of its military involvement in the region and has maintained a low military profile.

Within Latin America, China uses military engagement to boost goodwill, enhance understanding, and gain political leverage with regional governments. China's military engagement with the region involves arms sales, military exchanges and combined exercises, and participation in UN peacekeeping missions and HADR operations. Beijing is also building ties with the local defense and security establishment to protect Chinese investments and nationals in the region.[54]

---

[53] This paragraph draws from Zhang Yuzhe and Wang Ling, "Cheers, Fears for China's Next Step Overseas," *Caixin Online*, July 22, 2015.

[54] R. Evan Ellis, *China-Latin America Military Engagement: Good Will, Good Business, and Strategic Position*, Strategic Studies Institute, U.S. Army War College, August 2011.

China has very limited military presence in the region, and its presence has been mainly in the form of short-term riot police or peacekeepers for humanitarian missions and not combat personnel. Though Chinese investment in the region is growing and there have been cases of violence against Chinese workers and investments, Beijing has not deployed military assets to Latin America to protect its economic stakes.[55]

PRC Arms Sales

Although Latin America is not a large market for arms sales, PRC arms sales to the region increased dramatically in the 15 years through 2015. This has occurred despite the fact that many militaries in the region consider Chinese weapons to be inferior to Russian or Western arms and they are purchasing significantly more arms from Russia and the United States. China has made no arms sales to the Caribbean or Central America apart from Mexico, possibly because several countries in the Caribbean and Central America recognize the Republic of China on Taiwan instead of the PRC. The overwhelming majority, 88 percent, of Chinese arms sales to the region is to Venezuela; Bolivia comes in a distant second, making up just 8 percent of Chinese arms sales to the region. In total, PRC arms sales have been far lower than U.S arms sales; while China has sold $550 million worth of weapons since 2000, the U.S. has sold $4 billion worth of weapons, over seven times the volume of China's sales.[56]

China began selling arms to Venezuela in 2006 and has supplied nearly $500 million (in Trend Indicator Values, measured in 1990 constant dollars) worth of weapons to the country since then. While this volume of sales is substantial, it pales in comparison to Russian arms sales to Venezuela, which also began in 2006 but have since totaled more than $4 billion, more than eight times the volume of China's

---

[55] Colombia's FARC rebel group, for example, held four Chinese oil workers hostage for 17 months in 2011 and 2012. See "Columbia's FARC Release Chinese Hostages," *BBC News*, November 22, 2012.

[56] PRC arms sales data from SIPRI and measured in Trend Indicator Values based on 1990 constant dollars.

sales. Venezuela has received self-propelled artillery, transport aircraft (Y-8s),[57] and combat aircraft (mostly K-8s) from China. In November 2014, *HIS Jane's Defence Weekly* reported that Venezuela was the first foreign country to purchase the VN1 wheeled amphibious infantry fighting vehicle from China, which it acquired as part of a $500 million deal signed in 2012 and financed by Chinese loans offered in exchange for Venezuelan oil shipments.[58]

Although China sells arms to the region mainly to build regional goodwill and gain political leverage, Chinese arms have also been used for other purposes. Chinese weapons have been smuggled into Latin America and fallen into the hands of local paramilitary groups, including Columbia's Revolutionary Armed Forces of Colombia (FARC) guerilla group and Mexican drug cartels. It is unlikely that Chinese government and Chinese state-owned companies have been actively involved in such illegal operations, but they have not taken sufficient measures to prevent such from happening.[59] In March 2014, news reports indicated that Norinco VN-4 armored vehicles and Shaanxi Y-8 transport aircraft that the Venezuelan government had purchased from China were deployed against political protesters in major Venezuelan cities.[60]

PLA Military Diplomacy

Chinese Central Military Commission members have made just seven trips to Latin America since 2003, making the region the least visited by PRC military leaders among all others in the Developing World with the exception of Oceania. Five of those visits have occurred since

---

[57] "China's Y-8 Aircraft Poised to Land in South American Market," *People's Daily*, June 2, 2011.

[58] Richard D. Fisher Jr., and James Hardy, "Venezuela Signs Up for VN1, Hints at Chinese Amphibious Vehicles Buy," *IHS Jane's Defence Weekly*, November 23, 2014.

[59] R. Evan Ellis, "Chinese Organized Crime in Latin America," *PRISM*, Vol. 4, No. 1, December 2012, pp. 65–77.

[60] Zachary Keck, "Venezuela Uses Chinese Weapons in Crackdown," *The Diplomat*, March 7, 2014.

2009, suggesting that the region, while still a relatively low priority compared to other regions, is becoming increasingly important to China's military leaders. Of these seven total trips since 2003, CMC members visited nine different countries. Among the most frequently visited countries were Brazil, Colombia, Cuba, and Peru, each of which was visited twice during the period studied.

Combined Exercises

PLA troops have participated in four joint exercises with Latin American armed forces over the past few years: "Peace Angel-2010," a humanitarian medical rescue mission between PLA and Peruvian military medical teams; "Cooperation-2011," an urban anti-terrorism exercise between PLA Air Force and Venezuelan airborne troops; "Cooperation-2012," an anti-terrorism exercise between PLA Army and Colombian special forces; and a brief maritime joint exercise focusing on collaborative air defense between two PLA Navy warships and a few Chilean navy frigates and airplanes in 2013.[61] A *PLA Daily* article about "Peace Angel-2010" noted that the medical teams provided free medical service for local residents and conducted an hour-long humanitarian rescue drill during which they practiced first aid and decontamination, rapidly unpacking and setting up a field hospital, and preventing the spread of disease.[62]

PLAN Port Visits

In comparison to other regions in the Developing World, China has conducted the fewest port visits to countries in Latin America. Since 2000, China has visited just ten ports in the region. Notably, nine of those visits have occurred since 2009. As part of "Harmonious Mission 2011," the PLA Navy's *Peace Ark* hospital ship traveled to the Caribbean and Central America and made four weeklong port visits from

---

[61] *The Diversified Employment of China's Armed Forces*, 2013; "PLAN's Taskforce Conducts Maritime Joint Exercise with Chilean Navy," *China Military Online*, October 12, 2013.

[62] Yang Zurong, "Sino-Peruvian Joint Humanitarian Medical Rescue Operation Starts in Lima," *PLA Daily*, November 25, 2010.

October to November 2011, stopping in Cuba,[63] Jamaica,[64] Trinidad and Tobago,[65] and Costa Rica[66] to offer free medical treatment to local residents.

UN Peacekeeping Operations

Although the PRC left the United Nations Stabilization Mission in Haiti out of its 2013 Defense White Paper's list of the UNPKO in which the PRC had participated, China, in fact, sent 125 anti-riot police officers to Haiti to support the stabilization mission there in 2004.[67] China contributed peacekeepers to this mission in spite of Haiti's recognition of Taiwan, a fact that some PRC officials suggested was a sign of China's "growing diplomatic sophistication" and "peace-loving and responsible image."[68] Eight Chinese peacekeepers were killed during the devastating January 2010 earthquake.[69]

Military Operations Other than War

Again, despite the lack of diplomatic relations between the PRC and Haiti, the PRC sent substantial humanitarian assistance to Haiti following the January 2010 earthquake that killed roughly a quarter of a million people. In addition to the PRC government's contribution of $2.6 million cash, a 60-member search and rescue team, and a 40-member medical care and epidemic prevention team, the Chinese

---

[63] Zhang Yong, "China's PLA Navy 'Peace Ark' Hospital Ship Arrives at Havana, Cuba," *Xinhua News*, October 23, 2011.

[64] Zha Chunming, "Chinese Navy 'Peace Ark' Hospital Ship in Kingston, Jamaica," October 31, 2011.

[65] Embassy of the People's Republic of China in the Republic of Trinidad and Tobago, "'Peace Ark' Hospital Ship Starts Visit in Trinidad and Tobago," November 12, 2011.

[66] "Chinese Navy 'Peace Ark' Hospital Ship Arrives in Costa Rica," *Xinhua News*, November 24, 2011.

[67] "China to Send Anti-Riot Peacekeepers to Haiti," *China Daily*, June 5, 2004.

[68] Gill and Huang, 2009, pp. 5, 14.

[69] Wang Cong and Miao Xiaojun, "Bodies of Chinese Peacekeeping Police Killed in Haiti Earthquake Arrive Home," *Xinhua News*, January 19, 2010.

Red Cross donated $1 million in emergency aid.[70] An official from the UN mission in Haiti praised Chinese aid workers as "remarkably efficient" and "generous."[71] The PRC also evacuated 48 of its civilians from Haiti via charter flights.[72] In November 2012, China provided 17 million RMB worth of medicine, tents, terry blankets, water-purifying equipment, and electric generators to Cubans reeling from Hurricane Sandy.[73]

Conclusion

Although China has good relations with the region, Latin America is the least important developing region for China. It is geographically distant and comprises a small share of total Chinese trade. Chinese activities in the region are largely economic and political. The region is currently not part of China's Belt and Road Initiative, although there is potential to include it. There is limited PRC military engagement with the region and most of it is with Venezuela.

China is willing to increase its involvement in the region, but it is also clear-eyed about the problems associated with doing so and has not prioritized Latin America compared to other developing regions. Beijing is sensitive to the fact that Latin America is geographically adjacent to the United States and worries that Washington would resist Chinese attempts to develop close partnerships with regional countries. China is also concerned about the potential for volatility in the region and sees little opportunity for it to make significant inroads in a region that is so politically, economically, and culturally close to the West.

---

[70] Stephanie Ho, "China Sends Aid to Quake-Stricken Haiti," *VOA News*, January 23, 2010; "China Announces More Assistance to Haiti," Embassy of the People's Republic of China in the United States of America, January 21, 2010.

[71] Wu Chong, "UN: China 'Remarkably Efficient' in Haiti Aid," *China Daily*, January 20, 2010.

[72] Duchâtel, Bräuner, and Hang, 2014, p. 46.

[73] "Chinese Government Sends Relief Materials to Hurricane-Hit Cuba," *CCTV*, November 20, 2012.

Chinese efforts to engage more with the region is further hampered by its growing but still relatively limited number of experts on Latin America.

Overall, countries in Latin America have a largely positive view of China and its activities in the region, as shown by Pew polling on attitudes with the notable exception of Brazil (Table 9.1). In eight of the nine countries surveyed, larger proportions of the polled population had favorable views of China than unfavorable. People had the most positive views of China in Venezuela and least in Colombia. With the exception of Brazil and Colombia, more people also saw China's eco-

Table 9.1
Latin American Views of China, 2014

	General View of China		Is China's Economic Growth Good or Bad for Your Country?		Will or Has China Replaced the United States as Leading Superpower?	
	Favorable (%)	Unfavorable (%)	Good (%)	Bad (%)	Will or Has Replaced (%)	Will Never (%)
Venezuela	67	26	66	20	57	30
Chile	60	27	63	13	46	26
Nicaragua	58	19	74	13	50	35
Peru	56	27	54	23	52	20
El Salvador	48	25	54	26	51	36
Brazil	44	44	39	41	36	52
Mexico	43	38	38	36	54	30
Argentina	40	30	41	20	50	27
Colombia	38	32	30	45	46	37
Latin America median	50	30	51	26	49	33
Global median	49	32	53	27	49	34

SOURCE: Pew Research Center, Global Indicators Database, July 2014.

nomic growth as beneficial to their country than not. They view China as contributing to local economies and reducing poverty and inequality. Again with the exception of Brazil, most people believed that China has or will eventually displace the United States to become the leading superpower. There are, however, regional concerns of becoming too economically dependent on China.

Implications for the United States

China is not changing the regional balance of power in Latin America contrary to U.S. interests. China focuses mostly on pursuing economic opportunities in the region, which is in line with U.S. goals for the region. As in Africa, however, China's model of development and infrastructure financing could undermine U.S. efforts to promote good governance.

CHAPTER TEN

Pivotal Regional Partnerships

After reviewing the range of Chinese involvement in the Developing World on a region-by-region basis, we now examine China's relationships with what Beijing considers the pivotal state in each region. Although China has formally established partner relations (*huoban guanxi*) with many countries around the globe, Beijing deems some capitals to be more important than others and tends to dub these strategic partnerships (*zhanlue huoban*).[1] In fact, in almost every region examined in this study, China appears to have identified one particular state as being pivotal within its specific geographic region. These countries are considered pivotal because they possess "heft" as measured in terms of population, economy, defense, or geostrategic location, in terms of their posture vis-à-vis China and in terms of activities in their own neighborhoods.[2] Beijing believes these states are major players in their regions and key partners for China.[3]

---

[1] For more on partnerships, see, for example, Su Hao, "Zhongguo Waijiao De 'Huoban Guanxi' Kuangjia" ["The 'Partnership' Framework in China's Foreign Policy"], *Shijie Jishi* [*World Knowledge*], Vol. 5, 2000.

[2] See the discussion in Bruce Gilley and Andrew O'Neil, eds., *Middle Powers and the Rise of China*, Washington, D.C.: Georgetown University Press, 2014.

[3] Earlier scholarship on "pivotal states" in the Developing World focused on U.S. policy. This research emphasized that such states were "important [in their] neighborhood through extensive economic and/or political linkages," and as a result had the "potential to work significant beneficial or harmful efforts on their regions." Robert Chase, Emily Hill, and Paul Kennedy, introduction, in Chase, Hill, and Kennedy, eds., *The Pivotal States: A New Framework for U.S. Policy in the Developing World*, New York: W. W. Norton, 1999, p. 7.

In this chapter, we focus on specific bilateral relationships because it is at the state-to-state level that we can perhaps best assess how successful China has been in strengthening its position within a particular region and what objectives it has in mind. For each region, we assess which country China considers the pivotal partner because of, in China's view, the combination of its crucial significance to its particular neighborhood and China's interests. We further define such powers and explain our selections in subsequent sections.

Why does China seek to strengthen ties with particular states in the Developing World? There are many possible reasons, but the most significant appear to be geostrategic location, economic value, and sympathetic feelings toward China. The PRC works to build friendships with like-minded states that are influential in their own neighborhoods, not staunchly pro-U.S., and resource rich.

Since at least the 1980s, Beijing has consistently insisted that it does not seek allies. Indeed, China regularly contends that alliances are relics of an unenlightened Cold War mind-set and continually berates the United States for maintaining alliances in the Asia-Pacific and around the world.[4] From Beijing's perspective, alliances are targeted against a third country, and China strongly suspects that the raison d'être of U.S. alliances—at least those in the Asia-Pacific region—are to counter a rising China. In contrast to alliances, Beijing insists that China pursues partnerships with other states that are not aimed at threatening any third country.[5] Although some of these bilateral relationships have significant security dimensions, Beijing insists that none of these constitute military alliances.[6]

---

4 For example, the PRC Defense White Paper published in 2015 observes: "U.S. carries on its 'rebalancing' strategy and enhances its military presence and its military alliances in this [that is, the Asia-Pacific] region." See "I. National Security Situation" in *China's Military Strategy*, 2015.

5 According to the 2015 PRC Defense White Paper, "China's armed forces will continue to develop military-to-military relations that are non-aligned, non-confrontational and not directed against any third party" (see "VI Military and Security Cooperation" in *China's Military Strategy*, 2015).

6 See, for example, Su Hao, 2000.

Pursuing Partnerships

What are the key characteristics of a meaningful partnership? If Beijing labels a relationship a strategic partnership, then this signals that Beijing believes that ties with the other capital are comprehensive and long-term in scope.[7] In such circumstances, Beijing expects that the other country has explicitly acknowledged the legitimacy of China's rise, has demonstrated a willingness to coordinate common preferences, and has set aside any areas of disagreement.[8]

Especially important to China is the idea of having viable security partners that could help China protect its national interests. Unlike the United States, China does not have an established regional or global network of allies and partners with proven track records of security cooperation. Beijing feels quite vulnerable and almost alone in confronting its traditional and nontraditional security threats.

Which countries can China count on in a crisis? While the United States has battle-tested allies such as Australia, the United Kingdom, and South Korea and enduring alliances with countries such as Japan and Thailand, China has only one formal alliance of long standing—with North Korea. But this relationship does not provide Beijing much reassurance or peace of mind. While China and North Korea fought as comrades-in-arms during the Korean War, since the 1961 Treaty of Friendship, Cooperation, and Mutual Assistance, the two communist states have functioned as rather aloof "allies at arm's length."[9] The alliance is qualitatively different from those that the United States possesses and lacks even the most rudimentary characteristics of U.S. alliances. To the best of our knowledge, for example, the armed forces of China do not conduct field exercises or even command post exercises with the armed forces of North Korea, and there

---

[7] See Medeiros, 2009, p. 82.

[8] Scott L. Kastner and Phillip C. Saunders, "Is China a Status Quo or Revisionist State? Leadership Travel as an Empirical Indicator of Foreign Policy Priorities," *International Studies Quarterly*, Vol. 56. No. 2, June 2012, pp. 163–177.

[9] Andrew Scobell, *China and North Korea: From Comrades-in-Arms to Allies at Arm's Length*, Carlisle Barracks, Pa.: U.S. Army War College Strategic Studies Institute, 2004a.

is only the most cursory of coordination between the two defense establishments.[10]

But China does have a range of informal defense relationships with a variety of countries, and some of these have been quite extensive and enduring. In the second ring, Russia and Pakistan have had longstanding security relations with China. In the third ring, Bangladesh and Thailand have had ongoing defense cooperation with China. Finally, in the fourth ring, Iran and Venezuela both have continuing defense cooperation with China. Noteworthy is that China's deepest and most enduring defense relationships are with two states in the second ring—Russia and Pakistan.

Recently the PRC has officially articulated an intention: [t]o actively expand military and security cooperation, deepen military relations with major powers, neighboring countries and other developing countries, and promote the establishment of a regional framework for security and cooperation.[11]

Pivotal Regional Partners as Emerging Allies?

China appears to be seriously rethinking its disdain for alliances. Publicly, Beijing continues to insist that it does not want to build alliances, establish overseas military bases, or station Chinese troops outside of its borders. It has even declined to term its new installation in Djibouti a base; instead, it refers to the installation as a logistical support facility, although as already noted, others have subsequently described it as China's first overseas base. But there are good reasons to think that these firmly held principles of no alliances may not be immutable.[12] Although the capabilities of the PLA have been enhanced during recent decades, China's military remains constrained in terms of the distances across which it can project power and overstretched in terms of the expansive array of missions with which it has been

---

[10] Andrew Scobell and Mark Cozad, "China's Policy Toward North Korea: Rethink or Recharge?" *Parameters*, Vol. 44, No. 1, Spring 2014, p. 56.

[11] "II Strategic Guideline of Active Defense," in *China's Military Strategy*, 2015.

[12] See, for example, Feng Zhang, "China's New Thinking on Alliances," *Survival*, Vol. 54, No. 5, October-November 2012, pp. 239–148.

tasked, both within China's borders and around the country's immediate periphery.[13]

China's most pressing security concerns are domestic and around its periphery—China has charged its armed forces with protecting Chinese territory, preserving national unity, and countering terrorism and secessionism.[14] In addition, China has expanding overseas interests, especially economic ones, both in adjacent regions and states as well as in far-flung regions and countries across the globe.[15] Of particular concern to Beijing is how these interests can be protected. China has charged its own armed forces with rising to the challenge of protecting these interests.[16]

In short, Chinese civilian and military leaders face a dilemma about how to defend PRC citizens and property in the Asia-Pacific area and around the globe. At sea, Beijing has reluctantly been free-riding on the U.S. Navy, but it does not fully trust Washington and is unlikely to be satisfied with this arrangement as a permanent solution. On land, China is also in a bind, but the solution is far more complicated since conditions tend to be country-specific, so Beijing is far more dependent on individual states with wide-ranging capabilities and internal security situations.

One of the most important factors driving countries to form alliances is to balance against threats.[17] So what key threats does China face? According to official PRC documents and the writings of numerous Chinese analysts, the country confronts an extensive array

---

[13] See, for example, Andrew Scobell and Andrew J. Nathan, "China's Overstretched Military," *The Washington Quarterly*, Vol. 35, No. 4, Fall 2012, pp. 135–148.

[14] *China's Military Strategy*, 2015, "II Missions and Strategic Tasks of China's Armed Forces." See tasks 1, 2, and 7.

[15] As an example post-dating our study, China's highest grossing movie, at $608.6 million as of mid-August 2017, was *Wolf Warrior II*, starring Wu Jing as a Chinese special forces operative action hero rescuing Chinese nationals in Africa (Gaochao Zhang, "'Wolf Warrior 2' Becomes China's Highest-Grossing Film of All Time," *Los Angeles Times*, August 15, 2017; Joe Leydon, "Film Review: 'Wolf Warrior II'" *Variety*, August 11, 2017).

[16] *China's Military Strategy*, 2015, "II Missions and Strategic Tasks of China's Armed Forces." One of the eight tasks is: "To safeguard the security of China's overseas interests."

[17] Stephen Walt, *The Origins of Alliances*, Ithaca, N.Y.: Cornell University Press, 1988.

of threats. The PRC Defense White Paper published in 2015 states: "China, as a large developing country. . . . faces multiple and complex security threats . . . as well as traditional and nontraditional security threats [which] are interwoven."[18] In addition to the those posed by the militaries of other states, Beijing has identified a considerable range of nontraditional threats, including terrorism, transnational crime, water shortages, energy insecurity, and threats to domestic stability such as religious extremists, ethnic separatists, and political dissidents.[19]

Seeking Pivotal Regional Partnerships

China has argued for several decades that multipolarity is an ongoing trend in global politics.[20] And yet, the United States has remained the sole global superpower. Beijing views Washington as an essential partner but also a massive challenge. As noted earlier, China seeks to balance against the dominant influence of the United States. One important way to do this is for China to forge relationships with other powers around the world. Beijing's articulation of a new type of major power relations is not just intended for its relationship with the United States but also for its relations with other powers. On the global level, there are few states with significant hard or soft power willing and able to align with China. Most of the great powers are already aligned with the United States or reluctant to bandwagon with China. One of the few exceptions is Russia.

However, at the regional level, China finds more possibilities and has actively sought to woo regional powers around the world. China seeks states that are key actors in their own neighborhoods rather than those of global significance. We dub these pivotal regional partners (PRPs). China is looking for partnerships with regional powers. Such powers are different from what some scholars have labeled middle powers.[21] While a middle power is a second-rank power on the global stage,

---

[18] *China's Military Strategy*, 2015, "Part I: National Security Situation."

[19] *China's Military Strategy*, 2015, "Part I: National Security Situation."

[20] Medeiros, 2009, pp. 27–29.

[21] For discussion of middle power concept and middle powers as these relate to China, see Gilley and O'Neil, 2014.

below the level of a great power, a PRP is a key power in a particular region of the world, as judged from China's perspective. A PRP can be identified by assessing the level of attention China devotes to a country diplomatically, economically, or militarily along with the degree to which a country favors alignment with China over alignment with other great powers. For example, neither Pakistan nor Thailand would be considered middle powers or key secondary players on the global stage, but both would be good candidates for influential powers in their respective regions in the Asia-Pacific. While such a state should have significant diplomatic, economic, or military clout in its own neighborhood, what is most important is the quality or value of the bilateral relationship to China. Thus, it is the content and scope of the partnership itself that matters more than the characteristics of the state. We assess a PRP in terms of the value this relationship provides to China in a particular region.

In the following sections we examine China's PRPs in six regions. In five of the regions—Central Asia, South Asia, the Middle East, Africa, and Latin America—we identified only one pivotal partnership per region. In our sixth region, Southeast Asia, there is no clear single PRP, so we explore several possible candidate states. In our seventh region, Oceania, we cannot discern a PRP.

Two Tiers of Pivotal Regional Partnerships

China's strategic partnerships can be ranked largely according to where the pivotal state is located within the four rings of insecurity outlined in Chapter 2; the closer a state is to China geographically the higher the level of priority Beijing attaches to the relationship. Thus, top priority is afforded to those states within the second and third rings, countries that are closest at hand. This includes key states we identified within Southeast Asia: Indonesia, Malaysia, Thailand, and Vietnam. It also includes two of the five remaining PRPs: Russia and Pakistan. Here, Beijing has adopted a buffer strategy to maintain a stable zone with neutral or pro-China states. The goal is to deny presence or access to outside powers and counter threats to China's domestic stability (see

Chapter 2). The top priority is to maintain good relationships with PRPs within this belt.

A lesser but still important priority for China is strengthening ties with PRPs in the fourth ring. Iran might best be thought of as situated between China's third and fourth rings of insecurity—what some PRC analysts have dubbed "a strategic extension of China's periphery."[22] The Middle East has become a key region—almost certainly the most important geographic area outside of the Asia-Pacific region. China seeks friends that are influential but neither beholden to nor engaged in direct hostilities with the United States.

Two other PRPs found in the fourth ring are South Africa in Africa and Venezuela in Latin America. Africa and Latin America are both of growing importance to China, especially the former (see Chapter 8). Beijing needs good partners in each region. While there are other candidate PRPs in Africa and Latin America, China has clearly signaled its designation of a particular country in each continent. The Republic of South Africa has had the strongest economy in Africa, has been the continent's moral leader, and appears more engaged to coordinating responses to problems that afflict the continent. Since at least the 1990s, Beijing has singled out Pretoria for a long-term relationship. Meanwhile, China has engaged widely with an array of Latin American states, but one country stands out based on numerous economic and military indicators: Venezuela.

For each PRP, we examine the logic and history of the relationship, the role of the PRP in its own region, and the contours of China-PRP cooperation. We then assess the performance of the PRP to date and the future prospects of its partnership with China. Table 10.1 identifies each PRP by region and briefly notes the criteria for selection.

Rings 2 and 3: The Exceptions: Southeast Asia and Oceania

Southeast Asia and Oceania differ markedly from Central Asia, South Asia, the Middle East, Latin America, and Africa. While China maintains a PRP in each of these other regions, Southeast Asia contains no single standout country, based on an assessment of politico-economic

---

[22] See, for example, Li Weijian, 2004, p. 18.

Table 10.1
Pivotal Regional Partners by Region

Rings	Region	PRP	Criteria for Selection
2 & 3	Southeast Asia	None. Key states include	
		Indonesia	Most powerful state in region
		Malaysia	Most economically important to China
		Thailand	Long-standing, trusted partner
		Vietnam	Communist rival closer to United States
2 & 3	Central Asia	Russia	Dominant power with important security, cultural, political, and economic ties
2 & 3	South Asia	Pakistan	All-weather friend helping China with internal security, balancing against India, and diversifying trade routes
2 & 3	Oceania	None	
3 & 4	Middle East	Iran	Like China, millennia-old power; energy supplier, key part of Belt and Road, oppositional to United States
4	Africa	South Africa	BRICS member, most diversified and sophisticated African economy, continental leader
4	Latin America and the Caribbean	Venezuela	Energy rich, borrower, investment host, opposition to United States in support of multipolar world

SOURCE: Authors' assessment.

and military factors.[23] Meanwhile, in Oceania, the two largest states—Australia and New Zealand—are the most plausible, but they are both staunch U.S. security partners. This precludes either state having a robust PRP-like relationship. In short, there does not appear to be any viable candidate state in Oceania.[24]

[23] Security relations here refer to 1) whether the country is strategically likely to align with China (for example, the country does not have an overwhelming bias toward either Japan or the United States), and 2) if there are vibrant military-military relations, how much actual capacity and regional relevance does that actor have.

[24] For analysis of Australia as a Middle Power, see Thomas S. Wilkins, "Australia: A Traditional Middle Power Faces the Asian Century," in Gilly and O'Neill, 2014, pp. 149–170.

The geostrategic landscape of Southeast Asia is complicated by the ongoing territorial disputes between China and several countries in this region. Because of this, an important condition of relations for China is a state's stance vis-à-vis the maritime disputes in the South China Sea. Depending on the particular criterion employed, Beijing views several states as key but has no PRP. These key partners are Indonesia, Malaysia, and Thailand. In contrast, while Vietnam could be such a state, China's relationship with Vietnam is highly problematic, and there is a pervasive sentiment in Beijing that it has "lost Hanoi."

Indonesia

From the Chinese perspective, Indonesia is a prime regional partner, whether economically, politically, or militarily. For example, the IMF estimates Indonesia's GDP to be $895.7 billion as of 2015, far ahead of the next largest economy in the region—that of Thailand, valued at $386.3 billion. Its growth rate, meanwhile, has been respectable at around 5 percent per year since 2013, putting it just behind Vietnam and ahead of Malaysia. Politically, it is the only Southeast Asian country that is a member of the G20, allowing it to play an increasingly visible role in global governance. At the same time, it has been able to exercise "moderate" leadership within the region through such means as hosting the headquarters and secretariat of ASEAN in Jakarta and occasionally holding the organization's rotating presidency, which it last did in 2011. Combining economic and political factors, Indonesia, in the eyes of China, is also a critical link in the Maritime Silk Road and often held up as an exemplar of the "Asian community." Finally, it is true that Indonesia falls behind other, smaller neighbors in terms of certain military capabilities. Its naval capabilities, for example, are weaker than those of Singapore, Thailand, and Vietnam. However, since coming to office in October 2014, President Joko "Jokowi" Widodo has made naval modernization a priority, putting the country on track to become a regional naval power.[25]

Not surprising given these facts, Indonesia has been of particular interest to China in recent years, and during his state visit in Octo-

[25] Vibhanshu Shekhar and Joseph Chinyong Liow, "Indonesia as a Maritime Power: Jokowi's Vision, Strategies, and Obstacles Ahead," Brookings Institution, November 7, 2014.

ber 2013, Xi Jinping moved to further cement the relationship between the two countries by signing a comprehensive strategic partnership agreement with then president Susilo Bambang Yudhoyono. This makes Indonesia one of five entities within the region with which China has such an agreement—the others being Thailand, Vietnam, Malaysia, and ASEAN. In 2014, China also managed to get Indonesia to commit to investing roughly $33.6 billion into the proposed AIIB. Chinese leaders see great value in Indonesia, both in terms of salient cultural linkages—in part due to the large and influential Chinese community in Indonesia—and as a bridge to the rest of Southeast Asia. Indeed, Chinese leaders hope for, and actively seek to leverage their country's positive relations with Indonesia into, improved bilateral relations with countries elsewhere in the region. Indonesia's potential as a security partner further feeds into this; Chinese leaders believe that increased interactions in this area would not only have an important impact on the two countries' bilateral relationship but could also lead to improved security partnerships with other Southeast Asian countries.

Malaysia

Malaysia's importance rests with its status as the very first Southeast Asian country to normalize relations with China (in 1974). To this day, it remains a key state in Chinese strategies—both regionally and more globally, such as for the Belt and Road projects. In general, Malaysia has not actively balanced against the rise of China, and even its claims in the South China Sea have not led to significantly high bilateral tensions, such as has been the case with Vietnam or the Philippines.[26] This, in turn, has led Chinese leaders to view Malaysia as a moderate actor in the South China Sea; indeed, as a regional player with whom they can work and who is overall deserving of more attention. Certain commentators have even suggested that the Chinese government should officially reach out to Malaysia concerning their dispute.[27]

---

[26] Cheng-Chwee Kuik, "Making Sense of Malaysia's China Policy: Asymmetry, Proximity, and Elite's Domestic Authority," *Chinese Journal of International Politics*, Vol. 6, No. 4, December 2013, pp. 429–467.

[27] Yang Guanghai and Yan Zhe, "Nanhai Hangxing Ziyou Wenti De Lixing Sikao" ["A Rational Consideration of the Issue of Freedom of Navigation in the South Southeast Asia"], *The New Orient*, No. 5, December 2014.

Malaysia further plays an important role as a dealmaker within ASEAN and, as an added bonus, is not closely linked to the United States. Malaysia can also play a security role to the benefit of China. The two sides, for instance, issued a joint communiqué in May 2014 focusing on increased military cooperation through such activities as "exchange of high-level visits and meetings, joint exercises, personnel training, setting up a hot-line for communication between the two Armed Forces, and exchange of port-call visits by both navies."[28] Prior to this, on October 4, 2013, Xi Jinping arrived in Malaysia for a state visit and concluded it by signing a cooperative strategic friendship agreement with Prime Minister Najib Razak. It should be noted that just a day before, on October 3, Xi Jinping had signed a similar agreement with Indonesian President Yudhoyono, further highlighting Malaysia's importance to China. In terms of recent relations, Chinese commentators find it particularly disconcerting that U.S.-Malaysian cooperation has increased in scope but are confident that Malaysia will continue to remain closer to China, given their long history.[29]

Thailand

In the case of Thailand, Chinese leaders are not oblivious to its long-standing treaty alliance with the United States and so have often utilized the rhetoric of partnership without presuming that a future key regional partnership will necessarily manifest. That does not mean, however, that China has not proactively worked to strengthen its relationship with Thailand. In 2012, for example, the two countries signed a strategic partnership agreement. Certain Chinese commentators have, at the same time, made the argument that Thailand is vital to Chinese geo-economic strategic interests, with one even labeling it the

---

[28] *Joint Communiqué Between the People's Republic of China and Malaysia in Conjunction with the 40th Anniversary of the Establishment of Diplomatic Relations*, Ministry of Foreign Affairs of Malaysia, May 31, 2014.

[29] Liu Yanan, "Meima Guanxi Lishi Fazhan Zhong De Jinzhan Yu Wenti Yanjiu" ["Advances and Inquiries into the Historical Development of U.S.-Malaysia Relations"], *Theory Research*, Vol. 27, March 2014, pp. 34–35.

strategic fulcrum of Southeast Asia.[30] Zhou Fangzhi, a researcher at the Chinese Academy of Social Sciences' China Network for Asia-Pacific Research, further asserted in 2014 that the importance of Thailand to China is based on three key factors: its "flexible diplomatic position," its "highly adaptable society with comparatively fewer social tensions," and its "strong economy and complementarity with China."[31] The validity of the second point is questionable given the political instability that has prevailed in Thailand since 2006 as a result of the ongoing struggle between forces connected to former prime minister Thaksin Shinawatra and the conservative establishment comprised of the courts, the military, and the monarchy. However, on the last point, Chinese Premier Li Keqiang in October 2013 referred to Thailand as China's main trading partner in ASEAN during a speech to the Thai National Assembly.[32]

Leaders such as Li Keqiang have also further underscored the cultural overlap between the two countries and their equally strong military relations. Thailand was, for example, the first Southeast Asian nation "to establish a mechanism for defense and security consultation and to conduct joint military exercises and training with China."[33] Finally, there has been a growing vacuum in the traditional U.S.-Thai alliance that China has sought to exploit. The U.S. Department of State condemned the May 2014 military coup that brought General Prayuth Chan-ocha and his National Council for Peace and Order to power, and the United States has subsequently distanced itself from the new government because of concerns over the deteriorating state of democracy and human rights in Thailand. This turn of events has prompted Chinese leaders to significantly increase their outreach to

---

30 Zhou Fangzhi, "Zhongtai Guanxi: Dongmeng Hezuo Zhong Zhanlue Zhidian Zuoyong" ["China-Thailand Relations: Strategic Fulcrum Role in ASEAN Cooperation"], *Southeast Asian Affairs*, Vol. 3, 2014.

31 Zhou Fangzhi, 2014.

32 Li Keqiang, "May the Flower of China-Thailand Friendship Bear New Fruits," speech delivered to the National Assembly of Thailand, Bangkok, October 11, 2013.

33 Li Keqiang, 2013.

the new Thai government at the same time that their U.S. counterparts have decreased theirs.

Vietnam

In contrast to the results of any perceived geopolitical competition for Thailand, Chinese commentators argue that the United States has already succeeded in "winning over" Vietnam in its rebalance to Asia. Since the United States and Vietnam first normalized relations in 1995, they have steadily drawn closer together. This process culminated in July 2015 with a visit by Nguyen Phu Trong, secretary general of the Communist Party of Vietnam, to the United States, where he held a meeting with President Obama in the Oval Office. The meeting was not only unprecedented but a rare honor usually reserved for visiting heads of state and government. This event and others have firmly moved Vietnam away from having any kind of partnership with China. This is in spite of Vietnam's economic and political potential and the fact it had previously signed a strategic partnership agreement with China in 2008. However, it should be noted that relations between the leaders of the two countries were more conciliatory at the time. Nong Duc Manh and Hu Jintao, who became the general secretaries of their respective parties within a year of each other, made greater efforts at reconciliation and established more frequent contact at the beginning of their time in office.

As of 2014, however, Beijing is increasingly of the belief that Hanoi is destabilizing the region contrary to Chinese interests. For example, on September 3, 2015, Vietnam and the Philippines announced their signing of a strategic partnership.[34] The Philippines, further, has a strategic partnership with Japan (announced June 4, 2015) and a mutual defense treaty with the United States (signed August 30, 1951), meaning that Vietnam has now been drawn into a web of relationships that effectively aims to counter Chinese influence in Southeast Asia. It could, moreover, be argued that even before these recent developments and extending all the way back to the 1979 Sino-Vietnamese War, Vietnam had consistently and independently frustrated China

[34] "Philippines and Vietnam to Be 'Strategic Partners,'" *Straits Times*, September 4, 2015.

and that the brief thaw at the start of this century was more of an anomaly than anything else.

China's Key Southeast Asian States Taken Together

Based on these assessments, then, it is not possible to rank the key states; each is distinctive for a different reason. Indonesia, as the most powerful state within the region now and into the foreseeable future, is the most geostrategically important country in Southeast Asia. Thailand is perhaps most important politically to China, while Malaysia is currently of great importance economically. Vietnam is important because Chinese leaders essentially view it as a lost cause. It is certainly a key regional state acting as a spoiler for Chinese policies.

Overall, China sees developments within Southeast Asia as a whole as being pivotal, both for its regional strategy and for its global strategy. The new Belt and Road Initiative, the AIIB, and other efforts are more than economic in nature, as they have political implications for Chinese engagement in the Developing World. Regardless of the ongoing debate about whether Chinese actions indicate increasing foreign policy assertiveness,[35] recent regional activities in Southeast Asia show that Beijing's strategy is becoming more nuanced. Chinese perspectives of Indonesia, Malaysia, and Thailand being key regional players and of Vietnam being a lost cause may shift over time.

Rings 2 and 3 PRPs: A China-Russia Condominium in Central Asia?

Russia may not technically be a Central Asia state in our classification. Yet, by dint of its size, proximity, history, and enduring links to the six landlocked states that comprise the region—Mongolia, Kazakhstan, Kyrgyzstan, Tajikistan, Turkmenistan, and Uzbekistan—Moscow merits the title of Beijing's PRP for Central Asia. If Russia were excluded from consideration then Kazakhstan would be the logical selection, since

---

[35] Michael D. Swaine, "Perceptions of an Assertive China," *China Leadership Monitor*, No. 32, March 2010; David Shambaugh, "Coping with a Conflicted China," *The Washington Quarterly*, Vol. 34, No. 1. December 2011, pp. 7–27; Andrew Scobell and Scott W. Harold, "An 'Assertive' China? Insights from Interviews," *Asian Security*, Vol. 9, No. 2, Summer 2013, pp. 111–131; Iain Johnston, "How New and Assertive Is China's New Assertiveness?" *International Security*, Vol. 37, No. 4 (Spring 2013), pp. 7–48.

it is by far the largest Central Asian state in terms of territory, population, and economy, and it is by far China's most significant trading partner in the region. Yet, in terms of its population, economy, and military power, Russia dwarfs each of the aforementioned countries. Moreover, Russia's population is double the size of the aggregate populations of the six other states; Russia's economy is roughly 3.5 times the size of all six economies; Russia's military is roughly 5.6 times as large in terms of active personnel and 6.4 times in terms of paramilitary personnel and it possesses 1.3 times as many main battle tanks and 3.9 times as many fighter aircraft as all six of the Central Asian states combined. Most important, Russia holds significant influence over the region.

History and Logic

Being on good terms with Moscow is critical for Beijing because Russia occupies a sizeable piece of real estate along China's northern border. The geostrategic importance of Russia to China is comparable to the significance of Canada to U.S. national security. However, unlike Washington, Beijing cannot afford to take the stability or friendship of its large northern neighbor for granted. Turmoil in Russia or tensions with Moscow have produced great consternation in Beijing, especially during the mid to late portions of the Cold War (notably as the USSR disintegrated between 1989 and 1991) and tensions earlier, during the 1960s, 1970s, and 1980s. Russia offers China proximate sources of vital military technology and know-how as well as essential energy resources. An unstable or unfriendly Russia would be enormously troubling for China.

Role and Potential for Cooperation

Of greatest relevance is Russia's special status as a pivotal player in Central Asia. Indeed, Russia has long been the dominant power in the region, and Moscow remains key to the maintenance of stability in Central Asia. Although the six Central Asian states are no longer formally subordinate to Moscow, Russia continues to have considerable influence through its historical ties, ethnic Russian populations in most of these states, the prevalence of Russian language, and continued military, political, and economic links. Thus, Moscow plays a key role in maintaining order and structure in Central Asia. Russia maintains a quasi-alliance structure through the CSTO. Bilaterally and multilaterally, China and Russia cooperate in the region through mechanisms such as the SCO.[36]

China and Russia also tend to share similar perspectives on the posture and policies of the United States. Both Beijing and Moscow perceive the United States as overbearing, arrogant, and even threatening to their respective regimes. Not only can U.S. hard power be considered threatening but so, too, can U.S. soft power. Ideas such as democracy and universal human rights can seem as dangerous to the dictatorships in China and Russia as U.S. military capabilities. Finding common cause in countering these ideas and Washington-backed initiatives in arenas such as the United Nations Security Council can bring Beijing and Moscow together.

In terms of real substantive cooperation, coordination between Moscow and Beijing is quite limited. And yet rhetorical coordination and summitry, whether within the SCO or through BRICS heads of state meetings, can be significant for both states because symbolism matters enormously for both sets of leaders. Of particular note were the SCO and BRICS summits held in Ufa, Russia, in July 2015, which emphasized solidarity among "emerging markets and developing countries."[37] In Xi Jinping's one-on-one meeting with Vladimir Putin, the Chinese leader reportedly stressed that the two countries should continue their "high-level strategic coordination in the SCO" and indicated that Russia is included in China's plans for a "Silk Road Economic Belt."[38]

---

[36] Scobell, Ratner, and Beckley, 2014, pp. 30, 35.

[37] See Xi Jinping's July 9 speech at the BRICS summit in July 2015 at Xi Jinping, "Building Partnership Together Toward a Bright Future," speech given at the Seventh BRICS Summit, Ufa, July 9, 2015; see also, *VII BRICS Summit Ufa Declaration*, Ministry of Foreign Affairs of the People's Republic of China, July 9, 2015.

[38] See "Xi Jinping Meets with President Vladimir Putin of Russia," Ministry of Foreign Affairs of the People's Republic of China, July 8, 2015.

The two pillars of China's strategic partnership with Russia are military relations and energy cooperation. Yet even here, there are real limits—energy cooperation had been plagued by delays and a lack of Russian enthusiasm. But this suddenly changed with tensions with Europe over the crisis in Ukraine that prompted Putin to offer China a comprehensive and attractive energy deal hastily packaged during a visit to Beijing in November 2014. According to the terms of the deal, Gazprom would supply "as much as 30 billion cubic meters of gas annually from developments in West Siberia to China over 30 years . . . At the same time, another Russian producer, OAO Rosneft, agreed to sell a 10 percent stake in a Siberian unit to state-owned China National Petroleum Corp."[39] More important, it would also allow China to take Germany's place as Russia's biggest gas market.

China-Russia cooperation on Central Asia is funneled through the SCO. But cooperation might be too strong a word since the level and degree of interaction is quite modest. Indeed, coordination is probably a more accurate term. The SCO provides China with a multilateral umbrella to engage in bilateral cooperation with Central Asian states. Moreover, there appears to be a rough division of labor between Chinese and Russian engagement with the region; Moscow concentrates more on military activities, while Beijing is focused more on economic efforts.[40] Russian unease over growing Chinese economic power and influence in the five contiguous Central Asian states (excluding Mongolia) is readily discernible, but the SCO framework permits Moscow to have a ringside seat and a voice in its operations.

There is a significant military dimension to the relationship between Russia and China, the most visible manifestations of which are arms transfers and coproduction and joint exercises.[41] For instance, the Stockholm International Peace Research Institute in 2014 estimated that roughly 11 percent of Russia's arms exports go to China,

---

[39] James Paton and Aibing Guo, "Russia, China Add to $400 Billion Gas Deal with Accord," *Bloomberg*, November 9, 2014.

[40] Scobell, Ratner, and Beckley, 2014, p. 35.

[41] Note that the Chinese use the term *joint* to refer to exercises it conducts with other countries. Of course, this usage is very different to how the term is employed by the U.S. military.

making it Russia's second largest client after India, which receives 38 percent of these exports.[42] More recently, in May 2015, China and Russia conducted their very first joint exercises in the Mediterranean.[43] The two countries then followed up by conducting their first-ever joint amphibious exercise landing in the Sea of Japan, in August 2015.[44] The Russian and Chinese armed forces have engaged in an ongoing series of field exercises under the auspices of the SCO. Most of these have been multilateral with other member militaries, but there have also been at least three bilateral China-Russia military field exercises in the ten years running up to 2015—the 2005, 2009, and 2013 Peace Mission exercises. The combination of these interactions suggests a level of cooperation that is only matched by China's military-to-military ties with Pakistan. While noteworthy, Chinese-Russian military cooperation does not compare with the level of coordination and interoperability found between the U.S. military and allied militaries.

China's Defense White Paper issued in May 2015 identifies only two states by name—the United States and Russia. Russia is highlighted as a security partner of great interest to China. According to the document, Beijing is interested in sustaining and expanding its "exchanges and cooperation with the Russian military."[45]

Assessment and Prospects

Since the 1990s, cooperation between Russia and China has yielded real results that have proved mutually beneficial. This has been useful to both Moscow and Beijing. The SCO allows Russia and China to manage their relations, coordinate Central Asia initiatives, and respect Moscow's sensitivities to Beijing's greater clout in what has historically been a Russian sphere of influence. Among the common interests are

---

[42] Wezeman and Wezeman, 2015.

[43] Jonathan Marcus, "China-Russia Drills in Med Show Shifting Strategies," *BBC News*, May 11, 2015.

[44] Sam LaGrone, "China, Russia Land 400 Marines in First Joint Pacific Amphibious Exercise," *USNI News*, August 26, 2015.

[45] *China's Military Strategy*, 2015, "VI Military and Security Cooperation."

countering terrorism, extremism, and separatism as well as Western ideas of democracy and human rights.

However, "thinness" and "latent tensions" underlie Sino-Russian cooperation.[46] China's relations with Russia do not have the same breadth and scope of social and cultural interactions evident in PRC relationships with other states, such as the United States. Moreover, mutual suspicions and xenophobia are discernible just below the surface in both Russia and China. Thus, while there are prospects for a stronger partnership or alliance between China and Russia, the potential seems limited, barring the emergence of a daunting common threat.

Moreover, there are differences in how far Beijing and Moscow are willing to raise the temperature in their relations with Washington. While both countries seek to counter the influence of the United States and its allies, Russia is prepared to be far more provocative than China in words and deeds. Beijing is far more reluctant to antagonize Washington and European capitals, at least on matters that it does not deem to pertain directly to China's own core national interests. Most important for China is stability in Central Asia and cordial relations with all states in the region and, indeed, all around its periphery. Moscow seems keen to blend the CSTO and SCO and turn them into an Eastern alliance bloc to counter NATO. China, however, has displayed no interest in either of these endeavors.[47]

Rings 2 and 3 PRPs: China and Pakistan as Codependents in South Asia

Although India dominates the subcontinent in almost every way and clearly looms largest for China, it is not Beijing's PRP in the region.[48] Rather, it is Pakistan—India's nemesis—that has for decades been China's key partner in South Asia. In psychology, codependency is defined as a pathological relationship where two parties are overdependent upon each other to a degree that is unhealthy for both of them.[49] Each party has feelings of extreme insecurity and fears being alone.

---

[46] Medeiros, 2009, p. 105.

[47] Medeiros, 2009, pp. 140–141.

[48] For a thorough comparison of China and India, see Gilboy and Heginbotham, 2012.

[49] See, for example, Dr. Leon Seltzer's blog post, Leon F. Seltzer, "Codependent or Simply Dependent: What's the Big Difference?" *Psychology Today*, December 11, 2014.

This condition appears to define the relationship that China and Pakistan have had with each other since the 1960s. Both Beijing and Islamabad suffer from high anxiety and believe they have a dearth of reliable friends in other capitals. Accordingly, each views this partnership as essential to maintaining its own national security.[50]

China considers Pakistan a pivotal state that will decisively influence the course of events in surrounding countries, notably Afghanistan.[51] Moreover, Beijing also thinks of Islamabad as a longtime but deeply troubled ally on a geostrategic fault line between South and Central Asia—in a region where China has had few friends. Nevertheless, Pakistan has gradually declined in overall geopolitical significance as Beijing's diplomatic relations and economic ties with other capitals in South Asia and the Middle East have expanded. In particular, India looms ever larger as a major economic partner for China (see Chapter 6). Yet Islamabad continues to be Beijing's PRP in South Asia precisely because it is a counterweight to New Delhi.

History and Logic

China has enjoyed a warm relationship with Pakistan since the 1960s, with the leaders of both countries often referring to the bilateral relationship as an "all-weather friendship."[52] Yet, Beijing's support is more restrained than in the past. China's interests in Pakistan are increasingly regional and aimed at restraining Islamabad. Pakistan continues to be an important partner and a major arms market for Chinese defense firms, but Islamabad's value as China's conduit to the Islamic world or a Chinese facilitator on the global stage has been greatly reduced. In the twenty-first century, China has robust relationships with a variety of countries in the Middle East and, globally, has full diplomatic ties with all but 22 small countries as of 2015.[53]

---

[50] This appears to be the thesis of Small, 2015.

[51] For discussion of Pakistan as a pivotal state in South Asia for U.S. policy, see Hasan-Askari Rizvi, "Pakistan," in Chase, Hill, and Kennedy, 1999, pp. 64–87.

[52] This section draws on the analysis in Scobell, Ratner, and Beckley, 2014.

[53] Micro-states are those with populations of less than 500,000 people. For a list of countries that continue to formally recognize Taipei as the Republic of China, see Nathan and Scobell, 2012, p. 218.

During the early Cold War, China found itself surrounded by enemies. To the north and west were the Soviet Union and its client state Mongolia. To the south was India, which leaned toward the Soviet Union and was deemed hostile to China following the 1962 Sino-Indian border war. Border disputes with many of its neighbors, ethnic unrest, and fear of external invasion made China desperate for allies. In these circumstances, Pakistan became a fast friend, and the relationship proved mutually beneficial. Pakistan found an "all-weather friend" in a forbidding neighborhood, while China discovered a client to help check India, thereby helping to ameliorate the security situation on its southern border, and to act as a bridge to the Islamic world and the United States. Pakistan, for example, served as a key conduit in U.S.-China rapprochement.

Although Pakistan's value to China has substantially decreased over time, Islamabad's importance to Beijing is much more in regional terms and a negative sense than a positive sense in global terms. Beijing is more focused on suppressing Pakistan's potential to trigger instability on China's periphery than it is in enlisting Pakistani help in accomplishing broader geopolitical aims.[54] And while Chinese leaders continue to view Pakistan as a useful counterweight to India, they also worry that Pakistan might provoke India into a war through bellicose actions or through its own domestic instability.[55]

Role and Potential for Cooperation

Geopolitically, Pakistan has been the linchpin of China's South Asia policy.[56] This remains true, but as China's relations with India have improved, and economic interactions have dramatically expanded, Islamabad has been viewed as less of an asset and more of a liability. Moreover, growing instability within Pakistan is very worrying to

---

[54] Kardon, 2011, pp. 20–21.

[55] Thus, as Jing-Dong Yuan observes: "China's support of Pakistan in recent years has more to do with the concern of Pakistan falling apart that with Pakistan's value as a strategic counterweight to India." See Jing-Dong Yuan, "The Dragon and the Elephant: Chinese-Indian Relations in the 21st Century," *The Washington Quarterly*, Vol. 30, No. 3, Summer 2007, p. 139.

[56] This section draws on Scobell, Ratner, and Beckley, 2014.

China. Beijing is also concerned about Islamabad's role in post-2014 Afghanistan.[57]

Despite the significant liabilities Beijing sees in Islamabad, China believes it has no choice but to continue the policy it adopted in the late 1990s—close cooperation with Pakistan in support of three main security interests. First, China wants to ensure internal security by stifling connections between Uighurs in Xinjiang and radical Islamists in Pakistan. Second, China seeks to balance against India by maintaining an enduring security relationship with Pakistan. Third, China is keen to diversify its trade routes and expand economic opportunities.

Domestic Security: Containing Uighur Separatists. China's western Xinjiang province borders northwest Pakistan and is home to nearly ten million Uighurs, a Muslim people of Turkic origin and among whom separatist sentiment has historically run high. In the 1980s, hundreds of Uighurs crossed into Pakistan, enrolled in religious schools known as madrassas, and, with Chinese government training and arms, fought the Soviets in Afghanistan. Upon returning to Xinjiang via Pakistan, some joined violent Uighur nationalist groups.[58] Pakistan has contributed to Chinese efforts to fight Uighur separatists. In 2003, Pakistani forces killed Hasan Mahsum, the founder of the Uighur East Turkestan Islamic Movement, which the Chinese government had identified as the most threatening Uighur terrorist group. China and Pakistan have also signed agreements on information sharing, joint counterterrorism drills, and extradition of terrorist suspects.[59]

However, cooperation has not been seamless or trouble-free. Over the past 20 years, for example, China has frequently severed trade and transportation links with Pakistan by periodically shutting down border crossings, closing the Karakoram highway, and erecting security fences along the border to insulate Xinjiang from Islamists in Pakistan. Chinese analysts openly doubt the commitment and capabilities

---

[57] See, for example, Scobell, 2015, pp. 325–345.

[58] Cooley, 2002.

[59] See Ziad Haider, "Sino-Pakistan Relations and Xinjiang's Uighurs," *Asian Survey*, Vol. 45, No. 4, July/August 2005, pp. 535–537.

of Pakistan's security forces, even accusing them of warning Uighur groups to disperse prior to raids.[60] Moreover, Chinese leaders worry that Islamabad is too weak and unstable to secure Beijing's interests in Pakistan.[61]

Beijing has also become increasingly concerned about the safety of as many as 13,000 Chinese citizens working for some 60 companies in Pakistan.[62] The episode that raised China's ire was the Red Mosque incident in the summer of 2007. In June of that year, Muslim radicals seized seven Chinese massage parlor workers in Islamabad and took them hostage in a heavily fortified complex in the Pakistani capital. Strong Chinese pressure on then president Pervez Musharraf proved decisive in ending the incident. The result was a full-scale army assault on the Red Mosque compound, freeing some of the hostages at the cost of at least 100 deaths, including some of the hostages.[63] In contrast, U.S. pressure for Pakistani action against terrorists has often been ignored. The most prominent example of this was the U.S. effort to track down Osama Bin Ladin.[64] According to one expert on the China-Pakistan relationship, "Beijing's secretive ties with Pakistan are closer than most formal alliances."[65] The Red Mosque episode suggests that this is so. More recently, the relationship has been exemplified by Pakistan's agreement to assign a Pakistan army special secu-

---

[60] Andrew Small, "China's Caution on Afghanistan-Pakistan," *The Washington Quarterly*, Vol. 33, No. 3, June 24, 2010, p. 91.

[61] Small, 2010, p. 92.

[62] Kardon, 2011, p. 16; Sergei DeSilva-Ranasinghe, "Pakistan's Strategic and Foreign Policy Objectives," Future Directions International, Strategic Analysis Paper, May 5, 2011, p. 4; Syed Fazl-e-Haider, "Chinese Shun Pakistan Exodus," *Asia Times*, September 11, 2009.

[63] Small, 2015, prologue.

[64] The successful operation to seize the mastermind of the September 11, 2001, attacks on the United States was conducted by U.S. SOF without the knowledge or cooperation of Pakistani authorities. Moreover, U.S. intelligence discovered bin Laden's whereabouts without any assistance from Pakistan. Bin Laden, of course, was living in a walled compound in close proximity to a Pakistani military academy. It strains credulity to believe there was no complicity on the part of elements of the Pakistani military or intelligence services.

[65] Small, 2015, p. 1.

rity division of 10,000 troops to protect Chinese citizens working in Pakistan.[66]

Common Concerns: Keeping India in a Box. Both China and Pakistan view India as a rival (and in the case of Pakistan, as an existential threat). Although Beijing-New Delhi ties have improved, major problem areas persist—significant mutual distrust continues and border disputes remain unresolved.[67] China sees Pakistan as an extremely useful counterweight to India; New Delhi is the only capital that rivals Beijing in terms of population, geographic size, and economic and military heft.[68] The result is considerable wariness by Beijing of New Delhi's intentions and capabilities.[69]

China has, since the 1960s, pursued a "classic balance of power strategy," using Pakistan to confront India with a potential two-front war.[70] China's 2,500-mile border with India remains disputed, and although there has been no war since 1962, there are periodic border clashes. There exist some 400,000 square miles of disputed territory between China and India. In contrast, China and Pakistan have resolved their territorial dispute; in 1963, the two sides signed a border agreement that transferred 2,000 square miles of territory in Pakistan-held Kashmir to China.[71]

For decades, China has been Pakistan's most important and reliable weapons supplier (Figure 10.1). Between 1978 and 2008, for example, China sold roughly $7 billion in military equipment to Pakistan; it typically accounts for 40 percent of Pakistan's total arms purchases in any given year.[72] Twice, when the United States suspended arms aid

---

[66] Mateen Haider, "Army's Special Security Division to Protect Chinese Workers in Pakistan," *Dawn*, April 21, 2015.

[67] This section draws on Scobell, Ratner, and Beckley, 2014.

[68] For a systematic comparison of China and India, see Gilboy and Heginbotham, 2012.

[69] For a good overview of contemporary China-India relations, see Tanner, Dumbaugh, and Easton, 2011.

[70] Stephen P. Cohen, 2011, p. 60.

[71] Fravel, 2008, pp. 116–118.

[72] Stockholm International Peace Research Institute (SIPRI) Arms Transfers Database, 1978–2008.

to Pakistan, in 1965 and 1990, China stepped in to meet Pakistan's needs. Since the 1980s, Beijing has supplied Islamabad with considerable quantities of weaponry, including several hundred jet fighters, well more than 1,000 main battle tanks, and large quantities of surface-to-air and anti-tank missiles.[73]

During the mid-1970s, China began covertly assisting Pakistan's nuclear program. Beijing's help was aimed at countering New Delhi's nuclear program, which advanced with a nuclear test in 1974. This assistance reportedly included the design of a nuclear weapon and fissile material.[74] Then, during the 1980s, China also supplied assistance to Pakistan's efforts to develop missiles capable of carrying nuclear warheads. In 1988, China agreed to supply and train Pakistanis in the operation of the M-11 solid-fuel rocket, with a 185-mile range and carrying a 1,100-pound warhead.[75] The missiles arrived in 1995. In subsequent decades, China has sold Pakistan hundreds of jet fighters and signed agreements to sell frigates and submarines to Pakistan.[76]

Economic Cooperation. China is Pakistan's most important trading partner, but for Beijing, two-way trade with Islamabad is very modest.

---

[73] Stockholm International Peace Research Institute, *SIPRI Yearbook 1989: World Armaments and Disarmament*, London: Oxford University Press, 1989, p. 259; Aabha Dixit, "Enduring Sino-Pak Relations: The Military Dimension," *Strategic Analysis*, Vol. 12, No. 9, December 1989, pp. 981–990; Stockholm International Peace Research Institute, *SIPRI Yearbook 1994*, London: Oxford University Press, 1994, pp. 535–536; Stockholm International Peace Research Institute, *SIPRI Yearbook 1998*, London: Oxford University Press, 1998, p. 350; Richard Sharpe, ed., *Jane's Fighting Ships, 1997–1998*, London: Jane's Information Group, 1997, pp. 485–489.

[74] Garver, 2000, pp. 324–331. Pakistan, of course, carried out its own nuclear tests in 1998 and is currently believed to possess a small but significant nuclear arsenal.

[75] Garver, 2000, p. 237.

[76] Jeremy Scahill, "U.S. Delivering F-16s to Pakistan This Weekend," *The Nation*, June 24, 2010; Jeremy Page, "China to Fast-Track Jets for Pakistan," *Wall Street Journal*, May 20, 2011, p. 12; "Pakistan to Buy American F-16s, Chinese FC-10 Fighter Jets," *AFX News Limited*, April 13, 2006; Usman Ansari, "China Officially Offers Pakistan J-10 Variant," *Defense News*, August 3, 2011; "Pakistan Politics: Pakistan Tests a New Missile," *Economist Intelligence Unit ViewsWire*, April 8, 2011; Farhan Bokhari, Leslie Hook, and James Lamont, "A History of Military and Commercial Ties," *Financial Times*, December 20, 2010, p. 3.

Figure 10.1
China's Share of Pakistan's Arms Purchases, 1978–2012, Percent

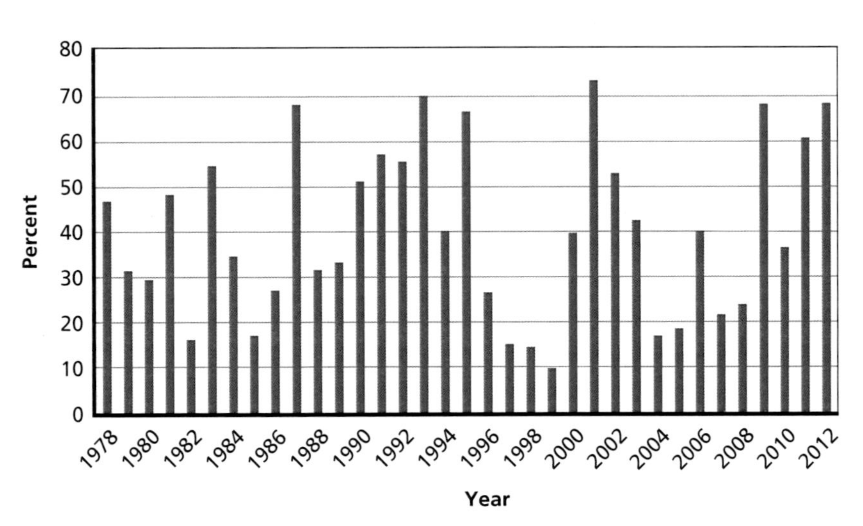

SOURCE: SIPRI Arms Transfers Database.
RAND *RR2273A-10.1*

In 2014, China's total annual goods trade with India was $70.6 billion, compared to $16.0 billion with Pakistan, meaning that trade with the latter amounts to only roughly 23 percent of trade with the former. Yet, Pakistan figures prominently in both parts of China's Belt and Road Initiative. During an April 2015 visit to Islamabad, Xi Jinping announced a $46 billion PRC plan to develop an ambitious China-Pakistan Economic Corridor. The oceanic dimension of the Belt and Road Initiative was already in process, with Pakistan's Gwadar port an important terminus in China's 21st Century Maritime Silk Road. The announcement of the CPEC also turned Pakistan into a central participant in the overland dimension as a segment of the land-based Silk Road Economic Belt. The CPEC involves upgrading the Karakoram Highway and building a natural gas pipeline over the Himalayas, among many other projects.[77]

---

[77] Scobell, Ratner, and Beckley, 2014, pp. 73–77; Ritzinger, 2105.

Assessment and Prospects

As of 2015, China's foreign policy toward Pakistan centers on a set of narrow but key interests that can be satisfied without enhancing Sino-Pakistani ties. Beijing's interests in domestic stability and economic security can be realized as long as Islamabad maintains a modest degree of political stability within its own borders and limits its meddling in the affairs of its neighbors (specifically, Afghanistan and India). And China's interest in checking India can be satisfied as long as Pakistan maintains some semblance of credible offensive military power. China is increasingly concerned about trends in Pakistan, instability, and the inability of Islamabad to control extremists who infiltrate into Xinjiang. But Beijing cannot afford to pull away. China finds its relationship with Pakistan extremely frustrating and troublesome. But abandonment does not seem to be an option because Beijing fears it would likely create more headaches and potentially even greater security problems for China. So, Beijing has signaled its intent to tighten its embrace of Islamabad by deciding to go ahead with CPEC. Even if not all of the massive infrastructure projects are actually built, the corridor will be a great boon to Pakistan.[78]

Meanwhile, Pakistan will continue to embrace China for the simple reason that Islamabad lacks any powerful and trusted friends except Beijing. Pakistan views the United States as fickle and unreliable, and ties between the two continue to be strained.[79]

Pakistan is almost certainly China's closest and most enduring PRP in any region. No other country has maintained such a good, sustained relationship with China as Pakistan has. The relationship has spanned six decades and endured many ups and downs. Indeed, few other countries have managed to retain friendly ties with China for prolonged periods. In the post-Mao era, the members of this select group are few: North Korea, Iran, and Pakistan. This is hardly an

---

[78] Ritzinger, 2015.

[79] For insights on this complex and tumultuous relationship, see the interview with Husain Haqqani, former Pakistan ambassador to Washington: Mark Landler, "Seeing Misunderstandings on Both Sides of U.S-Pakistan Ties," *New York Times*, October 23, 2013, p. A6. For more detail, see Haqqani's book: Husain Haqqani, *Magnificent Delusions: Pakistan, the United States, and an Epic History of Misunderstanding*, New York: Public Affairs, 2013.

impressive list and the states on it even less so, with the possible exception of Tehran.

Tier 2 PRP: A Limited China-Iran Partnership in the Middle East

China is a relative latecomer to the Middle East and has found it challenging to win footholds in the region (see Chapter 7). One of its most enduring partners in the region is Iran. While China has had good bilateral relationships with several other states, none of these bilateral ties has approached the scope and scale of Beijing's links with Tehran. And while China has developed a multifaceted relationship with Saudi Arabia, especially since the 1990s, the strength of this does not match the strength and durability of Beijing's strategic partnership with Tehran.[80]

History and Logic

China's relations with Iran have been good since the 1970s, weathering the overthrow of the Shah, and as with Beijing's ties with Islamabad, there has been cooperation on missile and nuclear programs. Despite good ties between post-Shah Iran and China, relations still do not compare to the closeness of China's relations with Pakistan. Nevertheless, analysts in Beijing and Shanghai have described Iran as a key partner for China in a tumultuous region.[81] The two countries have developed a level of trust built on cooperation in military and economic affairs during decades of ostracism by and financial sanctions on Tehran by Western capitals following the Islamic Revolution of 1979. Both China and Iran tend to think of themselves as millennia-old great powers and heirs to splendid ancient civilizations.[82]

Role and Potential for Cooperation

There is extensive across-the-board cooperation between China and Iran—economically, politically, and militarily. The economic dimension has become central to the Beijing-Tehran relationship—notably in terms of energy—especially since the 1990s. But in lieu of cash,

---

[80] Nathan and Scobell, 2012, p. 181.

[81] Discussions with Chinese analysts in Beijing and Shanghai, September 2014.

[82] See Garver, 2006.

China has paid for petroleum in kind with an array of Chinese-made consumer goods. This arrangement is satisfactory to China, but Iran would rather have the hard currency, while Iranian consumers complain about shoddy PRC-made products.[83] Since 2007, China has been Iran's largest trading partner, and as of 2014, Iran provides China with some 10 percent of its imported petroleum.[84] In addition, China has invested hundreds of millions of dollars in energy infrastructure, including oil refineries and chemical plants. Its investments have further extended into projects that do not directly benefit China. For example, during a state visit to Islamabad in April 2015, Xi Jinping signed an agreement with Pakistan Prime Minister Nawaz Sharif to build a gas pipeline that would bring natural gas from Iran to Pakistan and, theoretically, ease tensions between the two states.[85]

Meanwhile, a military relationship has endured since the 1980s, when China sold Iran conventional weapons, including missiles, during the Iran-Iraq War. As part of this security and military cooperation, Beijing also provided Tehran with both ballistic missile technology and nuclear technology. China ended the latter assistance during the 1990s in response to U.S. and Western pressure, but China continued to cooperate with Iran on missile technology.[86] These trends were also evident in China's relations with other countries, including Pakistan. Since 2008, China has been Iran's most important supplier of conventional arms, surpassing Russia. In the 2000s, Beijing provided Tehran with large numbers of anti-ship and anti-air cruise missiles, and in 2010, a Chinese-built factory reportedly began producing anti-ship cruise missiles in Iran.[87] A more recent indicator of ongoing military relations is a Sino-Iranian naval exercise in late 2014.[88]

---

[83] Scobell and Nader, 2016, pp. 37–38.

[84] Scobell and Nader, 2016, p. 44.

[85] Saeed Shah, "China to Build Pipeline from Iran to Pakistan," *Wall Street Journal*, April 9, 2015.

[86] Medeiros, 2007.

[87] Scobell and Nader, 2016, pp. 41–42.

[88] Scobell and Nader, 2016, p. 42.

China has also been active in diplomatic engagement and coordination with Iran. The two sides, for example, have consulted closely with each other on how to construct Belt and Road and also on how to connect Iran's "Look East" policy with China's own policy of opening up to the West.[89] China was also active in the P5+1 negotiations regarding Iran's nuclear program and acted supportively of Iran over the course of negotiations that began in February 2014 and concluded with the signing of the Joint Comprehensive Plan of Action in July 2015. During the final round of talks in Vienna, for instance, both China and Russia backed the lifting of the arms embargo against Iran.[90]

Assessment and Prospects

Despite the enduring bilateral partnership, there appear to be real barriers for the Beijing-Tehran partnership for several reasons. First, Iran has been a polarizing state in the Middle East. China is wary of further strengthening bilateral ties because it fears this would damage Beijing's surprisingly good relationships with other capitals in the region. Iran has tended to be perceived as a hotbed of radical Islam intent on expanding its influence and fomenting a fundamentalist Shia revolution in the neighborhood. Moreover, Tehran has a potent military machine and is on the threshold of acquiring nuclear weapons, unless the recently negotiated nuclear deal is successfully implemented and succeeds in halting Iran's progress toward a nuclear weapon.[91] As a result, many other states in the Middle East, including Saudi Arabia and Israel, view Iran as threatening. Second, tensions have arisen in the relationship. For example, Chinese companies have encountered many difficulties in recent years while trying to operate in Iran. Thus, while cooperation is significant and multifaceted, and will almost certainly continue, the partnership is very likely to remain limited.[92] In

---

[89] "President Hassan Rouhani of Iran Meets with Wang Yi," Ministry of Foreign Affairs of the People's Republic of China, February 16, 2015.

[90] Carol Morello, "Iran Talks Continue into Tuesday," *Washington Post*, July 13, 2015.

[91] For analysis, see Alireza Nader, "The Days After a Deal with Iran: Continuity and Change in Iranian Foreign Policy," Santa Monica, Calif.: RAND, Corporation, PE-124-RC, 2014.

[92] This conclusion draws on the analysis of Scobell and Nader, 2016, Chapter 5.

short, the prospects for enhanced cooperation in the military or political spheres seem modest.

Ring 4 PRPs: A China-South Africa Geo-Economic Partnership

The Republic of South Africa may not immediately come to mind as a pivotal state in Africa. Other African countries, such as Nigeria, have larger populations, and other countries, such as Angola, possess substantial reserves of petroleum and natural gas. But South Africa possesses one of the most significant economies in Africa with about 16 percent of the continent's GDP, just behind Nigeria.[93] Furthermore, South Africa's is the most diversified and sophisticated economy in sub-Saharan Africa. And Nigeria's outstripping South Africa's economy is new—until 2011, the South African economy was larger and may once again emerge as larger, depending on the weight of oil revenues in Nigeria's nominal GDP.[94]

History and Logic

Beijing and Pretoria formally established diplomatic relations in January 1998, and President Nelson Mandela made the first state visit to China by a South African head of state the following year. President Jiang Zemin reciprocated with an official trip to South Africa in April 2000. During Jiang's visit, the two governments signed the Pretoria Declaration on Partnership. Bilateral ties were officially upgraded to a strategic partnership in 2004 during the visit of PRC Vice President Zeng Qinghong, and were eventually further upgraded to a comprehensive strategic partnership in a nine-page document signed by heads of state Hu Jintao and Jacob Zuma in August 2010 in Beijing.

The foundation of relations with postapartheid South Africa was laid with China's longstanding rhetorical support for the anti-apartheid struggle, although Beijing did not directly support the African National Congress because of the latter's close ties to the Soviet Union. Nevertheless, China benefited from the perception that it was a longstand-

---

[93] Grimm et al., 2014, p. 16; and IMF data.

[94] GDP data are from the World Bank's World Development Indicators. From 2000 through 2010, Nigeria's nominal GDP averaged only 53 percent of South Africa's nominal GDP.

ing friend of the Developing World and Africa in particular. Beijing built upon this reputation by twice publicly supporting Pretoria's successful campaign to win a nonpermanent seat on the United Nations Security Council. Beijing's sponsorship of Pretoria's bid to become a member of the BRIC group further cemented China's special relationship with South Africa. In December 2010, Brazil, Russia, India, and China voted to admit South Africa as a member of the bloc. President Jacob Zuma then attended his first BRICS heads of state summit, held in Beijing in April 2011. The official title of the grouping also became BRICS, with the fifth letter—S—becoming capitalized to represent the new fifth member of the group—South Africa.

Role and Potential for Cooperation

There is a significant economic component to the partnership. South Africa ranks as China's "most significant trade partner on the continent"—China conducts about one-fifth of its two-way commerce with South Africa, and the country is one of Africa's top ten recipients of Chinese investment.[95]

South Africa may also have the largest community of expatriate PRC citizens on the continent. According to one leading expert, South Africa is a "prime destination" for PRC citizens.[96] Estimates of the number of PRC immigrants to Africa "since the early 1990s" range "anywhere from 300,000 to 750,000" with "perhaps a third" of this number headed to South Africa.[97] Both South African and Chinese analysts assess the number of PRC nationals living and working in the country as having grown dramatically in the twenty-first century. One South African estimate puts the number of Chinese nationals living in South Africa as of 2013 at between 350,000 and 500,000.[98] In 2007,

---

[95] Grimm et al., 2014, pp. 16, 17.

[96] Deborah Brautigam, *The Dragon's Gift*, New York: Oxford University Press, 2009, p. 154.

[97] Brautigam, 2009, p. 270. Note that more recently, as of 2017, this number has been in decline (Tom Hancock, "Chinese Return from Africa as Migrant Population Peaks," *Financial Times*, August 28, 2017).

[98] Grimm et al., 2014, Diagram 2 on p. 30. It is important to note that the PRC does not keep official statistics on the number of its citizens residing overseas. All estimates should be treated as speculative.

the PRC ambassador estimated that 100,000 Chinese lived in South Africa.[99] According to one Chinese researcher, "In recent years more and more [Chinese] entrepreneurs have come and settled here [in South Africa]."[100]

Moreover, Chinese businesses may find South Africa a useful "springboard and convenient base" to access other African states, given its strong financial services sector and other advantages.[101] In 2007, for example, a Chinese bank purchased a 20 percent stake in Standard Bank of South Africa—reportedly worth $5.5 billion.[102] In 1997, Hisense, a Chinese electronics company, purchased a Korean-owned factory in Johannesburg and began assembling televisions and DVD players. As of 2008, the factory was exporting to almost a dozen countries in sub-Saharan Africa, and Hisense started construction of a multimillion-dollar industrial park to manufacture refrigerators and washing machines.[103]

According to one—albeit biased—source: "South Africa is . . . a well-recognized and important player" in a variety of arenas from the African Union to the UNSC. But South Africa's standing is strongest on its own continent—the country has considerable moral authority and "arguably provides China's Africa engagement with legitimacy." The bottom line is that South Africa is widely considered to be a "continental leader."[104]

South Africa constitutes a "special case" of Chinese military assistance to the Developing World because, rather than simply being a consumer of Beijing's armaments, Pretoria has also sold military equipment to China. In the 1990s, South Africa bought "a modest quantity

[99] But he appeared to include all ethnic Chinese, not just PRC citizens. Cited in Deborah Brautigam, 2009, note 53 on p. 155 and p. 344.

[100] Feng Dan, "Zhongguo Yu Nanfei Guanxi Fazhan Xianzhuang Ji Wenti Duice Sikao" ["China and South Africa Relations—Current Developments and Policy-Related Considerations"], *Theory Research*, No. 11, 2013, p. 34.

[101] Grimm et al., 2014, p. 18.

[102] Medeiros, 2009, p. 150.

[103] Brautigam, 2009, p. 191.

[104] The quotes in this paragraph can be found in Grimm et al., 2014, p. 15–16, 16, respectively.

of Chinese arms" and also sold China approximately 2 million dollars worth of "nonsensitive military equipment."[105]

Assessment and Prospects

There are likely limits on how far this PRP can go. Chinese officials reportedly exhibited a "willingness to deepen bilateral relations," although they reported "relatively lukewarm" responses from South African counterparts."[106] Nevertheless, the Sino-South African partnership is likely to endure, cemented by the perception in Pretoria that Beijing is a reliable friend that views South Africa as the pivotal state—globally and regionally—located on a continent of increasing consequence to China. China's support for South Africa's admission to the BRICS is but one of the more recent indicators of growing importance of this Sino-African PRP.

Ring 4 PRPs: A China-Venezuela Military-Energy Partnership in Latin America

When thinking of a pivotal state in Latin America, Brazil is an obvious choice. The most populous country in the region with its largest economy, as well as a founding member of the BRICS bloc, seems like far and away the prime candidate. Certainly, Beijing sees Brazil as a key regional player (see Chapter 9), but a closer look at Chinese indicators of economic and military attention reveals that Caracas is of special interest to Beijing. Venezuela is the second largest oil producer in Latin America (after Mexico) and the sixth most populous state in the region (after Brazil, Mexico, Columbia, Argentina, and Peru). Most important, by some measures, it has the largest proved oil reserves in the world.[107]

History and Logic

The relationship took off in the 2000s when the late Hugo Chavez was looking for out-of-area patrons. In a different era (during the Cold

---

[105] David H. Shinn, "Military and Security Relations: China, Africa, and the Rest of the World," in Robert I. Rotberg, ed., *China into Africa: Trade, Aid, and Influence*, Washington, D.C.: Brookings Institution Press, 2008, p. 161.

[106] Grimm et al., 2014, p. 16.

[107] BP, *BP Statistical Review of World Energy 2015,* 64th Edition, June 2015.

War), Venezuela would have found a close friend in the Soviet Union. But in the twenty-first century, Moscow is weaker and less generous with its largesse. Beijing is actively looking for energy resources and opportunities for investment and cooperation. Most of the opportunities available are in states that, for ideological reasons or due to political instability, are unattractive or risky to corporations from developed states. Venezuela was one such state—rich in oil but led by the enigmatic socialist, populist Hugo Chavez, who came to power in 1999 and aligned his country with other left-leaning states in the region while forging close ties with communist-ruled Cuba. Chavez positioned himself as a latter-day Bolivarian champion of Latin America and implacable foe of the "imperialist" United States. China and Venezuela established a strategic partnership in 2001, and President Hu Jintao's visit to Caracas four years later cemented this. This partnership has proved enduring, as it survived the death of Chavez in 2013 and the leadership transition in China from Hu to Xi Jinping in 2012–2013.[108] In 2014, China and Venezuela officially upgraded their relationship to a comprehensive strategic partnership during President Xi's visit to Caracas.

Role and Potential for Cooperation

Beijing has minimal diplomatic coordination with Caracas but robust economic relations and security cooperation. As of 2013, the value of PRC foreign direct investment in Venezuela was estimated at $2.4 billion, making it the largest single destination of FDI in Latin America. Moreover, between 2005 and 2014, China loaned the country approximately $56 billion, with the collateral being mainly future oil shipments. This ten-year loan amount was more than the value of loans China provided its second largest debtor country in the region, Brazil, which received $22 billion (see Chapter 9). China has bought more petroleum from Venezuela than from any other state in Latin America, and Chinese imports of oil from Venezuela have grown from just over $4 million in 2000 to over $12 billion in 2013 (see Chapter 9).

Security-wise, Beijing and Caracas are active in a number of areas. This includes satellite launches and arms sales. Under Chavez,

[108] See Margaret Myers, "China's Unlikely Partnership with Venezuela," *International Relations and Security Network*, August 2014.

for example, Venezuela launched two satellites from China—one telecom satellite in 2008 and one remote sensing satellite in 2012. In October 2014, the new administration of President Nicolás Maduro signed an agreement with the state-owned China Great Wall Industry Corporation to launch a third satellite. This followed a state visit by Xi Jinping in July of the same year, when he declared that China would be expanding satellite technology transfer to Venezuela.[109] China has sold more armaments to Venezuela than to any other state in Latin America, almost $500 million since 2006. While the total amount and range of weapons systems provided are significant, Russian military sales dwarf these Chinese arms transfers. Since 2006, Moscow has sold Caracas more than $8 billion in weaponry. Beijing's goals are certainly economic, as Venezuela provides a good market for Chinese arms corporations, but it is the lure of access to energy resources that is crucial. Indeed, oil exports, rather than using cash, pay for some of the arms sales to Venezuela (see Chapter 9).

Venezuela is experiencing severe economic difficulties, and China is well aware of these problems. Beijing continues to support Caracas despite the grave risks because "there is money to be made," and many Chinese loans are "commodity-backed."[110] But the PRC is not prepared to write Venezuela a blank check. When Maduro flew into Beijing in January 2015 seeking additional Chinese emergency aid, he was disappointed; China simply offered to repackage an existing $20 billion credit for long-term investment.[111] As Venezuela's economic crisis is likely to get worse before it gets better, Caracas is likely to prove to be Beijing's most challenging PRP.

Conclusion

Some developing countries are more important to China than others, and individual PRPs are clearly identifiable in five of the seven regions

---

[109] "China to Help Venezuela Launch Third Satellite," *Xinhua News*, October 6, 2014.

[110] Myers, 2014.

[111] "Bello: The Dragon and the Gringo," *The Economist*, January 15, 2015, p. 36.

into which we have divided the Developing World: Central Asia, South Asia, the Middle East, Africa, and Latin America. It is noteworthy that only in Southeast Asia—arguably the most important region to China in the Developing World—can no single PRP be identified. Instead, Beijing seems to perceive four candidate states, depending on whether the primary criterion is economic, political, trustworthiness, or geostrategic risk. Economically, Malaysia appears to be China's top choice in Southeast Asia; politically, China considers Indonesia to be the most geostrategically important state in the region; in terms of being a trusted partner of longstanding reliability, China's clear favorite is Thailand; in terms of volatility and erratic behavior, China sees Vietnam as most problematic—a fraternal socialist state capable of behaving erratically in a proximate and very sensitive geostrategic locale.

For China, economics and geostrategic dimensions are key factors across the board. All of the PRPs identified in this chapter are likely to be enduring partnerships, but almost all of them—with the exception of South Africa—are fraught with considerable challenges. These challenges are especially evident in China's contemporary ties with Iran and Venezuela but are also present in its relations with Russia and Pakistan.

Perhaps not surprising, the most important PRPs are the two located inside China's second ring of insecurity. Russia and Pakistan are parked on the PRC's northern and western boundaries, respectively, and neither can be towed away if they break down. But Beijing would probably not really want to do this even if moving one or both was a viable option because it views each as playing a pivotal role in key regions on China's periphery. Indeed, maintaining the Russian and Pakistani PRPs is almost certainly viewed as essential from Beijing's perspective. Not so much because either enables China to do a lot; rather, both are important to China because the absence of constructive and cordial ties with these neighbors would have major adverse effects on Beijing's domestic security and China's standing in Central and South Asia.

With a record of decades-long mutually beneficial cooperation, China has built up a level of trust with Pakistan and Russia that it does not have in its relationships with many other states. While neither relationship is ideal from Beijing's perspective, both Moscow and Islamabad are known quantities, and experience has shown that China can work with each to manage security problems in ways that it can do with no other states. The bilateral defense relationships are as solid as Beijing has with any other capital. Furthermore, there is potential for one or the other to rise from a partnership to an alliance should the involved parties at some point feel it necessary. According to one Chinese analyst, "If China decides to develop formal alliances Pakistan would be the first place we would turn. It may be the only place we could turn."[112]

The second tier of PRPs contains only one state: Iran. Beijing's relationship with Tehran is important, enduring, but full of complexities. Significantly, Iran is the PRP in the region of perhaps greatest importance to China outside of its third ring (that is, Asia-Pacific). And Iran's importance is heightened because, geostrategically, China now appears to view the Middle East as part of its extended periphery because of economic and ethno-religious linkages that connect countries like Iran with Central and South Asia. The greatest impediment to further enhancement of the Sino-Iranian PRP, aside from the prickliness of Tehran's domestic politics, is Beijing's reluctance to risk harming its cordial relations with other regional powers, notably Saudi Arabia.

The third tier of PRPs is located farthest away—in China's outermost fourth ring. Of the two relationships in this ring, the steadiest and least demanding is Beijing's strategic partnership with Pretoria. The contours of this PRP are among the most difficult to appreciate because China is generally very active in countries across the African continent. Some analysts and researchers, therefore, tend to overlook China's relationship with South Africa completely.[113] And yet, for many Chinese strategists, Pretoria remains the most important capital in Africa.[114]

---

[112] Small, 2015, p. 181.

[113] One author, for example, barely makes passing mention of South Africa in a recent book that surveys China's involvement with Africa. See French, 2014.

[114] Conversations with Chinese analysts: 2008, 2015.

The other fourth ring PRP is in Latin America; arguably, this is the least important region in the Developing World for China. Venezuela is situated at the crossroads of Latin America, firmly in South America but proximate to Central America and touching the shores of the Caribbean Sea. While not an economic powerhouse on the order of Brazil or Mexico, Venezuela is a key oil producer. Moreover, it is a country in which China has disproportionately invested economically and militarily. The upshot is that Beijing has an enormous stake in Caracas. While China appears reluctant to throw unlimited amounts of money at Venezuela, it also seems unprepared to walk away or even distance itself from its Latin American partner. The political and economic crises in Venezuela appear chronic, and China's political leaders will face difficult decisions in the years ahead about how to handle this PRP.

Cooperation with other states has never been more important to the PRC than it is today. Growing Chinese interests overseas and ongoing competition with the United States require Beijing to be more engaged with countries across the globe and active in regions around the world. This will help protect its interests and build working relationships with like-minded countries to achieve favorable outcomes in these regions and counter U.S. influence in the Developing World.

CHAPTER ELEVEN

Conclusion

China has been more active economically, diplomatically, and militarily all across the Developing World since the 1990s. Beijing's activism has only increased in subsequent decades, and this report documents expanding Chinese involvement since 2000 through the early days of the Belt and Road Initiative in each of seven regions. China's presence in Southeast Asia, South Asia, Central Asia, Oceania, the Middle East, Africa, and Latin America and the Caribbean is likely to continue to expand under PRC President Xi Jinping. All indications are that Beijing remains intent on further global activism, especially in the Developing World. China's economic outreach has been reenergized by President Xi's 2013 announcements of the launch of what has become known as the Belt and Road Initiative and subsequent follow-through efforts, especially the founding of the Asian Infrastructure Investment Bank. Diplomatically, high profile travel by senior leaders seems to continue apace. China remains actively engaged in sustaining bilateral partnerships around the globe, as well as participating in multilateral forums, both at the regional and global levels. In the military realm, reforms are afoot to position the People's Liberation Army for greater reach beyond China's borders. In terms of defense diplomacy, port visits, combined field exercises, arms sales, and peacetime operational employments, the PLA is likely to remain engaged around the world. In recent years, these operational employments include participation in UNPKOs and periodic involvement in noncombatant evacuations.

Beijing's growing clout across the Developing World has not resulted in direct conflict or close cooperation with the United States. However, it does underscore two fundamental challenges for Washington where Beijing is concerned. The first challenge is how the United States handles the rise of China; the second challenge is how the United States persuades China to shoulder its fair share of great power responsibilities in upholding the international system.[1] With the exception of tensions in Southeast Asia, the United States and China appear to be partners in parallel—meaning that the two states work separately with no real collaboration in pursuit of similar ends. The end of this chapter explains and expands upon this concept.

Regions and Rings

For China, not all regions and countries are created equal. Chinese leaders perceive certain regions and countries to be more important than others. Beijing appears to be far more concerned with those regions that abut China's borders and that are in its immediate neighborhood than those further afield. Regions along its periphery, in China's second ring of security, are of greatest concern because instability there poses a direct and proximate threat to internal security—China's first ring. Foremost among these are Southeast Asia and Central Asia, with South Asia appearing to be of rising importance. Oceania is in China's third ring, and there is growing Chinese interest in this region. Beijing recognizes that key Chinese maritime trade routes pass through Oceania and wants to strengthen relations with islands in the region to protect Chinese trade and to prevent countries in the region serving as part of a second island chain aimed at containing or threatening China. Outside of the Asia-Pacific, in the fourth ring, are the Middle East, Africa, and Latin America and the Caribbean. These three regions are of lesser importance, although the Middle East is

---

[1] Thomas J. Christensen, *The China Challenge: Shaping the Choices of a Rising Power*, New York: W. W. Norton, 2015, p. 288.

garnering greater attention because of its energy resources and stability risks, and because in some respects it is considered to be part of a wider region intertwined with China's first, second, and third rings of security.[2]

Political Engagement by Region

China is increasing its political engagement with individual countries and leveraging existing regional institutions, such as ASEAN in Southeast Asia. It is also establishing new ones to engage with entire regions, such as the SCO for Central Asia and FOCAC for Africa.

In Southeast Asia, Beijing seeks to increase cooperation with its neighbors and regional influence through greater connectivity and trade, particularly through the Belt and Road effort and supporting economic initiatives that increase China's involvement in the region. Chinese strategists view the region as crucial to the success of the 21st Century Maritime Silk Road Initiative.[3] Through maritime cooperation, infrastructure loans, regional trade, and cultural outreach, Beijing hopes to bind China to its ASEAN neighbors. Nevertheless, China continues to press its territorial claims in the South China Sea even at the risk of damaging its relations with neighboring states.

Oceania is of much lesser importance, but even there, China seeks to win international support, facilitate political and economic cooperation—and isolate Taiwan. As China presses its territorial claims in the East and South China Seas, Beijing seeks to reassure Oceania that China is not a regional threat. Within the region, China prioritizes Australia and New Zealand, the largest geopolitical and economic actors in the region and the only two countries in the region with which China has signed comprehensive strategic partnerships. Although Australia and New Zealand are close U.S. allies, Beijing believes that political and economic exchanges could discourage both

---

[2] Andrew Scobell, "China's Search for Security in the Greater Middle East," in James Reardon-Anderson, ed., *The Red Star and the Crescent: China and the Middle East*, New York: Oxford University Press, 2018, pp. 13–35.

[3] "Dongnanya Zai 'Yi Dai Yi Lu' Jianshe Zhong Jiang Fahui Zhongyao Zuoyong," 2015.

from engaging in measures to contain China's growth or counter China's maritime claims.[4]

Beijing seeks to increase cooperation with its Central Asia neighbors and gain regional influence through greater connectivity and trade. China does not have conflicting relations with any of the Central Asian countries. Although Russia views Central Asia as its sphere of influence, Beijing and Moscow have found opportunities to collaborate on regional initiatives through the SCO, and Beijing sees Russia—although geographically on the periphery of Central Asia—as its pivotal partner in the region.

In South Asia, senior Chinese officials have made high-profile visits to Pakistan, Sri Lanka, and India to promote political engagement, trade, and investment. China's closest partner in the region is Pakistan, which Beijing sees as the key to countering New Delhi—long China's principal regional rival—especially as India grows stronger economically and more powerful militarily. China has little cultural influence in South Asia; indeed, it seems more concerned about the flow of the region's cultures—particularly Islam and Tibetan Buddhism—into China.

Beijing's relations with the Middle East have been growing strongly, as has the region's importance to China. Beijing has included the region as a link to Europe in its Belt and Road planning.[5] Emblematic of China's efforts to maintain good relations with all parties in the Middle East, the 21st Century Maritime Silk Road includes Israel, where China is building a new port in the Mediterranean city of Ashdod. Despite its strategic significance, China's senior leaders have generally refrained from visiting the Middle East, apparently because the current leadership considers the Middle East a hornet's nest to be

---

[4] Sun Junjian, "Aodaliya Dui Meiguo 'Chongfan Yatai' Zhanlue De Fan Ying" ["Australia's Response to the United States' 'Pivot to Asia' Strategy"]; "Zihuo Xieding Ling Zhong Ao Xingfen Meimei Danyou 'Yatai Zhanlue Luo Kong'" ["Free Trade Agreement Excites China, Australia, U.S. Media Worries About 'Asia-Pacific Strategic Failure'"], *Global Times*, July 19, 2015.

[5] *Vision and Actions on Jointly Building Silk Road Economic Belt and 21st-Century Maritime Silk Road*, 2015.

avoided.[6] Beijing views Iran and Saudi Arabia as its most important regional partners.

Relations with the 51 of Africa's 54 countries that recognize Beijing as of 2015 provide China with a strong dose of international legitimacy. Its commitment to avoid interfering in, or even passing judgment on, sovereign nations' behavior and policies allows it to pursue its political and economic interests across the continent with democrats and despots alike. China ensures ongoing high-level engagement with African countries in a range of disciplines through FOCAC, under the auspices of which China announces regional engagement strategies, launches educational and cultural initiatives, and unveils large bilateral trade, investment, and aid deals. China has also augmented its collaboration with the African Union as a way to give its engagement—particularly on security issues—greater regional impact and legitimacy.

The least important region for China is Latin America and the Caribbean, but China is engaged there as well. China's main political interest in the region is to win international support and legitimacy and to promote greater involvement by developing countries in multinational institutions. While China has actively reached out to the entire region, Brazil, Venezuela, and, at least until late 2015, Argentina have been priority countries for Chinese political, economic, and military engagement.

Economic Engagement by Region

China's economic exchange with most regions involves a heavy dose of resource trade. Southeast Asia stands out as different. With that region, China has extensive production networks and two-way trade in manufacturing inputs and finished projects. But relations in other regions go beyond resources, to investment, construction, and infrastructure development.

China's economic engagement with Southeast Asia in the past decade has been greater than with any other developing region. All ten members of ASEAN were among the 57 prospective founding members

---

[6] Liu Zhongmin, 2011.

of the China-led AIIB, widely seen as a vehicle for funding the Belt and Road Initiative. But the region is not solidly behind China in economic cooperation. Several countries are also signatories to the U.S.-led TPP trade deal, which excludes China. But in the spirit of not choosing sides, these same countries are negotiating partners in the Regional Comprehensive Economic Partnership, an ASEAN+6 (including China) trade deal that excludes the United States.

Beijing is principally interested in Oceania for its natural resources. China's trade with Oceania is dominated by trade with Australia and New Zealand, two economically advanced countries within a developing region, from which China imports mostly crude minerals and mineral fuels and to which it exports manufactured goods and machinery. Beijing's rapidly growing FDI in the region is concentrated almost entirely in Australia.

Central Asia is, by virtue of geography, the first stage in President Xi's Silk Road Economic Belt, and China has funded a range of infrastructure projects in the region. Although China dominates the region's trade, Chinese investment—which is concentrated overwhelmingly in the Kazakhstan hydrocarbon sector—represents a small share of overall FDI in the region. Beijing has pursued major mining, oil, and gas deals in the region, especially in Kazakhstan and Turkmenistan. As a result, whereas only 10 percent of Chinese imports from the region consisted of oil and gas in 2000, that figure had risen to 70 percent by 2013.

Somewhat like relations with Southeast Asia, but to a much lesser extent, China's imports from South Asia include a high proportion of manufactured items, most of which originate in India. Whereas most of China's regional trade is with India, most of its investment has gone to Pakistan. In large part, this investment has focused on building roads, railways, and an oil pipeline to connect China's Xinjiang province to the Pakistani port of Gwadar. This transportation infrastructure—critical components of the Belt and Road Initiative—would facilitate oil and gas imports from the Gulf and allow Chinese exports to be sent overland to a deepwater port on the Arabian Sea.

China's imports from the Middle East are dominated by mineral fuels (specifically, oil and related products), which comprise more than 80 percent of the total. Saudi Arabia alone provides one-third of China's Middle Eastern oil imports and 16 percent of its global oil imports. Iran, Iraq, and Oman are also significant sources of oil for China. China has invested significant amounts in Iran, Iraq, the UAE, and Saudi Arabia, particularly in the hydrocarbons sector and the petrochemical industry.

As with the Middle East, China's economic engagement in Africa has focused on gaining access to natural resources. But because of Africa's large population, there is also an effort toward creating markets for Chinese manufactured items, and developing manufacturing facilities that can take advantage of the continent's low labor costs and, in some cases, developed-country trade preferences. Eighty percent of Chinese imports from Africa—which have grown more than 20-fold since 2000—consists of fuel and raw materials. Although most of China's economic engagement has been undertaken by SOEs and state-backed finance institutions, private Chinese nationals are also pursuing economic opportunities in Africa independent of government-directed initiatives.[7] Africa receives nearly half of China's foreign aid, much of which is given in the form of concessional loans, and in some cases grants, intended for construction and infrastructure development tied to the purchase of Chinese goods and services.

Although Chinese trade with and investment in Latin America and the Caribbean has increased nearly 20-fold in the last decade, it is still low compared to other developing regions. Latin America has been a source of food and raw materials for Chinese manufacturing as well as an export market for Chinese manufactured goods and machinery. China seeks to strengthen trade with major regional economies and has been willing to provide significant financial support in exchange for resources.[8] To reduce the share of raw materials in China's trade with the region, Beijing is increasingly focusing its investment on infrastructure, agriculture, and local production of

---

[7] Mohan and Tan-Mullins, 2009, p. 589.

[8] China has provided billions of loans to oil-rich Venezuela and Ecuador. See "China Steps in to Support Venezuela, Ecuador as Oil Prices Tumble," 2015; "Venezuela to Get $5 Billion in Funding from China in Next Few Months," 2015.

value-added products. Countries that are more politically or financially isolated, such as Argentina through 2015, Bolivia, Ecuador, and Venezuela, have welcomed Chinese investment, but China has faced hurdles to investment in countries with strong labor laws, environmental safeguards, and otherwise strong (although at times selective) commitments to the rule of law, such as Brazil and Costa Rica.

Military Engagement by Region

Certain regions stand out for specific types of military activities. Central Asia is the region with the most military exercises, the Middle East is the region with the most PLAN port visits, while South Asia contains the greatest market for Chinese armaments. Southeast Asia, in contrast to other regions, has military flashpoints—specifically territorial disputes in the South China Sea.

Compared to other developing regions, Chinese military leaders have paid the most visits to Southeast Asia and have, particularly, focused on increasing ties with the Thai military, a close U.S. partner. Increasing maritime security cooperation, counterterrorism, and humanitarian assistance and disaster relief have driven a robust program of combined exercises, port visits, and other military activities.

China's military engagement in Oceania is small. However, its military leaders have visited the region more frequently in recent years. And in the twenty-first century, there have been joint exercises, particularly with Australia and New Zealand.

To avoid creating friction with Russia, which sees the former Soviet Central Asian republics as being squarely in its sphere of influence, China has refrained from providing significant military aid to Central Asia. It has, however, provided equipment and training to regional border security services to advance China's counterterrorism and anti-trafficking goals. China has engaged in a proactive program of high-level military visits, military-to-military exchanges, and combined exercises focused on anti-terrorism operations, suggesting that the region's security is a high priority for China.

Since 2000, China has been a key supplier of major conventional weapons to South Asia; Pakistan and Bangladesh purchased more than half of China's total arms exports from 2000 to 2014. China has sent high-level military officials PLAN vessels on visits to Sri Lanka in an attempt to make inroads in Colombo despite India's longstanding influence. Twelve of 18 combined exercises in the region were held with Pakistan, indicating the strong military alliance between the two countries.

China has sold few weapons to countries in the Middle East; these prefer U.S. military materiel. The principal exception is Iran, which has purchased Chinese anti-ship and antiaircraft cruise missiles and other armaments. Although China has conducted relatively few high-level military visits or combined exercises in the region, the Middle East hosted more PLAN port visits than any other region, principally because of Chinese participation in anti-piracy patrols off the coast of Somalia. The PLAN played a significant role in evacuating more than 500 Chinese nationals from Yemen in March 2015, an operation which China's ambassador in Sana'a called "a significant practice of major power diplomacy."

While China had long maintained a hands-off approach to security matters in Africa, regional instability has threatened Chinese investments in the region and citizens working in Africa. Accordingly, Beijing has recently taken a more proactive approach to security by building host nation capacity, making greater use of private Chinese security firms, and even using government assets and resources to evacuate Chinese citizens from conflict zones—steps that call into question China's commitment to noninterference when its own critical national interests are at stake. China has expanded its participation in UN and AU peacekeeping operations in the region, including those in Mali, Liberia, Congo, South Sudan, and Darfur, and PLAN ships have coordinated anti-piracy patrols in the Gulf of Aden with U.S. and EU navies.[9] This expansion culminated recently with the announcement of the establishment of a military facility in Djibouti, an installation that the Chinese do not refer to as a base but which can be considered one.

China has limited security interests in Latin America and the Caribbean and has modest military engagement there. China uses

---

[9] *The Diversified Employment of China's Armed Forces*, 2013.

military engagement—particularly arms sales, military exchanges, combined exercises, and humanitarian assistance—to boost goodwill, enhance understanding, and gain political leverage with regional governments. Beijing is also building ties with the local defense and security establishment to protect Chinese investments and nationals in the region.[10]

Pivotal Regional Partnerships

In terms of key countries, China appears to have clear favorites in each region of the Developing World, and Beijing has devoted significant attention to a handful of countries in Southeast Asia. Southeast Asia is the most complicated region for China. In recent years, China's activities in the South China Sea have provoked considerable concern among most countries of the region. Because China is also the most important trading partner and a key source of foreign direct investment for all these countries, governments of the region tend to be wary about how they respond to a more assertive China. Politically, Indonesia appears to be most important to Beijing, while economically, Malaysia seems to figure prominently for China, and militarily, Thailand is near the forefront. China senses greatest hostility from Vietnam and the Philippines, and it is no coincidence that these are the two countries most embroiled in maritime territorial disputes with China. But it is Hanoi that is of the greater concern because Beijing fears it is "losing" Vietnam and that the fraternal communist state is gravitating toward the United States geostrategically.

Of all the PRPs identified in this report, the most important to China are two within its second ring of security: Russia and Pakistan. Beijing has adopted a buffer strategy to maintain a stable zone with neutral or pro-China states that will deny access to outside powers and counter threats to China's domestic stability. Russia and Pakistan both do this. In addition, Pakistan helps China balance India in South Asia, although Sino-Indian relations have warmed recently.

---

[10] Ellis, 2011.

A high priority is attached to a single PRP within China's third ring of security, specifically Iran in the Middle East. Although Iran is located just beyond the Asia-Pacific ring, China seeks friends in the oil-rich Middle East that are influential but neither beholden to nor engaged in direct hostilities with the United States. A lesser but still important priority for China is strengthening ties with PRPs in the fourth ring, focusing on South Africa and Venezuela.

Ranking Regions by the Numbers

Our detailed examinations of Chinese involvement in seven different regions using a common template permit us to compare them using the same criteria (Table 11.1). An analysis of the movement and magnitude of China's economic, political, and military engagement can serve as indicators of Beijing's relative priorities of Developing World regions. Each dimension is represented by two data points. To assess economic engagement, we provide the total value of two-way trade in 2000 and 2014 and the total value of China's outward FDI in 2003 and 2012. To evaluate political engagement, we provide the number of senior leader visits (that is, PRC president, vice president, premier, minister of foreign affairs, and state councilor for foreign affairs) from 2003 to 2014 and the number of Confucius Institutes in 2014. To consider military engagement, we ranked the volume of arms sales from 2000 to 2014 and the number of military exercises the PLA conducted between 2000 and 2014, showing the dates of the first and last field exercise.

These data show that Southeast Asia is China's top priority region in the Developing World. Economically, Southeast Asia is far and away the most important of the seven regions, with the largest trade volume with the Developing World in 2014—$479.8 billion or 31.1 percent of China's total trade—and the recipient of the largest amount of China's outbound foreign direct investment in 2012: $28.2 billion, or 30.4 percent of China's total FDI in all seven regions. In terms of political attention, China sent more high-level leaders to Southeast Asia than to any other region of the Developing World (and far more than even to Africa when one compares the number of countries in each region:

Table 11.1
Chinese Economic, Political, and Military Engagement by Region

	Southeast Asia	Central Asia	South Asia	Africa	Middle East	Latin America	Oceania
Economic							
Trade $B (2000, 2014)	39.5 479.8	2.1 52.3	5.7 106.1	9.6 210.0	17.0 290.4	12.5 259.4	9.8 144.1
Investment $M (2003, 2012)	587 28,238	57 10,490	45 4,215	477 21,370	520 6,467	376 7,094	472 15,089
Political							
High level visits (2003–2014)	94	55	40	91	40	45	18
Confucius Institutes (2014)	25	11	8	34	11	32	16
Military							
Arms sales $M (2000–2014)	1,635	0	7,204	2,246	1,495	550	0
Field exercises	26 (2005–14)	27 (2002–14)	24 (2002–14)	3 (2009–14)	1 (2014)	4 (2010–13)	6 (2004–14)

SOURCE: Data sources described in the text.

NOTE: The countries with the highest levels of each indicator are highlighted in a darker color for each category.

ten versus 54, respectively). Between 2003 and 2014, top PRC leaders visited Southeast Asia countries 94 times, or 24.5 percent of all high-level visits to the Developing World. No other region—except Africa—comes close, certainly no other region in China's own neighborhood (see below). Southeast Asia ranks third in the number of Confucius Institutes—behind Africa and Latin America. On military measures of attention, Southeast Asia ranks third in volume of arms sales between 2000 and 2014, with $1.635 billion (behind South Asia and Africa), and second in the number of field exercises conducted between the PLA and regional militaries, with 26, behind only Central Asia.

Beyond the Asia-Pacific, Africa is China's second most important region in the Developing World and Beijing's most important region outside of the Asia-Pacific, at least according to this analysis of Chinese resource allocations. Note, however, that Africa also has the most countries, which would inflate some of the numbers. Africa was the second largest recipient of Chinese FDI (after Southeast Asia) in 2012, with $21.4 billion—almost a quarter of the total (23.0 percent) Beijing sends to the entire Developing World. Africa ranks fourth in terms of the value of the two-way trade China conducts with all seven of the regions—$210 billion in 2014 (behind Southeast Asia, the Middle East, and Latin America). Africa is also home to the largest number of Confucius Institutes of any single region: 34, or 24.8 percent of the total in the Developing World. Africa ranks second in terms of the most visited region by top-level PRC officials, well ahead of other regions, with 91 visits between 2003 and 2014, or 23.8 percent of the total. Africa ranks second only to South Asia in terms of the value of Chinese arms sales: $2.25 billion between 2000 and 2014. Although Africa ranks low in terms of the number of military exercises, if one includes other measures of military presence, such as the number of port visits between 2000 and 2014 (35), PLA operational deployments on UN peacekeeping missions in 2014 (seven), or building a naval facility in Djibouti in 2015, then this all only serves to underscore the level of importance Beijing attaches to Africa.

The Middle East ranks as China's third most important region in the Developing World and its second most important region outside of the Asia-Pacific region. By the numbers, Africa looms as more important, but if one factors in the Middle East's role as a critical source of China's imports, key linkages to China's internal security, and its geopolitical significance for China, then the Middle East at least rivals Africa's importance to Beijing. Nevertheless, the Middle East ranks ahead of Africa—and second only to Southeast Asia—in terms of the value of two-way trade China conducts with regions of the Developing World. However, the Middle East ranks sixth in terms of the amount of Chinese FDI, ahead only of South Asia. The political indicators, meanwhile, almost certainly do not do justice to the level of importance Beijing attaches to the region. The relatively low numbers of high-level political visits and Confucius Institutes in the region say more about Chinese political sensitivities and wariness where the Middle East is concerned.[11] Chinese military attention to the region is limited but noteworthy: $1.5 billion in arms sales between 2000 and 2014, as well as anti-piracy task forces in the Gulf of Aden since 2008, 44 port visits between 2009 and 2014—more than any other region, and small PLA detachments on UNPKOs make the PRC a small-time military player in the region.

Central Asia is China's fourth most important region in the Developing World and second most important developing region in the Asia-Pacific by the numbers. Economically, this region may not be hugely important—it ranks last in terms of the value of China's two-way trade—but it ranks fourth in terms of the value of Chinese investments in the seven regions. Politically, Central Asia is an important focus of PRC high-level leadership visits, ranking third behind Southeast Asia and Africa (although the number of Confucius Institutes is quite low). Militarily, Central Asia is considered particularly important at least in terms of the number of military exercises conducted in the region between 2002 and 2014: 27. This is the highest number the PLA conducted in any region of the world. This number becomes even more important given that the region has only seven countries, suggesting a high level of per-country activity. Arms sales, by contrast, are negligible.

South Asia is the fifth most important region in the Developing World and the third most important developing region in the Asia-Pacific. Economically, South Asia does not rate highly for China, with a low level of trade and ranking sixth, ahead of only Central Asia. Nevertheless, the region has a respectable volume of high-level leadership visits but ranks last in terms of the number of Confucius Institutes. It is in military metrics that South Asia truly stands out. It is number one in terms of the value of Chinese armaments sold in the Developing World, and South Asia ranks third in terms of the number of military exercises China conducts. Indeed, more than half of China's total arms sales in the Developing World between 2000 and 2014 were sold

[11] See Scobell and Nader, 2016.

to South Asian countries, and more than a quarter of China's military exercises between 2002 and 2014 were conducted with South Asia states—mostly with Pakistan.

While undoubtedly one of China's least important regions, Latin America and the Caribbean is of increasing significance to China. Economically the region is of growing importance and ranks fourth in terms of two-way trade in 2014 and fifth in terms of a recipient of Chinese FDI in 2012. Politically Latin America is a significant destination for high-level Chinese leaders—40—and ranks second only to Africa in terms of the number of Confucius Institutes. Moreover, the region takes on even greater political significance to China as home to a dozen states as of 2014 (Panama broke ties with Taipei in 2017) that continue to maintain ambassador-level diplomatic ties with Taiwan. This represents the largest single bloc of holdouts to recognizing the PRC and the government of China. Militarily, China's profile in the region is extremely small as measured by arms sales and field exercises.

While Oceania ranks last to China by the numbers as a region in the Asia-Pacific and low as a part of the Developing World, it is by no means unimportant to Beijing. Indeed, Oceania is of growing economic significance to China: it ranks third in terms of FDI—behind Southeast Asia and Africa—and fourth in the value of Beijing's two-way trade. Of course, much of this economic activity is focused on one country—Australia—but China is also economically engaged across this sprawling maritime region. Oceania plays host to the fewest number of senior leader visits but is home to a respectable number of Confucius Institutes. China also directs few military resources at the region, conducting only a handful of exercises and a negligible volume of arms sales.

The United States and China in the Developing World: Partners in Parallel?

Across the Developing World, the United States and China are, in general, neither in direct conflict nor working in close cooperation. But there is significant variation by region. In Southeast Asia, for example, Washington and Beijing are in a contentious mode over Chinese activities in the South China Sea and China's insistence that U.S. military vessels and aircraft must get permission prior to traversing disputed waters claimed by China. But outside of Southeast Asia (and Northeast Asia, among developed regions), the United States and China appear to be partners in parallel—meaning that the two states work separately with no real collaboration in pursuit of similar ends. As David Shambaugh notes, the two countries "pursue their interests and policies in an autonomous—rather than interactive—fashion with each other."[12] In some ways this is unfortunate. Although China is not yet a peer competitor of the United States, it can harm U.S. interests and the global system that has benefited most countries, including China; a challenge remains as to whether and how to encourage China to act as a cooperative partner.[13]

Notably, U.S. and Chinese interests do not seem to be in direct conflict in the Developing World, with the possible exception of Southeast Asia, where China's maritime territorial claims have resulted in tensions and confrontation. Further afield—in the fourth ring—China's sensitivities are not as raw and its national interests less vital. Significantly, it is beyond the first, second, and third rings where a number of cooperative efforts between the United States and China have borne fruit in recent years. For example, Washington and Beijing have cooperated diplomatically over finding a solution to the civil war in Sudan and slowing Iran's pursuit of nuclear weapons.[14]

Neither China nor the United States desires to conquer or occupy territories or build sprawling empires far from their respective homelands. While competition for markets and resources can become intense, war is unwanted and cooperation is not out of the question. For China's activities in the Developing World, the flag tends to follow

---

[12] Shambaugh suggests that the United States and China are "acting in parallel with each other around the world." These quotations are from Shambaugh, 2012, p. 76 and pp. 75–76.

[13] Christensen, 2015.

[14] For some succinct and trenchant discussion on U.S. and Chinese convergences on Sudan and Iran, see Elizabeth C. Economy and Michael Levi, *By All Necessary Means: How China's Resource Quest Is Changing the World*, New York: Oxford University Press, 2014, pp. 179–186.

trade and investment;[15] China's burgeoning economy is hungry for markets and resources, and the quest for both has led Chinese entrepreneurs and investors to range the world. Lagging behind the traders and adventurers have been investors belatedly keen to improve infrastructure from seaports to pipelines (and to get paid for doing so). Yet further behind—essentially stragglers—are warships, jet fighters, and armored personnel carriers deployed in an attempt to protect people, assets, and infrastructure beyond China's borders.

There may be some minimal security coordination, such as in the Gulf of Aden anti-piracy missions or in Afghanistan. These parallel efforts tend to occur within or at the fringes of existing frameworks, institutions, and regimes. There may also be opportunities for limited cooperation in UN peacekeeping; President Xi Jinping publicly committed China to a greater role in peacekeeping, including taking the lead in creating a standby force.[16] In any case, Beijing appears to be intent on increasing its military presence around the world engaged in noncombat operations, what one Chinese Middle East expert has called a "soft military footprint."[17]

The United States and China also act as partners in parallel as Beijing begins to operate in a parallel universe of institutions created by China. These entities, such as the AIIB, are Chinese creations, with China taking the leading role. The AIIB might compete with the Asian Development Bank or it might complement it instead. Another Chinese institution is the Shanghai Cooperation Organization that excludes the United States. China is not adamantly opposed to the United States joining, but it is not simply up to Beijing, because all the capitals of member states must be unanimous for a new member to be admitted.

The United States is not entirely immune from this game; until January 2017, the TPP trade deal was not designed to exclude China forever. Rather, there would have been opportunity for China to join

---

15 Economy and Levi, 2014, especially Chapter 9.

16 Michael Martina and David Brunnstrom, "China's Xi Says to Commit 8,000 Troops for U.N. Peacekeeping Force," *Reuters*, September 28, 2015.

17 Sun Degang, the deputy director of Shanghai International Studies University Middle East Institute has used this term. He is cited in Ghiselli, 2015, p. 14.

eventually after substantial reforms of its economy, reforms that would be politically difficult and require years to complete in the best of circumstances. As a result, the trade deal would have excluded China for many years had the U.S. not withdrawn and had Congress then agree to U.S. participation. Encouraging China's economic reforms in this way might ultimately have been to China's advantage and even beneficial to global economic growth, and that is a factor that adds to the complexity of the U.S.-China relationship and demands a longer-term perspective. The need for reforms may empower reformers within China, much as China's long effort to join the World Trade Organization empowered reformers. If the TPP were to be revived, then China's eventual on-ramp could be exactly the type of win-win situation that Chinese leaders advocate for throughout the world.

Two Caveats

There are two cautions about viewing the U.S.-China relationship in the Developing World solely through the lens of partners in parallel. First, the partners in parallel formulation is used at the risk of oversimplifying and mischaracterizing a complex reality. As noted, there are some regions where the United States and China are at loggerheads—in Southeast Asia, for example.

Second, in time of conflict or escalating tensions, these parallel Chinese and American operating trajectories are likely to start converging toward confrontation or diverging in the direction of estrangement. Parallelisms can and do persist in peacetime. But how might China act economically, diplomatically, and militarily in the Developing World vis-à-vis the United States in time of war or on the road to war? Both countries have strong desires to avoid answering this question firsthand, but both likely will need to consider it as China becomes more involved in the Developing World; as the Developing World continues to grow and gain greater weight in world economics and politics; and as the United States continues to face the immensely difficult problem of managing and improving the global rule-based system that it and its allies established and have led since the end of World War II.

APPENDIX A

Actors Involved in Shaping or Influencing Chinese Foreign Policy

In this appendix, we discuss the actors involved in shaping or influencing Chinese policy toward two regions: Southeast Asia and Latin America and the Caribbean. Southeast Asia is by far the most important Developing World region to China. In contrast, Latin America and the Caribbean is the least important. Accordingly, reviewing the various actors involved in shaping policy toward each region can give insight into how China manages its foreign policy priorities. Notably, foreign policy development and implementation are not necessarily seamless but, instead, include bureaucratic and political conflicts of interest and incentives that may cause Chinese entities to diverge from government directives.[1]

Southeast Asia

Chinese policy in Southeast Asia is shaped by a plethora of government, quasi-government, and nongovernment actors. There is significant Chinese attention to Southeast Asia within and outside the Chinese government and extensive engagement opportunities between China and its ASEAN counterparts.

At the top, President Xi Jinping and Premier Li Keqiang define China's relations with Southeast Asia. Since 2012, China has established

---

[1] Saunders, 2006.

a Central Maritime Rights Protection Leading Small Group (LSG) led by Xi to oversee Chinese activities in the South China Sea (as well as the East China Sea). The LSG is tasked with formulating and coordinating Chinese strategy to safeguard its maritime rights and interests and managing maritime territorial disputes. It includes senior representatives from 17 government branches, including the Ministry of Foreign Affairs, the State Oceanic Administration,[2] and the PLA Navy. There is also a Central Maritime Rights Protection LSG Office that provides research and helps convene meetings for the LSG. This office is housed within the CCP's Foreign Affairs Office, which is headed by State Councilor Yang Jiechi.[3]

There is significant high-level interaction between ASEAN and Chinese government actors that allows key Chinese government ministries to contribute to Chinese policy toward ASEAN. Since 1997, China and ASEAN have established a three-tiered dialogue and cooperation mechanism. The highest tier is the China-ASEAN leaders summit, which has occurred annually; the Chinese president or premier typically attends the summit. The second tier includes meetings between Chinese and ASEAN ministers. China has established 12 ministerial meetings that cover foreign affairs, commerce, culture, health, information, telecommunications, quality inspection and quarantine, transport, customs, procurator, youth affairs, and counter transnational crimes. The third tier consists of five types of working-level meetings between senior government officials: ASEAN-China Senior Officials Consultations (ACSOC), ASEAN-China Joint Cooperation Committee (ACJCC), China-ASEAN Joint Committee on Economic and Trade Cooperation, China-ASEAN Joint Committee on Scientific

---

[2] In 2013, China consolidated its handful of separate maritime law enforcement agencies under the administration control of the State Oceanic Agency and renamed them the Chinese Coast Guard. These changes were implemented to help streamline and integrate the agencies to allow China to implement a more coherent maritime policy. To date, institutional reorganization is still ongoing. See Lyle Morris, "Taming the Five Dragons? China Consolidates Its Maritime Law Enforcement Agencies," *China Brief*, Vol. 13, No. 7, March 28, 2013.

[3] Bonnie Glaser, "China's Maritime Rights Protection Leading Small Group—Shrouded in Secrecy," September 11, 2015, Asia Maritime Transparency Initiative.

and Technological Cooperation, and China-ASEAN Business Council (CABC).[4]

A range of economic actors are also involved in shaping Chinese policy toward the region. This includes, for example, the Chinese National Development and Reform Commission, state-owned banks such as the Development Bank of China and the Export-Import Bank of China, and state-owned enterprises such as the China National Offshore Oil Company.[5] It also involves new economic entities created by Beijing to facilitate greater investment and financial cooperation with the region, such as the China-ASEAN Fund on Investment Cooperation and the China-ASEAN Inter-Bank Association.[6] Chinese provincial and local governments are also reaching out to ASEAN, and some have signed formal cooperation agreements.[7]

On a day-to-day basis and within the Ministry of Foreign Affairs, Southeast Asia falls under the Department of Asian Affairs. The department covers Northeast Asia, Southeast Asia, and South Asia.[8] In 2009, China appointed an ambassador to ASEAN,[9] and in 2012, China established a diplomatic mission to ASEAN in Jakarta, Indonesia.[10] Current Chinese ambassador to ASEAN, Mr. Xu Bu, meets regularly with representatives to ASEAN.

---

[4] Qi Jianguo, "Cong Huangjin Shinian Dao Zuanshi Shinian" ["From the Golden Decade to Diamond Decade"], *Foreign Affairs Journal*, No. 113, Winter 2013.

[5] For CNOOC, see "Challenges and Opportunities of Offshore Development in South China Southeast Asia," Engineering and Construction Department, CNOOC, October 2014.

[6] Jiang Zhida, "Reconnecting China with Southeast Asia," *Beijing Review*, December 1, 2011.

[7] For example, see "Press Release—ASEAN Secretariat Enters into Cooperation Agreement with Guangdong Province, China ASEAN Secretariat," ASEAN, September 5, 2008.

[8] "Department of Asian Affairs," Ministry of Foreign Affairs of the People's Republic of China, webpage, undated.

[9] "Zhongguo-Dongmeng Guanxi (10+1)" ["China-ASEAN Relations (10+1)"], Ministry of Foreign Affairs of the People's Republic of China, February 2017.

[10] "Mission of the People's Republic of China to ASEAN Formally Inaugurated," Mission of the People's Republic of China to ASEAN, September 28, 2012.

Latin America and the Caribbean

At the top, President Xi Jinping and Premier Li Keqiang define China's relations with Latin America through statements and policies announced during their visits. Foreign Minister Wang Yi, Director of the National Development and Reform Commission Xu Shaoshi, Commerce Minister Gao Hucheng, and other Chinese leaders have been involved in the first China-CELAC Forum ministerial level meeting.[11] Chinese military leaders also visit the region to strengthen defense ties and relations. Unlike its involvement in Africa or the Middle East, China has not designated any special envoys to the region. Within China's Ministry of Foreign Affairs, the Department of Latin American and Caribbean Affairs is responsible for much of the day-to-day engagements with the region.

Outside of the government, China has fewer Latin America experts compared to experts on other developing regions. Many leading Latin America experts belong to the Institute of Latin American Studies at the Chinese Academy of Social Sciences, the country's premier think tank for the region.[12]

Economically, the China Development Bank (CDB)[13] and the Export-Import Bank of China (EXIM)[14] are involved in financing Chinese government-sponsored projects in the region.[15] A number of key Chinese state-owned enterprises, including China National Petroleum Corporation, also operate in the region and benefit from agreements Beijing helps facilitate and finance.[16] In some countries, Chinese state-

---

[11] "Ministry of Foreign Affairs Holds a Briefing for Chinese and Foreign Journalists on the First Ministerial Meeting of China-CELAC Forum," Ministry of Foreign Affairs of the People's Republic of China, January 5, 2015.

[12] Ariel C. Armony, "The China-Latin America Relationship: Convergences and Divergences," in Hearn and Leon-Manriquez, 2001, p. 25.

[13] L. Arias, "Costa Rica, China Sign Cooperation Agreements Worth Nearly $2 Billion," *Tico Times*, June 2, 2013.

[14] Isabella Cota, "China Lends Costa Rica $400 million on Xi Visit," *Reuters*, June 3, 2013.

[15] China is also injecting significant capital into both banks to support the country's "One Belt, One Road," initiative. See http://english.caixin.com/2015-04-21/100802136.html.

[16] Arias, 2013.

owned enterprises are wary of directly competing for large infrastructure projects and may be using proxies to increase Chinese investment.[17] In Nicaragua, for example, a Chinese billionaire entrepreneur, Wang Jing, has begun initial site work on constructing a $50 billion canal that, like the Panama Canal, will connect the Atlantic with the Pacific Ocean.[18] It is unclear the extent to which Wang is backed by the Chinese government, and he seems to be experiencing financial difficulties.

Given the large numbers of Chinese actors involved in Latin America, managing a coherent and centrally directed, top-down Chinese policy toward the region is not an easy task, and China may not necessarily have the bureaucratic capability to do so. Since 2010, MOFA's Department of Latin American and Caribbean Affairs—the main entity focused on the region—has experienced three different leadership changes, and the current Director General Zhu Qingqiao did not assume his current position until late 2014. In 2010, the department had approximately 80 staff working domestically and abroad, covering 33 countries.[19] The average staff age was less than 35 years old.[20] While it is likely that changes have occurred since then, the statistics suggest that China is not putting its most experienced officers into this department. The department is also likely stretched relatively thin in its duties to manage day-to-day relations and organize events, promote exchanges, and engage in translation work.[21]

---

[17] Lucy Hornby and Andres Schipani, "China Tilts Towards Liberal Latin American Economies," *Financial Times*, May 10, 2015.

[18] Carrie Grace, "Wang Jing: The Man Behind the Nicaragua Canal Project," *BBC News*, March 18, 2015.

[19] "Yang Wanming Jieshao Lameisi Gongzuo Ganbu Genju Xuyao Zai Guoneiwai Lunhuan" ["Yang Wanming Introduces Working Cadre of Latin America Division, Will Rotate Abroad and at Home Based on Needs"], *People's Daily Online*, November 23, 2010.

[20] "Yang Wanming: Qingnian Shi Waijiao Duiwu Gugan Lameisi Pingjun Nianling Bu Dao 35 Sui" ["Yang Wanming: Youths Are the Backbone of the Diplomatic Corps, Average Age of Latin America Division Is Less than 35"], *People's Daily Online*, November 23, 2010.

[21] "Yang Wanming Jieshao Lameisi Gongzuo Ganbu Genju Xuyao Zai Guoneiwai Lunhuan" ["Yang Wanming Introduces Working Cadre of Latin America Division, Will Rotate Abroad and at Home Based on Needs"].

References

"1 Nian You 16 Wan Duo Zhongguo Renmin 'Yimin' Mengjiala? Hai Zheng You Ke Neng" ["160,000 Chinese 'Immigrating' to Bangladesh in a Year? It Actually Is a Possibility"], *Aboluowang*, October 16, 2016. As of August 31, 2017: http://www.aboluowang.com/2016/1016/820201.html

VII BRICS Summit Ufa Declaration, Ministry of Foreign Affairs of the People's Republic of China, July 9, 2015. As of October 10, 2015: http://www.fmprc.gov.cn/mfa_eng/wjdt_665385/2649_665393/t1282066.shtml

2013 Statistical Yearbook of the Overseas Community Affairs Council, Republic of China (Taiwan), Overseas Community Affairs Council, Republic of China (Taiwan), September 2014. As of October 13, 2015: http://www.ocac.gov.tw/OCAC/Pages/VDetail.aspx?nodeid=51&pid=313

"Address of Wang Yang at the 2nd China-Pacific Island Countries Economic Development and Cooperation Forum and the Opening Ceremony of 2013 China International Show on Green Innovative Products and Technologies," Ministry of Commerce of the People's Republic of China, November 12, 2013. As of August 5, 2015:
http://english.mofcom.gov.cn/article/newsrelease/significantnews/201311/20131100386982.shtml

AFP, "China Boosts Africa Diplomacy," March 13, 2015. As of March 17, 2015: http://news.yahoo.com/china-boosts-africa-diplomacy-150407469.html

Aidoo, Richard, and Steve Hess, "Non-Interference 2.0: China's Evolving Foreign Policy Towards a Changing Africa," *Journal of Current Chinese Affairs*, Vol. 44, No. 1, 2015. As of March 31, 2015: http://nbn-resolving.org/urn/resolver.pl?urn:nbn:de:gbv:18-4-8175

Alden, Chris, *China in Africa*, London: Zed Books, 2007.

Alden, Chris, and Daniel Large, "On Becoming a Norms Maker: Chinese Foreign Policy, Norms Evolution and the Challenges of Security in Africa," *China Quarterly*, March 2015.

Allison, Simon, "Djibouti Welcomes China to the Playground of the Superpowers," *Daily Maverick*, May 14, 2015. As of May 15, 2015:
http://www.dailymaverick.co.za/article/2015-05-14-djibouti-welcomes-china-to-the-playground-of-the-superpowers/?utm_source=May+15+2015+EN&utm_campaign=5%2F15%2F2015&utm_medium=email#.VVXx2yFVhBc

Alterman, John B., and John W. Garver, *The Vital Triangle: China, the United States, and the Middle East*, Washington, D.C.: CSIS, 2008.

Amarsaikhan, B., "Two Countries' Servicemen Join in Military Exercises Against Terrorism," *Montsame National News Agency*, October 12, 2015. As of October 14, 2015:
http://en.montsame.mn/politics/two-countries-servicemen-join-military-exercises-against-terrorism

"Angola President Seeks More Non-Oil Deals in His Visit to China," *Bloomberg*, June 12, 2015. Available at:
http://www.bloomberg.com/news/articles/2015-06-12/angola-president-seeks-more-non-oil-deals-in-his-visit-to-china

Ansari, Usman, "China Officially Offers Pakistan J-10 Variant," *Defense News*, August 3, 2011.

Areddy, James T., "China Evacuates Citizens from Yemen," *Wall Street Journal*, March 30, 2015. As of October 10, 2015:
http://www.wsj.com/articles/china-evacuating-citizens-from-yemen-1427689845

Arias, L., "Costa Rica, China Sign Cooperation Agreements Worth Nearly $2 Billion," *Tico Times*, June 2, 2013. As of October 10, 2015:
http://www.ticotimes.net/2013/06/02/costa-rica-china-sign-cooperation-agreements-worth-nearly-2-billion

Armony, Ariel C., "The China-Latin America Relationship: Convergences and Divergences," in Adrian H. Hearn and Jose Luis Leon-Manriquez, eds., *China Engages Latin America: Tracing the Trajectory*, Boulder, Colo.: Lynne Rienner Publishers, 2001.

"ASEAN GDP and GDP Per Capita," *ASEAN Matters for America*, East-West Center, 2013. As of July 22, 2014:
http://www.asiamattersforamerica.org/ASEAN/data/gdppercapita

Asia Maritime Transparency Initiative, "Airpower in the South China Sea," Center for Strategic and International Studies, July 29, 2015. As of August 30, 2017:
https://amti.csis.org/airstrips-scs/

Asia Regional Integration Center, "Free Trade Agreements," webpage, Asian Development Bank, undated. As of October 14, 2015:
https://aric.adb.org/fta-country

Asian Development Bank, "Free Trade Agreements," Asia Regional Integration Center, 2015. As of November 28, 2015:
https://aric.adb.org/fta

Asian Infrastructure Investment Bank, "Prospective Founding Members," webpage, 2015a. As of November 28, 2015:
http://www.aiib.org/html/pagemembers/

———, "50 Countries Sign the Articles of Agreement for the Asian Infrastructure Investment Bank," June 29, 2015b. As of November 28, 2015:
http://www.aiib.org/html/2015/NEWS_0629/11.html

Athukorala, Prema-chandra, "Global Production Sharing and Trade Patterns in East Asia," Working paper No. 2013/10, Working Papers in Trade and Development, Arndt-Corden Department of Economics Crawford School of Public Policy, ANU College of Asia and the Pacific, June 2013.

Athukorala, Prema-chandra, and Jayant Menon, "Global Production Sharing, Trade Patterns, and Determinants of Trade Flows in East Asia," Working paper No. 41, ADB Working Paper Series on Regional Economic Integration, Asian Development Bank, January 2010.

Australian Department of Defence, "Minister for Defence—Statement—Freedom of Navigation in the South China Southeast Asia," October 27, 2015. As of November 10, 2015:
http://www.minister.defence.gov.au/2015/10/27/minister-for-defence-statement-freedom-of-navigation-in-the-south-china-Southeast Asia/

"The Awakening Giant," *The Economist*, February 8, 2014. As of April 8, 2015:
http://www.economist.com/news/middle-east-and-africa/21595949-if-africas-economies-are-take-africans-will-have-start-making-lot

Bao Haibin, "China-ASEAN Maritime Cooperation Fund," Ministry of Foreign Affairs of the People's Republic of China, March 2014. As of September 19, 2015:
http://ASEANregionalforum.ASEAN.org/files/Archive/21st/ARF%20Maritime%20Security%20Workshop%20on%20Preparedness%20and%20Response%20to%20Marine%20Pollution%20Incidents,%20Honolulu,%204-5%20March%202014/Annex%209%20-%20China-ASEAN%20Maritime%20Cooperation%20Fund.pdf

Barry, Ellen, "New President in Sri Lanka Puts China's Plans in Check," *New York Times*, January 9, 2015.

Bastians, Dharisha, and Gardiner Harris, "Chinese Leader Visits Sri Lanka, Challenging India's Sway," *New York Times*, September 16, 2014.

Bateman, Sam, "Australia and the US: Great Allies but Different Agendas in the South China Southeast Asia," *The Lowy Interpreter*, November 12, 2015. As of November 12, 2015:
http://www.lowyinterpreter.org/post/2015/11/12/Australia-and-the-US-great-allies-but-different-agendas-in-the-South-China-Southeast Asia.aspx

Baxter, Phil, "What Crunching the Data Tells Us About China's Naval Port Visits," *War Is Boring*, March 3, 2015. As of October 13, 2015:
https://medium.com/war-is-boring/what-crunching-the-data-tells-us-about-china-s-naval-port-visits-3ad0aec597c0

"BBC Brazil: Deals Show Waning US Influence," *China Daily*, May 21, 2015. As of June 25, 2015:
http://www.chinadaily.com.cn/world/2015livistsa/2015-05/21/content_20779416.htm

"BBC World Service Poll," *BBC*, June 3, 2014. As of July 2, 2015:
http://downloads.bbc.co.uk/mediacentre/country-rating-poll.pdf

Beauchamp-Mustafaga, Nathan, "The New Silk Road and Latin America: Will They Ever Meet?" *Jamestown China Brief*, Vol. 15, No. 5, March 6, 2015.

"Beijing Declaration of the First Ministerial Meeting of the CELAC-China Forum," China-CELAC Forum, January 23, 2015. As of May 22, 2015:
http://www.chinacelacforum.org/chn/zywj/t1230938.htm

"Beijing in 45b Yuan Global Media Drive," *South China Morning Post*, January 13, 2009. As of March 16, 2018:
http://www.scmp.com/article/666847/beijing-45b-yuan-global-media-drive

"Beijing's Africa Problem: 'No Blacks' Chinese Restaurant Shut Down in Kenya," *Mail & Guardian*, March 25, 2015. As of March 31, 2015:
http://mgafrica.com/article/2015-03-25-beijings-africa-problem-no-blacks-chinese-restaurant-shut-down-in-kenya/

"Bello: The Dragon and the Gringo," *The Economist*, January 15, 2015, p. 36. As of October 10, 2015:
https://www.economist.com/news/americas/21639549-latin-americas-shifting-geopolitics-dragon-and-gringo

Ben-Ari, Nirit, "On Bumpy Roads and Rails," *Africa Renewal*, April 2014. As of October 10, 2015:
http://www.un.org/africarenewal/magazine/april-2014/bumpy-roads-and-rails

Berlinger, Joshua, "Satellite Photos Reveal Underground Construction at Chinese Military Base," *CNN*, August 1, 2017. As of October 17, 2017:
http://www.cnn.com/2017/07/26/asia/china-military-base-djibouti-photos/index.html

Bessey, Bernice, "Ghana: Gov't to Re-Equip Armed Forces," *Ghanaian Chronicle*, September 10, 2008. As of October 10, 2015:
http://allafrica.com/stories/200809101037.html

"Big Fish in a Big Pond," *The Economist*, March 25, 2015. As of November 10, 2015:
http://www.economist.com/news/asia/21647169-chinese-aid-region-expandingas-its-immigrant-community-big-fish-big-pond

Bilateral Investment Treaty, Ministry of Commerce of the People's Republic of China, Department of Treaty and Law, 2011. As of November 28, 2015: http://tfs.mofcom.gov.cn/article/Nocategory/201111/20111107819474.shtml

"Biofuels Could Be Produced at Chinese Refinery in Limon, Says Costa Rica Oil Chief," *Tico Times*, January 10, 2015. As of May 19, 2015: http://www.ticotimes.net/2015/01/10/biofuels-would-be-produced-at-chinese-refinery-in-limon-says-costa-rica-oil-chief

Blanchard, Ben, "China, Kazakhstan Sign $23.6 Billion in Deals," *Reuters*, March 27, 2015. As of October 14, 2015: http://www.reuters.com/article/2015/03/28/us-china-kazakhstan-idUSKBN0MO02A20150328

———, "China Sends Troops to Open First Overseas Military Base in Djibouti," *Reuters*, July 11, 2017. As of August 23, 2017: http://www.reuters.com/article/us-china-djibouti-idUSKBN19X049

Blasko, Dennis J., "People's Liberation Army and People's Armed Police Ground Exercises with Foreign Forces, 2002–2009," in Roy Kamphausen, David Lai, and Andrew Scobell, eds., *The PLA at Home and Abroad: Assessing the Operational Capabilities of China's Military*, Carlisle, Pa.: U.S. Army War College Strategic Studies Institute, June 2010, p. 400. As of July 28, 2015: http://www.strategicstudiesinstitute.army.mil/pdffiles/PUB995.pdf

Bokhari, Farhan, Leslie Hook, and James Lamont, "A History of Military and Commercial Ties," *Financial Times*, December 20, 2010.

Bovingdon, Gardner, *The Uyghurs: Strangers in Their Own Land*, New York: Columbia University Press, 2010.

BP, *BP Statistical Review of World Energy 2015*, 64th ed., June 2015. As of December 5, 2015: http://bp.com/statisticalreview

Brandt, Jon, Nicole Adams, Christina Dinh, Devin Kleinfield-Hayes, Andrew Tuck, Derek Hottle, Nav Aujla, Kirsten Kaufman, and Wanlin Ren, "Chinese Engagement in Latin America and the Caribbean: Implications for US Foreign Policy," American University, School of International Service, December 2012.

Brant, Philippa, "Chinese Aid in the Pacific," Lowy Institute for International Policy, March 9, 2015. As of August 5, 2015: http://www.lowyinstitute.org/chinese-aid-map/

———, "One Belt, One Road? China's Community of Common Destiny," *The Interpreter*, Lowry Institute for International Policy, March 31, 2015. As of September 14, 2015: http://www.lowyinterpreter.org/post/2015/03/31/One-belt-one-road-Chinas-community-of-common-destiny.aspx

Brautigam, Deborah, *The Dragon's Gift*, New York: Oxford University Press, 2009.

———, "Is China Sending Prisoners to Work Overseas?" *China in Africa: The Real Story*, August 13, 2010. As of April 17, 2015:
http://www.chinaafricarealstory.com/2010/08/is-china-sending-prisoners-to-work.html

———, "The Chinese in Africa: *The Economist* Gets Some Things Right, Some Wrong," blog post, *China in Africa: The Real Story*, May 20, 2011. As of April 17, 2015:
http://www.chinaafricarealstory.com/2011/05/chinese-in-africa-economist-gets-some.html

"BRICS Countries Launch New Development Bank," *BBC News*, July 21, 2015. As of August 25, 2015:
http://www.bbc.com/news/33605230

"BRICS Pour Cash into the IMF in Exchange for Bigger Say," *RT*, July 19, 2012. As of December 8, 2014:
http://rt.com/business/imf-brics-funds-boost-153/

"Brief Introduction to the Shanghai Cooperation Organization," webpage, 2015. As of October 14, 2015:
http://www.sectsco.org/EN123/brief.asp

Brill Olcott, Martha, "China's Unmatched Influence in Central Asia," Carnegie Endowment for International Peace, September 18, 2013.

Broadman, Harry G., *Africa's Silk Road: China and India's New Economic Frontier*, Washington, D.C.: The World Bank, 2007. As of April 17, 2015:
https://openknowledge.worldbank.org/bitstream/handle/10986/7186/378950Africas0silk0road01PUBLIC1.pdf?sequence=1

Buckley, Chris, "Update 2—China Considers Seychelles Port Offer, Denies Base Plan," *Reuters*, December 13, 2011. As of August 23, 2017:
http://www.reuters.com/article/china-seychelles-navy-idUSL3E7ND2SG20111213

"Building and Enhancing the Strategic Partnership and Writing a New Chapter of Friendly Cooperation—Foreign Minister Yang Jiechi Talks About the Outcome of President Hu Jintao's Visits," Ministry of Foreign Affairs of the People's Republic of China, June 21, 2011. As of October 10, 2015:
http://www.fmprc.gov.cn/mfa_eng/topics_665678/hjtcxshfh_665754/t833247.shtml

Burke, Jason, and Tania Branigan, "India-China Border Standoff Highlights Tensions Before Xi's Visit," *The Guardian*, September 16, 2014. As of August 4, 2014:
https://www.theguardian.com/world/2014/sep/16/india-china-border-standoff-xi-visit

Bush, George H. W., *The China Diary of George H. W. Bush: The Making of a Global President*, Jeffrey Engel, ed., Princeton, N.J.: Princeton University Press, 2008.

Calabrese, John, "From Flyswatters to Silkworms: The Evolution of China's Role in West Asia," *Asian Survey*, Vol. 30, No. 9, September 1990.

Carr, Bob, "South China Southeast Asia Would Be a Lonely Patrol for Australia," *Financial Review*, November 11, 2015. As of November 12, 2015: http://www.afr.com/opinion/deputy-sheriff-would-ride-alone-20151111-gkw82e#ixzz3rFHQwq49

"The Central Conference on Work Relating to Foreign Affairs Was Held in Beijing," Ministry of Foreign Affairs of the People's Republic of China, November 29, 2014. As of October 12, 2015: http://www.fmprc.gov.cn/mfa_eng/zxxx_662805/t1215680.shtml

"Chairman of Chinese Delegation Teng Hsiao-ping's Speech at the Special Session of the U.N. General Assembly," *Peking Review*, April 19, 1974.

"Challenges and Opportunities of Offshore Development in South China Southeast Asia," Engineering and Construction Department, CNOOC, October 2014. As of September 14, 2015: http://www.cnoocengineering.com/dmft/1CNOOC/Challenges%20and%20Opportunities%20of%20Offshore%20Development%20in%20South%20China%20Southeast Asia.pdf

Chan, Felix K., "Chinese Submarines and Indian ASW in the Indian Ocean," *Geopolitcus*, November 24, 2014. As of August 4, 2017: https://www.fpri.org/2014/11/chinese-submarines-and-indian-asw-in-the-indian-ocean/

Chan, Minnie, "Live-Fire Show of Force by Troops from China's First Overseas Military Base," *South China Morning Post*, September 25, 2017. As of October 17, 2017: http://www.scmp.com/news/china/diplomacy-defence/article/2112780/live-fire-show-force-troops-chinas-first-overseas

Chanda, Nayan, *Brother Enemy: The War After the War*, New York: Harcourt Brace and Jonvanovich, 1986.

Chang, Amy, "Beijing and the Chinese Diaspora in Southeast Asia: To Serve the People," *NBR Special Report*, No. 43, June 2013.

Chang, Rachel, "There Will Never Be a Problem with Freedom of Navigation in South China Southeast Asia: Xi Jinping," *Strait Times*, November 7, 2015. As of November 10, 2015: http://www.straitstimes.com/singapore/there-will-never-be-a-problem-with-freedom-of-navigation-in-south-china-sea-xi-jinping

Chase, Robert, Emily Hill, and Paul Kennedy, "Introduction," in Chase, Hill, and Kennedy, eds., *The Pivotal States: A New Framework for U.S. Policy in the Developing World*, New York: W. W. Norton, 1999.

Chaziza, Modechai, "China's Policy in the Middle East Peace Process After the Cold War," *China Report*, Vol. 49, No. 1, 2013.

Chen Jian, *Mao's China and the Cold War*, Chapel Hill: University of North Carolina Press, 2001.

China-Africa Economic and Trade Cooperation, Information Office of the State Council, August 2013. As of May 18, 2015:
http://www.scio.gov.cn/zxbd/wz/Document/1344818/1344818.htm

China-Africa Think Tanks Forum, "The 2nd Meeting of the China-Africa Think Tanks Forum," conference report, Bisoftu, Ethiopia, October 12–13, 2012, p. 5. As of March 19, 2015:
http://dspace.africaportal.org/jspui/bitstream/123456789/34123/1/IPSS_China-Africa_Think_Tanks_Forum_Final_(2)[1].pdf?1

"China, Algeria to Jointly Push for Progress in Partnership," *China Daily*, February 8, 2015. As of October 10, 2015:
http://www.chinadaily.com.cn/world/2015-02/08/content_19521827.htm

"China and Africa Joint Southeast Asia Research and Exchange Program Formally Launched," website, March 31, 2010. As of April 23, 2015:
http://www.focac.org/eng/dsjbzjhy/t676571.htm

"China and Argentina in Currency Swap," *Financial Times*, March 21, 2009. As of June 25, 2015:
http://www.ft.com/intl/cms/s/0/eba6405c-1d7e-11de-9eb3-00144feabdc0.html#axzz3eT1UvemD

"China and Brazil Sign $30bn Currency Swap Agreement," *BBC News*, March 27, 2013. As of June 25, 2015:
http://www.bbc.com/news/business-21949615

"China Announces More Assistance to Haiti," Embassy of the People's Republic of China in the United States of America, January 21, 2010. As of April 13, 2015:
http://www.china-embassy.org/eng/xw/t653186.htm

"China-ASEAN FTA," *China FTA Network*, Ministry of Commerce of the People's Republic of China, undated. As of October 7, 2015:
http://fta.mofcom.gov.cn/topic/chinaASEAN.shtml

"China, Australia Agreed to Boost Military Ties," *Xinhua News*, December 2, 2014. As of November 10, 2015:
http://news.xinhuanet.com/english/china/2014-12/02/c_127271012.htm

"China, Australia Vow to Promote Bilateral Defense Cooperation," *Xinhua News*, November 4, 2015. As of November 10, 2015:
http://news.xinhuanet.com/english/2015-11/04/c_134784124.htm

China-Brazil Business Council, 2013, "Chinese Investments in Brazil from 2007–2012: A Review of Recent Trends," June 2013. As of October 10, 2015:
http://www.redalc-china.org/monitor/images/pdfs/Investigacion/24_CBBC-IDB_2013.pdf

China Construction Bank, "CCB Designated as the First RMB Clearing Bank in South America," May 26, 2015. As of June 25, 2015:
http://www.ccb.com/en/announcement/20150527_1432687603.html

"China, Costa Rica Agree to Enhance Ties," *China Daily*, June 6, 2013. As of May 19, 2015:
http://www.chinadaily.com.cn/china/2013xivisit/2013-06/04/content_16564706.htm

"China Donates Military Equipment to Namibia," *Star Africa*, March 31, 2015. As of May 18, 2015:
http://en.starafrica.com/news/china-donates-military-hardware-to-namibia.html

"China Formally Opens First Overseas Military Base in Djibouti," *Reuters*, August 1, 2017. As of October 17, 2017:
https://www.reuters.com/article/us-china-djibouti/china-formally-opens-first-overseas-military-base-in-djibouti-idUSKBN1AH3E3

"China FTA Network," Ministry of Commerce of the People's Republic of China, webpage, undated. As of November 13, 2015:
http://fta.mofcom.gov.cn/topic/enpakistan.shtml

"China-GCC FTA," Ministry of Commerce of the People's Republic of China, undated. As of March 18, 2018:
http://fta.mofcom.gov.cn/topic/engcc.shtml

"China in Central Asia: Rising China, Sinking Russia," *The Economist*, September 14, 2013.

"China-India Regional Trade Arrangement Joint Feasibility Study," Ministry of Commerce of the People's Republic of China, undated. As of October 10, 2015:
http://fta.mofcom.gov.cn/topic/enindia.shtml

China Institute of International Studies, "Tiujin 'Yidai Yilu' Nengyuan Ziyuan Hezuo De Waijiao Yunchou" ["Carry Forward 'One Belt One Road': A Diplomatic Plan for Cooperation on Energy and Natural Resources"], 2014.

"China Issues White Paper on Foreign Aid," *Xinhua News*, July 10, 2014. As of May 18, 2015:
http://china-wire.org/?p=35149

China-Latin America Financial Database, Inter-American Dialogue. As of July 22, 2015:
http://www.thedialogue.org/map_list/

"China-Latin American and Caribbean Countries Cooperation Plan (2015–2019)," China-CELAC Forum, January 23, 2015. As of May 19, 2015:
http://www.chinacelacforum.org/chn/zywj/t1230944.htm

"China Leads Nations Boosting IMF's Firewall to $456 Billion," *Bloomberg*, June 19, 2012. As of December 8, 2014:
http://www.bloomberg.com/news/2012-06-19/china-leads-nations-boosting-imf-s-firewall-to-456-billion-1-.html

"China-Maldives FTA," Ministry of Commerce of the People's Republic of China, undated:
http://fta.mofcom.gov.cn/list/chinamedfen/chinamedfennews/1/encateinfo.html

China National Petroleum Corporation, "Flow of Natural Gas from Central Asia," webpage, 2015. As of October 14, 2015:
http://www.cnpc.com.cn/en/FlowofnaturalgasfromCentralAsia/FlowofnaturalgasfromCentralAsia2.shtml

"China Overtakes US as Brazil's Top Trade Partner," *JOC*, March 24, 2014. As of June 12, 2015:
http://www.joc.com/international-trade-news/trade-data/south-america-trade-data/china-overtakes-us-brazil%E2%80%99s-top-trade-partner_20140324.html

"China, Pacific Island Countries Announce Strategic Partnership," *Xinhua News*, November 23, 2014. As of October 10, 2015:
http://www.chinadaily.com.cn/world/2014xiattendg20/2014-11/23/content_18961677.htm

"China-Pakistan FTA," Ministry of Commerce of the People's Republic of China, undated. As of October 10, 2015:
http://fta.mofcom.gov.cn/topic/enpakistan.shtml

"China Pushes 'One Belt, One Road,'" *CCTV*, March 8, 2015. As of October 2, 2015:
http://english.cntv.cn/2015/03/08/VIDE1425782526322272.shtml

"China Rolls Out Military Roadmap of 'Active Defense' Strategy," Ministry of National Defense of the People's Republic of China, May 26, 2015. As of August 24, 2015:
http://eng.mod.gov.cn/DefenseNews/2015-05/26/content_4586690.htm

"China Said to Seek Deeper Military Ties with Iran," *Radio Free Europe/Radio Liberty*, October 15, 2015. As of October 16, 2015:
http://www.rferl.org/content/china-said-seek-deeper-military-ties-iran-/27307251.html

"China Says Its Submarine Docked in Sri Lanka 'for Replenishment,'" *The Hindu*, November 28, 2014. As of *insert date*:
http://www.thehindu.com/news/international/world/china-says-its-submarine-docked-in-sri-lanka-for-replenishment/article6643129.ece

"China Seeks Role for Yuan in AIIB to Extend Currency's Global Reach," *South China Morning Post*, April 27, 2015. As of September 19, 2015:
http://www.scmp.com/news/china/economy/article/1766627/china-seeks-role-yuan-aiib-extend-currencys-global-reach?page=all

"China-Sri Lanka FTA," Ministry of Commerce of the People's Republic of China, undated. As of October 10, 2015:
http://fta.mofcom.gov.cn/list/ensri/enchinasrinews/1/encateinfo.html

"China, Sri Lanka Pledge Military Cooperation," *Xinhua News*, September 23, 2014. As of October 10, 2015:
http://eng.chinamil.com.cn/news-channels/china-military-news/2014-09/23/content_6150398.htm/

"China Steps in to Support Venezuela, Ecuador as Oil Prices Tumble," *Fortune*, January 8, 2015. As of June 12, 2015:
http://fortune.com/2015/01/08/china-steps-in-to-support-venezuela-ecuador-as-oil-prices-tumble/

"China, Suriname Sign Currency Swap Deal," *Global Times*, March 18, 2015. As of June 12, 2015:
http://www.globaltimes.cn/content/912757.shtml

"China to Allocate $3Bln to Kyrgyzstan—Reports," *RIA Novosti* (Moscow), September 11, 2013.

"China to Cooperate with Africa on Industrialization, Sanitation, Security: FM," *China Daily*, March 8, 2015. As of March 9, 2015:
http://www.chinadaily.com.cn/china/2015twosession/201503/08/content_19750684.htm?utm_medium=twitter&utm_source=twitterfeed

"China to Help Venezuela Launch Third Satellite," *Xinhua News*, October 6, 2014. As of October 10, 2015:
http://en.people.cn/n/2014/1006/c202936-8791034.html

"China to Send Anti-Riot Peacekeepers to Haiti," *Xinhua News*, June 5, 2004. As of April 30, 2015:
http://www.chinadaily.com.cn/english/doc/2004-06/05/content_336807.htm

"China, Trinidad and Tobago Pledge to Bolster Ties," *Xinhua News*, June 2, 2013. As of May 19, 2015:
http://news.xinhuanet.com/english/china/2013-06/02/c_132425348.htm

"China, Ukraine Set Up Strategic Partnership," *Xinhua News*, June 20, 2011, Ministry of Foreign Affairs of the People's Republic of China.

"China's African Policy," *Xinhua News*, January 12, 2006. As of May 18, 2015:
http://webcache.googleusercontent.com/Southeast Asiarch?q=cache:3NUK46t2xiYJ:news.xinhuanet.com/english/2006-01/12/content_4042521.htm+&cd=4&hl=en&ct=clnk&gl=us

China's Foreign Aid (2011), Information Office of the State Council, the People's Republic of China, April 2011.

China's Foreign Aid (2014), Information Office of the State Council, the People's Republic of China, July 2014.

"China's Hospital Ship Peace Ark Leaves Djibouti," *Xinhua News*, September 29, 2010. As of May 8, 2015:
http://news.xinhuanet.com/english2010/photo/2010-09/29/c_13536123_7.htm

China's Military Strategy, Information Office of the State Council of the People's Republic of China, May 2015.

"China's Peace Ark Arrives in Tanzania," *China Daily*, October 20, 2010. As of May 8, 2015:
http://www.chinadaily.com.cn/photo/2010-10/20/content_11434347.htm

"China's 'Peace Ark' Mission Proves Success in Seychelles," *Xinhua News*, October 30, 2010. As of May 8, 2015:
http://www.china.org.cn/world/2010-10/30/content_21236231.htm

"China's Policy Paper on Latin America and the Caribbean," *Xinhua News*, November 5, 2008.

"China's Position Paper on South China Southeast Asia," *China Daily*, December 7, 2014. As of August 25, 2015:
http://www.chinadaily.com.cn/china/2014-12/07/content_19037946.htm

China's Position Paper on the New Security Concept (July 31, 2002), Ministry of Foreign Affairs of the People's Republic of China, August 6, 2002. As of August 24, 2015:
http://www.fmprc.gov.cn/mfa_eng/wjb_663304/zzjg_663340/gjs_665170/gjzzyhy_665174/2612_665212/2614_665216/t15319.shtml

"China's Productivity Imperative," Ernst and Young, 2012. As of April 8, 2015:
http://www.ey.com/Publication/vwLUAssets/China_productivity_imperative_en/$FILE/China-Productivity-Imperative_en.pdf

"China's Xi Jinping Agrees $46bn Superhighway to Pakistan," *BBC News*, April 20, 2015. As of October 15, 2015:
http://www.bbc.com/news/world-asia-32377088

"China's Y-8 Aircraft Poised to Land in South American Market," *People's Daily Online*, June 2, 2011. As of April 30, 2015:
http://en.people.cn/90001/90776/90883/7398083.html

"Chinese Air Force Bayi Aerobatics Team Arrives in Russia with Seven J-10 Fighters," *People's Daily Online*, August 29, 2013. As of October 10, 2015:
http://en.people.cn/90786/8381578.html

"Chinese Army Rescuers Leave for Nepal After Quake," *Xinhua*, April 27, 2015. As of October 10, 2015:
http://english.gov.cn/news/international_exchanges/2015/04/27/content_281475097012802.htm

"Chinese Development Aid in Pacific Island Countries and Opportunities for Cooperation," United Nations Development Programme, China, Issue Brief No. 7, December 2014.

"Chinese Government Sends Relief Materials to Hurricane-Hit Cuba," *CCTV*, November 20, 2012. As of April 30, 2015:
http://english.cntv.cn/20121120/109301.shtml

"Chinese Hospital Ship 'Ark Peace' [sic] Arrives in Yangon," *Xinhua News*, Ministry of National Defense of the People's Republic of China, August 29, 2013. As of May 8, 2015:
http://eng.mod.gov.cn/Photos/2013-08/29/content_4463726.htm

"Chinese Hospital Ship Arrives in Cambodia for Goodwill Visit," *CNTV*, September 24, 2013. As of May 8, 2015:
http://english.cntv.cn/20130924/104726.shtml

"Chinese Hospital Ship 'Peace Ark' Provides Free Medical Checkups for Brunei Residents," Ministry of National Defense of the People's Republic of China, June 17, 2013. As of May 8, 2015:
http://eng.mod.gov.cn/Photos/2013-06/17/content_4455650.htm

"Chinese Navy 'Peace Ark' Hospital Ship Arrives in Costa Rica," *People's Daily Online*, November 24, 2011. As of April 30, 2015:
http://en.people.cn/90786/7655740.html

"Chinese Navy Warship Rammed Two Vietnamese Fishing Vessels," *USNI News*, August 7, 2015. As of September 19, 2015:
http://news.usni.org/2015/08/07/report-chinese-navy-warship-likely-rammed-two-vietnamese-fishing-vessels

"Chinese Premier Wen Jiabao Announces Eight New Measures to Enhance Cooperation with Africa," *Xinhua News*, November 9, 2009. As of April 23, 2015:
http://www.focac.org/eng/dsjbzjhy/t625619.htm

"Chinese President Expects Stronger Ties with Brazil, L. America," *Xinhua News*, July 17, 2014. As of June 12, 2015:
http://news.xinhuanet.com/english/china/2014-07/17/c_133491419.htm

"Chinese Soft Power in Africa," *Economist Intelligence Unit*, August 21, 2014. As of March 31, 2015:
http://country.eiu.com/article.aspx?articleid=332200817&Country=Chad&topic=Politics#.VRnNo9F_dYs.email

Chong, Wu, "UN: China 'Remarkably Efficient' in Haiti Aid," *China Daily*, January 20, 2010. As of April 13, 2015:
http://www.chinadaily.com.cn/world/haitiearthquake/2010-01/20/content_9350783.htm

Christensen, Thomas J., *The China Challenge: Shaping the Choices of a Rising Power*, New York: W. W. Norton & Company, 2015.

"Chronology of China's Belt and Road Initiative," *Xinhua News*, March 28, 2015. As of October 10, 2015:
http://www.xinhuanet.com/english/2015-03/28/c_134105435.htm

Clark, Helen, "Should Australia Fear An Influx of Chinese?" *South China Morning Post*, June 30, 2017. As of August 31, 2017:
http://www.scmp.com/week-asia/geopolitics/article/2100798/should-australia-fear-influx-chinese

Clemens, Morgan, "The Maritime Silk Road and the PLA: Part Two," *China Brief*, Vol. XV, No. 7, April 3, 2014.

———, "The Maritime Silk Road and the PLA: Part One," *China Brief*, Vol. XV, No. 6, March 19, 2015.

Cohen, Stephen P., *The Future of Pakistan*, Washington, D.C.: The Brookings Institution Press, 2011.

"Columbia's FARC Release Chinese Hostages," *BBC News*, November 22, 2012. As of July 6, 2015:
http://www.bbc.com/news/world-latin-america-20456716

Confucius Institute Headquarters, "About Confucius Institutes," Beijing, China, 2014. As of August 14, 2017:
http://english.hanban.org/node_7716.htm

"Confucius Institutes Around the Globe," University of Nebraska-Lincoln, October 13, 2015. As of November 10, 2015:
http://confuciusinstitute.unl.edu/institutes.shtml

Contessi, Nicola P., "China, Russia and the Leadership of the SCO," *China & Eurasia Forum Quarterly*, Vol. 8, No. 4, 2010.

Cooley, Alexander, *Great Games, Local Rules*, New York: Oxford University Press, 2012.

Cooley, John, *Unholy Wars: Afghanistan, America, and International Terrorism*, Sterling, Va.: Pluto Press, 2002.

"Costa Rica, China Sign Cooperation Agreements Worth Nearly $2 Billion," *Tico Times*, June 1, 2013. As of May 19, 2015:
http://www.ticotimes.net/2013/06/02/costa-rica-china-sign-cooperation-agreements-worth-nearly-2-billion

Cota, Isabella, "China Lends Costa Rica $400 Million on Xi Visit," *Reuters*, June 3, 2013. As of October 10, 2015:
http://www.reuters.com/article/2013/06/03/us-china-costarica-idUSBRE95218820130603

Craymer, Lucy, "Fiji Attracts Old Friends as China's Clout Grows," *Wall Street Journal*, October 30, 2014. As of November 10, 2015:
http://www.wsj.com/articles/fiji-attracts-old-friends-as-chinas-clout-grows-1414678386

"Defense Ministry's Regular Press Conference on August 28, 2014," Ministry of National Defense of the People's Republic of China, August 28, 2014. As of *insert date*:
http://eng.mod.gov.cn/Press/2014-08/28/content_4533190.htm

Denyer, Simon, "China Bypasses American 'New Silk Road' with Two of Its Own," *Washington Post*, October 14, 2013. As of October 10, 2015:
https://www.washingtonpost.com/world/asia_pacific/china-bypasses-american-new-silk-road-with-two-if-its-own/2013/10/14/49f9f60c-3284-11e3-ad00-ec4c6b31cbed_story.html

"Department of Asian Affairs," Ministry of Foreign Affairs of the People's Republic of China, webpage, undated. As of September 14, 2015: http://www.fmprc.gov.cn/mfa_eng/wjb_663304/zzjg_663340/yzs_663350/

DeSilva-Ranasinghe, Sergei, "Pakistan's Strategic and Foreign Policy Objectives," Future Directions International, strategic analysis paper, May 5, 2011.

Dezan Shira and Associates, "Understanding China's Double Tax Agreements," *China Briefing*, February 12, 2014. As of November 28, 2015: http://www.china-briefing.com/news/2014/02/12/understanding-chinas-double-tax-agreements.html

Ding Yifan, "China's IMF Contribution, A Move of Multiple-Layered Meaning," *China-US Focus*, July 13, 2012. As of December 8, 2014: http://www.chinausfocus.com/foreign-policy/chinas-imf-contribution-a-move-of-multiple-layered-meaning/

"Diplomatic Allies," Ministry of Foreign Affairs of the Republic of China (Taiwan), webpage, undated. As of May 11, 2015: http://www.mofa.gov.tw/en/AlliesIndex.aspx?n=DF6F8F246049F8D6&sms=A76B7230ADF29736

Dittmer, Lowell, and George T. Yu, eds., *China, the Developing World, and the New Global Dynamic*, Boulder, Colo.: Lynne Rienner Publishers, 2010.

The Diversified Employment of China's Armed Forces, Information Office of the State Council of the People's Republic of China, April 2013. As of October 10, 2015: http://en.people.cn/90786/8209362.html

Dixit, Aabha, "Enduring Sino-Pak Relations: The Military Dimension," *Strategic Analysis*, Vol. 12, No. 9, December 1989.

"Djibouti and China Sign a Security and Defense Agreement," *AllAfrica.com*, February 27, 2014. As of May 14, 2015: http://allafrica.com/stories/201402280055.html

"Djibouti President: China Negotiating Horn of Africa Military Base," *Defense News*, May 10, 2015. As of May 14, 2015: http://www.defensenews.com/story/defense/international/mideast-africa/2015/05/10/djibouti-president-china-negotiating-horn-africa-military-base/27082879/

"Dongnanya Zai 'Yi Dai Yi Lu' Jianshe Zhong Jiang Fahui Zhongyao Zuoyong" ["Southeast Asia Will Play an Important Role in the Construction of 'One Belt, One Road'"], Information Office of the State Council of the People's Republic of China, July 6, 2015. As of September 19, 2015: http://www.scio.gov.cn/ztk/wh/slxy/31200/Document/1440108/1440108.htm

Downs, Erica, "China Buys into Afghanistan," *SAIS Review*, Vol. 32, No. 2, Summer-Fall 2012.

Duchâtel, Mathieu, and Bates Gill, "Overseas Citizen Protection: A Growing Challenge for China," SIPRI, February 12, 2012. As of March 6, 2015: http://www.sipri.org/media/newsletter/essay/february12

Duchâtel, Mathieu, Oliver Bräuner, and Zhou Hang, "Protecting China's Overseas Interests: The Slow Shift Away from Non-Interference," SIPRI, Policy Paper 41, June 2014.

Economy, Elizabeth C., and Michael Levi, *By All Necessary Means: How China's Resource Quest Is Changing the World*, New York: Oxford University Press, 2014.

Eisenman, Joshua, "China's Post–Cold War Strategy in Africa: Examining Beijing's Methods and Objectives," in Joshua Eisenman, Eric Heginbotham, and Derek Mitchell, eds., *China and the Developing World: Beijing's Strategy for the Twenty-First Century*, Armonk, N.Y.: M.E. Sharpe, 2007.

Eisenman, Joshua, Eric Heginbotham, and Derek Mitchell, *China and the Developing World: Beijing's Strategy of the Twenty-First Century*, Armonk, N.Y.: M.E. Sharpe, 2007.

Eisenman, Joshua, Eric Heginbotham, eds., *China Steps Out: Beijing's Major Power Engagement with the Developing World*, New York: Routledge, 2018.

Ellis, R. Evan, *China-Latin America Military Engagement: Good Will, Good Business, and Strategic Position*, Strategic Studies Institute, U.S. Army War College, August 2011.

———, "Chinese Organized Crime in Latin America," *PRISM*, Vol. 4, No. 1, December 2012.

———, *China on the Ground in Latin America: Challenges for the Chinese and Impacts on the Region*, New York: Palgrave Macmillan, 2014.

Embassy of the People's Republic of China in the Republic of Trinidad and Tobago, "'Peace Ark' Hospital Ship Starts Visit in Trinidad and Tobago," November 12, 2011. As of April 30, 2015:
http://tt.chineseembassy.org/eng/zt/peaceark2011/t876460.htm

Erdbrink, Thomas, and Chris Buckley, "China and Iran to Conduct Joint Naval Exercises in the Persian Gulf," September 21, 2014. As of May 8, 2015:
http://www.nytimes.com/2014/09/22/world/middleeast/china-and-iran-to-conduct-joint-naval-exercises-in-the-persian-gulf.html

Erickson, Andrew S., and Austin M. Strange, *Six Years at Sea and Counting: Gulf of Aden Anti-Piracy and China's Maritime Commons Presence*, The Jamestown Foundation, June 2015. As of September 1, 2017:
http://www.andrewerickson.com/wp-content/uploads/2015/11/Erickson-Publication_Anti-Piracy_China_Jamestown-Book_GoA-Mission_6-Years_2015_Final.pdf

———, "China's Blue Soft Power: Anti-Piracy, Engagement, and Image Enhancement," *Naval War College Review*, Vol. 68, No. 1, Winter 2015, pp. 71–91. As of September 1, 2017:
https://www.usnwc.edu/getattachment/bf61b70c-dc5f-4f25-a7f0-b793face5e18/China-s-Blue-Soft-Power—Antipiracy,-Engagement,-a.aspx

Erickson, Andrew S., and Joel Wuthnow, "Barriers, Springboards and Benchmarks: China Conceptualizes the Pacific 'Island Chains,'" *China Quarterly*, Vol. 225, March 2016, pp. 1–22.

"Ethics Institute of South Africa, "Africans' Perceptions of Chinese Business in Africa: A Survey," Pretoria, 2014. As of April 20, 2015: http://www.ethicsa.org/index.php/resources/reSoutheast Asiarch-reports?download=106:african-perception-of-chinese-business-in-africa-august-2014

"Ethiopia Economic Outlook," African Development Bank Group, 2015, As of October 10, 2016: http://www.afdb.org/en/countries/east-africa/ethiopia/ethiopia-economic-outlook/

"Evacuation of Chinese Nationals from Yemen Completed," *CGTN America*, April 22, 2015. As of October 10, 2015: http://www.cctv-america.com/2015/03/31/evacuation-of-chinese-nationals-from-yemen-completed

"Expanding Global Footprint Forces China to Rethink Its Policy of 'Noninterference,'" *Japan Times*, June 16, 2015. As of October 12, 2015: http://www.japantimes.co.jp/news/2015/06/16/asia-pacific/expanding-global-footprint-forces-china-rethink-policy-noninterference/#.VhwYzuftAbE

Fazal-ur-Rahman, "Prospects of Pakistan Becoming a Trade and Energy Corridor for China," *Strategic Studies*, Vol. 28, No. 2, Summer 2007.

Fazl-e-Haider, Syed, "Chinese Shun Pakistan Exodus," *Asia Times*, September 11, 2009.

Feng Dan, "Zhongguo Yu Nanfei Guanxi Fazhan Xianzhuang Ji Wenti Duice Sikao" ["China and South Africa Relations—Current Developments and Policy-Related Considerations"], *Theory Research*, No. 11, 2013, p. 34.

Field, Michael, "China's 'Gift' Troubles New Prime Minister," *Nikkei Asian Review*, March 28, 2015. As of November 10, 2015: http://asia.nikkei.com/Politics-Economy/International-Relations/tonga

The Fifth Ministerial Conference of the Forum on China-Africa Cooperation, "Beijing Action Plan (2013–2015)," July 23, 2012, section 2.6. As of May 18, 2015: http://www.focac.org/eng/zxxx/t954620.htm

Final Communiqué of the Asian-African Conference of Bandung, April 24, 1955. As of April 8, 2015: http://franke.uchicago.edu/Final_Communique_Bandung_1955.pdf

The First Ministerial Conference of the Forum on China-Africa Cooperation, "Beijing Declaration of the Forum on China-Africa Cooperation," October 12, 2000. As of May 18, 2015: http://www.focac.org/eng/ltda/dyjbzjhy/DOC12009/t606796.htm

Fisher, Richard D., Jr., and James Hardy, "Venezuela Signs Up for VN1, Hints at Chinese Amphibious Vehicles Buy," *IHS Jane's Defence Weekly*, November 23, 2014. As of April 30, 2015:
http://www.janes.com/article/46091/venezuela-signs-up-for-vn1-hints-at-chinese-amphibious-vehicles-buy

Ford, Peter, "Why Chinese Workers Are Getting Kidnapped Abroad," *Christian Science Monitor*, February 1, 2012. As of April 7, 2015:
http://www.csmonitor.com/World/Asia-Pacific/2012/0201/Why-Chinese-workers-are-getting-kidnapped-abroad

"Foreign Minister Wang Yi Meets the Press," Ministry of Foreign Affairs, People's Republic of China, March 8, 2015. As of September 19, 2015:
http://www.fmprc.gov.cn/mfa_eng/zxxx_662805/t1243662.shtml

"Foreign Ministry Spokesperson Hua Chunying's Regular Press Conference on May 7, 2015," Ministry of Foreign Affairs of the People's Republic of China, May 7, 2015. As of August 24, 2015:
http://www.fmprc.gov.cn/mfa_eng/xwfw_665399/s2510_665401/t1261660.shtml

Forum on China-Africa Cooperation, "Forum on China-Africa Cooperation Beijing Action Plan (2007–2009)," November 16, 2006, para 2.5.2. As of April 10, 2015:
http://www.fmprc.gov.cn/zflt/eng/zyzl/hywj/t280369.htm

———, "Forum on China-Africa Cooperation Sharm El Sheikh Action Plan (2010–2012)," November 12, 2009, para 2.5.2. As of April 10, 2015:
http://www.focac.org/eng/dsjbzjhy/hywj/t626387.htm

———, "Declaration of the 1st Meeting of the China-Africa Think Tank Forum," November 23, 2011. As of March 18, 2015:
http://www.focac.org/eng/xsjl/zflhyjjljh/t880276.htm

———, "Forum on China-Africa Cooperation (FOCAC)," July 18, 2012. As of October 2, 2015:
http://www.focac.org/eng/dwjbzjjhys/t952503.htm

———, "FOCAC ABC," April 9, 2013. As of October 2, 2015:
http://www.focac.org/eng/ltda/ltjj/t933522.htm

———, "The First Joint Training Exercise Between the Two Armed Forces of Tanzania and China to Be Conducted," October 23, 2014. As of May 8, 2015:
http://www.mfa.gov.cn/zflt/eng/zxxx/t1203217.htm

———, "Ambassador Lu Observed Transcend 2014 Joint Training Exercise of Marine Corps Between China and Tanzania," November 15, 2014. As of May 8, 2015:
http://www.focac.org/eng/zxxx/t1211399.htm

"Four Chinese Military Aircraft to Join Nepal Earthquake Relief," *China Military Online*, April 27, 2015. As of *insert date*:
http://english.chinamil.com.cn/news-channels/2015-04/27/content_6463455.htm

Fransman, Marius, "Keynote Address to the Ambassadorial Forum on China–South Africa Diplomatic Relations at 15 Years," Pretoria, South Africa, September 19, 2013.

Fravel, M. Taylor, *Strong Borders, Secure Nation: Cooperation and Conflict in China's Territorial Disputes*, Princeton, N.J.: Princeton University Press, 2008.

Frazier, Mark W., "Quiet Competition and the Future of Sino-Indian Relations," in Francine R. Frankel and Harry Harding, eds., *The India-China Relationship: What the United States Needs to Know*, New York: Columbia University Press, 2004.

Freedom House, Map of Freedom 2014, 2014. As of April 9, 2015: https://www.freedomhouse.org/sites/default/files/MapofFreedom2014.pdf

French, Howard W., *China's Second Continent: How a Million Migrants Are Building an Empire in Africa*, New York: Knopf, 2014.

Frost, Alexander, "The Collective Security Treaty Organization, the Shanghai Cooperation Organization, and Russia's Strategic Goals in Central Asia," *China and Eurasia Forum Quarterly*, Vol. 7, No. 3, 2008.

"Full Text: China's Policy Paper on Latin America and the Caribbean," *Xinhua News*, November 6, 2008. As of October 10, 2015: http://www.chinadaily.com.cn/china/2008-11/06/content_7179488_2.htm

"Full Text of Foreign Minister Wang Yi's Speech on China's Diplomacy in 2014," *Xinhua News*, December 26, 2014. As of October 12, 2015: http://news.xinhuanet.com/english/china/2014-12/26/c_133879194.htm

Gady, Franz-Stefan, "Déjà Vu: Pakistan and Nigeria to Sign JF-17 Fighter Jet Deal in November," *The Diplomat*, September 19, 2016. As of August 4, 2017: http://thediplomat.com/2016/09/deja-vu-pakistan-and-nigeria-to-sign-jf-17-fighter-jet-deal-in-november/

Gadzala, Aleksandra, and Mark Hanusch, "African Perspectives on China-Africa: Gauging Popular Perceptions and Their Economic and Political Determinants," *Afrobarometer Working Paper*, No. 117, January 2010.

Gallagher, Kevin P., and Margaret Myers, "China-Latin America Finance Database," Washington, D.C.: Inter-American Dialogue, 2014.

Gamache, Lauren, Alexander Hammer, and Lin Jones, "China's Trade and Investment Relationship with Africa," USITC Executive Briefings on Trade, April 2013. As of April 8, 2015: http://www.usitc.gov/publications/332/2013-04_China-Africa%28Gamache HammerJones%29.pdf

Gardner, Frank, "US Military Steps Up Operations in the Horn of Africa," *BBC News*, February 7, 2014. As of July 28, 2015: http://www.bbc.com/news/world-africa-26078149

Garofano, John, and Andrea J. Dew, eds., *Deep Currents and Rising Tides: The Indian Ocean and International Security*, Washington, D.C.: Georgetown University Press, 2013.

Garver, John W., *Protracted Contest: China-India Rivalry in the Twentieth Century*, Seattle: University of Washington Press, 2000.

———, *China and Iran: Ancient Partners in a Post-Imperial World*, Seattle: University of Washington Press, 2006.

———, "China-Iran Relations: Cautious Friendship with America's Nemesis," *China Report*, Vol. 49, No. 1, 2013.

"General Liang Guanglie Calls on Secretary [of] Defence," Ministry of Defense, Sri Lanka, August 31, 2012. As of September 19, 2015:
http://www.defence.lk/new.asp?fname=General_Liang_Guanglie_calls_on_Secretary_Defence_20120831_06

Ghazvinian, John, *Untapped: The Scramble for Africa's Oil*, Orlando, Fla.: Harcourt, Inc., 2007.

Ghiselli, Andrea, "The Belt, the Road and the PLA," in *China Brief*, Vol. XV, No. 20, October 19, 2015.

Gilboy, George J., and Eric Heginbotham, *Chinese and Indian Strategic Behavior: Growing Power and Alarm*, New York: Cambridge University Press, 2012.

Gill, Bates, and Chin-Hao Huang, *China's Expanding Role In Peacekeeping: Prospects and Policy Implications*, SIPRI, Policy Paper 25, November 2009, p. 14. As of May 14, 2015:
http://books.sipri.org/files/PP/SIPRIPP25.pdf

Gilley, Bruce, and Andrew O'Neil, eds., *Middle Powers and the Rise of China*, Washington, D.C.: Georgetown University Press, 2014.

Gishkori, Zahid, "Economic Corridor: 12,000-Strong Force to Guard Chinese Workers," *The Express Tribune*, March 30, 2015. As of August 31, 2017:
https://tribune.com.pk/story/861078/economic-corridor-12000-strong-force-to-guard-chinese-workers/

Glaser, Bonnie, "China's Maritime Rights Protection Leading Small Group—Shrouded in Secrecy," September 11, 2015, Asia Maritime Transparency Initiative. As of September 14, 2015:
http://amti.csis.org/chinas-maritime-rights-protection-leading-small-group-shrouded-in-secrecy/

"Global Recovery Should Carry ASEAN Through the Economic Headwinds," *Forbes*, January 19, 2014. As of July 22, 2014:
http://www.forbes.com/sites/forbesasia/2014/01/19/global-recovery-should-carry-ASEAN-through-economic-headwinds/

Government Accountability Office Report, 2013.

Grace, Carrie, "Wang Jing: The Man Behind the Nicaragua Canal Project," *BBC News*, March 18, 2015. As of October 10, 2015:
http://www.bbc.com/news/world-asia-china-31936549

Green, Michael J., and Bates Gill, "Unbundling Asia's New Multilateralism," in Michael J. Green and Bates Gill, eds., *Asia's New Multilateralism: Cooperation, Competition, and the Search for Community*, New York: Columbia University Press, 2009.

Grimm, Sven, Yejoo Kim, and Ross Anthony with Robert Attwell and Xin Xiao, *South African Relations with China and Taiwan: Economic Realism and the 'One-China' Doctrine*, Stellenbosch, South Africa: Stellenbosch University Centre for Chinese Studies, February 2014.

Gu Jing, "China's Private Enterprises in Africa and the Implications for African Development," *European Journal of Development Research*, Vol. 21, No. 4. As of April 17, 2015:
http://www.palgrave-journals.com/ejdr/journal/v21/n4/pdf/ejdr200921a.pdf

Guest, Pete, "And Then There Were Three: China's Spending Power Entices Taiwanese Ally," *Forbes*, November 26, 2013. As of April 8, 2015:
http://www.forbes.com/sites/peteguest/2013/11/26/and-then-there-were-three-chinas-spending-power-entices-taiwanese-ally/

Guo Renjie, "PLAAF Aerobatics Team Stops Over in Thailand," *China Military Online*, March 25, 2015. As of October 10, 2015:
http://eng.mod.gov.cn/Photos/2015-03/25/content_4576647_3.htm

———, "Sri Lanka President Meets with Xu Qiliang," *China Military Online*, May 19, 2015. As of October 10, 2015:
http://eng.chinamil.com.cn/news-channels/china-military-news/2014-05/19/content_5909609.htm

Haboush, Mahmoud, "Middle Kingdom Visits Middle East as Chinese Navy Docks at Port Zayed," *The National*, March 25, 2010. As of October 10, 2015:
http://www.thenational.ae/news/uae-news/middle-kingdom-visits-middle-east-as-chinese-navy-docks-at-port-zayed

Haider, Mateen, "Army's Special Security Division to Protect Chinese Workers in Pakistan," *Dawn*, April 21, 2015. As of August 30, 2017:
https://www.dawn.com/news/1177322

Haider, Ziad, "Sino-Pakistan Relations and Xinjiang's Uighurs," *Asian Survey*, Vol. 45, No. 4, July/August 2005.

Hanauer, Larry, and Lyle Morris, *Chinese Engagement in Africa*, Santa Monica, Calif.: RAND Corporation, RR-521-OSD, 2014.

Hancock, Tom, "Chinese Return from Africa as Migrant Population Peaks," *Financial Times*, August 28, 2017. As of August 29, 2017:
https://www.ft.com/content/7106ab42-80d1-11e7-a4ce-15b2513cb3ff

Haqqani, Husain, *Magnificent Delusions: Pakistan, the United States, and an Epic History of Misunderstanding*, New York: Public Affairs, 2013.

Harding, Harry, *China's Second Revolution: Reform After Mao*, Washington, D.C.: Brookings Institution Press, 1987.

He Shengda, "Dongnanya Diqu Zhanlue Geju Yu Zhongguo—Dongmeng Guanxi" ["The Strategic Situation in the Southeast Asian Region and China-ASEAN Relations"], *Southeast Asia and South Asia Studies*, No. 1, 2014. As of September 19, 2015:
http://www.faobserver.com/NewsInfo.aspx?id=10871

He Wenping, "'One Belt, One Road' Can Find Place for Africa," *Global Times*, January 29, 2015. As of October 2, 2015:
http://www.globaltimes.cn/content/904823.shtml

Hearn, Adrian H., and Jose Luis Leon-Manriquez, "China and Latin America: A New Era of an Old Exchange," in Adrian H. Hearn and Jose Luis Leon-Manriquez, eds., *China Engages Latin America: Tracing the Trajectory*, Boulder, Colo.: Lynne Rienner Publishers, 2001.

Heath, Timothy, "Diplomacy Work Forum: Xi Steps Up Efforts to Shape a China-Centered Regional Order," *Jamestown China Brief*, Vol. 13, No. 22, November 7, 2013.

Herschelmann, Kerry, "First Algerian C28A Corvette Launched in China," *IHS Jane's Defence Weekly*, August 20, 2014. As of October 10, 2015:
http://www.janes.com/article/42238/first-algerian-c28a-corvette-launched-in-china

Hirono, Miwa, "China's Charm Offensive and Peacekeeping: The Lessons of Cambodia—What Now for Sudan?" *International Peacekeeping*, Vol. 18, No. 3, 2011.

Ho, Stephanie, "China Sends Aid to Quake-Stricken Haiti," *VOA News*, January 23, 2010. As of April 13, 2015:
http://www.voanews.com/content/china-sends-aid-to-quake-stricken-haiti-81465187/111449.html

Honan, Edith, "Kenya Corruption Watchdog Makes Allegations Against 175 Officials," *Reuters*, April 1, 2015. As of April 1, 2015:
http://www.reuters.com/article/2015/04/01/us-kenya-corruption-idUSKBN0MR1AI20150401

Hong Lei, "Foreign Ministry Spokesperson Hong Lei's Regular Press Conference on January 21, 2016," Ministry of Foreign Affairs of the People's Republic of China, January 21, 2016. As of August 23, 2017:
http://www.fmprc.gov.cn/mfa_eng/xwfw_665399/s2510_665401/t1333741.shtml

Hornby, Lucy, and Andres Schipani, "China Tilts Towards Liberal Latin American Economies," *Financial Times*, May 10, 2015. As of October 10, 2015:
http://www.ft.com/intl/cms/s/0/b73a606c-f46b-11e4-bd16-00144feab7de.html#axzz3aasy1X2r

Hou Liqiang, "Drive to Improve Vocational Education," *China Daily*, January 16, 2015. As of October 2, 2015:
http://www.chinadaily.com.cn/world/2015-01/16/content_19338097.htm

"How an Oil Rig Sparked Anti-China Riots in Vietnam," *CNN*, May 19, 2014. As of September 19, 2015:
http://www.cnn.com/2014/05/19/world/asia/china-vietnam-islands-oil-rig-explainer/

Howard, Brian Clark, "China Crushes Six Tons of Confiscated Elephant Ivory," *National Geographic*, January 7, 2014. As of October 10, 2015:
https://news.nationalgeographic.com/news/2014/01/140106-china-ivory-crush-elephant-conservation/

Hsiao, Russell, and Glen E. Howard, "China Builds Closer Ties to Afghanistan Through Wakhan Corridor," *China Brief*, Vol. 10, No. 1, January 7, 2010.

Hsu, Locknie, "Inward FDI in Singapore and Its Policy Context," *Columbia FDI Profiles*, Vale Columbia Center on Sustainable International Investment, Columbia University, 2012. As of October 7, 2015:
http://ccsi.columbia.edu/files/2014/03/Singapore_IFDI_-_FINAL_-_31_May_2012.pdf

Huang Meibo, and Qi Xie, "Forum on China-Africa Cooperation: Development and Prospects," *African-East Asian Affairs/The China Monitor*, Vol. 74, 2012.

Human Rights Watch, "'You'll Be Fired If You Refuse': Labor Abuses in Zambia's Chinese State-owned Copper Mines," 2011. As of April 17, 2015:
http://www.hrw.org/sites/default/files/reports/zambia1111ForWebUpload.pdf

"IMF Members' Quotas and Voting Power, and IMF Board of Governors," International Monetary Fund, October 12, 2015. As of October 12, 2015:
http://www.imf.org/external/np/sec/memdir/members.aspx

"India, Kazakhstan Sign Five Key Agreements," Press Trust of India, *The Hindu*, July 8, 2015. As of October 14, 2015:
http://www.thehindu.com/news/national/article7398943.ece

"Indonesia, China Committed to Infrastructure Co-Op: Indonesian Spokesman,"*Xinhua News*, April 24, 2015. As of October 10, 2015:
http://www.chinadaily.com.cn/world/2015xivisitpse/2015-04/24/content_20526739.htm

Inter-American Dialogue, China-Latin America Financial Database, 2015. As of July 22, 2015:
http://www.thedialogue.org/map_list/

International Crisis Group, "China's Central Asia Problem," *Asia Report*, No. 244, February 27, 2013.

"Japan and China Compete for Latin American Clout," *Asia Sentinel*, August 11, 2014. As of May 16, 2015
http://www.asiasentinel.com/politics/japan-china-compete-latin-american-clout/

Jia Qinglin, Chairman of the National Committee of the Chinese People's Political Consultative Conference, "Towards a Better Future with Stronger China-Africa Solidarity and Cooperation," speech to the 18th Ordinary Session of the Assembly of the African Union, Addis Ababa, January 29, 2012. As of April 10, 2015:
http://www.fmprc.gov.cn/mfa_eng/wjdt_665385/zyjh_665391/t903697.shtml

Jiang Zhida, "Reconnecting China with Southeast Asia," *Beijing Review*, December 1, 2011. As of September 14, 2015:
http://www.bjreview.com.cn/world/txt/2011-11/28/content_408374.htm

Jikkham, Patsara, and Wassana Nanuam, "Thailand, China Deepen Defence Ties," *Bangkok Post*, April 24, 2015. As of October 10, 2015:
http://www.bangkokpost.com/news/security/540599/thailand-china
-deepen-defence-ties

Johnston, Iain, "How New and Assertive Is China's New Assertiveness?" *International Security*, Vol. 37, No. 4, Spring 2013, pp. 7–48.

"Joint Action Plan Between the Government of the Federative Republic of Brazil and the Government of the People's Republic of China 2015–2021," *DefesaNet*, March 20, 2015. As of October 10, 2015:
http://www.defesanet.com.br/en/br_cn_e/noticia/19181/BR-CN
—-Joint-Action-Plan-BRAZIL-and-CHINA-2015-2021/

Joint Communiqué Between the People's Republic of China and Malaysia in Conjunction with the 40th Anniversary of the Establishment of Diplomatic Relations, Ministry of Foreign Affairs of Malaysia, May 31, 2014.

Joint Statement Between the People's Republic of China and Brunei Darussalam, Ministry of Foreign Affairs of the People's Republic of China, April 6, 2013. As of September 19, 2015:
http://www.fmprc.gov.cn/mfa_eng/wjdt_665385/2649_665393/t1029400.shtml

Jonson, Lena, "Russia and Central Asia," in Lena Jonson and Roy Allison, eds., *Central Asian Security: The New International Context*, Washington, D.C.: Brookings Institution Press, 2001.

Kardon, Isaac B., *China and Pakistan: Emerging Strains in the Entente Cordial Project 2049*, Washington, D.C.: Project 2049, 2011.

Karrar, Hassan H., *The New Silk Road Diplomacy: China's Central Asian Foreign Policy Since the Cold War*, Vancouver: University of British Columbia Press, 2009.

Kastner, Scott L., and Phillip C. Saunders, "Is China a Status Quo or Revisionist State? Leadership Travel as an Empirical Indicator of Foreign Policy Priorities," *International Studies Quarterly*, Vol. 56, No. 2, June 2012.

Katz, Andrew, "All the Presidents' Trips to Africa, Mapped," *Washington Post*, July 27, 2015. As of July 28, 2015:
https://www.washingtonpost.com/blogs/worldviews/wp/2015/07/24/all-the-u-s-presidents-trips-to-africa-mapped/?utm_source=July+28+2015+EN_02&utm_campaign=7%2F28%2F2015&utm_medium=email

Keck, Zachary, "Venezuela Uses Chinese Weapons in Crackdown," March 7, 2014. As of April 30, 2015:
http://thediplomat.com/2014/03/venezuela-uses-chinese-weapons-in-crackdown/

———, "China to Sell Saudi Arabia Drones," *The Diplomat*, May 8, 2014. As of October 10, 2015:
http://thediplomat.com/2014/05/china-to-sell-saudi-arabia-drones/

Kim, Samuel S., ed. *China and the World: Chinese Foreign Policy Faces the New Millennium*, 4th ed., Boulder, Colo.: Westview Press, 1998.

King, Kenneth, *China's Aid and Soft Power in Africa: The Case of Education and Training*, Suffolk, UK: James Currey, 2013.

Koch-Weser, Iacob, "Chinese Mining Activity in Latin America: A Review of Recent Findings," Inter-American Dialogue, September 24, 2014.

———, "Chinese Energy Engagement with Latin America: A Review of Recent Findings," Inter-American Dialogue, January 12, 2015.

Kuik, Cheng-Chwee, "Making Sense of Malaysia's China Policy: Asymmetry, Proximity, and Elite's Domestic Authority," *The Chinese Journal of International Politics*, Vol. 6, No. 4, December 2013, pp. 429–467. As of August 29, 2017:
http://cjip.oxfordjournals.org/content/early/2013/04/25/cjip.pot006.full

Kwok, Kristine, "China Offers Joint Drills with ASEAN in South China Southeast Asia to Check US Plan to Send Warships Near Spratly Islands," *South China Morning Post*, October 16, 2015. As of November 10, 2015:
http://www.scmp.com/news/article/1868814/china-offers-joint-drills-ASEAN-south-china-Southeast Asia-check-us-plan-send-warships?page=all

"Kyrgyzstan to Get 0.5 m Dollars Dollars of Chinese Military Aid," *Kabar News Agency*, November 12, 2007a, Bishkek (in Russian), translated by World News Connection, CEP20071112950147.

LaGrone, Sam, "Chinese Ships in Iran for Joint Exercises," *USNI News*, September 22, 2014. As of May 8, 2015:
http://news.usni.org/2014/09/22/chinese-ships-iran-joint-exercises

———, "China, Russia Land 400 Marines in First Joint Pacific Amphibious Exercise," *USNI News*, August 26, 2015. As of October 10, 2015:
http://news.usni.org/2015/08/26/china-russia-land-400-marines-in-first-joint-pacific-amphibious-exercise

Lammich, Georg, "China's Impact on Capacity Building in the African Union," paper presented at a workshop regarding South-South Development Cooperation Chances and Challenges for the International Aid Architecture, Heidelberg University, September 26–27, 2014. As of April 10, 2015:
http://www.uni-heidelberg.de/md/awi/ssdc_lammich.pdf

Landler, Mark, "Seeing Misunderstandings on Both Sides of U.S-Pakistan Ties," *New York Times*, October 23, 2013, p. A6.

Lanteigne, Marc, "In Medias Res: The Development of the Shanghai Cooperation Organization as a Security Community," *Pacific Affairs*, Vol. 79, No. 4, Winter 2006–2007.

"Latin America Set to Play Bigger Role for Chinese Firms," *China Daily*, September 12, 2014. As of June 12, 2015:
http://www.chinadaily.com.cn/business/2014-09/12/content_18585949.htm

Lee, John, "China Comes to Djibouti," *Foreign Affairs*, April 23, 2015. As of May 14, 2015:
https://www.foreignaffairs.com/articles/east-africa/2015-04-23/china-comes-djibouti

Lee, Karthie, "Chinese Private Security Firms Go Overseas: 'Crossing the River by Feeling the Stones,'" Frontier Services Group Analysis, September 8, 2014. As of April 7, 2015:
http://www.fsgroup.com/chinese-private-security-firms-go-overSoutheast Asias-crossing-the-river-by-feeling-the-stones/

Leins, Chris, "China's Evolving Ebola Response: Recognizing the Cost of Inaction," Atlantic Council, *New Atlanticist* blog, November 10, 2014. As of October 10, 2015:
http://www.atlanticcouncil.org/blogs/new-atlanticist/china-s
-evolving-ebola-response-recognizing-the-cost-of-inaction

Lewis, John W., Hua Di, and Xue Litai, "Beijing's Defense Establishment: Solving the Arms Export Enigma," *International Security*, Vol. 15, No. 4, Spring 1991.

Leydon, Joe, "Film Review: 'Wolf Warrior II'" *Variety*, August 11, 2017. As of August 29, 2017:
http://variety.com/2017/film/reviews/wolf-warrior-ii-review-1202524360/

Li, Anshan, "China and Africa: Policy and Challenges," *China Security*, Vol. 3, No. 3, Summer 2007.

"Li Calls for Manufacturing Shift in Peru," *China Daily*, May 24, 2015. As of June 12, 2015:
http://usa.chinadaily.com.cn/world/2015-05/24/content_20800968.htm

Li Keqiang, "Remarks by H.E. Li Keqiang, Premier of the State Council of the People's Republic of China at the 16th ASEAN-China Summit," Bandar Seri Begawan, Brunei, October 9, 2013. As of September 19, 2015:
http://www.fmprc.gov.cn/mfa_eng/topics_665678/lkqzlcxdyldrxlhy_665684/
t1089853.shtml

———, "May the Flower of China-Thailand Friendship Bear New Fruits," speech delivered to the National Assembly of Thailand, Bangkok, October 11, 2013. As of October 10, 2015:
http://english.gov.cn/premier/speeches/2014/08/23/content_281474983013254.htm

"Li Keqiang Arrives in Latin America with Promise of US$50 Billion in Infrastructure Investments," *South China Morning Post*, May 19, 2015. As of June 12, 2015:
http://www.scmp.com/news/china/diplomacy-defence/article/1802867/chinas-premier-arrives-latin-america-focus-investment

Li Keqiang and Dato'sri Mohd Najib Tun Abdul Razak, "Joint Communique Between the People's Republic of China and Malaysia in Conjunction with the 40th Anniversary of the Establishment of Diplomatic Relations," Beijing, May 31, 2014. As of August 29, 2017:
https://www.kln.gov.my/archive/content.php?t=8&articleId=4184783

"Li Keqiang Meets with President of the Council of the Nation Abdelkader Bensalah of Algeria," Ministry of Foreign Affairs of the People's Republic of China, September 4, 2015. As of October 10, 2015:
http://www.fmprc.gov.cn/mfa_eng/topics_665678/jnkzsl70zn/t1294311.shtml

"Li Keqiang Starts First Southeast Asia Visit," *Global Times*, October 9, 2013. As of September 19, 2015:
http://www.globaltimes.cn/content/816576.shtml

Li Weijian, "Zhongdong Zai Zhongguo Zhanlue Zhong De Zhongyaoxing Ji Shuangbian Guanxi" ["The Middle East's Importance in China's Strategy and Bilateral Relations"], *Western Asia and Africa*, No. 6, 2004, pp. 18–19.

Li Xiaokun and Li Lianxing, "Navy Looks at Offer from Seychelles," *China Daily*, December 13, 2011. As of May 14, 2015:
http://usa.chinadaily.com.cn/epaper/2011-12/13/content_14257718.htm

Li Xuanmin, "Gwadar Port Benefit to China Limited," *The Global Times*, November 23, 2016. As of August 4, 2017:
http://www.globaltimes.cn/content/1019840.shtml

Lin Hongyu, "'Haishang Sichou Zhi Lu' Guoji Zhanlue Yiyi Touxi" ["In-Depth Analysis of the International Strategic Value of the 'Maritime Silk Road'"], *People's Tribune*, September 1, 2014. As of October 12, 2015:
http://paper.people.com.cn/rmlt/html/2014-09/01/content_1476498.htm

Lin, Jeffrey, and P. W. Singer, "Biggest 'Anti-Terrorist' Exercise in the World Stars Chinese Drones, Russian Troops and a Ukraine-Inspired Wargame," *Popular Science*, September 2, 2014. As of October 10, 2015:
http://www.popsci.com/blog-network/eastern-arsenal/biggest-anti-terrorist-exercise-world-stars-chinese-drones-russian

———, "Did an Armed Chinese-Made Drone Just Crash in Nigeria?" *Popular Science*, January 28, 2015. As of October 10, 2015:
http://www.popsci.com/did-armed-chinese-made-drone-just-crash-nigeria

———, "Chinese Fighter Jets Fly South for Spring Break," *Popular Science*, March 25, 2015. As of October 10, 2015:
https://www.popsci.com/chinese-fighter-jets-fly-south-spring-break

Lin Piao, "Long Live the Victory of People's War!" *Peking Review*, September 3, 1965.

Lin Zhi, "Backgrounder: SCO Anti-Terror Military Drills," *Xinhua News*, September 9, 2010. As of October 10, 2015:
http://news.xinhuanet.com/english2010/world/2010-09/10/c_13489722.htm

Lin Zoe, "Off the Menu: China Moves to Protect Endangered Species," CNN.com, May 5, 2014. As of October 10, 2015:
https://www.cnn.com/2014/04/30/world/asia/china-wildlife-law/index.html

Liu Guangyuan, "Deepen China-Africa Media Cooperation and Enrich the China-Africa Community of Shared Destinies," speech at the seminar on China-Africa Media Cooperation on 18 November 2013, Chinese Embassy in Kenya, November 19, 2013.

Liu Zhongmin, "Zhongguo Bugai Zhuiqiu Zhong Dong Shiwu Lingdaozhe Jiaose" ["China Should Not Pursue a Leadership Role in Middle Eastern Affairs"], *Oriental Morning Post*, August 26, 2011. As of October 10, 2015:
http://news.ifeng.com/world/special/libiya/content-0/detail_2011_08/26/8706753_0.shtml

Liu Yanan, "Meima Guanxi Lishi Fazhan Zhong De Jinzhan Yu Wenti Yanjiu" ["Advances and Inquiries into the Historical Development of U.S.-Malaysia Relations"], *Theory Research*, Vol. 27, March 2014, pp. 34–35.

"Lizhu Zhoubian, Moupian Quanqiu" ["To Gain a Foothold on the Periphery, We Must Look for Opportunities Around the Globe"], *Xinhua News*, March 2, 2015. As of October 12, 2015:
http://news.xinhuanet.com/globe/2015-03/02/c_134030635.htm

Maasho, Aaron, "China Signs Deals with Ethiopia as Premier Starts Africa Tour," *Reuters*, May 4, 2014. As of October 10, 2015:
http://www.reuters.com/article/2014/05/04/china-africa-idUSL6N0NQ0LN20140504

MacDonald, Juli A., Amy Donahue, and Bethany Danyluk, *Energy Futures in Asia*, McLean, Va.: Booz Allen Hamilton, 2004.

Magnus, George, "China, the New Silk Road, Loud Thunder and Small Raindrops," May 15, 2015. As of October 14, 2015:
http://www.georgemagnus.com/china-the-new-silk-road-loud-thunder-and-small-raindrops/

"Malaysia Backs China over AIIB," *The Star Online*, August 28, 2015. As of October 10, 2015:
https://www.thestar.com.my/news/nation/2015/08/28/malaysia-backs-china-over-aiib-bank-will-rival-imf-and-top-institutions/

Malik, Mohan, "The Shanghai Cooperation Organization," in Sumit Ganguly, Joseph Liow, and Andrew Scobell, eds., *The Routledge Handbook of Asian Security Studies*, New York: Routledge, 2010.

Mandavia, Megha, "Why India Remains a Difficult Terrain for 7,000 Chinese Expatriates Living in the Country," *Economic Times*, August 31, 2015. As of August 31, 2017:
http://economictimes.indiatimes.com/news/politics-and-nation/why-india-remains-a-difficult-terrain-for-7000-chinese-expatriates-living-in-the-country/articleshow/48703439.cms

"Mapping China's New Silk Road Initiative" *Forbes*, April 8, 2015. As of October 10, 2015:
http://www.forbes.com/sites/ckgsb/2015/04/08/mapping-chinas-new-silk-road-initiative/

Marcus, Jonathan, "China-Russia Drills in Med Show Shifting Strategies," *BBC News*, May 11, 2015. As of October 10, 2015:
http://www.bbc.com/news/world-asia-china-32686956

Martina, Michael, and David Brunnstrom, "China's Xi Says to Commit 8,000 Troops for U.N. Peacekeeping Force," *Reuters*, September 28, 2015. As of October 10, 2015:
http://www.reuters.com/article/2015/09/29/us-un-assembly-china-idUSKCN0RS1Z120150929#sXaJF62dD1JlvI9Y.97

Masato, Masato, "Tanzania: Labour Ministry to Regulate Foreigner's Employment," *Daily News*, March 19, 2015. As of October 10, 2015:
http://allafrica.com/stories/201503190476.html

Mathews, Kuruvilla, "China and UN Peacekeeping Operations in Africa," in China-Africa Think Tanks Forum, "The 2nd Meeting of the China-Africa Think Tanks Forum," conference report, Bisoftu, Ethiopia, October 12–13, 2012. As of March 19, 2015:
http://dspace.africaportal.org/jspui/bitstream/123456789/34123/1/IPSS_China-Africa_Think_Tanks_Forum_Final_(2)[1].pdf?1

Matsiko, Haggai, "Is It Time for a China-Africa Command?" *The Independent* (Uganda), November 16, 2014. As of May 18, 2015:
http://www.independent.co.ug/news/news-analysis/9497-is-it-time-for-a-china-africa-command;
http://www.bbc.com/news/world-africa-25654155

Mazza, Jacqueline, *Chinese Migration to Latin America and the Caribbean,* Washington, D.C.: The Inter-American Dialogue, October 2016. As of August 31, 2017:
http://www.thedialogue.org/wp-content/uploads/2016/10/Chinese_Migration_to_LAC_Mazza-1.pdf

McNamee, Terence, "Africa in Their Words: A Study of Chinese Traders in South Africa, Lesotho, Botswana, Zambia and Angola," Brenthurst Foundation discussion paper 2012/03, April 2012.

Medeiros, Evan S., *Reluctant Restraint: The Evolution of China's Nonproliferation Policies and Practices, 1980–2004*, Stanford, Calif.: Stanford University Press, 2007.

———, *China's International Behavior: Activism, Opportunism, and Diversification*, Santa Monica, Calif.: RAND Corporation, MG-850-AF, 2009.

"MFA Press Statement: Introductory Calls on Minister for Foreign Affairs Minister Dr. Vivian Balakrishnan," Ministry of Foreign Affairs of Singapore, October 28, 2015. As of November 10, 2015:
http://www.mfa.gov.sg/content/mfa/media_centre/press_room/pr/2015/201510/press_20151028.html

Miller, Meredith, "China's Relations with Southeast Asia," Testimony for the U.S.-China Economic and Security Review Commission, May 13, 2015. As of August 24, 2015:
http://www.uscc.gov/sites/default/files/Miller_Written%20Testimony_5.13.2015%20Hearing.pdf

Miller, Travis M., "Is There Room for U.S.-China Cooperation on the Ebola Crisis? (Parts 1 through 3)," The Carter Center, *U.S. China Perception Monitor* blog, October 15, 2014. As of May 19, 2015:
http://www.uscnpm.org/blog/2014/10/15/is-there-room-for-u-s-china-cooperation-on-the-ebola-crisis-part-iii/

"Ministry of Foreign Affairs Holds a Briefing for Chinese and Foreign Journalists on the First Ministerial Meeting of China-CELAC Forum," Ministry of Foreign Affairs of the People's Republic of China, January 5, 2015. As of June 12, 2015:
http://www.fmprc.gov.cn/mfa_eng/wjbxw/t1226101.shtml

Minnie Chan, "PLA Air Force Joins Thai Military for Joint Drills," *South China Morning Post*, November 12, 2015. As of November 12, 2015:
http://www.scmp.com/news/china/diplomacy-defence/article/1878048/pla-air-force-joins-thai-military-joint-drills

"Mission of the People's Republic of China to ASEAN Formally Inaugurated," Mission of the People's Republic of China to ASEAN, September 28, 2012. As of September 14, 2015:
http://ASEAN.chinamission.org.cn/eng/stxw/t974688.htm

Mizokami, Kyle, "A Look at China's Growing International Arms Trade," *USNI News*, May 7, 2015. As of November 30, 2015:
http://news.usni.org/2015/05/07/a-look-at-chinas-growing-international-arms-trade

Mohan, Gilles, and May Tan-Mullins, "Chinese Migrants in Africa as New Agents of Development? An Analytical Framework," *European Journal of Development Research*, Vol. 21, No. 4, 2009. As of April 16, 2015:
http://www.palgrave-journals.com/ejdr/journal/v21/n4/pdf/ejdr200922a.pdf

Morello, Carol, "Iran Talks Continue into Tuesday," *Washington Post*, July 13, 2015. As of October 10, 2015:
https://www.washingtonpost.com/world/national-security/deal-in-iran-talks-imminent/2015/07/13/88656cfe-0952-44bd-9fe5-b71e7844bf43_story.html

Morris, Lyle, "Taming the Five Dragons? China Consolidates Its Maritime Law Enforcement Agencies," *China Brief*, Vol. 13, No. 7, March 28, 2013.

Mu Chunshan, "Revealed: How Yemen the Crisis Wrecked Xi Jinping's Middle East Travel Plans," *The Diplomat*, April 22, 2015. As of October 10, 2015:
http://thediplomat.com/2015/04/revealed-how-the-yemen-crisis-wrecked-xi-jinpings-middle-east-travel-plans

Mu Xuequan, "China's Drone Blasts Off Missile in SCO Anti-Terror Drill," *Xinhua News*, August 26, 2014. As of October 10, 2015:
http://news.xinhuanet.com/english/china/2014-08/26/c_126921067.htm

Murphy, Dawn Celeste, "Rising Revisionist? China's Relations with the Middle East and Sub-Saharan Africa in the Post–Cold War Era," dissertation, George Washington University, August 2012.

Myers, Margaret, "China's Unlikely Partnership with Venezuela," August 2014 International Relations and Security Network. As of October 10, 2015:
http://www.isn.ethz.ch/Digital-Library/Articles/Detail/?id=182309

Nader, Alireza, "The Days After a Deal with Iran: Continuity and Change in Iranian Foreign Policy," Santa Monica, Calif.: RAND, Corporation, PE-124-RC, 2014.

"Nanhai Zai Zhongguo Guofang Anquan Zhanlue Zhong Duju Zhongyao Diwei" ["The South Southeast Asia Holds a Uniquely Important Position in China's National Defense and Security Strategy"], *CRI Online*, August 14, 2015. As of September 19, 2015:
http://gb.cri.cn/42071/2015/08/14/8211s5067304.htm

Nanuam, Wassana, "Submarine Plan Resurfaces with Backing from Prawit," *Bangkok Post*, March 25, 2015. As of October 10, 2015:
http://www.bangkokpost.com/news/security/508086/submarine-plan-resurfaces-with-backing-from-prawit

Nathan, Andrew J., and Andrew Scobell, *China's Search for Security*, New York: Columbia University Press, 2012.

National Bank of the Republic of Kazakhstan, "Gross Inflow of Direct Investment in Kazakhstan from Foreign Direct Investors: Breakdown by Countries." As of October 10, 2015:
http://www.nationalbank.kz/?docid=469&switch=english

"Navy Hospital Ship 'Peace Ark' Arrives in Kenya," *China Daily*, October 14, 2010. As of May 8, 2015:
http://www.chinadaily.com.cn/photo/2010-10/14/content_11412199.htm

Nenge, Richard T., Takavafira M. Zhou, and Tompson Makahamadze, "Analysing the Extent to Which China Uses the Non-Interference Policy to Promote Peace and Security in Africa," in China-Africa Think Tanks Forum, "The 2nd Meeting of the China-Africa Think Tanks Forum," conference report, Bisoftu, Ethiopia, October 12–13, 2012. As of March 19, 2015:
http://dspace.africaportal.org/jspui/bitstream/123456789/34123/1/IPSS_China-Africa_Think_Tanks_Forum_Final_(2)[1].pdf?1

"New Asian Security Concept for New Progress in Security Cooperation," Ministry of Foreign Affairs of the People's Republic of China, May 21, 2014. As of October 12, 2015:
http://www.fmprc.gov.cn/mfa_eng/zxxx_662805/t1159951.shtml

"New Silk Road, New Dreams," *Xinhua News*, website, undated. As of October 10, 2015:
http://www.xinhuanet.com/world/newsilkway/index.htm

"Nigeria Acquiring New and Second-Hand Military Hardware," *Cameroon Concord*, March 30, 2015. As of April 3, 2015:
http://cameroon-concord.com/news/headlines/item/2889-nigeria-acquiring-new-and-second-hand-military-hardware

Niu Xinchun, "China's Interests in and Influence over the Middle East," *Contemporary International Relations*, Vol. 24, No. 1, January/February 2014.

Nzwilim, Fredick, "China Pledges $10 Million in Support of Wildlife Conservation in Africa," *National Geographic Voices* blog, May 13, 2014. As of March 19, 2015:
http://voices.nationalgeographic.com/2014/05/13/china-pledges-10-million-in-support-of-wildlife-conservation-in-africa/

"Obama Praises Ethiopia over Fight Against al-Shabab," *BBC News*, July 27, 2015. As of October 10, 2015:
http://www.bbc.com/news/world-africa-33671340

Okeowo, Alexis, "China, Zambia, and a Clash in a Coal Mine," *The New Yorker*, October 9, 2013. As of April 17, 2015:
http://www.newyorker.com/business/currency/china-zambia-and-a-clash-in-a-coal-mine

Oremus, Will, "China Is Finally Sending Its 'Peace Ark' to the Philippines," *Slate*, November 20, 2013. As of *insert date*:
http://www.slate.com/blogs/future_tense/2013/11/20/peace_ark_china_finally_sending_hospital_ship_to_philippines_after_typhoon.html

Organization for Economic Cooperation and Development, World Trade Organization, and World Bank Group, *Global Value Chains: Challenges, Opportunities, and Implications for Policy*, report prepared for submission to the G20 Trade Ministers meeting, Sydney, Australia, July 19, 2014. As of August 30, 2017:
https://www.oecd.org/g20/topics/trade-and-investment/gvc_report_g20_july_2014.pdf

Ori, Konye Obaji, "China Signs Deal with AU to Connect Africa's Big Cities," *The Africa Report*, January 28, 2015. As of October 10, 2015:
http://www.theafricareport.com/North-Africa/china-signs-deal-with-au-to-connect-africas-big-cities.html

"Overview of ASEAN-China (ACFTA)," Singapore government, 2014. As of October 7, 2015:
http://www.fta.gov.sg/fta_acfta.asp?hl=2

Pachios, Harold, "Let's Look at China's Role in the Iran Nuclear Deal," *The Hill*, August 21, 2015. As of October 10, 2015:
http://thehill.com/blogs/congress-blog/foreign-policy/251657-lets-look-at-chinas-role-in-the-iran-nuclear-deal

Pacific Islands Forum Secretariat, "About Us," webpage, undated. As of October 10, 2015:
http://www.forumsec.org/pages.cfm/about-us/

Page, Jeremy, "China to Fast-Track Jets for Pakistan," *Wall Street Journal*, May 20, 2011. As of October 10, 2015:
https://www.wsj.com/articles/SB10001424052748704083904576333192239624926

"Pakistan Politics: Pakistan Tests a New Missile," *Economist Intelligence Unit ViewsWire*, April 8, 2011.

"Pakistan, Kazakhstan Sign MOUs to Strengthen Trade Ties," *The Nation*, August 25, 2015. As of October 14, 2015:
http://nation.com.pk/national/25-Aug-2015/pakistan-kazakhstan-sign-mous-to-strengthen-trade-ties

"Pakistan to Buy American F-16s, Chinese FC-10 Fighter Jets," *AFX News Limited*, April 13, 2006.

Pan Guang, "The Role of a Multilateral Anti-Terror Mechanism in Central Asia," in Charles Hawkins and Robert R. Love, eds., *The New Great Game: Chinese Views on Central Asia*, Fort Leavenworth, Kan.: Foreign Military Studies Office, 2006.

Panda, Ankit, "China and Iran's Historic Naval Exercise," *The Diplomat*, September 23, 2014. As of May 8, 2015:
http://thediplomat.com/2014/09/china-and-irans-historic-naval-exercise/

———, "China Evacuates Foreign Nationals from Yemen," *The Diplomat*, April 6, 2015. As of May 8, 2015:
http://thediplomat.com/2015/04/china-evacuates-foreign-nationals-from-yemen/

Panfilova, Viktoriya, "Kyrgyzstan to Get 0.5 m Dollars of Chinese Military Aid," *Kabar News Agency*, November 12, 2007a, Bishkek (in Russian), translated by World News Connection, CEP20071112950147.

———, "China Will Dress Turkmenistani Army—Pekin Generously Credits Central Asian Countries," *Nezavisimaya Gazeta*, November 29, 2007b, Moscow (in Russian), translated by World News Connection, CEP20071129380002.

Parameswaran, Prashanth, "Beijing Unveils New Strategy for ASEAN–China Relations," *Jamestown China Brief*, Vol. 13, No. 21, October 24, 2013.

———, "Thailand Turns to China," *The Diplomat*, December 20, 2014. As of October 10, 2015:
http://thediplomat.com/2014/12/thailand-turns-to-china/

———, "China to Hold First Meeting with ASEAN Defense Ministers in Beijing," *The Diplomat*, June 3, 2015. As of September 19, 2015:
http://thediplomat.com/2015/06/china-to-hold-first-meeting-with
-ASEAN-defense-ministers-in-beijing/

———, "China's Peace Ark Completes First-Ever Australia Visit," *The Diplomat*, October 16, 2015. As of November 10, 2015:
http://thediplomat.com/2015/10/chinas-peace-ark-completes-first-ever-australia-visit/

———, "Indonesia Calls for South China Southeast Asia Restraint Amid US-China Tensions," *The Diplomat*, October 28, 2015. As of November 10, 2015:
http://thediplomat.com/2015/10/indonesia-calls-for-south-china-Southeast
Asia-restraint-amid-us-china-tensions/

Parello-Plesner, Jonas, and Mathieu Duchâtel, "How Chinese Nationals Abroad Are Transforming Beijing's Foreign Policy," *Caixin*, June 19, 2015. As of October 12, 2015:
http://english.caixin.com/2015-06-19/100821010.html

Patil, Sameer Suryakant, "Understanding the Phalcon Controversy," *Israel Journal of Foreign Affairs*, Vol. 2, No. 2, 2008, pp. 91–98.

Paton, James, and Aibing Guo, "Russia, China Add to $400 Billion Gas Deal with Accord," *Bloomberg*, November 9, 2014. As of October 10, 2015:
http://www.bloomberg.com/news/articles/2014-11-10/russia-china-add-to-400
-billion-gas-deal-with-accord

Paul, T.V., ed., *The China-India Rivalry in the Globalization Era*, Washington, D.C.: Georgetown University Press, forthcoming, 2018.

"'Peace Angel 2009' Kicks Off," *Xinhua News*, June 22, 2009. As of October 10, 2015:
http://english.sina.com/china/2009/0621/250031.html

"'Peace Ark' Hospital Ship Carries Out Remote Consultation for Philippine Patients," Ministry of National Defense of the People's Republic of China, *China Military Online*, December 9, 2013. As of October 10, 2015:
http://en.people.cn/90786/8479398.html

"'Peace Ark' Hospital Ship Participates in Joint Medical Tour in Indonesia," Ministry of National Defense of the People's Republic of China, September 12, 2013. As of May 8, 2015:
http://eng.mod.gov.cn/Photos/2013-09/12/content_4465460.htm

"Peace Ark Hospital Ship Returns to Zhoushan," *CCTV*, September 29, 2014. As of November 10, 2015:
http://english.cntv.cn/2014/09/29/VIDE1411990082504280.shtml

Pearson, Natalie Obiko, Sandrine Rastello, and David Tween, "Nepal Has Powerful Friends in High Places: India and China," *Bloomberg*, April 27, 2015. As of *insert date*:
http://www.bloomberg.com/news/articles/2015-04-27/nepal-has-powerful-friends-in-high-places-india-and-china

Pehrson, Christopher, *String of Pearls: Meeting the Challenge of China's Growing Power Across the Asian Littoral*, Carlisle Barracks, Pa.: U.S. Army War College Strategic Studies Institute, 2006.

Peng Fu, "China Focus: SCO Anti-Terror Drill Kicks Off in China," *Xinhua News*, August 24, 2014. As of May 4, 2015:
http://news.xinhuanet.com/english/china/2014-08/24/c_133580322.htm

Peng Yining, "Medics Soon at Work as Peace Ark Sails In," *China Daily*, November 26, 2013. As of October 10, 2015:
http://www.chinadaily.com.cn/2013-11/26/content_17131392.htm

Perlez, Jane, "China Offers Hospital Ship to the Philippines," *New York Times*, November 19, 2013. As of October 10, 2015:
https://sinosphere.blogs.nytimes.com/2013/11/19/china-offers-hospital-ship-to-the-philippines/

———, "China Surprises U.N. with $100 Million and Thousands of Troops for Peacekeeping," *New York Times*, September 28, 2015. As of August 31, 2017:
https://www.nytimes.com/interactive/projects/cp/reporters-notebook/xi-jinping-visit/china-surprisesu-n-with-100-million-and-thousands-of-troops-for-peacekeeping?mcubz=0

Perlez, Jane, and Chris Buckley, "China Retools Its Military with a First Overseas Outpost in Djibouti," *New York Times*, November 26, 2015. As of December 4, 2015:
http://www.nytimes.com/2015/11/27/world/asia/china-military-presence-djibouti-africa.html?_r=0

Perlez, Jane, and Yufan Huang, "Yemen Evacuation Shows Chinese Navy's Growing Role," *New York Times*, March 31, 2015. As of October 10, 2015: http://sinosphere.blogs.nytimes.com/2015/03/31/yemen-evacuation-shows-chinese-navys-growing-role/?_r=0

Pew Global Attitudes Project, "America's Global Image Remains More Positive than China's," Washington, D.C.: Pew Research Center, July 18, 2013.

Peyrouse, Sébastien, "Military Cooperation Between China and Central Asia: Breakthrough, Limits, Prospects," *China Brief*, Vol. 10, No. 5, March 5, 2010. As of October 10, 2015:
https://jamestown.org/program/military-cooperation-between-china-and-central-asia-breakthrough-limits-and-prospects/

"Philippines and Vietnam to Be 'Strategic Partners,'" *Straits Times*, September 4, 2015. As of August 29, 2017:
http://www.straitstimes.com/asia/philippines-and-vietnam-to-be-strategic-partners

Pi Xiaoqing, "China Wages Seen Jumping in 2014 Amid Shift to Services," *Bloomberg*, January 6, 2014. As of April 8, 2015:
http://www.bloomberg.com/news/articles/2014-01-06/china-wages-seen-jumping-in-2014-amid-shift-to-services-

"PLA Navy Submarine Visits Sri Lanka," *China Military Online*, September 24, 2014. As of October 10, 2015:
http://eng.chinamil.com.cn/news-channels/china-military-news/2014-09/24/content_6152669.htm

"PLAAF Aerobatic Team Arrives in Malaysia for Stunt Shows," *China Military Online*, March 12, 2015. As of October 10, 2015:
http://eng.mod.gov.cn/DefenseNews/2015-03/12/content_4574587.htm

"PLAN's Taskforce Conducts Maritime Joint Exercise with Chilean Navy," *China Military Online*, October 12, 2013. As of May 8, 2015:
http://english.chinamil.com.cn/special-reports/2007zgjdgjtm/2013-10/12/content_5625915.htm

"Premier Li Keqiang: Upgrade Practical Cooperation Between China and Latin America and the Caribbean Under the 3x3 Model," Ministry of the Foreign Affairs of the People's Republic of China, May 22, 2015. As of June 12, 2015:
http://www.fmprc.gov.cn/mfa_eng/zxxx_662805/t1266202.shtml

"Premier Li Keqiang's Keynote Speech at 10th China-ASEAN Expo," *Xinhua News*, September 4, 2013. As of September 14, 2015:
http://news.xinhuanet.com/english/china/2013-09/04/c_132688764.htm

"Premier Li: Latin America Is the New Global High Point," Information Office of the State Council of the People's Republic of China, May 26, 2015. As of June 25, 2015:
http://english.gov.cn/premier/photos/2015/05/26/content_281475115199503.htm

"Premier Zhou Enlai's Three Tours of Asian and African Countries," Ministry of Foreign Affairs of the People's Republic of China, undated. As of March 18, 2015: http://www.fmprc.gov.cn/mfa_eng/ziliao_665539/3602_665543/3604_665547/t18001.shtml

"President Hassan Rouhani of Iran Meets with Wang Yi," Ministry of Foreign Affairs of the People's Republic of China, February 16, 2015. As of October 10, 2015:
http://www.fmprc.gov.cn/mfa_eng/zxxx_662805/t1240340.shtml

"Press Release—ASEAN Secretariat Enters into Cooperation Agreement with Guangdong Province, China ASEAN Secretariat," ASEAN, September 5, 2008. As of September 14, 2015:
http://www.ASEAN.org/news/ASEAN-statement-communiques/item/press-release-ASEAN-secretariat-enters-into-cooperation-agreement-with-guangdong-province-china-ASEAN-secretariat-5-september-2008

Qi Jianguo, "Cong Huangjin Shinian Dao Zuanshi Shinian" ["From the Golden Decade to Diamond Decade"], *Foreign Affairs Journal*, No. 113, Winter 2013. As of September 14, 2015:
http://www.cpifa.org/q/listQuarterlyArticle.do?articleId=199

Rabi, Idan, "China VC to Invest $500m in Israel in 2015," *Globes*, June 3, 2015. As of October 16, 2015:
http://www.globes.co.il/en/article-chinese-vc-to-invest-500m-in-israel-in-2015-1001041922

Radlicki, Mikolaj, "From Sudan to Senegal, Africa's Head-Turning New Airports ... with a Helping Hand from Chinese Friends," *Mail & Guardian Africa*, March 6, 2015. As of October 10, 2015:
http://mgafrica.com/article/2015-03-03-africas-new-airports

Rajagopalan, Megha, "China to Send Elite Army Unit to Help Fight Ebola in Liberia," *Reuters*, October 21, 2014. As of October 10, 2015:
https://www.reuters.com/article/us-health-ebola-china/china-to-send-elite-army-unit-to-help-fight-ebola-in-liberia-idUSKBN0IK0N020141031

Rajagopalan, Megha, and Ben Blanchard, "China Evacuates Foreign Nationals from Yemen in Unprecedented Move," *Reuters*, April 3, 2015. As of October 10, 2015:
http://uk.reuters.com/article/2015/04/03/uk-yemen-security-china-idUKKBN0MU0HM20150403

Ramachandran, Sudha, "China's Pearl in Pakistan's Waters," *Asia Times Online*, March 4, 2005. As of October 10, 2015:
http://www.atimes.com/atimes/South_Asia/GC04Df06.html

Rejepova, Tavus, "Turkmenistan, China Reach New Energy Deals," *The Central Asia-Caucasus Analyst*, October 16, 2013. As of October 10, 2015:
https://www.cacianalyst.org/publications/field-reports/item/12834-turkmenistan-china-reach-new-energy-deals.html

Ritzinger, Louis, "The China-Pakistan Economic Corridor: Regional Dynamics and China's Geopolitical Ambitions," *Commentary*, Seattle, Wash.: National Bureau of Asian Research, August 5, 2015.

Saadi, Dania, "Sabic Retains Expansion Plans Despite Oil Drop," *The National*, January 12, 2015. As of October 16, 2015:
http://www.thenational.ae/business/energy/sabic-retains-expansion-plans-despite-oil-drop

Sakhuja, Vijay, "The Karakoram Corridor: China's Transportation Networks in Pakistan," *China Brief*, Vol. 10, No. 20, October 8, 2010.

"Satellite Images Suggest China 'Building Third Airstrip' in South China Southeast Asia," *CNN*, September 15, 2015. As of September 19, 2015:
http://www.cnn.com/2015/09/15/asia/china-south-china-Southeast Asia-airstrip/

Saunders, Phillip C., *China's Global Activism: Strategy, Drivers, Tools*, Institute for National Strategic Studies Occasional Paper No. 4, Washington, D.C.: National Defense University Press, October 2006.

"Say No to Ivory and Rhino Horn Chinese Cell Phone Users Told," WildAid, September 30, 2013. As of October 10, 2015:
http://www.wildaid.org.hk/news/say-no-ivory-and-rhino-horn-chinese-cell-phone-users-told

Scahill, Jeremy, "U.S. Delivering F-16s to Pakistan This Weekend," *The Nation*, June 24, 2010.

Scheives, Kevin, "China Turns West: Beijing's Contemporary Strategy Toward Central Asia," *Pacific Affairs*, Vol. 79, No. 2, Summer 2006, pp. 205–224.

Schiavenza, Matt, "What Is China's Plan for the Middle East?" *The Atlantic*, May 10, 2013. As of October 10, 2015:
http://www.theatlantic.com/china/archive/2013/05/what-is-chinas-plan-for-the-middle-east

Schmitt, Eric, "U.S. Signs New Lease to Keep Strategic Military Installation in the Horn of Africa," *New York Times*, May 5, 2014. As of July 28, 2015:
http://www.nytimes.com/2014/05/06/world/africa/us-signs-new-lease-to-keep-strategic-military-installation-in-the-horn-of-africa.html?_r=0

Scobell, Andrew, *China and North Korea: From Comrades-in-Arms to Allies at Arm's Length*, Carlisle Barracks, Pa.: U.S. Army War College Strategic Studies Institute, 2004a.

———, "Terrorism and Chinese Foreign Policy," in Yong Deng and Fei-ling Wang, eds., *China Rising: Power and Motivation in Chinese Foreign Policy*, Lanham, Md.: Rowman and Littlefield, 2004b, pp. 305–324.

———, China Ponders Post-2014 Afghanistan: Neither 'All In' nor Bystander," *Asian Survey*, Vol. 55, No. 2, March-April 2015.

———, "China's Search for Security in the Greater Middle East," in James Reardon-Anderson, ed., *The Red Star and the Crescent: China and the Middle East*, New York: Oxford University Press, 2018, pp. 13–35.

Scobell, Andrew, and Mark Cozad, "China's Policy Toward North Korea: Rethink or Recharge?" *Parameters*, Vol. 44, No. 1, Spring 2014.

Scobell, Andrew, and Scott W. Harold, "An 'Assertive' China? Insights from Interviews," *Asian Security*, Vol. 9, No. 2, Summer 2013, pp. 111–131.

Scobell, Andrew, and Alireza Nader, *China in the Middle East: The Wary Dragon*, Santa Monica, Calif.: RAND Corporation, RR-1229-A, 2016.

Scobell, Andrew, and Andrew J. Nathan, "China's Overstretched Military," *The Washington Quarterly*, Vol. 35, No. 4, Fall 2012.

Scobell, Andrew, Ely Ratner, and Michael Beckley, *China's Strategy Toward South and Central Asia: An Empty Fortress*, Santa Monica, Calif.: RAND Corporation, RR-525-AF, 2014.

"SCO's Purpose Is Not to Challenge NATO," *Global Times*, June 7, 2012.

The Second Ministerial Conference of the Forum on China-Africa Cooperation, "Addis Ababa Action Plan," September 25, 2009. As of May 18, 2015: http://www.focac.org/eng/ltda/dejbzjhy/DOC22009/t606801.htm

Seltzer, Leon F., "Codependent or Simply Dependent: What's the Big Difference?" *Psychology Today*, December 11, 2014. As of October 10, 2015: https://www.psychologytoday.com/blog/evolution-the-self/201412/codependent-or-simply-dependent-what-s-the-big-difference

Sesay, Terrence, "China Donates $4m Worth of Equipment to Liberian Military," *Africa Review*, February 27, 2014. As of May 18, 2015: http://www.africareview.com/News/China-donates-equipment-to-Liberian-military/-/979180/2223918/-/cguwx5z/-/index.html

"Set Aside Dispute and Pursue Joint Development," Ministry of Foreign Affairs of the People's Republic of China. As of September 19, 2015: http://www.fmprc.gov.cn/mfa_eng/ziliao_665539/3602_665543/3604_665547/t18023.shtml

Shah, Saeed, "China to Build Pipeline from Iran to Pakistan," *Wall Street Journal*, April 9, 2015. As of October 10, 2015: http://www.wsj.com/articles/china-to-build-pipeline-from-iran-to-pakistan-1428515277

Shambaugh, David, "Coping with a Conflicted China," *The Washington Quarterly*, Vol. 34, No. 1, December 2011, pp. 7–27.

———, *China Goes Global: The Partial Power*, New York: Oxford University Press, 2012.

Sharpe, Richard, ed., *Jane's Fighting Ships, 1997–1998*, London: Jane's Information Group, 1997, pp. 485–489.

Shear, David, "Statement of David Shear Assistant Secretary of Defense for Asian & Pacific Security Affairs," Senate Committee on Foreign Relations, May 13, 2015. As of September 19, 2015:
http://www.foreign.senate.gov/imo/media/doc/051315_Shear_Testimony.pdf

Shekhar, Vibhanshu, and Joseph Chinyong Liow, "Indonesia as a Maritime Power: Jokowi's Vision, Strategies, and Obstacles Ahead," Brookings Institution, November 7, 2014. As of August 29, 2017:
http://www.brookings.edu/research/articles/2014/11/indonesia-maritime-liow-shekhar

Shen Zhiliang, "Zhongla Guanxi: Guanfang Waijiao Yu Gonggong Waijia Bing Zhong" ["China-Latin America Relations: The Equal Importance of Official Diplomacy and Public Diplomacy"], *PR World*, Vol. 2, 2014.

Shi Yinhong, "Tuijin 'Yi Dai Yi Lu' Jianshe Yingyou Shenshen Xintai" ["In Advancing the Construction of 'One Belt, One Road,' We Must Be Prudent"], *People's Daily*, July 5, 2015. As of October 14, 2015:
http://world.people.com.cn/n/2015/0705/c1002-27256546.html

"Shibada Zhi Hou De Zhongguo Waijiao Xin Jumian" ["China's New Foreign Policy After the 18th Party Congress"], *Sina News*, January 9, 2014. As of October 28, 2014:
http://news.sina.com.cn/c/2014-01-09/111129197073.shtml

Shichor, Yitzhak, *The Middle East in China's Foreign Policy, 1949–1977*, New York: Cambridge University Press, 1979.

Shinn, David H., "Military and Security Relations: China, Africa, and the Rest of the World," in Robert I. Rotberg, ed., *China into Africa: Trade, Aid, and Influence*, Washington, D.C.: Brookings Institution Press, 2008.

Shivananda, H., "Sino-Myanmar Military Cooperation and Its Implications for India," *Journal of Defence Studies*, Vol. 5, No. 3, July 2011. As of November 30, 2015:
http://www.idsa.in/system/files/5_3_HShivananda.pdf

Small, Andrew, "China's Caution on Afghanistan-Pakistan," *The Washington Quarterly*, Vol. 33, No. 3, June 24, 2010.

———, *The China-Pakistan Axis: Asia's New Geopolitics*, New York: Oxford University Press, 2015.

Snow, Philip, *The Star Raft: China's Encounter with Africa*, Ithaca, N.Y.: Cornell University Press, 1988.

Song Yen Ling, "Fourth Line of Central Asia-China Gas Pipeline to Start Construction This Year," *Platts*, March 10, 2014. As of October 14, 2015:
http://www.platts.com/latest-news/natural-gas/beijing/fourth-link-of-central-asia-china-gas-pipeline-26749048

"South China Southeast Asia: Australia's Live Fire Exercise with China's Navy Could Be 'PR Disaster,' Expert Warns," *ABC News*, November 2, 2015. As of November 10, 2015:
http://www.abc.net.au/news/2015-11-02/south-china-Southeast Asia-live-fire-exercises-a-pr-disaster-says-expert/6903858

Southerland, Matthew, "U.S. Freedom of Navigation Patrol in the South China Southeast Asia: What Happened, What It Means, and What's Next," U.S.-China Economic and Security Review Commission, Issue Brief, November 5, 2015. As of November 10, 2015:
http://origin.www.uscc.gov/sites/default/files/ReSoutheast Asiarch/US%20Freedom%20of%20Navigation%20Patrol%20in%20the%20South%20China%20Southeast Asia.pdf

Spegele, Brian, "China Points Finger at Pakistan Again," *Wall Street Journal*, March 8, 2012. As of October 20, 2015:
https://www.wsj.com/articles/SB10001424052970204781804577266952254783484

"Sri Lanka Allows Chinese Submarine to Dock," *China Daily*, November 3, 2014. As of October 10, 2015:
http://www.chinadaily.com.cn/world/2014-11/03/content_18856943.htm

State Administration of Taxation of the People's Republic of China, "Zhongguo Shuishou Xieding Tanqian De Zongti Qingkuang" ["The Overall Situation of the Negotiation of China's Tax Treaty"], 2013. As of November 28, 2015:
http://www.chinatax.gov.cn/2013/n1586/n1904/n1933/n31845/n31870/n31871/c310353/content.html

"Statement by Ambassador Wang Yinfan, Permanent Representative of China to the United Nations, at the 56th Session of the General Assembly on the Issue of 'the Causes of Conflict and the Promotion of Durable Peace and Sustainable Development in Africa,'" December 3, 2001. As of March 19, 2015:
http://www.china-un.ch/eng/qtzz/wtojjwt/t85650.htm

Stats New Zealand—Taturanga Aotearoa, "2013 Census QuickStats About Culture and Identity," Wellington, April 15, 2014. As of August 31, 2017:
http://www.stats.govt.nz/Census/2013-census/profile-and-summary-reports/quickstats-culture-identity/birthplace.aspx

Steil, Benn, and Dinah Walker, "Are China's RMB Swap Lines an Empty Vessel," Council on Foreign Relations, May 21, 2015. As of June 25, 2015:
http://blogs.cfr.org/geographics/2015/05/21/swaplines/

Stockholm International Peace Research Institute, Arms Transfers Database, 1979–2008.

———, *SIPRI Yearbook 1989: World Armaments and Disarmament*, London: Oxford University Press, 1989.

———, *SIPRI Yearbook 1994*, London: Oxford University Press, 1994.

———, *SIPRI Yearbook 1998*, London: Oxford University Press, 1998.

Su Hao, "Zhongguo Waijiao De 'Huoban Guanxi' Kuangjia" ["The 'Partnership' Framework in China's Foreign Policy"], *Shijie Jishi* [*World Knowledge*], Vol. 5, 2000.

Sun Degang, and Yahia H. Zoubir, "China's Economic Diplomacy towards the Arab Countries: Challenges Ahead?" *Journal of Contemporary China*, Vol. 24, No. 95, 2015.

Sun Junjian, "Aodaliya Dui Meiguo 'Chongfan Yatai' Zhanlue De Fanying" ["Australia's Response to the United States' 'Pivot to Asia' Strategy"], *Contemporary International Relations*, No. 8, 2014. As of September 22, 2015: http://www.faobserver.com/NewsInfo.aspx?id=11087

Sun Zhiyuan, "'Yi Dai Yi Lu' Zhanlue Gouxiang De Sanzhong Neihan" ["The Three Major Details of the Strategic Concept of 'One Belt, One Road'"], Information Office of the State Council of the People's Republic of China, August 11, 2014. As of October 12, 2015:
http://www.scio.gov.cn/ztk/wh/slxy/31215/Document/1377654/1377654.htm

Sun Zhuangzhi, "SCO Summit in Tashkent Opens 'New Chapter,'" *People's Daily Online* (in English), June 12, 2010.

Swaine, Michael D., "China and the 'AfPak' Issue," *China Leadership Monitor*, No. 31, February 23, 2010. As of August 14, 2017:
http://carnegieendowment.org/2010/02/23/china-and-afpak-issue-pub-38880

———, "Perceptions of an Assertive China," *China Leadership Monitor*, No. 32, March 2010.

———, "Chinese Views and Commentary on Periphery Diplomacy," *China Leadership Monitor*, No. 44, July 2014.

———, "Xi Jinping's Address to the Central Conference on Work Relating to Foreign Affairs: Assessing and Advancing Major-Power Diplomacy with Chinese Characteristics," *China Leadership Monitor*, No. 46, Winter 2014.

Tang Jun, "Ying Jiang '21 Shiji Haishang Sichou Zhi Lu' Yanshen Zhi Lamei Diqu" ["The '21st Century Maritime Silk Road' Should Be Extended to the Latin American Region"], *The Contemporary World*, February 6, 2015. As of May 19, 2015:
http://cpc.people.com.cn/n/2015/0206/c187710-26521302.html

Tang Yingzi and Wang Xiaodong, "China Army Medics Join Ebola Battle," *China Daily*, November 15, 2014. As of October 10, 2015:
http://www.chinadaily.com.cn/china/2014-11/15/content_18918365.htm

Tanner, Murray Scot, Kerry Dumbaugh, and Ian Easton, *Distracted Antagonists, Wary Partners: China and India Assess their Security Relations*, Alexandria, Va.: Center for Naval Analyses, September 2011.

"Tanzania's MPs Approve Anti-Foreigner Law," *BBC News*, March 19, 2015. As of October 10, 2015:
http://www.bbc.com/news/world-africa-31965595

Taylor, Ian, *The Forum on China-Africa Cooperation (FOCAC)*, Abingdon: Routledge, 2011.

———, "From Santa Claus to Serious Business: Where Should FOCAC Go Next?" *African-East Asian Affairs/The China Monitor*, Vol. 74, 2012.

Taylor, Rob, "Australia Prepares Option of Sail-Through to Test China," *Wall Street Journal*, October 28, 2015. As of November 10, 2015:
http://www.wsj.com/articles/australia-prepares-option-of-sail-through-to-test-china-1446023112?alg=y&utm_content=buffer8335d&utm_medium=social&utm_source=twitter.com&utm_campaign=buffer

Tellis, Ashley J., C. Christine Fair, and Jamison Jo Medby, *Limited Conflicts Under the Nuclear Umbrella: Indian and Pakistani Lessons from the Kargil Crisis*, Santa Monica, Calif.: RAND Corporation, MR-1450-USCA, 2001.

Tepper, Aryeh, "China's Deepening Interest in Israel," *The Tower*, No. 30, September 2015. As of October 16, 2015:
http://www.thetower.org/article/chinas-deepening-interest-in-israel/

"Thai PM Meets with Chang Wanquan," *China Military Online*, February 9, 2015. As of October 10, 2015:
http://eng.chinamil.com.cn/news-channels/china-military-news/2015-02/09/content_6347163.htm

"Thai Warships Visit South China Southeast Asia Fleet," *China Military Online*, February 10, 2015. As of October 10, 2015:
http://eng.chinamil.com.cn/news-channels/china-military-news/2015-02/10/content_6348862.htm

"Thailand, China Agree to Deepen Military Ties," *Xinhua News*, April 24, 2015. As of October 10, 2015:
http://english.chinamil.com.cn/news-channels/china-military-news/2015-04/24/content_6459679.htm

"Thailand's Ambassador to China Signed Articles of Agreement of the Asian Infrastructure Bank," Asian Infrastructure Investment Bank, September 29, 2015. As of October 10, 2015:
https://www.aiib.org/en/news-events/news/2015/20150929_001.html

Thayer, Carl, "China-ASEAN Joint Development Overshadowed by South China Southeast Asia," *The Diplomat*, October 25, 2013. As of September 19, 2015:
http://thediplomat.com/2013/10/china-ASEAN-joint-development-overshadowed-by-south-china-Southeast Asia/

Till, Geoffrey, *Asia's Naval Expansion: An Arms Race in the Making?* London: International Institute for Strategic Studies, 2012.

Transparency International, *Corruption Perceptions Index 2014*, 2014. As of April 9, 2015:
http://www.transparency.org/cpi2014/results

Trofimov, Yaroslav, "In Africa, China's Expansion Begins to Stir Resentment," *Wall Street Journal*, February 2, 2007. As of April 17, 2015:
http://www.wsj.com/articles/SB117036261569895256

Tugendhat, Henry, "Chinese Training Courses for African Officials: A 'Win-Win' Engagement?" SAIS China-African Research Initiative Policy Brief No. 3, December 2014. As of April 10, 2015:
https://saiscari.files.wordpress.com/2014/10/sais-cari-brief-3-2014-tugendhat.pdf

United Nations, UN Comtrade Database, 2014.

———, "Current Peacekeeping Operations," webpage, undated. As of April 9, 2015:
http://www.un.org/en/peacekeeping/operations/current.shtml

———, *Non-Self-Governing Territories*, website, undated. As of October 10, 2015:
http://www.un.org/en/decolonization/nonselfgovterritories.shtml

———, *UN Missions Summary, Detailed by Country*, March 31, 2015. As of October 10, 2015:
http://www.un.org/en/peacekeeping/contributors/2015/mar15_3.pdf

United Nations Conference on Trade and Development, Bilateral FDI Statistics, webpage, 2014. As of November 28, 2015:
http://unctad.org/en/Pages/DIAE/FDI%20Statistics/FDI-Statistics-Bilateral.aspx

———, "China: Total Number of Double Taxation Agreements Concluded, 1 June 2011," 2011. As of November 28, 2015:
http://unctad.org/Sections/dite_pcbb/docs/dtt_China.PDF

———, *Investment Policy Hub: International Investment Agreements*, 2013. As of November 28, 2015:
http://investmentpolicyhub.unctad.org/IIA

United Nations Department of Economic and Social Affairs, Population Challenges and Development Goals, New York, 2005.

United Nations Development Programme, "The Ebola Virus Outbreak and China's Response," Issue Brief No. 6, December 2014. As of April 20, 2015:
http://www.cn.undp.org/content/dam/china/docs/Publications/UNDP-CH-SSC-December.pdf

United Nations General Assembly, Resolution 2758 (XXVI), October 25, 1971. As of April 8, 2015:
http://daccess-dds-ny.un.org/doc/RESOLUTION/GEN/NR0/327/74/IMG/NR032774.pdf?OpenElement

U.S. Department of Defense, "2010 Investment Climate Statement—Kyrgyz Republic," webpage, March 2010. As of October 10, 2015:
https://www.state.gov/e/eb/rls/othr/ics/2010/138095.htm

———, "Asia-Pacific Maritime Security Strategy," August 2015.

U.S. Energy Information Administration, "Country Analysis Brief: Iraq," U.S. Department of Energy, January 30, 2015.

———, "China," U.S. Department of Energy, May 14, 2015.

U.S. government official, "China and the US in Africa—Can Security Policy Promote Practical Cooperation?" Roundtable discussion, Johns Hopkins University School of Advanced International Studies, Washington, D.C., March 25, 2015.

Van Ness, Peter, *Revolution and Chinese Foreign Policy: Peking's Support of Wars of National Liberation*, Berkeley: University of California Press, 1971.

———, "China as a Third World State: Foreign Policy and Official National Identity," in Lowell Dittmer and Samuel S. Kim, eds., *China's Quest for National Identity*, Ithaca, N.Y.: Cornell University Press, 1993.

———, "China and the Third World: Patterns of Engagement and Indifference," in Samuel S. Kim, ed. *China and the World: Chinese Foreign Policy Faces the New Millennium*, 4th ed., Boulder, Colo.: Westview Press, 1998.

"Venezuela to Get $5 Billion in Funding from China in Next Few Months: PDVSA Official," *Reuters*, June 16, 2015. As of June 17, 2015:
http://www.reuters.com/article/2015/06/17/us-venezuela
-china-loan-idUSKBN0OX01O20150617

"Vietnam Gives Noncommittal Response to US Patrol in S. China Southeast Asia," *Voice of America*, October 29, 2015. As of November 10, 2015:
http://www.voanews.com/content/vietnam-gives-noncomittal-response-to-us
-patrol-in-south-china-Southeast Asia/3028642.html

Vision and Actions on Jointly Building Silk Road Economic Belt and 21st Century Maritime Silk Road, Beijing, March 28. 2015. Issued by the National Development and Reform Commission, the Ministry of Foreign Affairs, the Ministry of Commerce of the People's Republic of China with State Council authorization.

Vollgraaff, Rene, Amogelang Mbatha, and Mike Cohen, "Xi Unveils $60 Billion Funding Pledge at South Africa Summit," *BloombergBusiness*, December 4, 2015. As of December 4, 2015:
http://www.bloomberg.com/news/articles/2015-12-04/xi-announces
-60-billion-funding-package-as-china-summit-opens

"Waijiaobu Jie Feibin Yuenan Nanhai Feifa Qinquan Huodong: Yaoqiu Liji Tingzhi" ["Foreign Ministry Exposes Philippines and Vietnams Illegal Activities Infringing on Sovereignty in the South Southeast Asia, Demands Immediate End"], *Xinhua News*, April 29, 2015. As of September 19, 2015:
http://news.xinhuanet.com/world/2015-04/29/c_127748407.htm

"Waijiaobu Yazhousi Sizhang Luo Zhaohui Tan Zhongguo Zhoubian Waijiao Xin Zhengcheng" ["Chinese Ministry of Foreign Affairs' Department of Asian Affairs Director-General Luo Zhaohui Discusses New Directions in China's Neighboring Country Policy"], Ministry of Foreign Affairs of the People's Republic of China, December 27, 2013. As of October 28, 2014:
http://www.fmprc.gov.cn/mfa_chn/ziliao_611306/zt_611380/dnzt_611382/
wjdjtzt/ftsl/t1112428.shtml

Walt, Stephen, *The Origins of Alliances*, Ithaca, N.Y.: Cornell University Press, 1988.

Wang Cong, and Miao Xiaojun, "Bodies of Chinese Peacekeeping Police Killed in Haiti Earthquake Arrive Home," January 19, 2010. As of April 30, 2015: http://news.xinhuanet.com/english2010/china/2010-01/19/c_13142268.htm

Wang Fei-Ling, and Esi A. Elliot, "China in Africa: Presence, Perceptions and Prospects," *Journal of Contemporary China*, Vol. 23, No. 90, 2014. As of March 6, 2015:
http://www.tandfonline.com/doi/pdf/10.1080/10670564.2014.898888

Wang Jian-Ye, "What Drives China's Growing Role in Africa?" IMF Working Paper WP/07/211, October 2007. As of April 17, 2015:
https://www.imf.org/external/pubs/ft/wp/2007/wp07211.pdf

Wang Shengwei, "HK Must Embrace the 'One Belt, One Road' Initiative," *China Daily*, August 12, 2015. As of November 10, 2015:
http://www.chinadailyasia.com/opinion/2015-08/12/content_15302798.html

Wang Wei, "China and Africa Envision New Security Cooperation," *China.org.cn*, July 9, 2010. As of March 6, 2015:
http://www.china.org.cn/opinion/2010-07/09/content_20460645.htm

Wang Xuejun, "Developmental Peace: Understanding China's Policy Towards Africa in Peace and Security," Institute for Africa Studies, Zhejiang Normal University, September 12, 2014. As of April 8, 2015:
http://ias.zjnu.cn/uploadfile/2014/0912/20140912121304640.pdf

Wang Yi, "Creating a New Landscape for the Diplomacy with Neighboring Countries and Boosting the Asia-Pacific Regional Cooperation." Ministry of Foreign Affairs of the People's Republic of China, October 9, 2013. As of September 19, 2015:
http://www.fmprc.gov.cn/mfa_eng/topics_665678/xjpfwynmlxycx21apec_665682/t1088099.shtml

———, "Foreign Minister Wang Yi Talks about President Xi Jinping's Attendance at the G20 Summit and Visits to Three Countries Including Australia," Ministry of Foreign Affairs of the People's Republic of China, November 23, 2014. As of September 22, 2015:
http://www.fmprc.gov.cn/mfa_eng/topics_665678/xjpzxcxesgjtldrdjcfhdadlyxxlfjjxgsfwbttpyjjdgldrhw/t1214285.shtml

Wee, Vincent, "Malaysia Hoping to Tap on Chinese for New Port Investment," *Seatrade Maritime News*, June 12, 2015. As of October 10, 2015:
http://www.seatrade-maritime.com/news/asia/malaysia-hoping-to-tap-on-china-for-new-port-investment.html

"Wen's Speech at the China-Pacific Island Countries Forum," *China Daily*, April 5, 2006. As of August 5, 2015:
http://www.chinadaily.com.cn/china/2006-04/05/content_560573.htm

Wesley-Smith, Terence, "China in Oceania: New Forces in Pacific Politics," East-West Center, Pacific Islands Policy, No. 2, 2007.

Wezeman, Pieter D., and Siemon T. Wezeman, "Trends in International Arms Transfers, 2014," SIPRI Fact Sheet, March 2015. As of October 10, 2015: http://books.sipri.org/files/FS/SIPRIFS1503.pdf

"White Paper Details China's Foreign Aid Priorities," *Xinhua News*, July 10, 2014. As of May 18, 2015:
http://china-wire.org/?p=35146

Whitlock, Craig, "Remote U.S. Base at Core of Secret Operations," *Washington Post*, October 25, 2012. As of July 28, 2015:
https://www.washingtonpost.com/world/national-security/remote-us-base-at-core-of-secret-operations/2012/10/25/a26a9392-197a-11e2-bd10-5ff056538b7c_story.html

Wiemer, Calla, "The Economy of Xinjiang," in S. Frederick Starr ed., *Xinjiang: China's Muslim Borderland*, Armonk, N.Y.: M.E. Sharpe, Inc., 2004.

Wonacott, Peter, "China Inc. Moves Factory Floor to Africa," *Wall Street Journal*, May 14, 2014. As of April 8, 2015:
http://www.wsj.com/articles/SB10001424052702304788404579519631654112594

Wong, Edward, "China Quietly Extends Its Footprints Deep into Central Asia," *New York Times* (Washington edition), January 3, 2011.

———, "Security Law Suggests a Broadening of China's 'Core Interests,'" *New York Times*, July 2, 2015. As of August 24, 2015:
http://www.nytimes.com/2015/07/03/world/asia/security-law-suggests-a-broadening-of-chinas-core-interests.html?_r=0

World Bank, *World Development Indicators*, online database, last updated November 12, 2015. As of October 10, 2015:
http://databank.worldbank.org/data/reports.aspx?source=world-development-indicators

World Trade Organization, "Chronological List of Dispute Cases," website, Geneva, undated. As of August 31, 2017:
https://www.wto.org/english/tratop_e/dispu_e/dispu_status_e.htm

"Worldwide Confucius Institutes," Confucius Institute Online. As of October 13, 2015:
http://www.chinesecio.com/m/cio_wci/

Wu Jiao, and Zhang Yunbi, "Xi Proposes a 'New Silk Road' with Central Asia," *China Daily* (U.S. edition), September 8, 2013. As of October 10, 2015:
http://usa.chinadaily.com.cn/china/2013-09/08/content_16952304.htm

Wu, Yuwen, "China's Oil Fears over South Sudan Fighting," *BBC News*, January 8, 2014. As of October 10, 2015:
http://www.bbc.com/news/world-africa-25654155

Xi Jinping, "Speech by Chinese President Xi Jinping to Indonesian Parliament," Jakarta, Indonesia, October 3, 2013. As of September 19, 2015:
http://www.ASEAN-china-center.org/english/2013-10/03/c_133062675.htm

———, "Building Partnership Together Toward a Bright Future," speech given at the Seventh BRICS Summit, Ufa, July 9, 2015. As of October 10, 2015:
http://www.fmprc.gov.cn/mfa_eng/wjdt_665385/zyjh_665391/t1283789.shtml

"Xi Jinping Meets with President Vladimir Putin of Russia," Ministry of Foreign Affairs of the People's Republic of China, July 8, 2015. As of October 10, 2015:
http://www.fmprc.gov.cn/mfa_eng/zxxx_662805/t1280313.shtml

"Xi Jinping Meets with Prime Minister Abdelmalek Sellal of Algeria," Ministry of Foreign Affairs of the People's Republic of China, April 29, 2015. As of October 10, 2015:
http://www.fmprc.gov.cn/mfa_eng/zxxx_662805/t1260832.shtml

Xiang Bo, "'Peace Mission-2014' Scale: More than Ever," *Xinhua News*, August 28, 2014. As of *insert date*:
http://news.xinhuanet.com/english/china/2014-08/28/c_133603431.htm

"Xinhua Insight: Chinese Peacekeeping Troops Show Responsibility, Professionalism," *Xinhua News*, April 19, 2015. As of October 10, 2015:
http://english.chinamil.com.cn/news-channels/china-military-news/2015-04/19/content_6449481.htm

"Xinjiang Pipeline Oils Wheels," *The Standard*, December 14, 2009.

Yan Meng and Zhang Qian, "China's J-10 Presence at Russian Air Show Shows Good Relationship Between the Two Militaries," *People's Daily Online*, August 28, 2013. As of October 10, 2015:
http://en.people.cn/90786/8380185.html

Yang Guanghai and Yan Zhe, "Nanhai Hangxing Ziyou Wenti De Lixing Sikao" ["A Rational Consideration of the Issue of Freedom of Navigation in the South Southeast Asia"], *The New Orient*, No. 5, December 2014.

Yang Jiechi, "The Evolving International Pattern and China's Diplomacy," China Institute of International Studies, August 22, 2011. As of October 12, 2015:
http://www.ciis.org.cn/english/2011-08/22/content_4425488.htm

"Yang Wanming Jieshao Lameisi Gongzuo Ganbu Genju Xuyao Zai Guoneiwai Lunhuan" ["Yang Wanming Introduces Working Cadre of Latin America Division, Will Rotate Abroad and at Home Based on Needs"], *People's Daily Online*, November 23, 2010. As of June 12, 2015:
http://politics.people.com.cn/GB/1027/13291811.html

"Yang Wanming: Qingnian Shi Waijiao Duiwu Gugan Lameisi Pingjun Nianling Bu Dao 35 Sui" ["Yang Wanming: Youths Are the Backbone of the Diplomatic Corps, Average Age of Latin America Division Is Less than 35"], *People's Daily Online*, November 23, 2010. As of June 12, 2015:
http://politics.people.com.cn/GB/1027/13292293.html

Yang Yao, "Chinese Security Company Makes Foray into Africa," *China Daily Africa*, October 31, 2014. As of April 7, 2015:
http://africa.chinadaily.com.cn/weekly/2014-10/31/content_18836367.htm

Yang Zurong, "Sino-Peruvian Joint Humanitarian Medical Rescue Operation Starts in Lima," *PLA Daily*, November 25, 2010. As of April 30, 2015:
http://eng.chinamil.com.cn/news-channels/china-military-news/2010-11/25/content_4341860.htm

Yarger, Harry R., *Strategic Theory for the 21st Century: The Little Book on Big Strategy*, Publication 641, Strategic Studies Institute, U.S. Army War College, Carlisle, Pa., February 2006.

"'Yi Dai Yi Lu' Huo You Li Yu Jiefangjun Gaige" ["'One Belt One Road' Might Benefit PLA Reforms"], *Huanqiu Shibao* [*Global Times*], October 21, 2015. As of October 10, 2015:
http://whw360.org/2015/102213W592015.html

"'Yi Dai Yi Lu' Jiang Shi Weilai 30 Nian Zhongguo Dui Wai De Da Zhan Lue" ["'One Belt, One Road' Will Be China's Grand Diplomatic Strategy for the 30 Years to Come"], *Guangming Daily*, February 26, 2015. As of September 19, 2015:
http://theory.gmw.cn/2015-02/26/content_14922530.htm

"'Yi Dai Yi Lu' Zheng Gaixie Quanqiu Jingji Bantu" ["'One Belt, One Road' Is Remaking the Global Economic Map"], *People's Daily Overseas Edition*, December 29, 2014. As of September 19, 2015:
http://paper.people.com.cn/rmrbhwb/html/2014-12/29/content_1515437.htm

Yu Chang Sen, "The Pacific Islands in Chinese Geo-Strategic Thinking," paper presented to the conference on "China and the Pacific: the View from Oceania," National University of Samao, Apia, Samoa, February 25–27, 2015. As of August 13, 2015:
http://www.victoria.ac.nz/chinareSoutheast Asiarchcentre/programmes-and-projects/china-symposiums/china-and-the-pacific-the-view-from-oceania/10-Yu-Changsen-The-Pacific-Islands-in-Chinese-Geo-strategic-Thinking.pdf

Yu Jincui, "Overseas Evacuation Attests to Nation's Responsibility," *Global Times*, March 31, 2015. As of October 10, 2015:
http://www.globaltimes.cn/content/914865.shtml

Yu Lintao, "Vibrant Integration," *Beijing Review*, January 22, 2015. As of June 12, 2015:
http://www.bjreview.com.cn/world/txt/2015-01/19/content_664488_2.htm

Yuan, Jing-Dong, "The Dragon and the Elephant: Chinese-Indian Relations in the 21st Century," *The Washington Quarterly*, Vol. 30, No. 3, Summer 2007.

"Yuenan Deng Guo Zai Nai Hai Fengkuang Tianhai Xifang Shi Er Bu Jian Zhi Pi Zhongguo" ["Vietnam and Other Countries Reclaim Land like Mad in the South Southeast Asia, West Ignores and Criticizes Only China"], *Sina News*, June 21, 2015. As of September 19, 2015:
http://mil.news.sina.com.cn/2015-06-21/1048833592.html

Yun Sun, "March West: China's Response to the U.S. Rebalancing," Brookings Institution, January 31, 2013. As of October 10, 2015:
http://www.brookings.edu/blogs/up-front/posts/2013/01/31-china-us-sun

———, "Xi Jinping's Africa Policy: The First Year," Brookings Institution *Africa in Focus* blog, April 14, 2014. As of April 10, 2015:
http://www.brookings.edu/blogs/africa-in-focus/posts/2014/04/10-jinping-africa-policy-sun

———, "Inserting Africa into China's One Belt, One Road Strategy: A New Opportunity for Jobs and Infrastructure?" Brookings Institution, March 2, 2015. As of November 10, 2015:
http://www.brookings.edu/blogs/africa-in-focus/posts/2015/03/02-africa-china-jobs-infrastructure-sun

———, "The Limits of U.S.-China Cooperation in Africa," Brookings Institution *Africa in Focus* blog, April 6, 2015. As of May 19, 2015:
http://www.brookings.edu/blogs/africa-in-focus/posts/2015/04/06-limit-us-china-cooperation-in-africa-sun

Zerba, Shaio H., "China's Libya Evacuation Operation: A New Diplomatic Imperative—Overseas Citizen Protection," *Journal of Contemporary China*, Vol. 23, No. 90, 2014. As of March 6, 2015:
http://www.tandfonline.com/doi/pdf/10.1080/10670564.2014.898900

Zha Chunming, "Chinese Navy 'Peace Ark' Hospital Ship in Kingston, Jamaica," October 31, 2011. As of April 30, 2015:
http://english.cntv.cn/20111031/106073.shtml

Zhang Feng, "China's New Thinking on Alliances," *Survival*, Vol. 54, No. 5, October-November 2012.

Zhang Gaochao, "'Wolf Warrior 2' Becomes China's Highest-Grossing Film of All Time," *Los Angeles Times*, August 15, 2017. As of August 29, 2017:
http://www.latimes.com/business/hollywood/la-fi-ct-china-box-office-wolf-warrior2-story.html

Zhang Yong, "China's PLA Navy 'Peace Ark' Hospital Ship Arrives at Havana, Cuba," *Xinhua News*, October 23, 2011. As of April 30, 2015:
http://eng.chinamil.com.cn/special-reports/2011-10/23/content_4701787.htm

Zhang Yunbi, "Over 500 Chinese Nationals Evacuated from Yemen," *China Daily*, March 30, 2015. As of October 10, 2015:
http://www.chinadaily.com.cn/china/2015-03/30/content_19953138.htm

Zhang Yuzhe, and Wang Ling, "Cheers, Fears for China's Next Step Overseas," *Caixin Online*, July 22, 2015. As of October 14, 2015:
http://english.caixin.com/2015-07-22/100831560.html

Zhao Huasheng, *Zhongguo De Zhongya Waijiao* [China's Central Asian Diplomacy], Beijing: Shishi Chubanshe, 2008.

Zhen, Summer, "Chinese Firm Takes Control of Gwadar Port Free-Trade Zone in Pakistan," *South China Morning Post*, November 11, 2015. As of August 4, 2017: http://www.scmp.com/business/companies/article/1877882/chinese-firm-takes-control-gwadar-port-free-trade-zone-pakistan

Zheng Wang, *Never Forget National Humiliation: Historical Memory in Chinese Politics and Foreign Relations*, New York: Columbia University Press, 2012.

"Zhiku Luntan: Yi Dai Yi Lu Tiaozhan Yu Jiyu Dongnanya Zhongyao" ["Think Tank Forum: The Challenges and Opportunities of One Belt, One Road, Southeast Asia Is Important"], CRNTT News, June 23, 2015. As of September 19, 2015:
http://hk.crntt.com/doc/1038/1/0/5/103810576.html?coluid=7&kindid=0&docid=103810576&mdate=0624085409

"Zhongguo Buying Gaogu Lamei De Zhanlue Yiyi" ["China Should Not Overestimate Latin America's Strategic Value"], *Financial Times* (China), January 21, 2015. As of July 2, 2015:
http://m.ftchinese.com/story/001060237

"Zhongguo-Dongmeng Guanxi (10+1)" ["China-ASEAN Relations (10+1)"], Ministry of Foreign Affairs of the People's Republic of China, February 2017. As of October 10, 2015:
http://www.mfa.gov.cn/chn//pds/wjb/zzjg/yzs/dqzz/dnygjlm/zghdny/t575554.htm

"Zhongguo Haijun Jianting Biandui Fu Yemen Cheli Zhongguo Gongmin" ["Chinese Naval Detachment Sails to Yemen to Evacuate Chinese Nationals"], Ministry of National Defense of the People's Republic of China, March 30, 2015. As of October 10, 2015:
http://news.mod.gov.cn/headlines/2015-03/30/content_4577471.htm

"Zhongguo Haijun Jianting Biandui Shouci FangwenYilang" ["Chinese Navy Ship Formation Visits Iran for the First Time"], PRC government web portal, September 20, 2014. As of May 8, 2015:
http://www.gov.cn/xinwen/2014-09/20/content_2753578.htm

"Zhongguo Haiyao Fuhuo Nanmei De Xin" ["China Still Needs to Capture South America's Heart"], *Think.China.cn*, August 20, 2014. As of July 2, 2015:
http://www.china.com.cn/opinion/think/2014-08/20/content_33289051.htm

"Zhongguo Hexin Liyi Bu Rong Tiaozhan" ["China's Core Interests Are Not to Be Challenged"], *Xinhua News*, May 25, 2015. As of August 24, 2015:
http://news.xinhuanet.com/world/2015-05/25/c_1115401978.htm

"Zhongguo Lamei Luntan Rang Meiguo Zhuakuang" ["China-Latin America Forum Drives America Mad"], *Creaders.net*, January 10, 2015. As of May 19, 2015:
http://news.creaders.net/china/2015/01/10/1476467.html

"Zhongguo Qudai Meiguo Chengwei Aodaliya Zui Da Waizi Laiyuan" ["China Replaces the U.S. as Australia's Largest Source of Foreign Investment"], *Sina News*, April 30, 2015. As of March 18, 2018:
http://finance.sina.com.cn/money/forex/whqqscgd/20150430/184922086629.shtml

"Zhongguo Shi Lamei Waijiao 'Taipingyang Zhanlue' De Youxian Mubiao" ["China Is the Primary Target of Latin America Foreign Policy's 'Pacific Strategy'"], *People's Daily*, May 15, 2015. As of October 10, 2015:
http://world.people.com.cn/n/2015/0515/c1002-27007845.html

"Zhongmei Zai Nanhai Wenti Shang Bu Ying Tiaozhan Duifang De Hexin Li Yi" ["China and America Should Not Challenge Each Other's Core Interests in the South Southeast Asia"], *CRI International*, August 11, 2015. As of August 24, 2015:
http://gb.cri.cn/42071/2015/08/11/8211s5063147.htm

Zhou Bo, "China-ASEAN Hotlines: The Best Fruits in an 'Early Harvest,'" *China-US Focus*, August 20, 2015. As of September 19, 2015:
http://www.chinausfocus.com/foreign-policy/china-ASEAN-hotlines-the-best-fruits-in-an-early-harvest/

Zhou Fangzhi, "Zhongtai Guanxi: Dongmeng Hezuo Zhong Zhanlue Zhidian Zuoyong" ["China-Thailand Relations: Strategic Fulcrum Role in ASEAN Cooperation"], *Southeast Asian Affairs*, Vol. 3, 2014.

Zhu Yongbiao, "Zai Zhongya Zhongguo Laodong Quanyi Mianlin De Fengxian" ["The Risks Facing Chinese Labor Rights in Central Asia"], *Journal of Xinjiang Normal University*, No. 4, 2017.

Zhu Zhe, "China, Mexico Boost Relations," *China Daily*, June 5, 2013. As of October 10, 2015:
http://www.chinadaily.com.cn/china/2013xivisit/2013-06/05/content_16573196.htm

Zhuang Guotu, "Dongnanya Huaqiao Renshuliang De Xin Gusuan" ["A New Estimate of the Ethnic Chinese Population in Southeast Asia"], *Journal of Xiamen University (Arts & Social Sciences)*, General Serial No. 193, No. 3, 2009, pp. 62–69. As of August 31, 2017:
http://www.ims.sdu.edu.cn/cms/attachment/110522075043.pdf

"Zihuo Xieding Ling Zhong Ao Xingfen Meimei Danyou 'Yatai Zhanlue Luo Kong'" ["Free Trade Agreement Excites China, Australia, U.S. Media Worries About 'Asia-Pacific Strategic Failure'"], *Global Times*, July 19, 2015. As of October 10, 2015:
http://world.huanqiu.com/exclusive/2015-06/6723949.html